The Practical Guide to Athletic Training

Ted Eaves, MS, LAT, ATC, CSCS

North Carolina Agricultural and Technical State University
Greensboro, NC

JONES AND BARTLETT PUBLISHERS
Sudbury, Massachusetts
BOSTON   TORONTO   LONDON   SINGAPORE

World Headquarters
Jones and Bartlett Publishers
40 Tall Pine Drive
Sudbury, MA 01776
978-443-5000
info@jbpub.com
www.jbpub.com

Jones and Bartlett Publishers Canada
6339 Ormindale Way
Mississauga, Ontario L5V 1J2
Canada

Jones and Bartlett Publishers International
Barb House, Barb Mews
London W6 7PA
United Kingdom

Jones and Bartlett's books and products are available through most bookstores and online booksellers. To contact Jones and Bartlett Publishers directly, call 800-832-0034, fax 978-443-8000, or visit our website, www.jbpub.com.

Substantial discounts on bulk quantities of Jones and Bartlett's publications are available to corporations, professional associations, and other qualified organizations. For details and specific discount information, contact the special sales department at Jones and Bartlett via the above contact information or send an email to specialsales@jbpub.com.

The author, editor, and publisher have made every effort to provide accurate information. However, they are not responsible for errors, omissions, or for any outcomes related to the use of the contents of this book and take no responsibility for the use of the products and procedures described. Treatments and side effects described in this book may not be applicable to all people; likewise, some people may require a dose or experience a side effect that is not described herein. Drugs and medical devices are discussed that may have limited availability controlled by the Food and Drug Administration (FDA) for use only in a research study or clinical trial. Research, clinical practice, and government regulations often change the accepted standard in this field. When consideration is being given to use of any drug in the clinical setting, the health care provider or reader is responsible for determining FDA status of the drug, reading the package insert, and reviewing prescribing information for the most up-to-date recommendations on dose, precautions, and contraindications, and determining the appropriate usage for the product. This is especially important in the case of drugs that are new or seldom used.

Production Credits
Acquisitions Editor: Shoshanna Goldberg
Editorial Assistant: Kyle Hoover
Production Manager: Julie Champagne Bolduc
Production Assistant: Jessica Steele Newfell
Marketing Manager: Jessica Faucher
V.P., Manufacturing and Inventory Control: Therese Connell
Composition: Publishers' Design and Production Services, Inc.

Interior and Cover Designs: Kristin E. Parker
Photo Research Manager and Photographer: Kimberly Potvin
Senior Photo Researcher and Photographer: Christine McKeen
Assistant Photo Researcher: Bridget Kane
Cover Image: © Jones and Bartlett Publishers. Photographed by Kimberly Potvin.
Printing and Binding: Courier Stoughton
Cover Printing: Courier Stoughton

Library of Congress Cataloging-in-Publication Data
Eaves, Ted.
  The practical guide to athletic training / Ted Eaves. — 1st ed.
    p. cm.
  Includes index.
  ISBN 978-0-7637-4633-9 (pbk. : alk. paper)
1. Sports injuries. 2. Athletic trainers. 3. Sports injuries—Prevention. 4. Physical education and training.
5. Physical fitness. I. Title.
  RD97.E28 2009
  617.1'027—dc22
                                                                                2008025967

6048

Printed in the United States of America
13 12 11 10 09   10 9 8 7 6 5 4 3 2 1

This book is dedicated to my girls—Jenny, Caroline, and Natalie—all my love.

Contents

Preface

The Practical Guide to Athletic Training was created as an introductory text detailing the practical knowledge and skills needed to be successful in an athletic setting. It is not intended as a definitive resource for all injuries and illnesses. This guide details common injuries and the special tests and rehab protocols that should be utilized to address those injuries. Information regarding rare illnesses and injuries is omitted so that the text can be kept to an appropriate length. Some serious conditions that deserve an athletic trainer's consideration are not found in these pages. However, these conditions are less common and, therefore, less applicable to an introductory text.

The material found here has been divided into five sections.

Section I: Administrative Foundations

This section focuses on the profession of athletic training and information essential to success in the field. Chapter 1 discusses many questions students ask prior to entering an athletic training education program. These same questions often are discussed again as a student nears graduation and begins the quest for employment. This section also discusses the many administrative duties that a professional athletic trainer will encounter. Specifically the guide addresses budgeting, insurance, and risk management strategies, including documentation, liability, protective equipment, and environmental concerns.

Section II: Assessment and Treatment of Injuries

This section focuses on the various injuries an athlete may incur and the healing process associated with those injuries. It discusses appropriate treatment protocols to improve the athlete's ability to return to play safely. This section also examines the importance of assessment and the proper techniques to utilize during the evaluation.

Section III: Lower Body Evaluation

This section provides a detailed analysis of each major region of the lower body and injuries that are common to those regions. It discusses appropriate tests, treatments, and rehabilitation protocols for long-term situations or postsurgical cases in each region of the lower body.

Section IV: Upper Body Evaluation

This section is an overview of the upper body and its common injuries. Similar to Section III, this section discusses tests, treatments, and rehab protocols specific to each region in the upper body.

Section V: General Medical Conditions

The final section offers an overview of many disorders and illnesses that an athlete may face. There are abundant opportunities for disease transmission in athletics today. Proper management of these diseases and disorders provides the athletic trainer with the best potential for a healthy athletic population.

Acknowledgments

I would like to thank my family for their support, patience, and understanding during the writing process. It is through your love and encouragement that this is possible. I also would like to thank my friends and colleagues—Tim Botic, Emily Canfield, Kim Humphrey, and Jed Siebel—who were willing to revise and edit the rough draft. You helped me to make it better.

I would like to thank the students who helped to transpose the manuscript to a computer format. I appreciate everyone's efforts that helped to make this textbook a reality, especially Laura Darby McNally, who volunteered her time to help with many of the photographs in this book.

Thank you also to the reviewers of this edition. Your voices, criticism, and support have truly made this a better text:

- Gary E. McIlvain, MS, ATC, Marshall University
- Gina L. Kraft, MS, ATC, Oklahoma Baptist University
- Jayne A. Willett, PhD, ATC, California State University–Sacramento
- Shawn D. Felton, MEd, ATC, LAT, Florida Gulf Coast University
- Earl R. "Bud" Cooper, EdD, ATC, CSCS, Georgia College and State University
- Brian Razak, MS, LAT, ATC, Fort Hays State University
- Mary J. Barron, PhD, ATC, Georgia Southern University
- Jeff Roberts, MS, ATC, NASM-PES, San Jose State University
- Joseph A. Beckett, EdD, ATC, Eastern Kentucky University
- Matthew Rothbard, MS, ATC, Towson University
- Mary McLendon, MS, ATC, Mississippi State University
- Lisa S. Jutte, PhD, LAT, ATC, Ball State University
- Rick Proctor, EdD, LAT, ATC, High Point University
- Bruce E. Fischbach, MSS, ATC, University of South Dakota

Administrative Foundations

Introduction to Athletic Training

Students face many questions when they first consider a career in athletic training. What is an athletic trainer? How do I become one (and a good one, at that)? What would my job responsibilities be? Where would I work? These are all important issues to contemplate as a student ponders what his or her future may hold.

When a student enters an athletic training education program (ATEP), and again as he or she prepares to graduate and enter the workforce, these questions arise, becoming even more pertinent as they affect the student's future livelihood. This chapter addresses these questions for all athletic training students, regardless of where they are in their education. The goal of the chapter, and this text in general, is to help students recognize the roles and responsibilities of an athletic trainer and what can be expected from the profession. With this information, students can make an informed decision about whether to pursue a career in the athletic training or sports medicine field.

What Is an Athletic Trainer?

The National Athletic Trainers' Association (NATA) defines athletic training as "practiced by athletic trainers, health care professionals who collaborate with physicians to optimize activity and participation of patients and clients. Athletic training encompasses the prevention, diagnosis and intervention of emergency, acute, and chronic medical conditions involving impairment, functional limitations, and disabilities."[1]

The NATA definition provides a strong technical understanding of athletic training and the athletic trainer; however, it does not reach to the heart of the profession. Athletic trainers are part of an American Medical Association (AMA) recognized allied health field that has direct access to patients, often at the onset of injury. The athletic trainer is an expert in preventive medicine, emergency care, injury assessment, treatment protocols, therapeutic exercise, the psychological impacts of injury, and return-to-play criteria. An athletic trainer will be the primary contact for an injured athlete throughout the duration of the injury and the athlete's recovery.

The successful athletic trainer also manages the team as a whole from its first practice until the end of the season. The athletic trainer's responsibility is to decrease the risk of **acute injuries** and prevent the onset of **chronic injuries**. This is accomplished through developing stretching and strengthening programs, proper equipment fitting, and

acute injury An injury with sudden, traumatic onset.

chronic injury Injury with gradual onset and long duration.

Fast Fact

It is critical that all members of the sports medicine team use the proper terminology for athletic trainers and the profession of athletic training. The term *trainer* has long been associated with this field because it is easy to use in conversation and at practices or competition. However, there are many types of trainers, including personal, horse, and dog trainers. Athletic trainers receive specialized education from an accredited undergraduate or graduate program. This differentiation is very important to specify in terminology because it will assist staff in gaining and maintaining the respect of the medical community and their patients.

<table>
</table>

TABLE 1.1

MEMBERS OF THE SPORTS MEDICINE TEAM

Physicians	Exercise physiologists
Dentists	Biomechanists
Podiatrists	Nutritionists
Nurses	Sport psychologists
Physician assistants	Coaches
Physical therapists	Strength and conditioning specialists
Massage therapists	
Occupational therapists	Social workers
Athletic trainers	Chiropractors

evaluation of field conditions. The athletic trainer also should be actively involved in team practices to ensure that athletes maintain proper hydration and to help avoid heat- or cold-related illnesses. Essentially, the profession, in conjunction with the supervising physician, is responsible for the management of the overall health and well being of the members of all assigned athletic teams or patients in a nonathletic setting.

Who Else Is Involved in the Sports Medicine Team?

Athletic trainers are a key element in maintaining the health and well being of athletes and other patients. Many other people are also involved and can directly benefit the patients and their health care. The group of individuals tasked with this responsibility is collectively known as the *sports medicine team*. The team consists primarily of the coaching staff, team physicians, and athletic trainers.

The sports medicine team is responsible for the prevention and treatment of all athletic injuries along with the other ancillary job duties that are discussed later in this chapter. Many other health care professionals fall under the sports medicine umbrella and may play important roles in an athlete's health care. These members are listed in **Table 1.1**.

This text is beneficial not only for future athletic trainers, but for all members of the sports medicine team. The administrative roles and responsibilities discussed in the subsequent chapters pertain to anyone working in the sports medicine field, whereas the injury management sections will benefit all future sports medicine professionals in the evaluation, assessment, and rehabilitation of injuries in their patients.

How Do I Become an Athletic Trainer?

First, a student must select a college that offers an accredited athletic training education program (ATEP) to become certified as an athletic trainer. These programs offer an athletic training major with an established core of coursework. The ATEP curriculum has been reviewed and approved by the Commission on the Accreditation of Athletic Training Education (CAATE). If a college or university's program does not have CAATE accreditation, graduates of the ATEP will not be allowed to sit for the athletic training certification exam and cannot practice as athletic trainers.

Throughout their 4 years, students in an accredited ATEP will become increasingly involved in the education program through both coursework and clinical education. Although each college or university may list their courses differently, athletic training programs all follow the same basic guidelines. The first year begins with a course providing an introduction to athletic training, a course involving first aid and cardiopulmonary resuscitation (CPR) certification, and a basic athletic training techniques class. These courses offer a brief glimpse into the life of an athletic trainer and aid the student in determining if this is a profession worth pursuing. After the introductory year, the student will complete courses in upper and lower body evaluation, therapeutic modalities, general medical conditions, rehabilitation and therapeutic exercise, and organization and administration.

The athletic training student also must complete required classes through the Kinesiology or Biology departments. Some common courses required of athletic training

majors include human anatomy and physiology, exercise physiology, biomechanics, nutrition, sports psychology, and the history/philosophy of sport. Each of these classes offers essential knowledge for the athletic training student. This information, when integrated with the educational tools developed as part of the athletic training program, provides the student with the foundation to develop into a competent professional.

Along with their coursework, students also must complete a clinical program that further enhances their athletic training knowledge, skills, and abilities. The clinical portion of the educational program offers the student an opportunity to learn from—and interact with—a variety of health care professionals, as well as complete clinical rotations in practical settings both inside and outside of the college/university.

Fast Fact

The first sports physician is considered to be Herodicus, who treated patients and athletes with therapeutic exercises and diet. Herodicus practiced in Athens during the 5th century B.C. He trained other physicians in his medical techniques, including Hippocrates—the founder of modern medicine and the namesake of the Hippocratic oath.[2]

Some clinical rotations may include physical therapy clinics, general medical offices, orthopedic surgery observations, local high school athletic training programs, and on-campus sports teams. Each rotation is intended to provide the student with a general idea of the different job settings for athletic trainers and what may be best suited to the student's individual interests. The rotations also offer an excellent opportunity for students to learn from various clinical instructors outside of the classroom.

The successful student is able to take what was taught in the classroom and utilize that information in a real-world setting. The opportunity to work with athletes throughout the practice and game schedule, as well as in the off-season, provides the student with critical thinking skills and the ability to adapt to unforeseen situations. Without the ability to translate academic knowledge into real-life solutions, a student is unlikely to succeed as an athletic trainer.

■ Entry-Level Master's Degree Programs

An alternative path to certification that is gaining popularity among athletic training students is the entry-level master's degree program. These programs accept students who have a bachelor's degree and are interested in becoming certified as an athletic trainer. These students either did not have accredited athletic training programs at their undergraduate institutions or are interested in the field but were not involved in athletic training earlier. The entry-level master's program is completed in 2 years and offers the student the ability to take the Board of Certification (BOC) exam, which is an opportunity only offered to graduates of accredited programs at either the undergraduate or graduate level. Meanwhile, the advanced degree also allows the student to teach at the collegiate level and provides additional opportunities for employment. The entry-level graduate program is an area that promises to be a strong facet of athletic training education.

■ BOC Certification

Upon completing his or her degree in athletic training, the student is well prepared to take a certification examination administered by the BOC, the only accredited certification agency for athletic trainers.[3] Successfully passing the computer-based exam is mandatory for those who wish to become certified athletic trainers and work in the profession.

The exam is designed to determine the knowledge base of the student and includes practical scenarios in which the student must determine the proper course of action. The certification exam is intended to assess whether the student has achieved an acceptable degree of knowledge

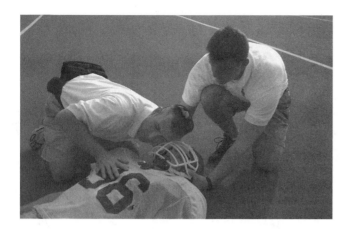

and skill to be classified as an entry-level athletic trainer. The exam does not determine the overall quality and skill level of the individual, nor should it be the final educational goal of the student. Successful athletic trainers are constantly learning in a bid to improve themselves and their abilities.

With that in mind, the BOC requires that the certified athletic trainer achieve 75 units of continuing education during a 3-year span. The continuing education unit (CEU) requirements must be met every 3 years to maintain certification throughout an athletic trainer's career. These CEUs are obtained through attendance at local, regional, and national conventions; participation in approved seminars; completion of research and publications; and completion of collegiate-level sports medicine–related courses. Each athletic trainer also is required to maintain an annual certification in emergency cardiac care through an approved provider, although CEUs are no longer awarded for this certification. An athletic trainer who does not complete the CEU requirements will forfeit his or her certification and the ability to work in the field as an athletic trainer.

Graduate School

Upon successful graduation from college at the undergraduate level and completion of the BOC exam, many athletic trainers choose to return to school for their master's degrees. The graduate degree provides additional employment opportunities for an athletic trainer, especially for such positions as a head athletic trainer or clinical faculty. In fact, 70% of certified athletic trainers have a master's degree or more advanced degree.[4]

Many schools prefer their athletic training staff to teach in the ATEP curriculum or in the Kinesiology department if there is not an athletic training major. Teaching at the collegiate level in most institutions requires a master's degree, further highlighting the need for postgraduate study. Certified athletic trainers can also benefit from the additional experience they gain while studying for their master's degree in graduate school.

Colleges and universities may offer graduate assistantships that help defray the cost of the graduate program in exchange for athletic training assistance in their intercollegiate program or other local facilities (e.g., local college, high school, clinic). The graduate assistantship (GA) positions benefit both the institution—which adds a certified athletic trainer to its staff—and the individual—who gains valuable experience and earns funding for tuition and living expenses.

State Practice Regulations

In an attempt to protect the profession of athletic training and its members, many states have now adopted rules and regulations that govern the practice of athletic training. There are four current forms of state regulation: licensure, certification, registration, and exemption. See **Table 1.2** for a list of states and their regulation. Each form of regulation benefits the profession of athletic training by restricting practice to approved members.[5]

Licensure is the most restrictive of the four forms of legislation and is the most prevalent version across the country (36 states currently have licensure regulations). Licensure limits the practice of athletic training to only those individuals who have met the minimum requirements determined by the specific state. Licensure protocols detail the roles and responsibilities of athletic trainers and limit the practice of those roles to qualified, registered athletic trainers. Any individual found to be practicing athletic training skills without a license or utilizing the athletic training title inappropriately is subject to fines and censure rules.

Certification restricts the practice of athletic training only to those individuals who are registered as athletic trainers; however, it does not place any restrictions on the use of the title athletic trainer or athletic training.

Registration protocols dictate that an athletic trainer must register with the state prior to practicing or beginning work. This registration places the athletic trainer on a list of practitioners that are available, but does not dictate roles and responsibilities and neither does it require the individual to demonstrate proficiency. There are no protections in place to restrict the use or practice of athletic training to only qualified staff.

Exemption regulations recognize that athletic trainers perform duties that are similar to other members of the sports medicine team. However, it does not require the athletic trainer to comply with the practice acts of those other professions. Instead, the legislation exempts the athletic trainer from those practice acts and allows the individual to perform those tasks that are within the athletic training scope of practice.[5]

TABLE 1.2

STATE REGULATION OF ATHLETIC TRAINING

Licensure	Certification
Alabama	Kentucky
Arizona	Louisiana
Arkansas	New York
Connecticut	Pennsylvania
Delaware	South Carolina
Florida	
Georgia	**Registration**
Idaho	Minnesota
Illinois	Oregon
Indiana	
Iowa	**Exemption**
Kansas	Colorado
Maine	Hawaii
Massachusetts	Oregon
Michigan	
Mississippi	**No Regulation**
Missouri	Alaska
Montana	California
Nebraska	Maryland
Nevada	West Virginia
New Hampshire	
New Jersey	
New Mexico	
North Carolina	
North Dakota	
Ohio	
Oklahoma	
Rhode Island	
South Dakota	
Tennessee	
Texas	
Utah	
Vermont	
Virginia	
Washington	
Wisconsin	

Data from: National Athletic Trainers' Association. *NATA State Regulatory Boards.* Retrieved August 22, 2007, from http://www.nata.org.

What Does It Take to Be a Good Athletic Trainer?

■ Attributes

A true professional in the field is capable of establishing a strong relationship with each athlete without regard to sex, race, creed, or ethnic background. *There is no room in athletic training for discrimination.* Building a relationship with the athletes can be difficult at times, especially with complicated individuals. Nevertheless, the athletic trainer must be knowledgeable in the field and professional in his or her attitude while maintaining an approachable personality. A successful athletic trainer develops a rapport with the athletes and gains their respect rather than adopting a controlling attitude and demanding the athletes' respect.

Although developing a strong relationship with the student-athletes is essential, it is just as imperative to create a collegial relationship with the coaching staffs of assigned sports. Becoming an integral part of the team begins with establishing an understanding that everyone associated with the team is focused on the best interests of the athletes.

As important as a friendly, adaptable personality is to the individual, there are many other traits that also are essential to the successful athletic trainer.

Hardworking/Dedication

An individual who is successful in athletic training is always hardworking and dedicated to the profession. Throughout the years, athletic trainers have developed a reputation for long hours in a variety of conditions. Along with the traditional practice and game coverage—the obvious job responsibilities that everyone recognizes—there also are hours spent in the athletic training room completing treatments and rehabilitations, updating necessary documentation, and overseeing various administrative tasks such as budget, insurance, and inventory.

The hardworking reputation is well earned because extensive hours and weekend assignments are common, but that should not deter students from entering the field. Many rewards offset the time that is required of the profession. The hours become worthwhile when you consider the relationships that an athletic trainer develops with the coaches and athletes; the sense of accomplishment that arises when an athlete returns to play from an injury; the effect the athletic trainer has on the lives of the athletes; and finally, the potential material and emotional rewards that arise from successful seasons. These, and many other reasons, are why athletic trainers are so dedicated to their field and why students continue to enter the profession.

However, there is a strong risk for **burnout** in athletic trainers in all settings. The long hours and sometimes stressful situations can overcome even the strongest individual. It is crucial that each and every athletic trainer sets a limit to how much he or she works (within reason) and develops hobbies and outside interests. Spending time on enjoyable pursuits outside of the athletic training room can be extremely beneficial and can decrease the stress and

> **burnout** Fatigue, frustration, or apathy that results from prolonged stress, overwork, or intense activity.

potential burnout. It also is vital that all athletic trainers make time for their family and friends. It often is difficult to balance work and family, but it is important that the job does not consume the individual and that there is time to spend with spouses and children especially.

◼ Strong Organization/Time Management

Successful athletic trainers are able to develop a practical organizational system for themselves and their facility, as well as understand how to prioritize and manage time so that they are able to complete all of the assigned tasks. A strong organizational system is necessary when considering the many roles that an athletic trainer plays. Whether this system is neat and orderly is not the principal concern. As long as the individual who is utilizing the system understands it and can locate what is needed, then almost any useful system is acceptable.

It is important for the athletic trainer to be organized so that all documentation and paperwork is in order and accessible. A common concern for athletic training—and the medical field in general—is the threat of lawsuits and legal issues. Proper documentation and good organization both play a role in minimizing the risk of lawsuits.

Time management also is an essential attribute for the successful athletic trainer. As mentioned before, many tasks require a dedicated time commitment. Without proper management, these tasks either would not be completed or require additional time from the athletic trainer. To be successful, the athletic trainer will learn to allocate appropriate amounts of time to each task, as well as complete all assigned tasks in a timely manner—an equally important trait.

◼ Professionalism

The successful athletic trainer always is professional and appropriate in his or her behavior. When discussing professionalism, it is important to examine both attitude and appearance.

Attitude

The attitude of athletic trainers is their portrayal to everyone they meet. A professional attitude begins with ethical behavior. An athletic trainer must always uphold the highest standards of conduct and integrity. The NATA developed a code of ethics for its members to follow. This code was established with five basic principles in mind:

1. Members shall respect the rights, welfare, and dignity of all individuals.
2. Members shall comply with the laws and regulations governing the practice of athletic training.

much more enjoyable. Students, athletes, and staff will all be more comfortable around the athletic trainer and find him or her easier to work with if the individual is upbeat and not overly serious or agitated.

Another aspect of professionalism is ensuring that an athletic trainer's clinical skills are always at the highest level. Developing a strong foundation of skills prior to certification and then making a conscious effort to improve oneself through continuing education will ensure that an athletic trainer is both competent and capable to fulfill all expected roles and responsibilities. The athletes deserve the best health care available, and an integral component of that is striving to be a better professional.

The final aspect of professional behavior is developing or maintaining an empathetic attitude. An athletic trainer is frequently in attendance when an athlete is injured, whether seriously or not. The athletic trainer must provide a support structure for the injured athlete and help to alleviate the physical or mental anguish that occurs. A fine line, in this situation, arises between offering sympathy and support for the injured athlete and becoming the sole emotional outlet for the athlete or developing an attachment to the athlete that may become detrimental to both people involved. The athletic trainer should involve other members of the sports medicine team (e.g., team doctor, psychologist, nurse, physician assistant) along with the athlete's family to ensure that the injured individual receives the best care possible.

Appearance

The other component of professionalism relates to the appearance of the athletic trainer. The first, and often lasting, impression that an individual provides athletes, parents, staff, and anyone else he or she comes in contact with is created by his or her appearance. Although proper attitude and behavior establish the athletic trainer's credibility with the athletes and create a strong rapport with the team, it is the athletic trainer's appearance that often will dictate the level of respect and patient response that he or she receives.

3. Members shall accept the responsibility for the exercise of sound judgment.
4. Members shall maintain and promote high standards in the provision of services.
5. Members shall not engage in conduct that constitutes a conflict of interest or that adversely reflects on the profession.[6]

The concept of professionalism, however, extends beyond ethical conduct. It also includes the bearing and manner of an athletic trainer. The successful individual is calm and collected in adverse situations. There are many opportunities in athletics for injuries to develop into serious medical emergencies. Maintaining a professional attitude helps keep the patient calm and confident in the athletic trainer's skills and can prevent a serious situation from becoming much worse.

An athletic trainer also should have an appropriate sense of humor. Working extended hours can lead some individuals toward burnout. Maintaining a positive attitude and a sense of humor will help to decrease the stress that is present and make the environment and the job setting

> ### Fast Fact
>
> Galen, the team physician at the gladiatorial school in ancient Rome during the 2nd century, is considered by many to be the original athletic trainer. Galen was one of several early physicians to emphasize proper training habits to improve physical conditioning.[2]

An athletic trainer should dress in business casual attire, which consists of khaki pants or shorts and a polo shirt. This is appropriate clothing for practices, athletic training room coverage, and outdoor events. Occasionally, indoor events will require dress attire, usually consisting of a coat and tie or a suit for men and a dress or business attire for women. The choice of clothing for these events often is dictated by the coach and should be appropriate for the specific event. For instance, a sport that has numerous incidents of bleeding (e.g., wrestling, boxing) may not be the appropriate environment for a tie.

In conclusion, professional individuals conduct themselves with the utmost level of conduct and present themselves in appropriate attire. This level of professionalism is essential to being a successful athletic trainer and will lend itself to a long, productive career in the field.

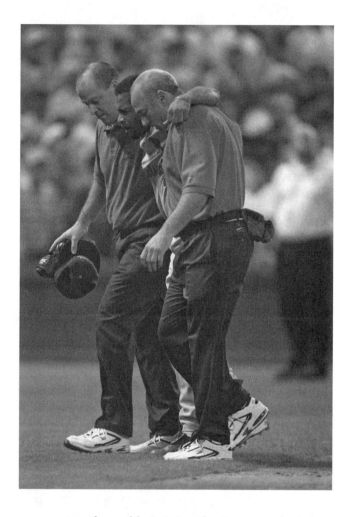

 ## What Are the Roles of an Athletic Trainer?

As mentioned earlier in the chapter, an athletic trainer has numerous roles and responsibilities—outlined in the BOC role delineation study—that are completed throughout the day. He or she is an expert in prevention; clinical evaluation and diagnosis; immediate care; treatment, rehabilitation, and reconditioning of all athletic injuries; organization and administration; and professional responsibility.

■ Prevention

An athletic trainer's first and foremost responsibility is the prevention of athletic injuries. The ability to prevent injuries decreases workload and often can directly lead to increased success for the team. Proper stretching routines, in-season health maintenance, off-season conditioning programs, proper nutrition and hydration, appropriate protective equipment fitting, and field maintenance all play a role in the prevention of injuries. It is important for the athletic trainer to incorporate other members of the sports medicine team who are involved with the athletes in the prevention of injuries. This may include coaches, physical education teachers, strength and conditioning specialists, and many others. Each of these individuals is able to play a role in preventing injuries, which will benefit athletes throughout their seasons and their careers.

■ Clinical Evaluation and Diagnosis

Of course, not all injuries can be prevented. Often, joint sprains, muscle strains, and overuse injuries can be avoided with the programs mentioned previously; however, there will always be injuries involved with athletic events. The assessment of an athletic injury begins once the injury has occurred. Assessment in athletic training consists of the evaluation of an injury utilizing the patient's history, objective tests, and analysis of the symptoms and findings. The athletic trainer will complete observation of the injured area, manual muscle testing, measurements of range of motion, palpation techniques, and special tests specific to the area of the body that is injured. With this information in hand, the staff member then is able to assess the injury and determine the proper treatment or referral to the team physician.

The assessment is the first step in the management of an injury once it occurs. Without proper testing and anatomic knowledge, the athletic trainer could misinterpret the injury and potentially cause further harm. The proper assessment of the injury places the athlete on the road to recovery and return to play.

■ Immediate Care

Along with the evaluation and assessment of injuries, the athletic trainer also is responsible for the management of acute injuries through the use of appropriate first aid techniques. All athletic trainers are required—through continuing education—to be certified in emergency cardiac care and first aid. These courses are offered by a number of national groups including the American Red Cross (CPR/AED for the Professional Rescuer) and the American Heart Association (BLS Healthcare Provider). As part of immediate care, the athletic trainer should have an established emergency action plan that provides a step-by-step process for treating serious injuries. Emergency action plans are discussed in more detail in Chapter 2.

■ Treatment, Rehabilitation, and Reconditioning

The treatment of athletic injuries takes up a large portion of an athletic trainer's workday. Athletes with injuries should attempt to receive at least two treatments each day if class, work, and practice schedules permit. These treatments typically involve some form of therapeutic modality use along with an individual stretching and strengthening program. The therapeutic modality use, which is discussed in Chapter 6, is beneficial in decreasing pain, swelling, and

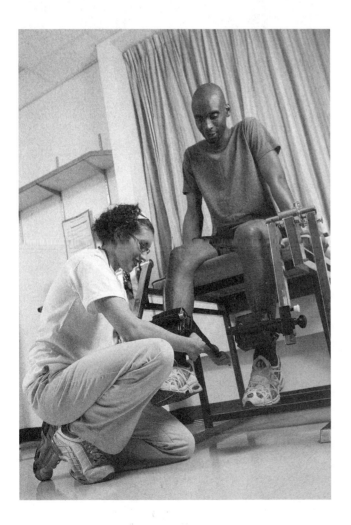

spasm, while the stretching and strengthening programs increase range of motion (ROM), strengthen muscles, and improve balance and proprioception—all of which are affected by injury. The treatment that an athlete receives provides the opportunity to continue practice or return to play without risking his or her health and well being.

Rehabilitation implies a program that is developed for an athlete who has a long-term injury or surgical repair that will prohibit him or her from returning to competition for a lengthy amount of time. Treatment programs are considered a form of rehab and can assist an athlete's return to play at 100% health. The difference between treatment and rehabilitation, for the purposes of this text, is the length of the program. A rehabilitation program ensures that the athlete with a serious injury progresses appropriately for his or her ability and level of function.

An athletic trainer must tread a fine line between pushing the athlete to improve and going too far. It is important to break through physical and psychological barriers, but the athletic trainer must make certain that the athletes do not push themselves too hard too quickly and cause further injury or complications. The rehabilitation protocol utilized for athletes should be created individually to meet their needs and long-term goals.

Several sample rehabilitation protocols for specific injuries are provided throughout the text. These protocols are intended as examples to demonstrate a potential procedure for each injury.

■ Organization and Administration

An athletic trainer will have numerous administrative roles throughout his or her career. A staff member at a high school, college, or university may oversee the budget for the department; conduct inventory control and supply orders; maintain documentation and paperwork; and complete any number of other tasks. All staff members are expected to maintain proper medical documentation for their sports and athletes.

■ Professional Responsibilities

Athletic trainers should strive to continuously improve professionally. This may be done through continuing education credits; maintaining a working knowledge of current and cutting-edge techniques; involvement with athletic training organizations at the state, regional, and national levels; and the promotion of the profession of athletic training.

It is through the individual member's efforts that the profession continues to grow and gain respect and standing in the medical community and in the general public. This may be achieved through something as simple as working in an appropriate and professional manner. Or, it could include additional responsibility as a researcher, educator, or spokesperson for the profession. No matter what role is played, every member needs to do his or her part to make athletic training as strong a profession as possible.

Other Roles of an Athletic Trainer

■ Insurance Coordinator

As part of their administrative duties, many athletic trainers are asked to coordinate the insurance submissions for the athletic department. Most institutions offer secondary insurance coverage for their athletes. This insurance requires that proper claim forms be submitted along with all bills and primary insurance documentation. The many facets of insurance are discussed in more detail in Chapter 2.

■ Drug Testing Coordinator

Most National Collegiate Athletic Association (NCAA) Division I institutions and many NCAA Division II and III organizations, National Association of Intercollegiate Athletics (NAIA) groups, and high schools have developed internal drug testing programs for their athletes. The concern that has led to these programs is that some of today's athletes are using recreational drugs and performance-enhancing substances. To ensure a level playing field and to protect athletes from these dangerous substances, institutions are conducting random testing throughout the academic year. These tests are performed in conjunction with mandatory testing conducted by the NCAA and NAIA both during the year and at championship tournaments. A member of the athletic training staff is assigned to coordinate all drug testing to certify random sampling without tampering. This staff member also oversees all penalties associated with a positive test.

■ Counselor

An athletic trainer obviously is involved with an athlete's injury and return to play. Throughout this time, he or she is an integral component of the athlete's physical rehabilitation as well as his or her mental healing. Although an athletic trainer should never take the place of a trained counselor or psychologist, it is important for the athletic trainer to assist in the athlete's progression through the five stages of grief that are associated with significant injuries: denial, anger, bargaining, depression, and acceptance.

Each individual will proceed through these stages at different speeds. It is important that the athletic trainer is available for the athlete at this time and ensures that the injury does not propel the athlete into a depressed state. The athletic trainer is there to support the athlete, be a good listener, and offer referral to the proper clinician who can help the athlete through this difficult time.

Where Are Athletic Trainers Employed?

Athletic trainers, as allied health professionals, are found in work settings throughout the medical field, not just with sports teams. In fact, more than 50% of the NATA's certified athletic trainer members are currently employed outside of school athletic programs.[4] With the wide array of skills that a certified member possesses, the athletic trainer is capable of succeeding in any number of environments. These environments continue to expand and change almost daily with the emergence of new opportunities that utilize staff in unique settings. The following are several of the possible settings available to today's athletic trainer. No one job setting is better than any other; instead, each individual must decide for himself or herself which setting is most appropriate for his or her career.

■ College/University

The college and university setting is the traditional workplace associated with athletic training. Throughout the foundation of the profession, colleges and universities were leading sources of employment for athletic trainers. Colleges and universities come in all sizes and shapes with athletic departments ranging from a few sports to more than 50 varsity and club offerings. The athletic trainer at a college or university supervises the practices and games for assigned sports along with various other campus and local events. The collegiate setting is appropriate for an individual with the ability to develop a close relationship with a group of dedicated student athletes. The sports aspect of the profession is obviously emphasized in this environment.

■ High School

The high school athletic trainer is very similar in job description to the collegiate staff member. These individuals often work with the freshmen, junior varsity, and varsity programs that a school offers to its students. Many athletic trainers in the high school setting also are employed as teachers at their specific institution. The educational component of the position may be the athletic trainer's primary role, or it can act as a supplement to the individual's salary and position at the school. The role of the athletic trainer is dependent on the institution. Many high schools are only able financially to hire an athletic trainer for the athletic teams if that individual is primarily a teacher. Other schools are able to hire full-time athletic trainers for the athletics program without a teaching requirement.

High school athletic training is associated with long hours and lower salary ranges than some environments (**Table 1.3**), although most staff members are provided the same summer vacation the students receive. The rewards are similar to the collegiate setting except that in the high school setting, the athletic trainer often has the opportunity to have a true impact on a student's life during a pivotal developmental stage. Whether the impact is in the student's future professional interests, in the quality of life, or understanding of the world, the influence that a teacher/athletic trainer may have is incredible.

■ Professional Sports

Quite possibly the most popular career goal for athletic training students, the professional athletics environment is the toughest field in which to gain employment.

Few positions are available compared to the job settings discussed previously (approximately only 3% to 5% of athletic trainers are employed in the professional setting), and there are numerous candidates for each position. The professional realm is high intensity and high reward—both salary and supplemental benefits—especially with successful organizations. The student who does enter this field should expect long hours with a great deal of travel. Employment in this environment, more so than any other, is based greatly on networking. Completing internships and volunteer opportunities is essential to becoming a viable candidate. A student interested in the professional realm has to pay his or her dues to become qualified and generate an opportunity for a staff position.

■ Clinic

The athletic trainer in the clinical setting specializes in rehabilitation techniques and return-to-play/work criteria. These individuals assist all populations, both athletic and nonathletic, in their treatment and rehabilitation for acute and chronic injuries and postsurgical cases. This setting is traditionally associated with higher salaries than the previously discussed environments, as well as more stable hours and working conditions. (It rarely rains or snows in the clinic). The difference in the time commitment is seen most often in weekend coverage, which tends to be optional in the clinical setting.

The clinic athletic trainer is rewarded with the opportunity to see his or her clients return-to-play/work after a serious injury. The difficulty found with this position is the decreased opportunity to develop long-term relationships with the clients. Whereas most athletes in the previous settings are a member of the team for 4 or more years, the clients in a clinic complete their rehabilitation within a matter of weeks or months.

■ Clinic Outreach

One specific subenvironment in the clinical setting is the outreach programs available in certain districts. Many high schools currently hire part-time staff members that work in a clinic in the morning and a high school in the afternoon for practices and games. This environment offers the benefit of slightly better hours than the traditional high school setting along with a change of scenery during each workday.

This position allows the high school to develop a relationship with a physician's office or rehabilitation clinic, which eventually will benefit both parties. The high school is able to offer supplemental income to the athletic trainer rather than finance a full-time staff member. This relationship often is universally beneficial for everyone involved.

TABLE 1.3

2005 NATA ATHLETIC TRAINING SALARY SURVEY

Work Setting	Average Total Annual Income	Work Setting	Average Total Annual Income
Amateur Sports	$41,045	Hospital–Orthopedics	$47,100
Clinic–Hospital-Based Clinic	$43,341	Hospital–Other	$39,236
Clinic–Outpatient/Ambulatory/Rehab	$43,223	Independent Contractor	$45,100
Clinic–Physician-Owned Clinic	$42,688	Industrial/Occupational–Clinic	$47,371
Clinic–Secondary School/Clinic	$35,227	Industrial/Occupational–Ergonomics	$43,714
Clinic–Other	$42,782	Industrial/Occupational–Health/Wellness/ Fitness	$38,750
College–Two-Year-Faculty/Academic/ Research	$51,022	Industrial/Occupational–Other Capacity	$49,940
College–Two-Year-Prof. Staff/Athletics/ Clinic	$37,678	Law Enforcement	$51,000
College–Two-Year-Split Appointment	$35,596	Military–Active Duty	$46,500
College/University–Faculty/Academic/ Research	$51,647	Military–Civilian	$49,900
		Professional Baseball–Men	$32,827
College/University–Professional Staff/ Athletics/Clinic	$37,617	Professional Basketball–Men	$42,125
College/University–Split Appointment	$39,103	Professional Football	$80,111
Corporate–Business Sales/Marketing	$52,178	Professional Hockey	$47,000
Corporate–Ergonomics	$39,333	Professional Performing Arts	$56,135
Corporate–Health/Wellness/Fitness	$49,012	Professional Soccer	$45,750
Corporate–Patient Care	$36,505	Recreational Sports	$36,345
Government	$50,716	Secondary School–High School (Private)	$41,000
Health/Fitness/Perform–Enhancement/ Sports Club	$39,759	Secondary School–High School (Public)	$43,884
Hospital–Administration	$73,832	Secondary School–Middle School (Private)	$39,833
Hospital–Emergency Department	$57,000	Secondary School–Middle School (Public)	$36,972
		Youth Sports	$46,296

Adapted from: National Athletic Trainers' Association. (2005, June). *NATA News*, 22–23.

■ Industrial

The industrial setting for athletic training is constantly expanding and creating new opportunities. An industrial athletic trainer works with a specific company or corporation to provide medical care for its employees. The athletic trainer often is directly employed at the plant or facility to provide acute care/treatment for injuries, ergonomic assessments to prevent chronic injuries, and rehabilitation for those employees who are recovering from medical issues. These athletic trainers benefit the companies by providing

first aid care to the employees, ensuring that they can work safely and efficiently, and decreasing insurance premiums by providing on-site rehabilitation services.

Industrial athletic trainers typically earn higher salaries than athletic trainers in an athletic setting do and have established work hours that rarely deviate from an assigned schedule. The industrial athletic trainers also may develop stronger relationships with their patients than staff at a clinic do because of the continuity of employment. The concern in the industrial setting is the lack of motivation to return to work that some patients may have. It is difficult to rehabilitate an individual who does not wish to improve.

■ Military

A relatively new realm of athletic training is the military setting. The staff in this environment often works with a specific unit, base, or ship treating the injuries that occur during training or combat. The military has recognized the benefit of athletic trainers in the treatment and rehabilitation of this specialized population, and it has expanded the career opportunities for staff members in the armed services. The athletic trainer provides the ability to motivate the injured individual while preventing him or her from exceeding safe limitations and causing further injury. These positions offer a competitive salary with excellent government benefits but may require deployment with the assigned unit or ship.

■ Academic Faculty

Academic faculty in athletic training is undergoing a renaissance of sorts with the recent requirement that all students graduate from an accredited athletic training program. Certainly, there were professors in colleges and universities prior to the new accreditation requirement. However, the need for program directors, clinical coordinators, and other faculty has risen dramatically since 2004 when the accreditation regulations were implemented.

The faculty at an institution is responsible for the classroom education and clinical supervision of the athletic training students. A master's degree or doctorate plus 5 years of experience as a certified athletic trainer are prerequisites for most faculty positions. With a doctoral degree, many athletic training faculty members become eligible for tenure, which essentially ensures continued employment at the institution as long as the individual wishes to stay. A great deal of time must be invested to earn the required degrees and become proficient in all of the required athletic training competencies, but the salary is higher than for most clinical athletic trainers, and with tenure, the faculty are all but assured a permanent position.

What Are the Current/ Future Trends That Athletic Trainers Will Face?

The field of athletic training is growing and constantly evolving. With the recent educational changes and the increasing opportunities for athletic trainers outside of the traditional settings, the field today is dramatically dif-

ferent from how it was even 10 years ago. Many issues on the horizon will certainly cause the same level of change for the profession and for sports medicine in general in the decades to come.

The NATA and athletic trainers nationwide have been and will continue to be focused on increasing the visibility and understanding of the profession. Local community efforts in conjunction with national marketing campaigns, such as National Athletic Training Month (March), and numerous research endeavors help demonstrate the scope of practice and capabilities of athletic trainers. Included in the goal of increased visibility is the hope that employers recognize the value of athletic trainers and create more job opportunities for staff members. Increased visibility may lead to an increase in the number of secondary schools that hire athletic trainers for their sports coverage or potentially to developing new territories for athletic trainers to find job opportunities, such as the military, corporations, and industry.

The NATA, CAATE, and the BOC are working together to develop, reorganize, and hone educational programs and competencies so that athletic training students continue to receive the best level of education possible so that they can then provide their future patients with the highest standard of care.

State athletic training organizations continue to focus on improving or implementing regulatory protocols for athletic trainers today and in the future. It is vital to the profession that state regulation continuously evolves and provides the appropriate protection and privileges for athletic trainers.

Finally, third-party reimbursement and Medicare reimbursement are priority topics nationally for athletic training administrators. Third-party reimbursement provides insurance payments to athletic trainers for care—specifically rehabilitation services—that is rendered within the appropriate scope of practice. Many insurance companies, including Medicare, do not provide reimbursement for athletic trainers, only for physical therapists and physicians. The NATA is leading a strong legislative push to allow athletic trainers to be reimbursed for their services in clinical setting and, eventually, in athletic settings as well.

Great progress has been made by athletic trainers on many fronts in the past several decades; however, it will take even more effort by all professionals and members of the sports medicine team to ensure that athletic training continues to grow and thrive.

With the basics of athletic training set, the following chapters focus on specific aspects that are critical to the professional in the field. As mentioned before, the focus of this text is on the college/university and high school settings. This by no means detracts from the other settings, which are equally important to the overall profession.

CHAPTER REVIEW

1. List the roles of an athletic trainer.
2. Describe the classes that are required for an athletic training education program.
3. What are the CEU requirements to maintain athletic training certification?
4. List the traditional employment settings for athletic trainers.
5. List the four forms of state regulation.
6. What does the acronym CAATE stand for?

CRITICAL THINKING

How can you work to improve and promote the field of athletic training?

REFERENCES

1. Strategic Implementation Team. (2007, December). Strategic Implementation Team defines profession. *NATA News,* 14.
2. Starkey C, Johnson G. *Athletic Training and Sports Medicine*, 4th ed. Sudbury, MA: Jones and Bartlett, 2006.
3. Board of Certification. *BOC Mission & Vision*. Retrieved August 23, 2007, from http://www.bocatc.org.
4. National Athletic Trainers' Association. *Facts About Athletic Training*. Retrieved August 23, 2007, from http://www.nata.org.
5. National Athletic Trainers' Association. *NATA State Regulatory Boards*. Retrieved August 22, 2007, from http://www.nata.org.
6. National Athletic Trainers' Association. *NATA Code of Ethics*. Retrieved March 15, 2006, from http://www.nata.org.

Administration

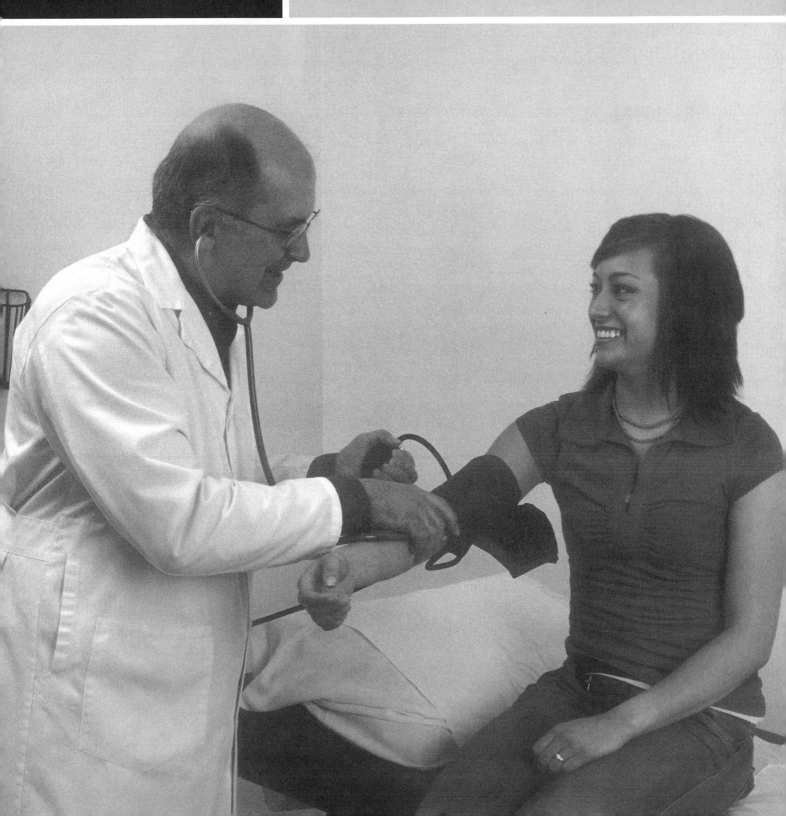

The administration of an athletic training program is a time-consuming—sometimes onerous—task that is an integral factor in promoting a smooth-running department. The business aspect of athletic training may not be the job most students envision when they consider their future in the field. However, it is an essential responsibility because the proper administration of the department can ensure fiscal responsibility through budgeting and insurance filing, while proper documentation helps to minimize risk and liability. Throughout this chapter, the various aspects of the administration of athletic training and the role that they play in a staff member's daily life are discussed.

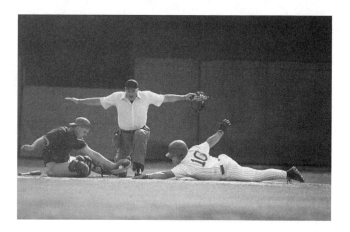

 ## Budgeting

A **budget** is a financial system of operation that allocates resources for disposable and durable goods and services.[1] These monies are usually available in the form of appropriations from the athletic department or institution in general. The size and type of budget often is dependent upon the size of the athletic program and the school. For instance, larger institutions and more athletes should indicate higher budget allocation. Along with the increased budget comes an expectation for a higher standard of care for the athletes, as well as increased breadth and quality of equipment and supplies to serve them.

Proper record keeping in regard to budgetary allocations and expenses allows the department to evaluate its spending criteria and determine if they are maximizing the available funds. One athletic trainer in the department should be responsible for budget oversight. This ensures appropriate expenditure protocol and may avoid any spending outside the realm of the budget. Having one predetermined person responsible for the budget can protect the program from irresponsible ordering or misappropriation of funds.

■ Budget Allocations

There are two basic types of budget allocations found in the athletic training setting. The first is the day-to-day operating budget.[1] This contains funds that are allocated for supplies and equipment utilized in the normal operation of the department. Some materials that fall into this category are taping and first aid supplies; long-term treatment and rehabilitation equipment such as crutches and walking boots; and maintenance, calibration, and repair of modality and exercise equipment. This budget may fluctuate with the budget of the institution.

The second type of allocation is frequently titled capital expenditures. This budget is a long-term expense and is intended for items not generally purchased.[1] Depending on the size of the athletic training budget, the capital expense can range from modality units to taping and treatment tables or can progress to items in excess of $50,000 to $100,000 (e.g., isokinetic machines, X-ray units). The capital budget also may include funds allocated for future construction projects or renovation of athletic training facilities. This budget tends to develop over a number of years through fund-raising or bond initiatives and is not as accessible as the operating budget.[1]

■ Budget Programs

There are numerous techniques used in developing budgets and accessing the funds. Many times, the protocol for determining which budget system is utilized is assigned by the institution. The athletic training department then follows the same budget program as the rest of the school.

Line Item Budget

The first type of budget program to be discussed is the line item budget—a commonly used method for athletic departments. This system allocates funds by categories for each sport and department. Typical athletic training items would include taping supplies, expendable or disposable supplies, student materials, operations, travel, and professional development.[1] Under each classification, there may be numerous subcategories to allow for more concise bookkeeping and follow-up. The funds in each category are rarely transferable to other subgroups. This can be difficult if costs in one category are extremely high for a given year. The line item system does not account for long-term planning and appropriation. This budget is renewed each year without rollover of any remaining funds.

> **budget** An estimate of expected income and expense for a given period in the future.

Zero-Based Budget

A second type of budget system often used in athletic training programs is the zero-based budget.[1] This system is developed on the basis of the performance of the program in question. Each year the department must demonstrate its needs and justify the expenses that it expects to incur. The benefit of the zero-based budget is, with proper planning, the allocation can increase in a given year or be developed with long-term goals in mind. The detriment of the system is a constant need to justify any and all expenditures. It also necessitates a great deal of forethought and planning, and it results in difficulty with managing unexpected expenses.

■ Budget Process

When developing the budget for a department, it is important to consider both what materials and supplies you will need throughout the year and what materials are already on hand.[1] Prior to creating a supply order, it is paramount to complete an **inventory**, a listing of which supplies are available and in what quantities. This inventory should be completed on an annual basis at the very least; it is preferable, however, to complete an evaluation more often, either every athletic season or academic semester. A thorough catalog of all materials not only allows you to develop an idea of which supplies to order, but also ensures that supplies are not disappearing more quickly from the facility than expected. An inventory should be maintained as a continuous system, placing each inventory in a side-by-side manner allowing for a multiyear analysis. Trends and patterns of use will develop throughout the years, making it easier for the staff to create orders for supplies.

When creating a supply order, it is beneficial to the athletic trainer to request bids from several distributors. Often the price for supplies that is listed in the distributed catalog is intended for an individual who is purchasing single items or for schools who are ordering a small number of supplies. When there is a large-scale order being

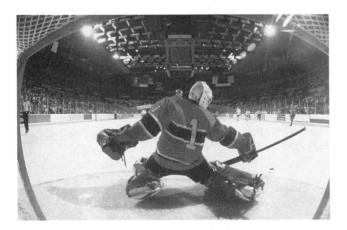

created, the company may be willing to offer a discount in exchange for your business. By soliciting several suppliers for a bid price, an athletic trainer is able to secure the best deal and, as a result, save money in the budget for other expenditures.

To fully utilize the bid process for the athletic training room, it is best to determine three to five companies that are interested in developing a long-term relationship with your institution. Once the supply order has been developed, the athletic trainer should submit this order to the bid department of each company that has been selected. The company then will return the order with their best price listed for each item. Depending on the individual institutional philosophy, the athletic training staff may elect to choose the best overall bid price for all of the supplies or the best price for each individual item.

Once the items have been selected, the staff will create a purchase order and complete the process by placing the order with the selected companies. It is important that the athletic trainer is straightforward with the companies that are solicited for bid requests. Each company should know the policy of the department and the protocol for what supplies are purchased from which company. This will ensure that there is no ill will if a bid is not accepted.

■ Personnel Management

One of the head athletic trainer's most important roles in the administration of the athletic training room is the oversight of personnel. Without proper personnel management, the athletic training room and team coverage can quickly become disorganized, unproductive, and a genuine mess.

The traditional athletic training staff will consist of a team of full-time and part-time certified athletic trainers, graduate assistant athletic trainers, and athletic training students who are there for the opportunity to gain practical experience during their education. Each staff member should be given responsibilities consistent with his or her time allocation for athletic training.

Full-time staff members should be the primary athletic trainers for the institution. They will generally be assigned to cover the collision, contact, or other high-risk sports.[1] Full-time staff members may also be assigned ancillary duties that can include budget oversight, inventory, physician coordination, health programming, drug testing, and so forth. There may be full-time staff members with

inventory A complete listing of stock on hand that is created annually.

teaching responsibilities in addition to their duties in the athletic training room. These staff members may have scheduling issues for team coverage based on class conflicts that will need to be addressed. In this situation, it would be appropriate to assign teaching responsibilities to staff that are not traveling with a team during the semester in which a course is taught.

Part-time and graduate assistant athletic trainers are being utilized at an increasing rate in both the collegiate and high school settings. These employees will tend to work fewer hours in the athletic training room than the full-time staff and be given fewer team and ancillary responsibilities. Part-time staff may have other assignments within the institution or the local community. For instance, a part-time employee may be a component of a rehabilitation clinic's high school outreach program or the athletic trainer may be a faculty member with a dual appointment who is allotted a set time for athletic coverage within his or her academic duties.

This position, as opposed to a full-time employee with teaching responsibilities, will face the challenge of teaching an allotted course load, conducting research, completing the requirements for tenure, and offering his or her services to the athletic training department. Care should be taken with dual appointment employees to ensure that they are able to meet all of these expectations productively without excessive stress or hours.

Part-time athletic trainers often are utilized to provide coverage for teams that the full-time staff cannot cover otherwise or offer athletic training room hours during traditional practice times. The part-time staff offers a valuable service to the athletic training program without the budgetary cost of adding full-time staff members.

The head athletic trainer is responsible for the management of the entire staff so that the athletic department receives the medical coverage required for their program and athletes, while the well being of each and every athletic training staff member is protected as much as possible. It often is a juggling act for the head athletic trainer to ensure that both of these requirements are met to the satisfaction of all parties.

Situations also may arise where the head athletic trainer and/or other staff members are required to take a leadership role in conflict management. Whether that conflict occurs between staff members, coaches, administrators, or athletes is inconsequential. The athletic training staff must make every effort to reach an agreement or at least an understanding between the involved parties so that the issue is resolved and the atmosphere of the athletic training room is not affected negatively.

Liability

Lawsuits have become extremely familiar in today's society. It has reached a point that people will utilize a lawsuit almost as a "feeling-out" process to see if a settlement is possible with or without a hope for winning the case.

The most frequent legal problem an athletic trainer will face is **liability**. Liability is responsibility for one's actions, specifically when those actions cause harm or injury.[2] Liability can be proven through negligent behavior, failure to inform a patient of all pertinent information, breach of contract, or assault and battery. Of those causes, the athletic training profession is most often liable for **negligence**.[2]

---

liability The state of being legally responsible for the harm one causes another person.

negligence The failure to use ordinary or responsible care.

Fast Fact

For more information on legal issues and recent lawsuits related to sports participation, please visit http://www.gym2jury.com. This Web site discusses current legal issues in athletics, recommends publications that provide in-depth discussions of sports law, and offers consulting services if a lawsuit arises.

■ Negligence

Two forms of negligence may occur—**omission** or **commission**. Omission is a failure to act in a given situation. Athletic trainers, because of their certifications and knowledge of emergency care, have a responsibility to act if a medical issue arises. Commission, on the other hand, occurs when the athletic trainer acts in an improper manner. Because of the advanced training that athletic trainers receive, they are expected to treat a patient appropriately in any medical situation or summon advanced personnel if needed.

To prove negligence in court, the patient must demonstrate that four criteria were met. First, there must be a duty to act for the defendant. The duty to act is an obligation recognized by the law requiring a person to conform to a certain standard of conduct for the protection of others.[3] This standard of conduct is developed by each state as a defined scope of practice and a standard of care for all health professions. The National Athletic Trainers' Association (NATA) has created its own standard of care for the athletic training profession (**Table 2.1**). An athletic trainer, when certified, falls under this scope of practice, which determines which tasks the athletic trainer may and may not complete. As a member of an institution, the athletic trainer then will be given job responsibilities within the scope of practice. The duty to act arises out of the job description and the responsibilities associated with the treatment of athletes.[4–7]

The second criterion of negligence is a breach of duty. This criterion is proven when the athletic trainer, who is improperly completing his or her job, violates the standard of care that was discussed earlier. The breach of duty can occur in prevention, standard of care, or disclosure. In regard to prevention, if an athletic trainer allows practice to occur in unsafe environmental conditions (e.g., heat/cold, poor field condition), then there is a breach of duty. The other two aspects—standard of care and disclosure—have been discussed previously.

Causation is the third criterion for negligence. Causation is defined as when an athletic trainer's actions lead

---

omission When a person fails to perform a legal duty.

commission When a person commits an act that is not legally his or hers to perform.

causation The determination that the actions of a person led to damage and to what extent the person is responsible for the damage caused.

vicarious liability When one person is liable for the negligent actions of another person, even though the first person was not directly responsible.

TABLE 2.1
ATHLETIC TRAINING STANDARDS OF PRACTICE
1. Direction—all care performed under the direction of a physician
2. Prevention
3. Immediate Care
4. Clinical Evaluation and Diagnosis
5. Treatment, Rehabilitation, and Reconditioning
6. Program Discontinuation—once the patient has received optimal benefit
7. Organization and Administration

Data from: Board of Certification. *BOC Standards of Practice.* Retrieved September 4, 2007, from http://www.boatc.org.

to the damage incurred and to what extent that person is responsible for the damage. The results of the action must be considered foreseeable to the average individual with the same level of knowledge and certification. If the actions are considered unforeseen by a prudent and reasonable athletic trainer, then this criterion has not been met.

The fourth and final criterion under negligence is damage. If the athlete does not suffer residual damage, then his or her injury does not qualify for negligent behavior, even if the athletic trainer acted in an improper manner. A lawsuit arguing negligence can be successful only if all four criteria have been met.

Vicarious Liability

Another concern for staff members in negligence cases is known as **vicarious liability**. Head athletic trainers or full-time staff members may be held liable for the actions of athletic trainers who are under their supervision (e.g., part-time staff, graduate assistants). Vicarious liability results when one athletic trainer acts in a negligent manner while under the supervision of another staff member. Legally, both athletic trainers are liable for the actions of the negligent staff member.[8]

This also may occur in athletic training education programs, when certified athletic trainers are held liable for the actions of their students. It is important in either situation to provide the appropriate training to all members of the athletic training program and also provide suitable supervision for junior staff members or athletic training students.

Good Samaritan Law

The final consideration to be discussed under liability is the **Good Samaritan law**. This protocol states that if an individual comes to the aid of an injured party—even without a duty to act—and stays within the appropriate standard of care, then they are protected from legal actions. The law does not condone negligent behavior from the assisting party, but does protect the individual if injuries occur from appropriate care.

A frequent benefit of this law for athletic trainers is during voluntary coverage where the athletic trainer is not involved with his or her traditional employment. Each state may have different variations of the Good Samaritan law. It is important for all athletic trainers to determine the level of legal protection that their home state provides.

■ Avoiding Litigation

There are numerous preventive steps that may be taken by an athletic trainer to reduce the likelihood of a lawsuit (**Table 2.2**). These steps are intended to be completed prior to any incident and do not provide legal benefit in cases involving negligence. Each athletic training staff should review the institution's policies and procedures and determine which specific protocols should be developed to minimize the risk of a lawsuit.

■ Liability Insurance

Most employers at the high school and collegiate levels offer liability insurance for their staff. This insurance protects the staff from the punitive damages they may incur as the

result of a lawsuit. It also preserves the individual's personal assets from inclusion in the legal proceedings.

It is highly recommended that all athletic trainers purchase some form of liability insurance to protect their personal interests if they will be volunteering or working outside of their traditional employment. Liability insurance purchased individually also may act as surplus coverage beyond that offered by the employer. The NATA offers a policy for purchase by its members to serve as personal liability insurance. It provides $2 million per incident and $4 million per year for all incidents. The traditional institution coverage ranges from $100,000 to $200,000 per incident.[2]

■ Emergency Action Plan

A key component to protecting an athletic training staff from liability is developing an **emergency action plan (EAP)**. The EAP is a well-developed and deliberate protocol that details the necessary steps required to afford an injured athlete with the optimal level of care. In the event of serious injuries, prompt medical care is essential to provide the athlete with the best chance for survival.

The EAP is an institution's written policy that lists who will render emergency care and who will control the spectator aspect of the situation, which may include fans, teammates, coaches, or family members. The EAP

TABLE 2.2
STEPS TO AVOID LITIGATION
1. Develop a list of job expectations.
2. Maintain CPR/first aid certification.
3. Develop an emergency action plan.
4. Obtain consent form/waiver.
5. Conduct preparticipation physicals.
6. Document all injuries.
7. Consistently update education.
8. Periodically inspect facilities and equipment.
9. Maintain effective lines of communication

Source: Pfeiffer RP, Mangus BC. *Concepts of Athletic Training*, 5th ed. Sudbury, MA: Jones and Bartlett, 2008.

Good Samaritan law Provides limited protection against legal liability to any individual who voluntarily chooses to provide first aid.

emergency action plan (EAP) A written document that details the standard of care required in an emergency at a specific institution.

also discusses what type of care should be initiated in life-threatening situations. In the event that an ambulance is required, the plan lists who will contact the ambulance and meet emergency medical personnel when they arrive at the facility. Finally, the EAP should note which institutional staff must be notified during an emergency, whether that is campus security, the dean of students, or the athletic director.[1]

It is essential that the EAP be reviewed annually to make certain that the information is accurate and up-to-date. The athletic training staff also should schedule mock emergencies to prepare both the certified athletic trainers and the athletic training students in case a medical emergency does arise during practice or competition.

 ## Medical Insurance

Because of the high costs of medical care in the United States today, **insurance** has become more and more important for both the athlete and the athletic department. Several different types of medical insurance available are discussed in this section.

There are two basic forms of insurance policies: medical and health insurance. *Medical insurance* covers a predetermined percentage of an individual's medical expenses that result from illnesses and injuries. On the other hand, *health insurance* covers the same medical costs, as well as preventive care such as wellness programs. These types of insurance in the athletic setting can be purchased

either by the athlete or the institution that sponsors the sports program.[2]

If the athlete or the athlete's parents purchase an insurance policy to cover medical expenses, it is considered the **primary insurance coverage**, or the first dollar coverage.[2] The primary policy is responsible for the initial review and payment of expenses related to illness or injury. As mentioned before, this policy covers only a predetermined percentage of the expenses. To cover the remaining costs, the institution may purchase a secondary (accident) coverage policy for its students.

A **secondary insurance** policy is responsible for the remaining portion of the medical expenses incurred with any athletic injury. The National Collegiate Athletic Association (NCAA) now requires all member athletic departments to provide secondary insurance coverage for their athletes. This rule was instituted prior to the 2005–2006 academic year.[9] The new policy ensures that all athletes at NCAA institutions are provided with some form of coverage for their medical expenses.

Because secondary insurance policies do not cover medical expenses until the primary insurance has reviewed the injury, many institutions require that their athletes purchase some form of insurance as their primary coverage to protect the athlete from incurring debt as a result of any athletic injuries. This insurance may be purchased individually or through the school. Neither the NCAA nor the National Federation of State High School Associations requires the athlete to obtain primary insurance coverage, although it is recommended that an athlete purchase an individual policy. It is dependent upon the school or district association to determine the level of insurance coverage expected of its athletes.[2,10]

There are several **exclusions** found in the accident policies purchased by athletic departments. An exclusion is a situation that is specifically outlined in the policy as not covered by the insurance company.[2] The basic insurance covers any injury sustained in competition, established practices, or team travel. Nonaccident or chronic injuries that result from sports participation, such as sports hernias, stress fractures, or overuse injuries, often are considered an exclusion and as such are not covered under the school's secondary policy.

Another type of exclusion found in athletic accident policies is the **preexisting condition**. A preexisting condition is an injury that has occurred previously and may predispose an athlete to reinjury. For instance, an athlete with a ligament sprain prior to the season may not be covered if reinjury occurs during the season. An average time frame for a preexisting condition to be considered in the payment decision is 6 to 12 months from medical clearance to participate. From then on, an injury may be considered a new occurrence.

---

insurance The act of insuring property, life, one's person, and so on against loss or harm arising in specified contingencies and in consideration of a payment proportionate to the risk involved.

primary insurance coverage All expenses related to an injury that an insurance company provides within a policy.

secondary insurance Insurance coverage that provides for the remaining expenses once a primary coverage plan has completed its payments.

exclusions A specific situation that is not covered by an insurance policy.

preexisting condition A condition that is present prior to the current injury that predisposes an individual to damage. Preexisting conditions often are considered exclusions for insurance policies.

When determining the payment of an accident claim, an insurance company will follow the policy of what is usual, customary, and reasonable (UCR). The insurance company will evaluate what is a usual fee for the service rendered. It then will examine the customary fee in the geographic area in question and finally a reasonable fee for the specific service. The UCR will determine the amount of the bill that the insurance company will cover with the remainder assessed to the individual or the institution.[2]

■ Types of Health Care Coverage

Insurance companies offer many different types of health care coverage to individuals who purchase a policy. The branch of health care coverage that we focus on is managed care organizations because it has become increasingly popular, as health care costs have risen.

There are four traditional types of managed care organizations. They are health maintenance organizations (HMOs), preferred provider organizations (PPOs), point-of-service plans (POSs), and exclusive provider organizations (EPOs). Each of these services has benefits and detriments, which are discussed.

Health Maintenance Organizations

The health maintenance organization (HMO) is an established group of health care professionals that offers services to an enrolled population. The HMO covers 100% of the costs for all services as long as those services are rendered in the preassigned facility. The disadvantage of this system occurs when the enrolled individual is not able to receive treatment at the specified facility. This is especially important for collegiate athletes who attend school away from home. The athlete or the secondary insurance will be charged a large portion of the bill (if not all of it) if the athlete is unable to return home for evaluation.[9]

Preferred Provider Organization

A preferred provider organization (PPO) offers a larger network of health care providers for its members than the traditional HMO does. The enrolled member receives a list of approved providers throughout the network, which often consists of a state or geographic region of the country. If services are received through any approved provider, then the insurance covers 80% to 100% of the cost. The member has the opportunity to leave the network for treatment but receives less benefit.[11]

A benefit to enrolling in a PPO versus an HMO is the direct access to medical specialists. In a PPO, if the specialist is in-network, the member can schedule appointments directly with the specialist without any loss of benefit. An HMO, on the other hand, assigns each member to a doctor—usually a primary care physician—who acts as the "gatekeeper." This doctor is the initial point of contact for any illness or injury and will then refer the member to the appropriate specialist (whether it is a cardiologist, neurologist, orthopedic surgeon, or another type of specialist). The fee coverage decreases if the patient does not follow protocol and see the gatekeeper physician first.

Point of Service

The point-of-service plan (POS) is a combination of both the HMO and the PPO. The POS offers its members the HMO-style network of providers and the referral structure, but also allows for services to be performed out of network as does the PPO. This plan offers more flexibility than the traditional HMO does, but also maintains the network of providers and easy access that the HMO offers.[11,12]

Exclusive Provider Organization

The exclusive provider organization (EPO) is similar to the PPO in that it provides a broad network of physicians who are directly affiliated with the insurance company. The member can see any of the providers in-network and the insurance will cover the expenses. However, the member must obtain services from an approved physician to receive payment. Unlike the PPO, the providing physician may not be allowed to treat a patient who is not a member of the organization. This obviously limits the providers and would make it extremely difficult for these physicians to be affiliated with an athletic department.[2]

■ Deductible/Co-Pay

In many of these managed care organizations, the members may be required, as part of their coverage, to pay either a **deductible** or a **co-pay**. The deductible is a predetermined monetary amount that each member must pay before the insurance begins its reimbursement. There is usually a separate deductible for different types of service, such as emergency room visits, surgeries, childbirth, or general services.

A co-pay is a preassigned fee that the member is responsible for at each visit. Again, this fee may be different for each type of service. Both deductibles and co-pays are eligible for payment by the secondary insur-

> **deductible** The amount for which the insured is liable on each injury before an insurance company will make payment.
>
> **co-pay** A relatively small fixed fee required by a health insurer to be paid by the patient at the time of each office visit, outpatient service, or filling of a prescription.

ance policy. It is important that the athlete keep receipts and documentation to submit to the secondary plan for reimbursement.

■ Catastrophic Insurance Coverage

A catastrophic insurance policy consists of a plan that covers any injury so severe that the patient's quality of life is dramatically compromised. The care of this type of patient is extremely expensive, often requiring 24-hour supervision or an extended stay at a medical facility. The NCAA purchases a catastrophic insurance plan for all of its member institutions to provide for any traumatic injuries that occur to the covered athletes. The maximum payout for the NCAA plan is $20 million in lifetime benefits after a $75,000 deductible is reached. The premium for this plan is purchased with the proceeds from the Division I basketball championships.[13]

■ NCAA Regulations Regarding Medical Claims

The NCAA has developed a policy for its member institutions that determines what medical care is allowed for its athletes. Certain medical treatments are not permissible under the NCAA guidelines. Treatments such as dental work outside of accidental injury, treatment for any illness or injury that is not the direct result of athletic participation, or payment for prescribed eyewear cannot be filed with the institution's insurance policy. Inappropriate claims are considered NCAA rules violations and can result in infractions placed on the school and the athletic department.[10,14]

 ## Documentation

Documentation and record keeping are essential to ensure and demonstrate that each athlete has consistently received the best care possible. Documentation also assists in protecting the athletic trainer in the event that legal issues arise at any point in his or her career. The documented information that should be kept on file for an institution's athletes includes personal, insurance, and medical materials.

The personal information consists of basic demographic information, such as name, birth date, year in school, address, and phone number, as well as emergency contact information in the event that a parent or guardian needs to be reached.

The insurance information for each athlete should be kept on file and updated annually. The athletic trainer

must have the company name and address, the name of the policy holder (in case it is through a parent or guardian), the group name or number, and the policy number. The athletic trainer also should record the type of coverage and any regulations regarding benefits—for instance, if referrals or preauthorization is required.

The medical data in the file is the most pertinent information for the staff to utilize on a daily basis. This information begins when the athlete enters school and completes a previous medical history form and preparticipation physical exam. It continues throughout his or her career with information regarding injury evaluations, treatment and rehabilitation records, and office notes from doctors' visits. The medical information develops into a detailed history of the athlete's medical status throughout his or her time at an institution.

All medical records should be kept as accurately as possible for each and every athlete. In the event of a lawsuit, the injured party's lawyer has the right to subpoena the person's medical records from both the athletic training room and the team physician's office. The medical record is the definitive documentation for detailing which steps were taken in the evaluation of an injury and what care was offered to the athlete. Each institution must create a policy for what exactly is defined as an injury—for instance, whether *every* issue that arises is considered an injury, or if time lost/missed activities are taken into account. Once that policy is developed, the athletic trainer must take special care to complete the necessary documentation for every single injury. Without precise detail in all documents, it can be difficult for an athletic trainer to prove in court that he or she provided the optimal level of care for the injured athlete.

The athlete's record should be kept on file by the athletic trainer for several years after the completion of the athlete's career. The length of time these records should be kept is dependent upon the state in which the institution's campus is situated. Each state has a set of laws

questionnaire that requests the personal injury/illness history of the incoming athlete, the medical history of that individual's close family, and an orthopedic and head injury history for the student.

The personal medical history examines the injuries and illnesses that an athlete has faced throughout his or her life. In this section, it is important to focus on cardiac abnormalities, diabetes, allergies (especially those that result in severe or life-threatening reactions), asthma, prescription medications that the athlete may take consistently (e.g., amphetamine [Adderall], montelukast sodium [Singulair], blood pressure medications), and any other conditions that may inhibit or disqualify an athlete from competition.

The family medical history covers any potential conditions that can be inherited from close relatives. This may include sickle cell traits, cardiac or pulmonary issues, cancers, and/or any sudden deaths—especially at a young age. See **Figure 2.1** for an example of physical examination paperwork.

The orthopedic and head injury history details the athlete's previous ailments in the musculoskeletal system including surgeries, hospital stays, concussions, and lingering symptoms from previous injuries.

A physician and a member of the athletic training staff will review the information in the previous medical history upon completion and highlight medical red flags for further inspection or referral. After the athlete's first year when the initial history form is completed, he or she will only need to submit a health update form for each year thereafter. The athlete should update the initial history with any significant illnesses or injuries that have occurred during the previous academic year.

known as the **statute of limitations**. This statute assigns a time frame that an injured individual has to file a claim or lawsuit against another party. The time frame outlined in the statute of limitations is what should determine the length of time that records are kept on file. Depending on the state in question, this time frame will generally run from 1 to 8 years.[2]

■ Preparticipation Documentation

The athlete's medical record is a continuously evolving document that can be described as a work in progress until the athlete has completed his or her career at an institution. The following documents contain the information that should be included in the medical record.

Previous Medical History

All incoming athletes, prior to the first practice of the season, must complete a previous medical history. Typically, this form is filled out as part of the school's preparticipation physical exam. The medical history is a detailed

Physical Examination

The physical examination consists of a thorough physician evaluation accompanied by a blood pressure and pulse check, vision assessment, and height/weight measurement. This information, along with the medical history, assists the team physician in determining the athlete's ability to compete in a sport.

There are certain illnesses and injuries that are not conducive to competing in athletics or that demand special care and consideration prior to the initiation of practices and competition. These athletes, in conjunction with the athletic trainer and team physician, will determine during the preparticipation physical exam if participation is viable or appropriate regarding the injury or illness in question.

statute of limitations A statute defining the period within which legal action may be taken.

GREENSBORO COLLEGE: NEW ATHLETE PHYSICAL FORM

Date of Exam: _____

Name _____ Sex _____ Age_____ Date of Birth _____

Sport(s) _____ SSN _____

Campus Address _____

Cell Phone ( ) _____ Home Phone ( ) _____

In case of emergency, contact: Name _____ Relationship _____

Phone (H) ( ) _____ (W) ( ) _____

Please answer the following questions by circling yes or no. If yes, explain what, where, and when.

1. Have you had a medical illness or injury since your last check up or sports physical? Yes No

   If yes, explain _____

2. Do you have an ongoing or chronic illness? Yes No

   If yes, explain _____

3. Have you ever been hospitalized overnight? Yes No

   If yes, explain _____

4. Have you ever had surgery? Yes No

   If yes, explain _____

5. Are you currently taking any prescription or non-prescription (over the counter) medications or pills or using an inhaler? Yes No

   If yes, explain _____

6. Have you ever taken any supplements or vitamins to help you gain or lose weight or improve your performance? Yes No

   If yes, explain _____

7. Do you have any allergies (including pollen, medicine, food, or stinging insects)? Yes No

   If yes, explain _____

8. Have you ever had a rash or hives develop during or after exercise? Yes No

   If yes, explain _____

9. Have you ever passed out during or after exercise? Yes No

   If yes, explain _____

10. Have you ever been dizzy during or after exercise? Yes No

    If yes, explain _____

11. Have you ever had chest pain during or after exercise? Yes No

    If yes, explain _____

12. Do you tire more quickly than your friends during exercise? Yes No

    If yes, explain _____

13. Have you ever had racing of your heart or skipped heartbeats? Yes No

    If yes, explain _____

14. Have you had high blood pressure or high cholesterol? Yes No

    If yes, explain _____

15. Have you ever been told you have a heart murmur? Yes No

    If yes, explain _____

FIGURE 2.1 Greensboro College: New Athlete Physical Form.

16. Has any family member or relative died of heart problems or of sudden death before age 50?   Yes   No

    If yes, explain _____

17. Have you had a severe viral infection (like myocarditis or mononucleosis) within the last month?   Yes   No

    If yes, explain _____

18. Has a physician ever denied or restricted your participation in sports for any heart problems?   Yes   No

    If yes, explain _____

19. Have you ever had a head injury or concussion?   Yes   No

    If yes, explain _____

20. Have you ever been knocked out, become unconscious, or lost your memory?   Yes   No

    If yes, explain _____

21. Have you ever had a seizure?   Yes   No

    If yes, explain _____

22. Do you have frequent or severe headaches?   Yes   No

    If yes, explain _____

23. Have you ever had numbness or tingling in your arms, hands, legs, or feet?   Yes   No

    If yes, explain _____

24. Have you ever had a stinger, burner, or pinched nerve?   Yes   No

    If yes, explain _____

25. Have you ever had a heat related illness (including cramps, dizziness, or fainting)?   Yes   No

    If yes, explain _____

26. Do you cough, wheeze, or have trouble breathing during or after activity?   Yes   No

    If yes, explain _____

27. Do you have asthma?   Yes   No

    If yes, explain _____

28. Do you have seasonal allergies that require medical treatment?   Yes   No

    If yes, explain _____

29. Do you use any special protective or corrective equipment or devices that aren't usually used for your sport or position (such as knee brace, special neck roll, foot orthotics, retainer for your teeth, or hearing aid)?   Yes   No

    If yes, explain _____

30. Have you had any problem with your eyes or vision?   Yes   No

    If yes, explain _____

31. Do you wear glasses, contacts, or protective eyewear?   Yes   No

    If yes, explain _____

32. Have you broken or fractured any bones or dislocated any joints?   Yes   No

    If yes, explain _____

33. Have you had any other problems with pain or swelling in muscles, tendons, bones, or joints?   Yes   No

    If yes, explain _____

34. Do you have any menstrual irregularities, problems, or missed periods?   Yes   No

    If yes, explain _____

35. Do you have any other medical concerns that you would like addressed?   Yes   No

    If yes, explain _____

I hereby state that, to the best of my knowledge, my answers to the above questions are complete and correct.

Signature of Athlete _____   Date _____

FIGURE 2.1   *(Continued)*

Disqualification from participation may be recommended by the team physician to protect the athlete and the athletic department from future issues. The athlete may choose to follow up with a specialist for a second opinion or, in some cases, sign a waiver that would allow participation despite the increased risk associated with the injury or illness. Waivers are discussed in more detail below.

The NCAA, effective in 2007, now requires that all incoming athletes receive a complete physical within 6 months prior to participation their first year.[10] This is best conducted on campus with the team physicians if possible. Family physicians or other doctors may complete the physical process for incoming athletes; however, it is beneficial to the athletic training staff to meet all new athletes and introduce them and their medical history to the team physicians. It is up to the discretion of each individual school whether the athletes receive a physical any of the subsequent years during their career.

Concussion Assessment

Because of the prevalence of concussions in athletics, many athletic training departments are now completing concussion assessments on athletes in contact sports. The assessment evaluates the cognitive abilities of each athlete prior to any incidence of injury at the institution. Through various memory and analytical tests, the staff can develop a baseline value, which is then compared to post-injury data during the season.

This comparison is useful in assessing cognitive deficits that result from a concussive injury exclusive from any preexisting deficits that were present. There are several established concussion assessment programs, with both electronic and paper versions, available for purchase and use by the athletic training department.

Waiver

After completion of the medical history and preparticipation physical exam, the athlete should sign some form of **waiver** or release of liability. The waiver should state the risks inherent in athletic competition and that the athlete is aware of these risks and chooses to voluntarily participate (legally known as **assumption of risk**). The waiver also can include authorization for release of medical

> **waiver** An intentional relinquishment of some right or interest.
> **assumption of risk** An individual, through either express or implied consent, assumes that some risk or danger will be involved in a particular undertaking.

information so that the athletic training staff may request office notes from physicians.

For schools with institutional drug testing policies, there may be a section on the waiver for authorization to conduct drug testing on the athlete. This section should be openly discussed with the athletic population in an educational session at the beginning of the academic year so that all questions about the drug testing policy may be answered.

Those athletes who have medical conditions that could limit or disqualify them from participation occasionally may be able to sign a waiver requesting the opportunity to play with the medical condition and releasing the institution from any liability that may result from further injury. These waivers have been successfully utilized in court cases, but do not entirely shield the athletic training staff or the institution from litigation and a legal victory for an injured athlete.[15]

■ Injury Evaluation

Any injury that is assessed in the athletic training room must be recorded on an injury evaluation form. The athlete's name, sport, date of injury, affected body part, and the specific injury complaint should be listed at the top of the form. The remainder of the form should be completed in Subjective, Objective, Assessment, and Plan (SOAP) note format. A sample injury report is shown in **Figure 2.2**.

■ SOAP Notes

Athletic injury assessment has long been based on the SOAP note format that was developed by Dr. Lawrence Reed for medical note taking. The acronym SOAP stands for Subjective, Objective, Assessment, and Plan.[2,16] Throughout the SOAP note, the athletic trainer can save space and time by utilizing standard abbreviations that are universally understood and accepted in the medical community. Some of the more pertinent abbreviations for use by athletic trainers are listed in **Table 2.3**.

Subjective

The subjective portion of the assessment details the information that the patient provides for the current condition. The chief complaint, previous history, mechanism of injury (MOI), sounds or feelings at the time of injury, and descriptions of pain and functional deficits should all be included in this section of the evaluation.

Objective

The objective information includes the observations and tests conducted by the athletic trainer or physician to determine the nature of the injury. These tests include

INJURY REPORT

Name: _____ Date: _____ Sport: _____

Injury Occurred During: ( ) Practice ( ) Scrimmage ( ) Game ( ) Other _____

Playing Surface: ( ) Turf ( ) Grass ( ) Hard court Location: _____

Time of Injury: ( ) 1st ( ) 2nd ( ) 3rd ( ) 4th ( ) OT ( ) Quarter ( ) Half

Mechanism of Injury: ( ) Running ( ) Cutting ( ) Jumping ( ) Kicking

                         ( ) Twisting ( ) Throwing ( )Catching

                         ( ) Direct contact with: ( ) Opponent ( ) Equipment ( ) Surface

Location of Injury: ( ) Toe ( ) Foot ( ) Ankle ( ) Shin/calf ( ) Knee ( ) Thigh/hamstring

                         ( ) Hip/groin ( ) Abdomen ( ) Back ( ) Chest ( ) Neck ( ) Head/face

                         ( ) Shoulder ( ) Upper arm ( ) Lower arm ( ) Wrist

                         ( ) Hand ( ) Finger/thumb

Side: ( ) Left ( ) Right ( ) N/A

History of Present Injury or Illness _____

_____

_____

_____

_____

_____

Objective _____

_____

_____

_____

_____

Assessment _____

_____

_____

_____

_____

Plan _____

_____

_____

_____

_____

Referral: ( ) Team Ortho ( ) Team Internist ( ) Emergency room/Urgent care ( ) Other: _____

Special Tests Recommendation: ( ) X-ray ( ) MRI ( ) Bone scan ( ) Other _____

_____

Reporting Athletic Training Staff Member

FIGURE 2.2 Injury Report.

TABLE 2.3

MEDICAL ABBREVIATIONS

AAROM	Active assistive range of motion	PROM	Passive range of motion
ADL	Activities of daily living	PTP	Painful to palpation
AP	Anterior-posterior	PWB	Partial weight bearing
AROM	Active range of motion	QD	Once daily
ASAP	As soon as possible	QID	Four times a day
Ath.	Athlete	R	Right
BID	Twice a day	RESP	Respiratory
B	Bilateral	r/o	Rule out
BP	Blood pressure	ROM	Range of motion
BPM	Beats per minute	RROM	Resistive range of motion
CC	Chief complaint	Rx	Treatment, prescription
C/O	Complains of	s/p	Post-surgery
CV	Cardiovascular	SOB	Shortness of breath
CWP	Cold whirlpool	Surg.	Surgery
Dx	Diagnosis	Sx	Symptoms
E.R.	Emergency room	TAB	Tablet
FROM	Full range of motion	TID	Three times a day
FWB	Full weight bearing	TTP	Tender to palpate
Fx	Fracture	Tx	Treatment
HR	Heart rate	WK	Week
Hx	History	WNL	Within normal limits
Jt.	Joint	WT	Weight
L	Left	WWP	Warm whirlpool
LOC	Loss of consciousness	1+	Mild
LROM	Loss/lack of range of motion	2+	Moderate
MD	Medical doctor	3+	Severe
MEDS	Medications	$\bar{c}$	With, W/
NEG/-	Negative	$\bar{s}$	Without, W/O
NWB	Non-weight bearing	>	Greater than
$\bar{p}$	Pain	<	Less than
POS/+	Positive	=	Equal
POST-OP	After surgery	~	Approximately
PRE-OP	Before surgery	%	Percent
PRN	As needed	↑	Increase

range of motion (ROM), manual muscle testing (MMT), reflexes, palpation, swelling, discoloration, and special tests for specific injuries. The types of tests, as well as the results, should be recorded in this section along with any other relevant information discovered during the evaluation.

Assessment

The assessment section consists of the athletic trainer's professional opinion of the injury based on the information accrued throughout the evaluation. This section is specifically entitled *assessment* to differentiate the determination of an injury by an athletic trainer versus a physician's diagnosis. This is an important distinction to bear in mind because of the aforementioned scope of practice. Athletic trainers who make a "diagnosis" are stepping out of the bounds of the scope of practice and opening themselves to legal action.

Plan

The plan is the final portion of the SOAP note. This section describes the treatment or rehabilitation plan for the athlete and the goals to be achieved prior to return to play.

■ Post-Injury Documentation

Treatment Log

A treatment log is completed each time an athlete receives any form of therapy in the athletic training facility. This information is either recorded on the original SOAP note or on a separate log sheet that also may be utilized as a check-in form. The athletic trainer should record the type of treatment provided and any notes of progress or decline in the athlete's condition. The progress notes should be specific and objective so that any staff member can examine the document and assist the athlete.

Rehabilitation Log

The rehabilitation log is similar to the treatment sheet except that it is utilized for an athlete recuperating from a long-term injury. The rehabilitation log records the therapeutic exercises and treatments that are completed daily during the athlete's progression to a return to play. This log can be taken from one athletic training facility to another or into the weight room dependent on the functional level of the injured student. The athletic trainer adds and discontinues exercises as the athlete progresses toward recovery.

■ Computers

The computer has become an integral facet of the athletic training room, as it has throughout society. As a result, most facilities now utilize their office computers to some degree for record keeping. Each individual institution and its staff determine the extent of computer usage for records and may choose to use any of a number of medical software programs that are available (e.g., Sportsware, SIMS).

These packages offer treatment logs, injury evaluation and follow-up forms, coaches' reports, and many other paperwork options for the athletic trainer. These computer programs allow easy access to records with much less storage space; however, they do require a great deal of time for data entry. The programs can be difficult to update during the busiest times of the day, resulting in treatment data that is not recorded. There also is the risk of losing data because of computer malfunction or theft. The athletic trainer must remember to back up data in several different formats to guarantee that no information is lost under any circumstance.

■ Confidentiality

It is important to remember that no matter what form of record keeping is utilized, the athletic trainer is always required to maintain complete confidentiality for all athletes' records. All documents must be kept in locked file cabinets or password-encoded files on the computer. The office where the file cabinets or computer is housed also should be locked when not in use to further ensure confidentiality.

The Health Insurance Portability and Accountability Act (HIPAA) places a monetary fine and jail term as punishment for any confidentiality violations to protect both athletic and nonathletic injury information. The athletic training staff and students may discuss the information as part of daily operations, but they may not discuss any injury information outside of the athletic training "family." This confidentiality agreement includes coaches, teammates, and the media unless the injured athlete has given written permission for the release of information to specific individuals.

Unfortunately, athletic training has been plagued by legal concerns and liability issues, as has the entire medical community. The benefit of these legal problems, though, is the consistent improvement in the health care system that has resulted. It is essential that the staff follow proper guidelines to ensure that all athletes receive the best care possible with the proper procedures and record keeping.

CHAPTER REVIEW

1. What are the two types of budget allocations used in athletic training?
2. What four criteria are needed to prove negligence?
3. What is an emergency action plan?
4. List the four types of health care coverage.
5. List the traditional stations found in a physical examination.
6. What are the four components of a SOAP note?
7. What does the acronym HIPAA stand for?

CRITICAL THINKING

How would you handle a difficult coach or co-worker?

REFERENCES

1. Anderson MK, Hall SJ, Martin M. *Sports Injury Management*, 2nd ed. Baltimore: Lippincott, Williams, & Wilkins, 2000.
2. Rankin JM, Ingersoll CD. *Athletic Training Management: Concepts and Applications*, 3rd ed. Boston: McGraw-Hill, 2006.
3. Pfeiffer RP, Mangus BC. *Concepts of Athletic Training*, 5th ed. Sudbury, MA: Jones and Bartlett, 2008.
4. Hawkins J, Appenzeller H. Legal aspects of sports medicine. In Mueller F, Ryan A (Eds.): *Prevention of Athletic Injuries: The Role of the Sports Medicine Team*. Philadelphia: FA Davis, 1991.
5. Osbourne B. (2001). Principles of liability for athletic trainers: managing sport-related concussion. *Journal of Athletic Training*, 36(3):316–321.
6. West SA, Ciccolella ME. (2004). Issues in the standard of care for certified athletic trainers. *Journal of Legal Aspects of Sport*, 14(1):64–74.
7. Board of Certification. *BOC Standards of Professional Practice*. Retrieved September 4, 2007, from http://www.bocatc.org.
8. Leverenz LJ, Helms LB. (1990). Suing athletic trainers: part I, a review of the case law involving athletic trainers. *Athletic Training*, 25(3):212–216.
9. Copeland J. (2005, July 18). Protective Custody: Requirement to maintain insurance certification among significant efforts to manage risk. *The NCAA News Online*. Retrieved September 29, 2006, from http://www.ncaa.org.
10. Klossner D., ed. *2006–2007 NCAA Sports Medicine Handbook*. Indianapolis, IN: NCAA, 2006.
11. Anderson E. (1995, September). Managed care terminology. *NATA News*, 12–13.
12. Prentice WE. *Arnheim's Principles of Athletic Training: A Competency-Based Approach*, 12th ed. Boston: McGraw-Hill, 2006.
13. National Collegiate Athletic Association. *NCAA Catastrophic Injury Insurance Program 2006–2007 Benefits Summary*. Retrieved September 29, 2006, from http://www.ncaa.org.
14. National Collegiate Athletic Association. *2006–2007 NCAA Divisions I, II, and III Manuals*. Indianapolis, IN: NCAA, 2006.
15. Anonymous. (2002). Court upholds liability waivers. *Journal of Physical Education, Recreation, & Dance*, 73(7):11.
16. Kettenbach G. *Writing SOAP notes*, 3rd ed. Philadelphia: FA Davis, 2004.

Protective Equipment

The first aspect of an athletic trainer's roles and responsibilities is the prevention of injury in athletes. Although not all injuries can be prevented, steps can be taken to decrease the risk or incidence of injuries. A principal component of that prevention is the proper fitting and maintenance of protective equipment. The National Collegiate Athletic Association (NCAA) requires specific equipment for selected sports (**Table 3.1**). The mandatory equipment has been proven effective in the protection of athletes and the prevention of injuries common to each individual sport.

The athletic trainer's responsibility, in conjunction with any equipment personnel, is to ensure that the institution purchases all necessary protective equipment for its athletes and that the equipment is fitted properly to provide optimal protection. Specific protective equipment and proper fitting protocols are discussed later in this chapter.

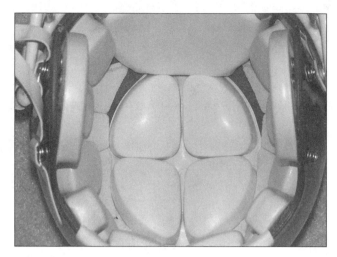

FIGURE 3.1A   Appropriate padding inside the helmet.

Football Helmets

An essential, and somewhat obvious, first step in proper football helmet fitting is to have the athlete present for the fitting session with the hairstyle and facial hair that he or she intends to maintain during the season. A player that intends to have long hair during the season should have long hair for the fitting session. A player that undergoes a dramatic hairstyle change after the initial fitting should be refitted because the hairstyle change can drastically alter the fit of the helmet.

The athletic trainer should visually examine all equipment, not just helmets, to ensure that there are no obvious defects and that the equipment has been inspected and approved by the appropriate organization prior to fitting any equipment. The governing body responsible for safety inspections of football helmets is the National Operating

Committee on Safety for Athletic Equipment (NOCSAE).[1] NOCSAE-approved football helmets have the NOCSAE sticker affixed to the back of the helmet approving it for use. All equipment must be checked for a visible approval sticker for liability reasons. Serious legal repercussions may occur if a helmet is issued to a student athlete without NOCSAE inspection or the approval sticker.

The athletic trainer should continue the visual examination of the equipment by searching for cracks in the outer shell of the helmet; inspecting the inner shell to determine if all of the proper padding is installed and has appropriate rebound response to compression (**Figure 3.1A**); and inspecting the facemask for visible defects. The outer shell of the helmet and the facemask must be sturdy enough to withstand the collision forces that occur throughout a football season. The interior padding should be whole, without any tears or cracks, and have appropriate compression and rebound tendency to absorb the impact forces from a direct blow. Faulty padding may lead to improper force absorption and increased injury, including lacerations from torn padding.

Once the helmet is deemed safe for use, the athletic trainer should have the athlete wet his or her hair to simulate the sweaty conditions present during practices and games. Next, measure the circumference of the head using a cloth tape measure (**Figure 3.1B**). The measurement is taken directly above the eyebrows of the athlete and the tape is wrapped around the head at the skull's widest point. Most helmet manufacturers provide a tape measure specifically for fitting purposes. A helmet-specific tape measure is labeled in both inches and helmet sizes. When used to measure the head, the tape will align with the range for each helmet size (Small–XX Large). The measurement provides an approximate size for trial,

TABLE 3.1

NCAA-MANDATED PROTECTIVE EQUIPMENT

Sport	Equipment	Sport	Equipment
1. Baseball	a. A double-earflap protective helmet while playing; helmet must carry the NOCSAE mark. b. All catchers must have throat guard on their mask. c. All catchers must wear protective helmet while playing.	8. Women's lacrosse	a. Goalkeepers must wear helmet with facemask, throat protector, mouthpiece, and chest protector. b. Field players should wear eye protectors. c. Mouthpiece that covers upper teeth.
2. Basketball	None.	9. Men's lacrosse	a. Protective helmet equipped with facemask and secure chinstrap. b. Mouthpiece that is a highly visible color. c. Gloves, shoulder pads, shoes, jersey. d. Throat and chest protector for a goalie.
3. Fencing	a. Masks with meshes of maximum 2.1 mm and from wires with a minimum gauge of 1 mm diameter. b. Gloves that cover the competitor's sword arm, halfway up the forearm. c. Protective jacket or vest. d. Ladies must wear a protective jacket made of metal. e. Underarm protector.	10. Rifle	a. Shooters and workers should wear hearing protectors and shooters should wear protective eyewear.
4. Field hockey	a. Goalkeepers must wear body and wraparound throat protector, pads, kickers, gloves, helmet, elbow pads. b. Mouth guards. c. Wraparound throat protector and helmet for player designated as "kicking back."	11. Soccer	a. Shin guards under socks.
		12. Skiing	a. Giant slalom racers must wear helmets designed for ski racing.
5. Football	a. Knee pads that cover the knee; no pads may be worn outside the pants. b. Face masks and helmets with a secure chinstrap; helmets must carry a warning label and must be approved by NOCSAE. c. Shoulder pads, hip pads with tailbone protectors, and thigh guards. d. Properly fitted mouthpiece.	13. Softball	a. Catcher must wear foot-to-knee shin guards. Helmet with built-in throat protector and chest protector. b. Double-earflap protective helmet while playing.
		14. Swimming/diving	None.
		15. Track and field	None.
6. Gymnastics	None.	16. Volleyball	None.
7. Ice hockey	a. Helmet with secure facemask. b. Facemask that protects eyes and face. c. Mouthpiece.	17. Water polo	a. Cap with protective ear guards.
		18. Wrestling	a. Protective ear guards.

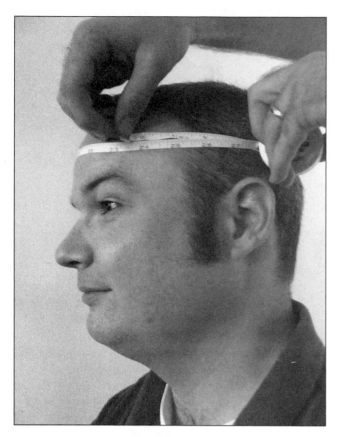

FIGURE 3.1B First measure the circumference of the head to determine the general helmet size.

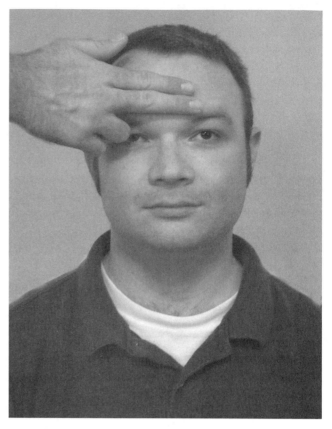

FIGURE 3.1C The front of the helmet should be approximately 2 finger-widths above the eyebrows.

but having the athlete physically wear the helmet is the preferred method for determining the exact fit for each individual.

After finding the approximate size, have the athlete place the helmet on his or her head to see if it is appropriate. Helmets vary slightly even within a specific size. An athlete may have to try several different helmets or different brands to find the best possible fit. Many different brands of helmet are available in the sporting goods market. Some helmets may be more effective for a specific athlete because of style preference, comfort, or injury history. Newer helmet models have been designed to decrease (but not eliminate) the risk for concussions and other head injuries. Athletes with a history of head injuries may wish to utilize these newer helmets even though they are more expensive, which may be a consideration for institutions with smaller budgets.

To put the helmet on, the athlete holds it upside down and grasps the ear holes on each side of the helmet. Have the athlete pull gently on the ear holes to widen the opening, provide easier access for the head, and decrease friction on the ears. Next, have the athlete place the helmet on his or her head beginning at the back of the skull and

pulling forward until the helmet is properly situated on the head.

The helmet should have a snug fit, but not be too tight for the athlete. The front of the helmet should rest one to two finger-widths above the athlete's eyebrows (**Figure 3.1C**). A distance from eyebrows to helmet greater than two finger-widths will cause the athlete discomfort because the helmet will be too tight on the top of the head. If there is less distance than one finger-width, then there is a danger the helmet will slip down over the eyes of the athlete and block vision or cause injury to the eyes or nose.

The alignment of the ear holes and back of the helmet should be examined once the front of the helmet is properly fitted. The ear holes should be even with the athlete's ears so that the padding of the helmet does not impinge on any part of the ear or ear lobe. The back of the helmet must be long enough to cover the base of the skull protecting the vulnerable brain stem from injury.

The athletic trainer also must check the detachable jaw/ear pads on the sides of the helmet to ensure a snug fit between the ear pads and the side of the jaw. There only should be enough room between the jaw and the pads on both sides to slide a tongue depressor through the

FIGURE 3.1D You should be able to slide a tongue depresser between the cheek and the pad to ensure a proper fit.

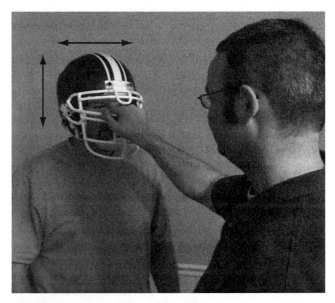

FIGURE 3.1E The helmet and head should move in unison when the helmet is shifted up, down, and side to side.

gap (**Figure 3.1D**). If the pads are too tight or too loose, remove them and try a different pad thickness until the correct fit is found.

After the helmet is aligned properly with a comfortable fit, the athletic trainer can test the helmet to make sure it is appropriate for athletic competition. The athlete will buckle the chinstrap to the proper position, which should be snug yet comfortable. Once the helmet is in place and the chinstrap is buckled, the athletic trainer should grasp the facemask in one hand and forcibly pull the helmet up, down, and side to side. The helmet should stay in contact with the head at all times and allow little movement of the helmet in any direction, with relation to the head, during the test (**Figure 3.1E**).

If the helmet moves too far up, down, or to the sides, then either the padding or the helmet is not appropriate for the athlete. Try adjusting the size of the pads or adding/removing air from the individual pads to determine if a better fit is possible. Once the helmet is adjusted to minimize movement in all directions, it can be cleared for use for the athlete. Each athlete's helmet size and fit are different and require an individual test prior to being approved for play (**Table 3.2**).

TABLE 3.2
HELMET FITTING PROTOCOL
1. Identify inspection sticker from appropriate governing body.
2. Visually inspect for noticeable defects and proper padding.
3. Athlete should be present with in-season hairstyle.
4. Measure head circumference to determine approximate size.
5. Have the athlete place the helmet on his or her head.
6. Helmet should be 1–2 finger-widths above the eyebrows.
7. Ensure that ear holes line up appropriately and the back of the helmet covers the base of the skull.
8. There should be only a tongue depressor's width between the jaw and padding without being too tight.
9. There should be 3 finger-widths between the facemask and the tip of the nose.
10. Chinstrap should be comfortable and snug when buckled.
11. The helmet and head should maintain good contact during movement in all directions.

FIGURE 3.1F The facemask should be approximately 3 finger-widths away from the nose.

FIGURE 3.2 Ice hockey helmet.

Facemasks

Each position in football requires a different, unique style of facemask. During the fitting process, the athlete should be given a facemask appropriate to his or her role on the field. If a facemask is changed, check to make sure that the clips attaching the facemask to the helmet are tightened and the facemask does not shift. The facemask should sit three finger-widths from the nose to protect from injury during contact (**Figure 3.1F**).

Ice Hockey/Lacrosse/ Goalkeeper Helmets

Each NCAA sport requiring a helmet incorporates similar fitting protocols as that discussed for the football helmet. Ice hockey (**Figure 3.2**), men's lacrosse, and certain goalkeeper helmets, for instance, must first be inspected for the certification sticker guaranteeing the equipment has met all safety standards. The governing bodies for these sports include the American Society for Testing and Materials (ASTM), the Canadian Standards Association (CSA), and the Hockey Equipment Certification Council (HECC).[1,2] These governing bodies inspect and test the equipment to ensure the safety of the helmets.

Following a visual inspection to rule out any defects, the helmet is fitted and tested in a similar manner as a football helmet is. Ice hockey and men's lacrosse helmets tend to be less snug than football helmets; however, proper fitting procedures still need to be followed.

Baseball/Softball Batting Helmets

Baseball and softball do not require individual fittings for batting helmets because the standards are developed more for the safety and the integrity of the helmet rather than the unique fit for each athlete (**Figure 3.3**). Still, all helmets must be examined and approved for use in competition both by the governing body and the athletic trainer. The batting helmet is designed with a flap on both sides that is intended to cover and protect the ears and side of the head. The batter is better protected if he or she chooses a helmet that fits snugly around the forehead and jaw, which allows the helmet to more efficiently absorb the force of impact. Helmet inspections should be performed at the beginning of the season and routinely throughout the year.

FIGURE 3.3   Baseball batting helmet.

Shoulder Pads

Prior to fitting the athlete, shoulder pads should be inspected for any defects that could increase the risk of injury (**Figure 3.4**). When assigning shoulder pads to the athletes, any additional padding the athlete intends to wear should be taken into account. Injuries requiring additional padding should be identified during the preparticipation physical exam or annual health check prior to the season. Previous neck and shoulder injuries can be further protected with optional padding such as cowboy collars, neck rolls, or shoulder harnesses. The team physician, in conjunction with the athletic trainer, can determine what is best for the athlete to prevent further damage.

Once the additional equipment has been assigned, the athletic trainer asks each athlete which position the

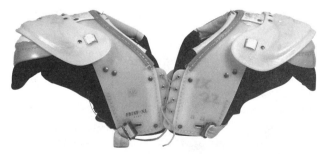

FIGURE 3.4   Football shoulder pads.

athlete expects to play during the season. Each position has unique styles of shoulder pads to improve performance and protect from the impacts associated with the athlete's role on the team. After the athlete's position has been determined, the athletic trainer can measure the individual to develop a baseline size for fitting.

To fit the individual, the athletic trainer stands behind the athlete in a position to measure shoulder width. Begin measurement at one shoulder tip (acromion) and measure across the shoulder and upper back to the tip of the opposite shoulder. This measurement provides a size range (S–XXXL) for the athlete. Each set of shoulder pads may fit differently, even within a size range. The athlete should try on several different sets of pads to determine the most comfortable pair.

When the athlete has found a set of shoulder pads that feels comfortable and is appropriate for the specific position, the athletic trainer can evaluate the pads to guarantee a proper fit (**Table 3.3**). Examine the neckline to ensure that there is a ½- to ¾-inch space between the neck and the pads. The padding around the neck and chest should also cover the sternoclavicular (SC) joint on both sides.

TABLE 3.3

SHOULDER PAD FITTING PROTOCOL

1. Visually inspect for noticeable defects and proper padding.
2. Determine the position the athlete will play.
3. Measure the shoulder width from acromion to acromion.
4. Have the athlete try on the appropriate shoulder pads.
5. There should be a ½- to ¾-inch space between the neck and the padding.
6. Padding must cover the sternoclavicular joint.
7. The deltoid muscle and acromioclavicular joint must be covered.
8. There should be 2–3 finger-widths between the padding and the AC joint.
9. The deltoid muscle must be completely covered by the padding.
10. The back of the pads must completely cover the scapula.
11. Have the athlete connect the underarm straps and put on helmet.
12. There should be adequate range of motion in the shoulders while the pads and helmet are on.

The pads are too large for the athlete if the SC joints are visible or the pad spacing is too wide around the neck.

The athletic trainer then evaluates the padding that covers the shoulder, verifying that the acromioclavicular (AC) joint and deltoid muscle are both protected. There are two levels of padding at the shoulder joint. The lower level is in position to protect the AC joint. To validate this pad, palpate underneath the padding and check for an appropriate gap between the pads and AC joint (two to three finger-widths). The gap protects the AC joint from injury by absorbing the force of impact. The upper level of padding is a flap that extends beyond the lower level to the base of the deltoid muscle. The upper padding shields the deltoid muscle from injury and offers added protection to the acromion and the AC joint.

The athletic trainer then evaluates the back of the shoulder pads to determine if they are the correct length. The back of the shoulder pads must be long enough to extend past the lowest point of the scapula to protect the shoulder blade from injury. Once the visual examination is complete and the pads are appropriately positioned, have the athlete buckle or snap the underarm straps into place and check for both snugness and comfort.

Final shoulder pad fitting should be performed while wearing a helmet. The athletic trainer then has the athlete raise his or her arms above the head. The pads should allow for an adequate range of motion based on the demands of the athlete's field position. The neck of the pads should not cause discomfort while the athlete is wearing a helmet. Follow-up checks during the season are suggested to ensure that proper fitting continues throughout practice and competition.

Catcher/Goalkeeper Equipment

Catchers and goalkeepers in a variety of sports are required to utilize equipment entirely different from their teammates. The equipment is designed to protect the athlete from low-mass, high-velocity objects such as a ball or puck. Although each sport requires specific equipment for this position, chest protectors, shin guards, and helmets are fairly universal.

Sports Bras

Within the past several decades, there has been a dramatic increase in the prevalence of women who are active in sports and recreation. Because of this increase and the resultant increase in demand, there has been a great deal of research into the effectiveness of sports bras. Sports bras are designed to minimize the vertical and horizontal motion of the breasts during activity. The proper sports bra should provide support and compression of the breasts to decrease stretching of the **Cooper's ligament**, the primary support structure of the tissue.[1]

There are many different types of sports bras available. Each athlete should try on several different brands and different levels of compression to determine which model provides the proper support and is the most appropriate for that athlete. Unsuitable or nonsupportive sports bras should be avoided because they may cause abrasions to the skin and nipples during activity.

Prophylactic/Post-Injury Bracing/Padding

Athletes may wish to wear **prophylactic braces** to prevent frequent injuries that occur in their chosen sport. The athlete utilizes these braces for protection even if there is no previous history of injury. Ankle, knee, and shoulder braces are especially common in activities such as football, basketball, and volleyball. Prophylactic braces are discussed in more detail in specific chapters dedicated to each joint.

Following an injury, an athlete may require or benefit from bracing, padding, or splinting to protect the injured area. Numerous post-injury braces that have been designed specifically for athletes (e.g., Donjoy, Breg, Bledsoe) are on the market. The athletic trainer should investigate which brace is appropriate for the athlete and his or her specific injury. If a brace, pad, or cast is utilized post-injury, it must adhere to the safety guidelines dictated by the NCAA for each individual sport. In general, the special protective equipment must be necessitated on genuine medical grounds and designed so that it creates no danger for other players.

Athletic trainers often are required to create or design this protective padding for their injured athletes. A certain level of creativity is needed for fabricating protective padding because the padding needs to benefit the athlete, be appropriate for the specific injury, and not cause injury to other participants. This padding can be fabricated from a

Cooper's ligament A strong ligamentous band that provides support for the breast tissue.

prophylactic braces Braces used to prevent or protect from injury.

FIGURE 3.5   Types of padding.

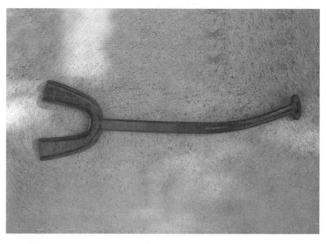

FIGURE 3.6   Generic mouthguard.

variety of resources available in the athletic training room, including both soft and hard materials. Soft materials include felt and foam padding, which may be found in several levels of thickness and density (**Figure 3.5**). The athletic trainer can determine the appropriate level of thickness or density based on the needs of the athlete and what is necessary for the injury.

Hard materials include different types of casting materials, splints, and foot orthotics. An athletic trainer or team physician can utilize these materials to protect the current injury and decrease the risk for reinjury during competition. In most sports that have guidelines governing special protective equipment, the brace, cast, or splint must be covered by a protective neoprene sleeve or at least one half inch of closed-cell, slow-rebounding foam to prevent the injured athlete from inflicting harm on other players.[3]

Mouth Guards

The piece of protective equipment mandated by the NCAA for the most sports is the intraoral mouth guard.[3] Use of a mouth guard to cover the entire upper row of teeth is required or recommended for numerous sports and their athletes. Research has shown that mouth guards decrease the incidence of traumatic injury to the teeth and reduce the force of impact that can cause lip lacerations, jaw fractures, and concussions.[4]

Three types of mouth guards are available to athletes. The stock mouth guard is the cheapest and least effective version of mouth guard available. The stock mouth guard may be found in any sporting goods or all-purpose

store offering athletic equipment. The stock type is sold preformed to a generic mouth mold and is not customizable to the individual athlete. The stock mouth guard is uncomfortable for the athlete, may restrict breathing and speech, and is difficult to retain in the mouth.[4]

The second type of mouth guard is a moldable mouth guard also available in sporting goods stores for general purchase (**Figure 3.6**). This mouth guard, often referred to as a "boil-n-bite," is easily moldable for each individual athlete. To size a mouth guard to a specific athlete, the mouth guard is placed in hot water that has been brought to a boil and removed from the heat source. The athlete then holds the mouth guard in the hot water for an amount of time specified by the manufacturer, typically 10 to 20 seconds.

Once the mouth guard is pliable, the athlete removes it from the water, lets it cool for a few seconds, and then places it in his or her mouth in a comfortable position along the top row of teeth. The athlete bites down on the mouth guard and sucks the air out of his or her mouth to mold the mouth guard to the teeth. Once the mouth guard has cooled, it will maintain that molding.

The athlete then may remove the mouth guard from his or her mouth and trim the molar ends to an appropriate length. The end of the mouth guard should align with the last molar. A mouth guard that is too long may decrease breathing ability and verbalization, as well as produce a gag reflex. However, the athlete should be counseled not to shorten the mouth guard to the point that any of the teeth are not protected. A too short mouth guard does not allow for proper impact absorption and decreases the mouth guard's ability to prevent injury. Most commercial mouth guards have preset marks on them to allow for equal shortening on each side.[4]

FIGURE 3.7 Custom-fit mouthguard.

The third type of mouth guard is the custom-fit dental mold guard (**Figure 3.7**). The custom-fit molds are the most comfortable version for the athletes and provide the highest level of protection from injury.[4] Custom-fit mouth guards are precisely fitted to a mold of the athlete's upper teeth and are considerably more comfortable than commercial versions.

Making a custom mouth guard requires a dentist to personally fit each athlete. The dentist creates a mold from the athlete's dental impression. The impression has to be exact or else the mouth guard will not fit the athlete. After the dental mold is completed, a member of the athletic training staff can create at least one mouth guard (and often a backup) for each athlete using a specialized tool that combines heat and a vacuum to mold a plastic square into the customized mouth guard. The process might be difficult to implement for smaller sports programs because it is both cost- and time-prohibitive.[4]

Eyewear

The equipment safety governing bodies—ASTM or CSA—must approve any protective eyewear utilized in athletics.[2] The eyewear used in competition should be made of impact-resistant plastic that helps to dissipate any force that is placed upon it during activity. As with other protective equipment, the eyewear should be fitted properly to the athlete.

Many athletes today opt to wear contact lenses rather than prescription glasses/goggles during competition. Contact lenses are allowed for use in practices and competition, but the NCAA does not permit its member institutions to purchase contacts for their athletes. Unlike most protective equipment, contact lenses are considered an extra benefit that could lead to a rules violation if the school purchases them for an athlete.

CHAPTER REVIEW

1. What is the most common piece of protective equipment required by the NCAA?
2. What equipment is required for football athletes?
3. List the governing bodies that oversee the safety standards for protective equipment.
4. List the three types of mouth guards.
5. *True* or *False*: An institution may purchase contact lenses for its athletes.

CRITICAL THINKING

What would you do if you suspected some of your team's equipment was defective?

REFERENCES

1. Prentice WE. *Arnheim's Principles of Athletic Training: A Competency-Based Approach*, 12th ed. Boston: McGraw-Hill, 2006.
2. Pfeiffer RP, Mangus BC. *Concepts of Athletic Training*, 5th ed. Sudbury, MA: Jones and Bartlett, 2008.
3. Klossner D, ed. *2007–2008 NCAA Sports Medicine Handbook*. Indianapolis, IN: NCAA, 2007.
4. Berry DC, Miller MG. (2001). Athletic mouth guards and their role in injury prevention. *Athletic Therapy Today*, 6(5):52–56.

Environmental Considerations

FIGURE 4.1   Proper field evaluation is essential.

Another important component of injury prevention is maintaining safe practice and competition facilities, as well as monitoring other environmental concerns. Although not often considered part of the traditional job description of an athletic trainer, ensuring safe facilities often can prevent injuries to your athletes.

A routinely scheduled walk-through and assessment of the facility can identify safety hazards such as potholes, divots, sprinkler heads, rocks, broken glass, or other dangerous conditions. Any one of these hazards can cause injury to an unsuspecting athlete. Removing these risks or marking them for repair will benefit the athletic trainer as well as the athletes by preventing potential issues. This safety walk-through (**Figure 4.1**) should be conducted at the beginning of the preseason and every few days thereafter to spot new hazards.

The safety walk-through should be conducted for both outdoor and indoor facilities. Although less common at indoor complexes, safety hazards can arise—especially as the facility ages. The athletic trainer should evaluate the proximity of the bleachers and walls to the playing surface along with protective padding or barriers to guarantee that unsafe conditions are identified and mitigated.

Exertional Heat Illness

A threat to an individual's well being that occurs frequently in athletics and is related to environmental conditions is exertional heat illness, or **hyperthermia**. Hyperthermia occurs when an individual's body temperature is elevated above normal levels, and it may lead to complications such as cognitive deficits, temperature regulation dysfunction, organ damage, and possible death. There are four main categories of exertional heat illness: dehydration, heat cramps, heat exhaustion, and heat stroke. These conditions are serious and may become life-threatening if not treated properly. It is the athletic trainer's responsibility to assess his or her athletes for signs of hyperthermia and to take appropriate action. Because of the serious nature of heat-related illness, it is critical for the athletic trainer to use every measure available, including proper practice management and established participation guidelines, to prevent athletes from reaching any level of hyperthermia.

■ Dehydration

The first category of exertional heat illness is **dehydration**. Dehydration has many deleterious effects by itself but, more important, may be a precursor to more serious heat illnesses. Our bodies sweat to allow for temperature regulation through evaporative cooling. This is essential for maintaining safe body temperatures, but sweating also causes fluids to be lost, leading to dehydration. Because of the intense physical effort required to compete in athletics, there usually is some level of dehydration in every athlete during activity.

The first sign of dehydration is feeling thirsty—a symptom everyone is familiar with, even outside of athletic competition. Mild dehydration is easily remedied by ingesting fluids. However, once water loss decreases body weight by more than 2%, decrements in performance may be noticeable because the body begins to react in a manner that protects vital organs from damage.[1] Symptoms of dehydration can include:

- Thirst
- Dry mouth

hyperthermia Elevated body temperature.

dehydration Deprivation of water; reduction of water content in the body.

- Irritability
- Headache
- Dizziness
- Excessive fatigue
- Frequent, dark urination
- Decreased urine output
- Increased **urine viscosity** (fluid is more dense)

If an athlete begins to show these symptoms or other unusual behavior, he or she should be removed from play, taken inside or to a cooler environment, and rehydrated with either water or a sports drink. The athletic trainer should monitor the athlete's symptoms; if the symptoms resolve, then the athlete can return to play. However, if the symptoms continue, then the athlete should seek medical attention prior to returning to activity.

In cases of dehydration or other forms of hyperthermia, a **sports drink** may be more appropriate for rehydrating the athlete. Sports drinks are specially designed beverages intended to replenish **electrolytes**, sugar, and other nutrients that are lost through sweating.[2] Drinking water replaces any fluid that is lost during activity; however, consuming too much water can actually deplete electrolyte and mineral stores, leading to other medical issues such as **exertional hyponatremia**, which is discussed later.

Heat Cramps

The second category of exertional heat illness is heat **cramps**. Muscle cramps that result from activity in a hot environment are not uncommon in athletic settings and often occur as a result of dehydration and/or excessive electrolyte loss. Electrolytes are minerals—such as sodium, calcium, and potassium—that are used for essential body processes. These elements are lost through excessive perspiration and can result in heat cramps or other heat-related illnesses. The signs and symptoms of heat cramps are:

- Muscle spasm in the major muscles of the arms and legs
- Dehydration
- Profuse sweating

Fast Fact

Cool water is the most effective hydration tool during practice. Cool water (55° to 65°) is absorbed faster into the body than cold or warm water.[3]

An athlete suffering from heat cramps should be removed from play, taken to a cooler environment if possible, and given water or sports drinks to replenish fluid levels. The athlete should have the cramping muscle stretched and massaged, which helps to relieve the spasm. Ice bags or ice massage also can be utilized to relieve the muscle cramp.

If the cramping ceases, the athlete may return to activity; however, the individual should be monitored closely because he or she may continue to spasm/cramp throughout the remainder of activity. If the symptoms do not resolve, the athlete should seek medical attention.

Many obscure remedies have been championed to decrease the incidence of heat cramps. For instance, pickle juice, mustard, and Alka-Seltzer all have been suggested as cures for cramping either prior to competition or after the muscle spasm has begun. These methods are minimally successful simply because they replace minerals (typically sodium) that are lost with sweating. The traditional sports drink has been shown to be just as effective at replenishing these minerals and tends to taste quite a bit better.[3]

Heat Exhaustion

Heat exhaustion is the third category of exertional heat illness and greatly increases the risk of serious injury for the athlete. Heat exhaustion is not life-threatening by itself, but it can easily progress to heat stroke, which can be fatal. The signs and symptoms for heat exhaustion are listed and compared to those of heat stroke in **Figure 4.2**.

The proper treatment for heat exhaustion is, as with the other heat illnesses, immediate removal from activity. The athlete should be moved to a cool environment,

urine viscosity The thickness or density of the urine, which increases as the water content in the body decreases and dehydration increases.

sports drink A drink intended to quench thirst faster than water can and replenish sugar and minerals lost through physical activity.

electrolytes Salts and minerals found in the body that conduct electricity and that are needed to maintain body fluid function.

exertional hyponatremia A condition that occurs when an athlete's blood sodium levels decrease either as a result of overhydration or inadequate sodium intake. If not treated, this condition may become fatal.

cramps Painful muscle spasms caused by prolonged contraction.

heat exhaustion A form of reaction to heat resulting from severe dehydration.

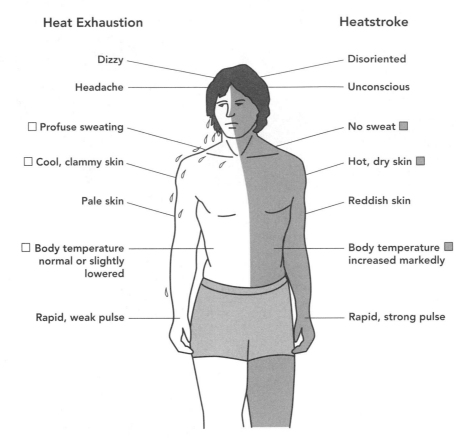

FIGURE 4.2 Heat illness symptoms.
Source: Booher JM, Thibodeau GA. *Athletic Injury Assessment*, 4th ed. Boston: McGraw-Hill, 2000. Reprinted with permission.

preferably with air conditioning, if available. Have the athlete drink fluids if he or she is able to ingest them without vomiting.

If the athlete is wearing a helmet or pads, remove the equipment to improve airflow and allow the athlete's sweating to be more effective in reducing core body temperature. Also, remove or loosen clothing and place ice bags or cold towels (**Figure 4.3**) on the athlete on the back of the neck, in the armpits, and in the groin region, specifically where there are major blood vessels.[3]

The athletic trainer should monitor the athlete's **vital signs**, including temperature (rectal temperature is the most reliable, but inappropriate to measure during an on-field assessment). If the athlete has not shown improvement after approximately 30 minutes, then he or she should be seen by a physician to possibly receive intravenous (IV) treatment to replenish lost fluids.

An athlete who has suffered heat exhaustion should not return to play for the remainder of the day. If the athlete receives IV fluids, he or she should be held out of play for an additional day to allow for recuperation.[4]

■ Heat Stroke

The fourth and final category of exertional heat illness is **heat stroke**. This condition is very dangerous and can potentially lead to death. Heat stroke occurs when the core body temperature reaches or exceeds 104°. At this temperature, internal organ systems begin to overheat and eventually fail.

Management of heat stroke requires quick activation of the emergency medical services (EMS) system. The athletic trainer should have an athletic training student, coach, or another staff member contact 9-1-1 and request an ambulance to the scene. The athletic trainer should

vital signs The pulse rate, temperature, and respiratory rate of an individual.

heat stroke A severe and often fatal illness produced by exposure to excessively high temperatures, especially when accompanied by marked exertion.

FIGURE 4.3 Use of ice towels.

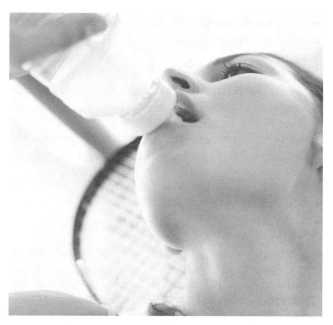

FIGURE 4.4 Proper hydration.

constantly monitor vital signs and remain with the athlete throughout treatment and until advanced medical personnel arrive.

If properly trained personnel are available—including certified athletic trainers—the athlete should be placed in a cold whirlpool or tub of cold water to rapidly decrease the core body temperature. When the athlete's temperature reaches 106° or higher, the body begins to shut down internal organs because they are overheating and essentially cooking. A rapid decrease in temperature to 101° to 102° protects the athlete from internal organ damage and does not pose a high risk of sending the athlete into shock.[4]

If cold-water immersion is not available, move the athlete into a cool environment, preferably air-conditioned, and remove equipment and clothing. Wrap the athlete in cold towels and place ice bags in the armpits, groin, and neck (areas with a high blood flow). Treat the athlete

Fast Fact

Many people—even some medical professionals—are concerned that the rapid decrease in temperature resulting from cold-water immersion is too much of a shock to the system and could further injure the athlete. However, with the increased core temperature, the athlete is already in a life-threatening situation. The risks associated with cold-water immersion are minimal in comparison with the issue already at hand.[4]

for shock and monitor vital signs until the ambulance arrives.

■ Other Heat Illnesses

Most heat illness classifications list only the four types of hyperthermia discussed here. There are, however, two other heat-related illnesses that should be considered in this discussion: heat syncope and exertional hyponatremia.

Heat Syncope

Heat syncope is attributed to peripheral vasodilation, blood pooling, diminished venous return, dehydration, cerebral edema, or reduction in cardiac output.[4] Heat syncope often occurs after long periods of standing in hot or humid environments or a rapid rise to an upright position following rest. The athlete with this condition becomes disoriented, dizzy, and may even lose consciousness briefly. An athlete suffering from heat syncope should be treated in the same manner as with any other heat illness.

The athlete should be removed from the hot environment and placed in an air-conditioned room, if possible. The athlete should be given fluids and monitored until the symptoms resolve (**Figure 4.4**). The athlete should be removed from practice for the remainder of the day

heat syncope A reaction to heat that causes the individual to faint and momentarily lose consciousness.

and instructed to replenish fluids and eat healthy meals before the next practice.

Exertional Hyponatremia

Exertional hyponatremia is a relatively rare condition that occurs when the sodium level in the body reaches critically low levels (less than 130 mmol/L).[5] Hyponatremia typically occurs either when an athlete replenishes lost fluid with water or low-sodium beverages (known as water intoxication), or an athlete does not replenish fluid losses appropriately following activity. The low sodium levels can lead to intracellular swelling, which can cause neurologic and physiologic dysfunction, potentially leading to death.[5]

Athletes suffering from hyponatremia present with disorientation, headache, vomiting, **lethargy**, localized swelling in the extremities, pulmonary **edema**, cerebral edema, and/or seizures.[5] The best treatment for this illness is prevention through replenishment of fluids lost with beverages that contain an appropriate amount of sodium. If an athlete presents with these symptoms, he or she must be referred immediately to a physician for treatment. Hyponatremia can quickly lead to fatal symptoms if not treated in a timely manner.

 ## Prevention of Heat Illness

Utilizing simple prevention techniques can help to minimize or eliminate all forms of exertional heat illness. The National Athletic Trainers' Association (NATA) has developed preseason workout guidelines that decrease the risk of heat illness for athletes.[4] The first aspect of these guidelines is the use of a weight chart for all preseason athletes. A weight chart is a daily record of pre- and postpractice weights for each athlete and the amount of weight lost during practice. The lost weight is primarily fluid loss that needs to be replaced prior to the next practice. For every pound of weight lost during practice, the athlete should consume 20 to 24 ounces of fluid to replace it.[4] It is not uncommon to lose 5 to 10 pounds or more during a single practice, especially for larger athletes.

The weight lost during practice is an important indicator of the level of dehydration present in each athlete. But even more important is the comparison of postpractice weight to the next session's prepractice weight. This measure demonstrates whether the athlete is replenishing the lost fluid/weight during rest periods between sessions. If the athlete does not replenish the lost fluid, then he or she will be at a disadvantage for the next practice and at an increased risk for heat illness.

The next policy guideline is a rather obvious one: consume fluids in abundance. It is best if the athlete consumes 17 to 20 ounces of fluid (either water or sports drink) 2 to 3 hours prior to activity and 7 to 10 additional ounces 10 to 20 minutes prior. The athletes should also consistently consume fluids throughout practice—approximately 7 to 10 ounces every 10 to 20 minutes.[3] After activity, the athlete should consume the amount of fluid needed to replace the weight lost during practice or play.

■ Acclimatization

The National Collegiate Athletic Association (NCAA) also has established preseason protocols to help protect athletes from heat illnesses. Based on the concept of acclimatization, which is the process of adapting to and developing a tolerance for heat, the NCAA has created a preseason schedule intended to prevent heat illnesses in the colle-

> **lethargy** A state of physical and mental fatigue that is characterized by decreased motivation, muscle weakness, and general exhaustion.
> **edema** Swelling as a result of the collection of fluid in connective tissue.

giate athlete. There is a 5-day **acclimatization** period that limits the amount of practice time for athletes during the opening days of a team's preseason. After the acclimatization period, the team cannot schedule consecutive days of two-a-day practices—instead alternating between one and two practices each day.[6]

In regard to football, the NCAA has established a staggered equipment schedule to enhance the athlete's ability to acclimate to the weather. A football team can only practice with helmets, shorts, and shirts the first two days; helmets and shoulder pads the next two days; and full equipment for the remainder of the preseason.[6]

It also is important for all athletes to wear appropriate attire during hot weather practices. Loose-fitting, absorbent, and light-colored clothing can assist in the evaporation process and improve the athlete's ability to regulate body temperature.[4] Specific materials are now available that wick moisture away from the body and increase the evaporation of the athlete's sweat. The coaching staff should consider uniforms and practice clothing made from this material, if budgets allow.

The acclimatization period is intended to benefit all athletes, especially those who may be more susceptible to heat illness. Athletes who are obese, out of shape, unaccustomed to hot weather, have a previous history of heat illness, or have other short- or long-term illnesses are more likely to be negatively affected by the heat. The acclimatization period allows the athletes to become acclimated to the weather and prepare their body to combat heat illnesses.

Acclimatization is a gradual adaptation to the setting that is intended to adjust the individual's internal systems to ensure success in the environment. Because it is a gradual process, acclimatization should begin for the athlete well before preseason practices start. An athlete who is preparing for a hot preseason should conduct as much activity as possible outside in the months leading up to the start of training camp. Running or playing outside allows the athlete's body to adapt to being active in a hot environment and prepares the athlete for the activities that will occur during preseason. It is important for all athletes to attempt to become acclimated to the weather as much as possible prior to starting practice. Previous acclimatization greatly benefits the athlete's body and decreases the risk for heat illness.

■ Heat Index

Another facet of heat illness prevention consists of athletic trainers monitoring the **heat index** and providing practice suggestions based on the results. The heat index is a mathematical equation, incorporating both temperature and **humidity**, which determines how hot it feels to the body.

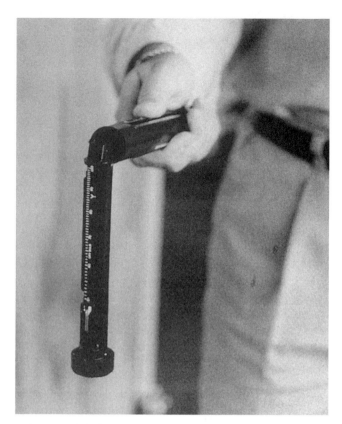

FIGURE 4.5 Sling psychrometer.

Temperature and humidity are measured using a device known as a **psychrometer** (**Figure 4.5**). There are different varieties of psychrometers available, including manual and digital models. These instruments are very effective for assessing temperature and humidity at the site of the practice or competition. Temperature is found with the dry bulb component of the psychrometer whereas the humidity reading uses a combination of both a dry bulb and a wet bulb (a thermometer with the bulb covered in a

acclimatization Physiologic adaptations of an individual to a different environment, especially climate or altitude.

heat index A measurement of the air temperature in relation to the relative humidity.

humidity The amount of water vapor in the air, usually expressed as relative humidity.

psychrometer An instrument for determining relative humidity by the reading of two thermometers, one with a wet bulb and one with a dry bulb.

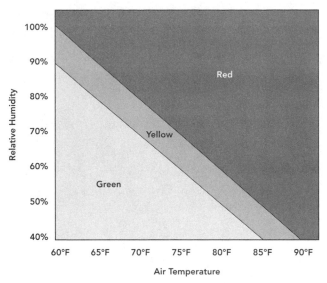

FIGURE 4.6 Heat index chart.
Source: Booher JM, Thibodeau GA. *Athletic Injury Assessment*, 4th ed. Boston: McGraw-Hill, 2000. Reprinted with permission.

wet strip of cloth). Once both dry and wet bulb numbers are determined, the instrument ascertains the heat index through an associated mathematical formula. **Figure 4.6** shows a scale that aligns temperature with humidity and provides a risk stratification for consideration when practicing in the given temperature and humidity.

There are three risk categories for the heat index relating to participation: green, yellow, and red. Each level is accompanied by practice suggestions that should be incorporated to protect the team and individual athletes from heat illness.

The green level is considered a safe zone where practice can be completed with normal rest and water breaks.

The yellow level is one for moderate concern. Heat and/or humidity are increasing along with the potential for heat illness. Practice should be scheduled outside of the hottest portion of the day (10 AM to 5 PM), preferably in the early morning or late evening. Normal rest and water breaks should be combined with a 5-minute break in the middle of practice. This break should be a sit-down rest period in the shade if possible. The rest period is intended to be a time for recuperation and rehydration and should not be utilized for team or position meetings.

Finally, the red level is the danger zone. The heat index has reached the point where coaches should consider canceling practice or practicing without equipment. The practice should be held in the early morning or late evening and rest breaks should be offered every 20 to 30 minutes. The potential for heat illness in this range is extremely high and dangerous for athletes.

As shown in Figure 4.6, it does not necessarily have to be extremely hot outside for the heat index to fall in the red zone. High humidity also can lead to a dangerous heat index. Humidity is the percentage of moisture found in the air. As that percentage increases, it becomes more difficult for the body to regulate core temperature because there is too much moisture in the air and sweat does not evaporate effectively enough to cool the body. This increases body temperature and increases the risk of heat illness. Therefore, the ambient temperature can be relatively mild with high humidity and the practice could still be listed in the red zone. Both temperature and humidity should be considered when determining practice considerations and the safety of the athletes.[7]

The Kentucky High School Athletic Association has placed a great deal of emphasis on heat-related illnesses and has developed a heat index policy that provides an excellent protocol for athletic trainers to follow. This policy may be found at http://www.khsaa.org/sportsmedicine.

Any heat index guideline should be considered in conjunction with the region of the country in which it is applied. Some areas, such as Florida, have a large percentage of days where the heat index is at the red, dangerous level. However, many of the athletes in this region are acclimatized to the heat and may safely participate under these conditions. Other athletes who are from more mild climates may not be acclimatized at all and should be watched closely for signs of heat illness, even when the heat index is in the green or yellow zones.

Cold-Related Illness

On the opposite end of the spectrum from heat illness is the risk for cold-related illness, or **hypothermia**. Hypothermia is a decreased body temperature that can lead to serious complications if not properly treated. Hypothermia is not seen as often in athletes, but it may occur, especially in fall sports with late-ending seasons, spring sports with early preseasons, or in colder regions of the country. Cold temperatures and wind can combine to make athletes competing in outdoor activities susceptible to hypothermia. See **Figure 4.7** for a wind chill chart to determine the risk level for hypothermia. Hypothermia should be considered just as life-threatening as heat illnesses.

The signs and symptoms of hypothermia are:

- Shivering (the first sign)
- Decreased motor control
- Slurred speech

hypothermia Decreased body temperature.

FIGURE 4.7 Wind chill chart.

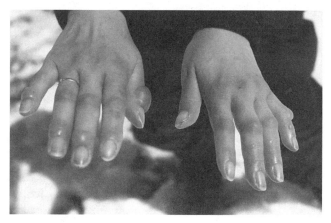

FIGURE 4.8 Frostbite.

- Loss of memory
- Decreased core temperature[9,10]

In more serious cases, symptoms can increase to include:

- Stiffness
- Blue skin (**cyanosis**)
- Decreased respiration
- Decreased pulse
- Unconsciousness[9,10]

Any individual with these symptoms should be moved to a warm environment and wrapped in blankets or hot packs. You should remove any wet clothes, replacing them with dry, warm material. As body temperature increases, monitor vital signs and seek medical assistance if the symptoms do not improve.

■ Frostnip and Frostbite

The cold-related illnesses that may occur separately or in conjunction with hypothermia are **frostnip** and **frostbite**. Both are caused by an overexposure of the skin to the environment and are most commonly seen in the fingers and toes.

Frostnip is the first stage of overexposure and involves freezing of the superficial tissues of the open areas. Signs and symptoms include pain and burning sensation, reddening of the skin, and decreased blood flow. Frostbite (**Figure 4.8**) is more extensive than frostnip is and can affect the deep tissue as well as the superficial. Signs of frostbite include loss of sensation, loss of movement, and gray, black, or green skin.[9]

The same treatment protocol is utilized for both frostnip and frostbite. Remove the individual from the cold environment and remove any wet clothing. Place the person in warm blankets and dry material. If a specific area is affected (e.g., fingers, toes), place that area in tepid, room-temperature water to gradually rewarm the tissue. Do not use hot water because the affected skin is very sensitive to high temperatures and hot water will cause a great deal of pain and possible tissue damage if the individual has lost sensation and cannot tell if it is too hot.[9]

Finally, if frostbite is suspected, seek medical assistance. Frostbite often can lead to tissue death and decay that, if left untreated, will spread throughout the extremity unchecked, destroying more and more tissue. Even if treated properly, amputation of affected parts may be necessary if the level of frostbite is severe.[9]

■ Air Quality

The quality of the air that athletes breathe during practice is a serious issue in some regions, especially urban areas. The air that we breathe may contain such noxious chemicals as ozone, carbon monoxide, sulfur dioxide, nitrogen dioxide, lead, and other fine particles.[8] Exercising under these conditions places an individual at greater risk for health damage, mostly because during exercise, athletes tend to breathe more through their mouth, bypassing

cyanosis A slightly bluish or purple discoloration of the skin caused by a reduced amount of blood hemoglobin.

frostbite Local tissue destruction resulting from exposure to extreme cold.

frostnip Local tissue destruction resulting from exposure to extreme cold. Usually seen as a precursor to frostbite.

the first line of defense—the nose. The nose acts as an air filter, removing the dangerous chemicals from the air prior to its arrival in the lungs.[8]

To avoid the risks involved with poor air quality, it is important to attempt to practice in the mornings or evenings when the pollution levels are lowest. The athletic trainer also should monitor the **air quality** at the practice facility to ensure that events are postponed or canceled if the air quality is unsafe. This will protect the athletes and coaches from contact with harmful substances in the air. Athletic trainers in urban settings or high-risk environments should be especially aware of air quality and its implications for practices and games.[8] Air quality indexes are available on numerous weather-related Web sites and through local news broadcasts.

 ## Lightning Safety

An environmental hazard that especially affects outdoor sports is thunderstorm and lightning activity (**Figure 4.9**). The NATA has developed a position statement that contains guidelines and procedures for this manner of inclement weather.[11] The position statement is intended to be a guide for each institution to develop an inclement weather protocol to meet the program's specific needs. These guidelines are based on the concept of **flash-to-bang ratio**—a method used to estimate the proximity of lightning. The position statement outlines recommendations for when to postpone an outdoor practice or event and seek shelter, as well as when it is safe to resume the activity.

The athletic trainer supervising an outdoor sport should use a reliable weather resource either on the Internet (for example, http://www.weather.com) or television/radio (for example, the National Weather Service or local weather broadcasts) to determine the threat for inclement weather each day prior to practice or competition. A risk of thunderstorms should place the staff on notice for the duration of an event so that all athletic trainers and athletic training students can be alert for flashes of lightning and sounds of thunder.

Once a lightning strike is spotted, the athletic trainer should count the number of seconds that elapse between the lightning strike and the thunderclap (the time from flash to bang). Once the elapsed time has been determined, divide the number of seconds by 5. This provides an estimate of the distance (in miles) that the lightning strike is from the observer. If the flash-to-bang ratio is within 6 miles (30 seconds), there is an increased risk to the athletes and spectators at the site, and the event should be postponed.[11,12] Research has demonstrated that light-

FIGURE 4.9 Lightning.

ning strikes can make contact with the ground from as far away as 5 miles from the source of the lightning. If the flash-to-bang ratio is 3 miles or less (< 15 seconds), then the field should be vacated immediately and all athletes and spectators ushered to safe refuge.[12]

The safest place for individuals to seek shelter during a thunderstorm is an indoor facility. If there is no available facility, the recommendation is to seek shelter inside an automobile. If neither of these options is available, it is suggested that each person find a low-lying area, such as

air quality A measurement of the pollutants in the air; a description of the healthiness and safety of the atmosphere.

flash-to-bang ratio Number of seconds from a lightning flash until the sound of thunder, divided by 5; used as an indicator of the proximity of a thunderstorm.

FIGURE 4.10   Lightning detector.

a ditch, and crouch in the smallest posture possible (fetal position). This limits the contact surface that the individual has with the ground and decreases the amount of current that enters the body if lightning strikes nearby.

Lightning tends to strike the tallest object in the area, so avoid trees or telephone poles. Also, avoid standing on a hill or near large metal objects such as bleachers. Metal is an excellent conductor of electricity and increases the risk for strike as well as the severity of the injury. Finally, if at all possible, attempt to avoid standing water or large

> **lightning detector** Equipment that detects the presence and proximity of lightning strikes produced by thunderstorms.

bodies of water because they also can increase the risk of strike.[12]

An alternative method for assessing the risk of inclement weather is a portable **lightning detector** or a permanent lightning prediction system. Lightning detectors/predictors are quite useful tools and may be utilized as part of the inclement weather protocol by individual institutions. The lightning detector (**Figure 4.10**) senses the electromagnetic signature of lightning strikes and provides an indication of the proximity of a storm to your location. A lightning prediction system measures the amount of static electricity in the air and predicts when a strike may occur before it does. Lightning detectors/predictors are good alternatives to calculating the flash-to-bang ratio; however, there is a potential for false-positive readings or warnings with undefined storm distances.

■ Suspension/Resumption of Play Decision

When a practice or competition is threatened by inclement weather, it is essential to know who is responsible for the suspension of play decision as well as when to return to play. The decision-making process should be outlined in each program's inclement weather policy and discussed prior to an event with the proper officials.

The athletic trainer should be the person responsible for determining when it is no longer safe to practice outside. In competition settings, though, it often is the decision of the game officials using advice from athletic trainers. Resumption of play decisions tend to follow the same guidelines as suspension of play, with athletic trainers resuming practice and game officials resuming competition.

The NATA has recommended that 30 minutes should elapse from the last lightning strike before any play is allowed to continue.[11] This allows the storm to pass and decreases the risk for injury or death from a lightning strike. All of these details should be evaluated and delineated in each school's inclement weather policy to avoid any confusion at the time of the storm.

CHAPTER REVIEW

1. What are the four categories of exertional heat illness?
2. Which athletes are more susceptible to heat illnesses?
3. Define a *heat index*.
4. Which illness is more serious, frostnip or frostbite?
5. How far from its source can lightning strike?
6. *True* or *False*: Trained personnel must supervise cold-water immersion.

CRITICAL THINKING

How would you address a coach to alter a practice because of a high heat index?

REFERENCES

1. Inter-Association Task Force on Exertional Heat Illnesses. (2003, June). Inter-Association Task Force on Exertional Heat Illnesses consensus statement. *NATA News,* 24.
2. Wikipedia. *Sports Drink.* Retrieved January 4, 2008, from http://www.wikipedia.org.
3. Casa DJ, Armstrong LE, Hillma S. (2000). National Athletic Trainers' Association position statement: fluid replacement for athletes. *Journal of Athletic Training,* 35(2):212.
4. Binkley H, Beckett J, Casa D, Kleiner D, Plummer P. (2002). National Athletic Trainers' Association position statement: exertional heat illnesses. *Journal of Athletic Training,* 37(3):329.
5. Gatorade Sports Science Institute. *Dehydration and Heat Injuries: Identification, Treatment, and Prevention, 1997.* Retrieved May 16, 2008, from http://www.gssiweb.com.
6. National Collegiate Athletic Association. *2007–2008 NCAA Divisions I, II, and III Manuals.* Indianapolis, IN: NCAA, 2007.
7. Klossner D, ed. *2007–2008 NCAA Sports Medicine Handbook.* Indianapolis, IN: NCAA, 2007.
8. American Lung Association. *Air Quality and Exercise.* Retrieved January 4, 2008, from http://www.lungusa.org.
9. Schottke D. *First Responder: Your First Response in Emergency Care,* 4th ed. Sudbury, MA: Jones and Bartlett, 2007.
10. Pfeiffer RP, Mangus BC. *Concepts of Athletic Training,* 5th ed. Sudbury, MA: Jones and Bartlett, 2008.
11. Walsh K, Bennett B, Cooper M. (2000). National Athletic Trainers' Association position statement: lightning safety for athletics and recreation. *Journal of Athletic Training,* 35(4):471.
12. Bennett B. (1997). A model lightning safety policy for athletics. *Journal of Athletic Training,* 32(3):251.

Assessment and Treatment of Injuries

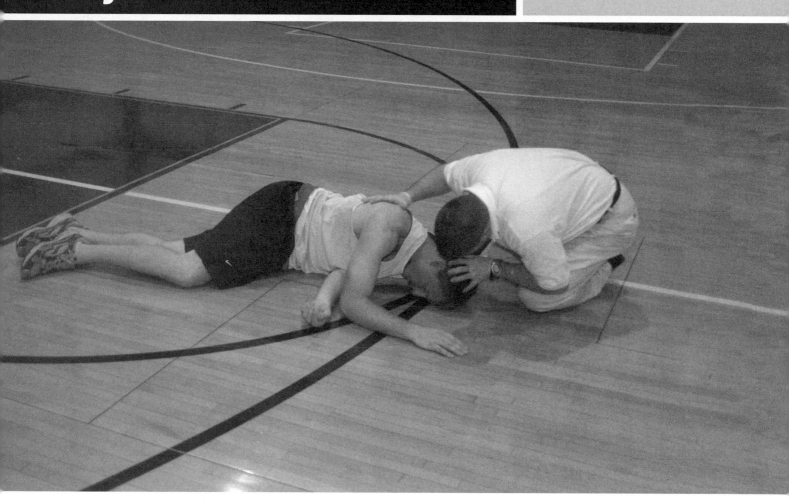

Mechanism of Injury

To truly understand the specific injuries that are discussed in the upcoming chapters, it is important to first learn about the general types of injuries that occur in athletics. In this chapter, we identify the categories of injuries that occur and develop a basic understanding of the healing process of the body.

Athletic Injuries

Athletic trainers traditionally have classified athletic injuries into two categories: acute and chronic. The acute injury classification contains injuries that are associated with a sudden onset or traumatic incident.[1] Once these injuries occur, athletes demonstrate signs and symptoms immediately. The signs and symptoms that result from acute injuries include pain, **swelling**, loss of range of motion or function, loss of strength, and **discoloration**.

Chronic injuries, on the other hand, are described as having a gradual onset with symptoms progressively increasing over time. There is usually no traumatic incident associated with chronic problems. In hindsight, however, many athletes can pinpoint a time or day that symptoms began.

Chronic injuries develop steadily as consistent, repetitive force is placed on the body part throughout activity.[2] This force leads to a breakdown of tissue that ultimately becomes a debilitating injury. Because of the gradual onset of chronic injuries, they often are described as overuse injuries, suggesting continuous abuse of the injured area rather than a single traumatic incident.

To differentiate the types of tissue that are found in the body and that can be injured during athletic competition, we can separate all structures into two categories: **soft tissue** and **bony tissue**. *Soft tissue* is somewhat of an

---

swelling An enlargement of an injured area usually resulting from increased fluid.

discoloration A change in color from what is normally seen in an individual.

soft tissue Any part of the body that is not associated with the bones of the body, including muscles, ligaments, tendons, connective tissue, and skin.

bony tissue Any part of the 206 bones that make up the human body.

compression A pressure or squeezing force directed through a body in such a way as to increase density; a force that crushes tissue.

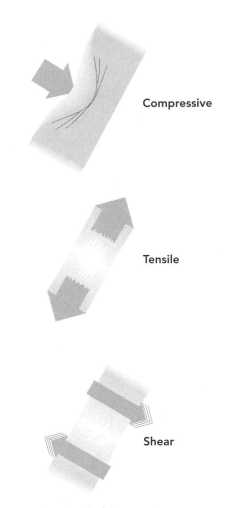

FIGURE 5.1 Mechanical forces of injury.

overarching term in that it encompasses the majority of the components in the body. Muscles, tendons, ligaments, joint capsules, and skin all fall into this category because they are pliable and easily stretched or contracted. *Bony tissue*, on the other hand, is composed of the 206 bones that are found in the human body. This category is distinct in that the bones do not have the elastic capabilities of the soft tissue and do not tend to stretch or bend, except in minimal amounts or as a result of injury.

■ Injury-Causing Forces

Three principal forces on the body can cause injury to both soft and bony tissue: compression forces, tension, and shearing (**Figure 5.1**).[3,4]

Compression

Compression is a force that causes a crushing of the tissue. Both soft and bony tissues are capable of withstanding a certain degree of compression. However, once the pressure exceeds that limit, an injury occurs. **Contusions** and **fractures** are injuries that are often associated with compression forces.

Tension

Tension forces are those that stretch tissue in any given direction. The body again is capable of withstanding a certain degree of tension before failure and injury occur. Common injuries associated with tension forces are **sprains** and **strains**.

Shearing

The third force is known as **shearing**. Shearing is a motion that occurs across the tissue in a manner not expected or anticipated. The shearing force tears at the tissue and causes injury because either it is not in the same direction as the tissue's strength is aligned or the force exceeds the strength of the injured fibers. Injuries associated with shearing forces are skin wounds, disc injuries in the back, and some forms of fractures.[3]

Acute Soft Tissue Injuries

As you can imagine with the number of structures that fall into the soft tissue category, numerous forms of soft tissue injuries can occur. The injuries discussed here are associated with specific soft tissue structures. The particular names of each injury allow for a general understanding throughout the medical community of which structure is affected.

> **contusion** Compression injury involving an accumulation of fluid in a muscle; a bruise.
> **fracture** A disruption in the continuity of a bone.
> **tension** Force that pulls or stretches tissue.
> **sprain** Injury to the ligaments of the body.
> **strain** Injury to the muscle, tendon, or the junction between the two.
> **shearing** Force that moves across the parallel organization of the tissue.
> **closed wound** An internal injury that does not disrupt the continuity of the skin.
> **ecchymosis** Black and blue skin discoloration caused by internal bleeding.
> **hematoma** A collection of blood and other fluids that is found at an injury site.

■ Contusion

Contusion is the appropriate medical term for what is normally called a bruise (**Figure 5.2**). One of the most common injuries found in athletics, contusions develop after a direct blow to the skin and underlying tissue, causing what is known as a **closed wound**. A closed wound does not penetrate the skin or produce external bleeding. The force of the direct blow causes damage and bleeding within the tissue that then result in the black and blue coloring known as **ecchymosis**—the primary symptom associated with a bruise. Contusions occur very frequently in all sports and can develop after contact with other players, equipment, or the playing surface.[2]

Many contusions are minor injuries that should be treated with modalities and avoidance of reinjury. However, serious complications can occur, especially if the compression force affects vital organs such as the brain, liver, or kidneys. If the injury is left untreated or does not heal properly, there may be a pooling of the blood that was released from the tissue. This pooling of blood is called a **hematoma**. By itself, a hematoma is not a life-

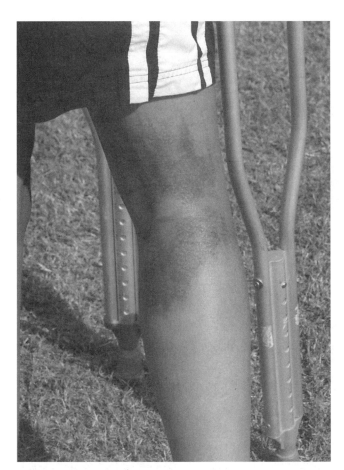

FIGURE 5.2 Contusion.

threatening or serious injury, but if the blood is placing pressure on vital tissues or is left untreated, then it can become dangerous for the injured athlete.

If a hematoma in the muscle tissue is left untreated, it may develop into a condition known as **myositis ossificans**. Myositis ossificans is the development of bony formations within the muscle tissue, causing tearing and damage to the affected fibers.

■ Skin Wounds

Injuries that occur to the skin, also known as **open wounds**, tend to be relatively obvious in that there is external bleeding and damage to the protective outer layer of the body. There are several different categories of skin wounds (**Figure 5.3**), all labeled to distinguish the mechanisms of injury that cause the damage.

Abrasion

An **abrasion** is the tearing or scraping of the skin resulting from friction caused by contact with a rough surface. The injury often is shallow because the topmost layers of skin are torn away.

Laceration

A **laceration** is a cut on the skin that is associated with uneven, jagged edges of tissue. This type of wound results from contact with sharp objects not intended for cutting such as metal, glass, or protective equipment.

Incision

An **incision** also is a cut on the skin, but it is one with smooth edges of tissue. Incisions are seen in surgeries or as a result of an injury caused by sharp objects such as knives.

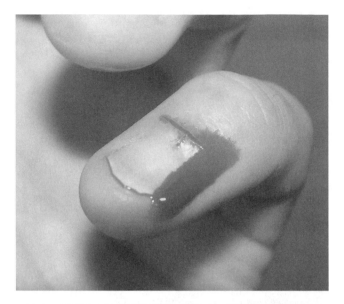

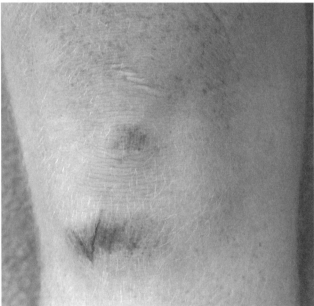

FIGURE 5.3 Types of skin wounds.

Avulsion

An **avulsion** injury that occurs anywhere in the body is described as a tearing away of one tissue from another (e.g., tendon from bone, skin from skin). The force causing the injury must be extreme because tissue that was once connected together is torn apart.

Puncture

A **puncture** wound is a penetration of the skin by some manner of sharp object. This wound does not injure a large surface area of tissue, but it can be very deep depending on the force applied.

> **myositis ossificans** Inflammation in the muscle that is marked by formation of a bony mass within the muscle.
>
> **open wound** An injury that disrupts the continuity of the skin and causes external and/or internal damage to the body.
>
> **abrasion** An injury resulting from scraping; the result of rubbing or abrading.
>
> **laceration** A torn or jagged wound caused by blunt trauma.
>
> **incision** A cut; a surgical wound.
>
> **avulsion** Forcible tearing away of a part or a structure.
>
> **puncture** Piercing of the skin with a pointed object.

■ Sprain

A sprain is an injury to any one of the ligaments found in the body. A **ligament** is a structure composed of connective tissue that attaches one bone to another at a joint. Sprains occur as a result of a motion that forces the joint into an abnormal position and places stress on the ligament. All sprains result in damage to the ligament structure whether the damage is microscopic or macroscopic. Damage to the structure can range from a few **collagen** fibers to a full-thickness rupture.

Athletes tend inappropriately to describe these injuries as "tears." Although this is true to a degree, the implication of the word *tear*, and the concern that is fittingly associated, is not suitable for most ligament injuries. Ligament injuries occur in any of the major joints including the ankle, knee, hip, wrist, elbow, and shoulder. Sprains are classified in three categories based on the level of damage to the tissue.

GRADE I

First-degree sprains are minor injuries. These sprains cause the least amount of ligamentous damage and produce mild symptoms in conjunction with minimal disability. There is little instability in the joint or laxity within the ligament. Most athletes who suffer a grade I sprain may return to activity anywhere from a few minutes post-injury to approximately 2 weeks depending on the site of injury and response to treatment.

GRADE II

Second-degree sprains are more debilitating than a grade I injury. These sprains cause moderate damage to the ligament and cause more pain and loss of function in the injured joint. Swelling and **instability** are increased with this injury and the athlete faces an increased treatment and rehabilitation time prior to return to play. General recovery times for second-degree sprains last from 2 to 4 weeks—again depending on the injury site and response to treatment.

GRADE III

A third-degree sprain is associated with a complete tear or disruption of the ligamentous tissue. The pain and swelling are significant and the loss of function is obvious because the **stability** of the joint has been completely compromised. Third-degree sprains have a lengthy recovery time and may require surgery to reestablish the integrity of the ligament, the stability of the joint, and the ability to compete successfully in athletics. A recovery time of 4 to 6 weeks is typical for nonsurgical recuperation, whereas 4 to 6 months is more appropriate for surgical cases.[5]

■ Dislocation/Subluxation

A **dislocation** of a joint is the displacement of one bone from another in a joint surface. Two categories of dislocations are seen in athletics. The first is known as a **subluxation**. A subluxation occurs when the bones are only partially displaced and may return, on their own volition, to the proper anatomical position. A dislocation (or **luxation**) occurs when the bone is entirely displaced from its joint surface.[3] Whereas a subluxation tends to return to its normal placement, a dislocation requires reduction by a physician or trained medical personnel.

Dislocations and subluxations, because they occur at the joint, injure the ligaments that provide stability. In fact, dislocations are often considered third-degree sprains, although a joint can dislocate without completely disrupting the ligaments and a third-degree sprain can occur without a dislocation. High incidences of dislocation occur at the fingers and shoulders.[3] However, wherever there is a joint, a dislocation injury is possible.

■ Strain

A strain is an injury to a **muscle**, **tendon**, or the junction between the two. A strain occurs as the result of an excessive dynamic force that the athlete places on the muscle or tendon during activity.[5] A tendon is the tissue that attaches a muscle to the nearby bone. As with sprains,

ligament A band of tissue, usually white and fibrous, serving to connect bones and fulfill other bodily functions.

collagen The main protein found in connective tissue in the body.

instability A joint's inability to function under the stresses encountered during functional activities.

stability The resistance of various musculoskeletal tissue that maintains the integrity of a joint or other skeletal structure.

dislocation A displacement of a part, especially a bone, from its normal position.

subluxation Incomplete or partial dislocation of a bone from a joint.

luxation A complete dislocation of a bone from a joint.

muscle A tissue composed of muscle fibers, the contraction of which produces movement in the body.

tendon A composite of dense, tough, inelastic, white, fibrous tissue, serving to connect a muscle with a bone or part.

there are three grades of strains determined by the level of damage.

GRADE I

A first-degree strain has the least amount of damage and disability. The athlete often considers it a pulled muscle or a tweak. There are minimal symptoms and return to play can occur relatively quickly with a similar time frame to sprains—anywhere from minutes to approximately 2 weeks.

GRADE II

A second-degree strain causes a moderate level of damage to the muscle or tendon. Symptoms increase with more pain, swelling, loss of strength or **flexibility**, and muscle spasm found in the injured area. Occasionally, there is a palpable deficit found in the muscle belly resulting from damage to the muscle fibers. Recovery time for a grade II injury ranges from a few days to 3 to 4 weeks.

GRADE III

A third-degree strain suggests a large amount of tissue damage—potentially including complete disruption of the muscle or tendon. The symptoms are dramatic with a significant loss of strength and function and the appearance of an obvious deficit that is visible through the skin. The injury requires a significant recovery time and could involve surgery to allow for a return to full function.

 ## Acute Bony Tissue Injuries

Bony tissue injuries that have a sudden onset can be described in a single category: fractures. A fracture is a break or crack in the bone that causes immediate pain and loss of function directly related to the injury site. There are two fundamental types of fractures—closed and open.

A **closed fracture**, sometimes called a simple fracture, is an injury to the bone that does not penetrate the skin. In an **open fracture** or **compound fracture**, the bone does penetrate the skin and is considered more serious because of external bleeding and an increased risk for **infection**.[5] Fractures can be further classified by the damage incurred within the bone. **Figure 5.4** shows the different types of fracture that may occur to the bony tissue.

Numerous signs and symptoms are associated with fractures. As with most acute injuries, there is obvious pain at the onset. Fractures may be differentiated from soft tissue injuries by the presence of immediate discoloration and swelling over the injury site.[1] Because of the swelling around the injury and the various types of fractures, there may or may not be a **deformity** visibly present. With most fractures, there is an immediate loss of function in the injured area, and the athlete blatantly shields and protects the injury from further damage.

Finally, there may be a grating sound or feeling (**crepitus**) that occurs as the ends of the fractured bone grind against each other during movement. The athletic trainer should listen/feel for crepitus but should not attempt to shift the bone in an effort to generate crepitus because this will cause a significant increase in pain for the athlete and

flexibility Capable of being bent or moved repeatedly without injury or damage.

closed fracture An uncomplicated fracture in which the broken bones do not pierce the skin.

open fracture A fracture in which broken bone fragments lacerate soft tissue and protrude through an open wound in the skin.

compound fracture A fracture in which the broken bone is exposed through a wound in the skin.

infection Invasion of pathogenic microorganisms, which may produce subsequent tissue injury and progress to overt disease through a variety of mechanisms.

deformity A deviation from the normal shape or size of a body part.

crepitus Crackling or crunching sound or sensation characteristic of a fracture when the bone's ends are moved.

Fast Fact

Tendons and ligaments are very similar in concept and can be easily confused. It is important to remember that ligaments connect bone to bone, while tendons connect muscle to bone. The injury classifications also can be confusing (sprains vs. strains). One way to remember the difference is that a strain has a *T* in it that can stand for tendon.

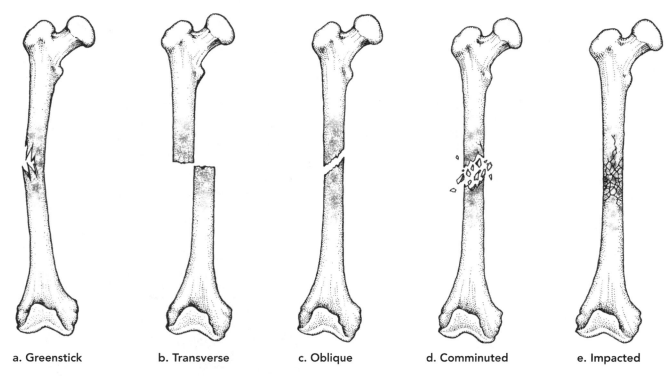

| a. Greenstick | b. Transverse | c. Oblique | d. Comminuted | e. Impacted |

FIGURE 5.4 Types of fractures.

may cause further damage to the bone and surrounding tissue.[2]

If these symptoms occur, it is important to refer the athlete to a physician for X-rays to determine if a fracture is indeed present. Return to play is dependent on the severity of the fracture and the location of the injury in regard to how much it is utilized in a given sport or at a specific position. For instance, a fractured arm may not hinder a soccer field player from returning quickly, but a goalkeeper will be unable to play for an extended period of time.

 ## Chronic Soft Tissue Injuries

Chronic injuries (those with a gradual onset) have a high frequency rate in the soft tissue structures of the body. In some joints and muscles, chronic issues are more common even than acute injuries. Treatment protocols for all soft tissue injuries are pretty consistent, including ice, rest, ultrasound, stretching, and a rehabilitation program.

■ Fasciitis

Fasciitis is an inflammation of the **fascia**—the connective tissue that supports and separates muscle. The most

recognized form of this injury is plantar fasciitis, or inflammation of the fascia in the sole of the foot. Fasciitis is a very painful injury that develops over time with repeated body movements that irritate the tissue. Because of the chronic **inflammation** that has developed over a lengthy period, it can take a significant amount of time to rehabilitate. Symptoms include pain, loss of motion, and minimal swelling.

■ Tendinitis/Tenosynovitis

Tendinitis is an extremely common chronic injury that is associated with almost all of the major tendons in the body. It is an inflammation of the tendon caused by repeated abuse to the affected joint. Tendinitis is seen in all sports and with all age groups and levels of athletes. Signs and

fasciitis Inflammation of the fascia surrounding portions of a muscle.

fascia Fibrous membrane that covers, supports, and separates muscles.

inflammation Pain, swelling, redness, heat, and loss of function that accompany musculoskeletal injuries.

tendinitis Inflammation of a tendon.

symptoms include pain, swelling, and loss of motion or strength during activity. As with fasciitis, tendinitis may take some time for symptoms to resolve, especially if the athlete continues to participate with pain.

Tenosynovitis is fairly analogous to tendinitis with the exception that it affects the tissue sheath that surrounds the tendon. Tenosynovitis may be either an acute or chronic condition. The symptoms are similar in both injuries—including pain, swelling, and loss of motion. However, tenosynovitis is differentiated by a squeaking sound that is made as the tendon passes through the inflamed sheath during motion or activity.

■ Bursitis

Bursitis is most often seen in the knee, shoulder, or elbow.[3] This injury is an inflammation of the **bursa sac**, a fluid-filled pouch that sits between two bony structures to prevent friction or degradation of the bone and its surrounding soft tissue (**Figure 5.5**). Bursitis may occur acutely, but it is more frequently the result of chronic irritation. Signs and symptoms are highlighted by swelling (a great deal of swelling in acute cases), pain, and loss of motion. Bursitis is treated with a compression wrap to reduce swelling, along with the other soft tissue injury treatments. Athletes may choose to compete with bursitis if their symptoms allow.

 Chronic Bony Tissue Injuries

As is the case with acute bony tissue injuries, there is only one chronic injury present in bony tissue: **stress fractures**. Stress fractures are quite prevalent in both athletes and nonathletes alike, especially in the lower body and foot. Traditionally, runners have been more prone to this injury than athletes in any other weight-bearing sport.[6] However, this injury has received more notice in the past

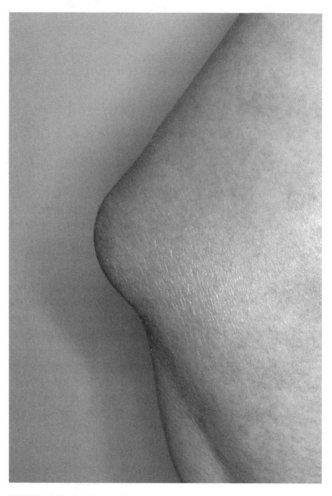

FIGURE 5.5 Elbow bursitis.

several years as athletes in the high-revenue sports (i.e., football, basketball) have had an increased incidence of stress fractures.

Stress fractures are a gradual eroding of the bone caused by repeated stress. The athlete will complain of pain with activity, tenderness, and localized swelling over the injury site. If not properly diagnosed and treated, this injury can develop into a frank, or true, fracture. Treatment for this injury depends on the severity and location of the fracture, the type of sport, and the individual athlete. A

Fast Fact

Many theories have been advanced as to why stress fractures occur so frequently in athletics—including physiological concerns, gender, shoe design, decreased rest and recovery time, increased off-season programming, and ground/court conditions.[6,7] No single factor has been isolated, but research is continuing into this injury and its risk factors.

tenosynovitis Inflammation of a tendon sheath.
bursitis Inflammation of a bursa.
bursa sac A fibrous sac membrane typically found between tendons and bones; acts to decrease friction during motion.
stress fracture A fracture resulting from repeated loading with relatively low magnitude forces.

follow-up with a physician for an X-ray can help to rule out a true fracture or soft tissue injury. Stress fractures often are difficult to see on X-ray and are only visible once healing has begun.[2] Most physicians who are concerned that an athlete is suffering from a stress fracture will order an **MRI** or **bone scan** to assist in diagnosis.

The Healing Process

The **healing process** that occurs following an injury is divided into three phases: the inflammatory phase, the repair phase, and the remodeling phase. The athletic trainer who is treating and rehabilitating an injured athlete must understand these phases or risk inhibiting the process and slowing a resolution of symptoms and return to play. Each phase of the healing process works concurrently with the others to ensure the proper environment for the complete repair of the injured area.

The Inflammatory Phase

The **inflammatory phase** of the healing process (**Figure 5.6**) begins immediately following the onset of injury. As soon as the tissue is damaged, the body reacts to protect the injured area and prevent further harm. No matter what type of tissue is injured, the inflammatory phase is initiated within minutes and lasts anywhere from 24 hours to 96 hours post-injury.[2,3]

Immediately following injury, blood flow to that area is decreased (**vasoconstriction**) and pain and loss of function symptoms occur. A few minutes after the injury occurs, blood flow is returned to the injury site and increases (**vasodilation**) dramatically—up to 10 times more than normal blood flow.[8] This increased blood flow constitutes the swelling and inflammation often seen with injury and acts as a catalyst or trigger for the healing process to begin within the damaged area. The swelling, pain, and loss of function all decrease the athlete's desire and ability to move and participate. This is the body's method of protecting itself from further damage.

As the buildup of fluids increases with both the primary damage to the cellular structure and the resulting inflammation, the pressure causes a decrease in oxygen flow. This lack of oxygen in the injured area leads to further cell death known as **secondary hypoxic injury**.[9]

The trauma that is sustained during injury, both primary and secondary, causes the death of millions of cells throughout the damaged area. The principal responsibility of the inflammatory phase is to protect the injured area and begin the removal of those dead cells and other waste associated with injury.[9] Numerous substances and chemicals arrive at the injury site during this phase to complete the process, most notably **histamine**—a powerful inflammatory chemical.[2]

The best treatment for the athlete during the inflammatory phase is rest, ice, compression, and elevation (**RICE**). The RICE treatment protects from further injury while allowing the phase to run its course and prepare the injured area for repair. **Compression** and **elevation** specifically can minimize the damage that results from secondary hypoxic injury. Immediate treatment can reduce the amount of fluid found in the area and decrease the amount of cellular damage that occurs post-injury.[9] Early return to participation can inhibit the body's ability to heal and could cause more damage that would then lead to increased recovery time.

In chronic injuries, the inflammatory phase also occurs with the initial onset of injury. However, the response does not completely remove the debris or the injury-causing

---

MRI Magnetic resonance imaging; a noninvasive diagnostic procedure that provides detailed sectional images of the internal structure of the body.

bone scan Diagnostic imaging that detects bone abnormalities through the use of radioactive material that collects at tumors, fractures, and infections.

healing process A series of predictable reactions to injury that is designed to repair the damaged tissue.

inflammatory phase The first phase of the healing process characterized by swelling, pain, redness, and loss of range of motion. This phase lasts from 24 to 72 hours.

vasoconstriction Constriction of the blood vessels, as by the action of a nerve.

vasodilation Dilation of the blood vessels, as by the action of a nerve.

secondary hypoxic injury Additional cellular breakdown and death as a result of a lack of adequate oxygen supply around the primary area of injury.

histamine A powerful stimulant of gastric secretion, a constrictor of bronchial smooth muscle, and a vasodilator that causes a fall in blood pressure.

RICE Rest, ice, compression, and elevation.

compression A pressure or squeezing force directed through a body in such a way as to increase density; a force that crushes tissue.

elevation The height to which something is elevated above a point of reference such as the heart.

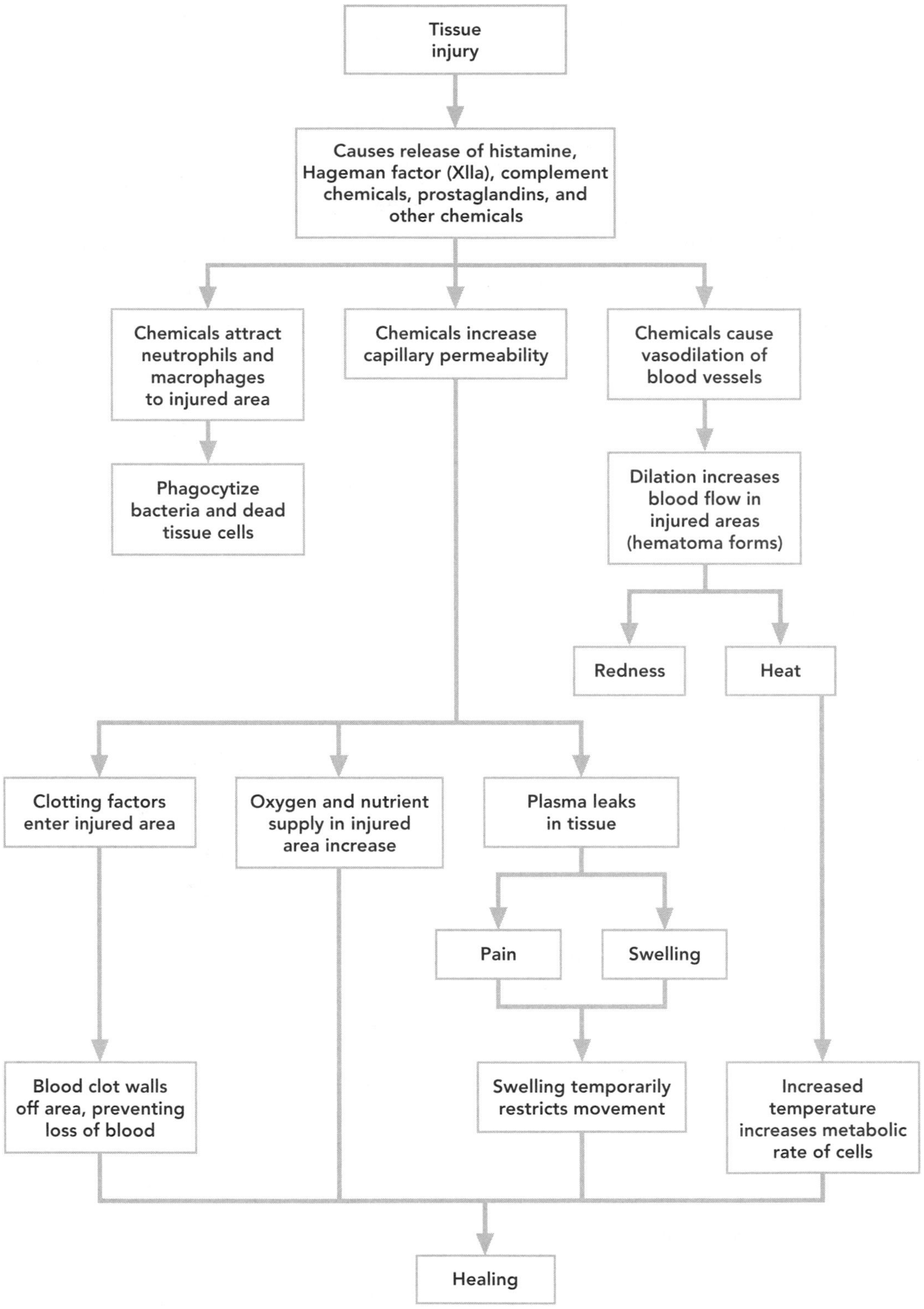

FIGURE 5.6 The inflammatory process.

elements. Because some substances remain in the affected area, the body does not continue to the repair phase and the inflammation remains. Because it is repeated trauma that causes chronic injuries, the inflammatory process continues to develop and degrade the tissue in a repetitive manner, which then causes the signs and symptoms that were discussed.

■ The Repair Phase

The **repair phase** begins while the inflammatory phase is still active. During this second phase, the last of the debris is removed, the site is prepared for recovery, and new cells are generated to replace those lost during the trauma. Connective tissue and collagen fibers (known as **fibroblasts**) arrive to strengthen the injured area.[2,9] These fibers are placed randomly throughout the area to protect the site from any and all abuse. The repair phase typically begins around day 2 or 3 and can continue for anywhere from 2 to 6 weeks.[3]

Unlike the inflammatory phase where the same process occurs no matter what type of tissue is involved, the repair phase of healing is slightly different for bony tissue versus soft tissue. In bony tissue injuries, **osteoblasts** take the place of fibroblasts and create new bone tissue in the injured area. **Osteoclasts** also enter the affected area at this time in an attempt to remove the damaged bony tissue.

These two cellular organisms work in unison to remove debris and repair the injured tissue. Osteoblasts create a fibrous vascularized tissue, known as a **callus**, that reconnects the two ends of the fractured bone.[4] The callus is progressively strengthened from a weak immature tissue back into the strong bony tissue that was present before the injury. This strengthening occurs during both the repair phase and the final phase, known as remodeling.

■ The Remodeling Phase

The **remodeling phase** is the last and longest phase in the healing process. Depending on the injury, this phase may last from a few months to more than a year. The fibroblasts or osteoblasts—depending on the type of injured tissue—that were lain down entirely at random during the repair phase are now realigned and remodeled to allow for maximum protection and optimal use for each specific athlete. The collagen fibers are reabsorbed and reestablished according to the stresses placed on the affected area.

Wolff's law describes this process, stating that tissues respond to physical demands, remodeling and adapting to the stress placed on them.[9] As the athlete progresses through his or her treatment and rehabilitation, those demands change from walking to running to sport-specific movements. With the increase in the stress placed upon the healing injury, the fibers align in a manner that is most conducive to the athlete and the activities in which the athlete is involved. In other words, the stress that is placed on the fibers alters them to create the best possible alignment for that athlete.

repair phase The second phase of the healing process, characterized by initial tissue repair and new tissue generation. This phase begins 48 to 72 hours after the injury and lasts for approximately 2 weeks.

fibroblasts A cell present in connective tissue capable of forming collagen fibers.

osteoblasts Bone-producing cells.

osteoclasts Cells that reasorb bone.

remodeling phase The third and final phase of the healing process, characterized by scar tissue formation and connective tissue maturation. This phase begins 48 to 72 hours after the injury and may last for up to a year.

Wolff's law A law that states that bone and soft tissue will respond to the physical demands placed upon them, causing the formation of collagen to remodel or realign along the lines of stress, thus promoting healthy joint biomechanics.

callus Localized thickening of skin epidermis owing to physical trauma. Fibrous tissue containing immature bone tissue that forms at fracture sites during repair and regeneration.

CHAPTER REVIEW

1. What are the three injury-causing forces?
2. What is a hematoma?
3. List the types of skin wounds.
4. What is the difference between a sprain and a strain?
5. What is a fracture?
6. What does RICE stand for?
7. What are the three phases of the healing process?
8. What does Wolff's law state?

CRITICAL THINKING

How does your approach change from a major injury (e.g., fracture) to a minor one?

REFERENCES

1. Starkey C, Johnson G. *Athletic Training and Sports Medicine*, 4th ed. Sudbury, MA: Jones and Bartlett, 2006.
2. Pfeiffer RP, Mangus BC. *Concepts of Athletic Training*, 5th ed. Sudbury, MA: Jones and Bartlett, 2008.
3. Prentice WE. *Arnheim's Principles of Athletic Training: A Competency-Based Approach*, 12th ed. Boston: McGraw-Hill, 2006.
4. Anderson MK, Hall SJ, Martin M. *Sports Injury Management*, 2nd ed. Baltimore: Lippincott, Williams, & Wilkins, 2000.
5. Booher JM, Thibodeau GA. *Athletic Injury Assessment*, 4th ed. Boston: McGraw-Hill, 2000.
6. Jones BH, Thacker SB, Gilchrist J, Kimsey JD, Sosin DM. (2002). Prevention of lower extremity stress fractures in athletes and soldiers: a systematic review. *Epidemiologic Reviews*, 24(2):228–247.
7. Bennell K, Matheson G, Meeuwisse W, Brukner P. (1999). Risk factors for stress fractures. *Sports Medicine* (Auckland, NZ), 28(2):91–122.
8. Lachmann S. *Soft Tissue Injuries in Sport*. Oxford, England: Blackwell Scientific, 1988.
9. Starkey C. *Therapeutic Modalities for Athletic Trainers*. Philadelphia: F. A. Davis, 1993.

Therapeutic Modalities

When discussing the treatment aspect of an athletic trainer's responsibilities, **therapeutic modalities** constitute a vast majority of the methods practiced. Throughout the healing process and rehabilitation, an athletic trainer can utilize a number of different therapeutic modalities. Certain modalities may be more appropriate for individual athletes depending on where the athlete is in the healing process. Therapeutic modalities also may be used for prevention of injuries and can offer assistance in decreasing symptoms from minor aches and pains. We discuss modalities as divided into four main categories: cryotherapy, thermotherapy, electrotherapy, and massage (**Table 6.1**).

Cryotherapy

Cryotherapy consists of any treatment that is associated with decreasing local body temperatures. Cryotherapy is especially important in the inflammatory phase of the healing process, in general pain management, and in treatment for chronic conditions. Often considered an athletic trainer's best friend, cryotherapy reduces the swelling in an injured area, which is a by-product of inflammation, while still allowing the tissue healing and repair to occur. When cold elements are applied to an acute injury, **metabolism** in the injured area is decreased, which minimizes the secondary hypoxic injury to tissue surrounding the injury site.[1] The less tissue that is damaged, the faster an athlete can recover and return to play.

The basic theory behind cryotherapy is that applying the cold element to the body decreases blood flow (vasoconstriction), muscle spasm around the injury site, and nerve conduction velocity, which can lessen the level of pain that the athlete is feeling.[1,2] All of the benefits of cryotherapy make it a useful tool for treating many different types of injuries. You will see cryotherapy included in the treatment protocols of specific athletic injuries in later chapters.

In the practical setting, cryotherapy often is written as the acronym RICE, which incorporates rest, ice,

therapeutic modalities Any treatment conducted on an injured area that is intended to promote healing and minimize or reduce symptoms.

cryotherapy Cold application.

metabolism The chemical processes occurring in a living organism that are necessary for the maintenance of life.

TABLE 6.1

THERAPEUTIC MODALITY CHART

Modality Type	Indications	Contraindications
Cryotherapy		
Ice bag, ice massage, cryo-cuff, cold immersion	Acute injuries, swelling, pain management	Decreased/increased sensitivity to cold, loss of sensation, cold allergy
Thermotherapy		
Moist heat packs, warm whirlpool, paraffin bath, ultrasound, phonophoresis	Chronic injury, prepractice treatment	Acute injuries, sensitivity to heat, loss of sensation, active infection, cancer, pregnancy (ultrasound)
Electrotherapy		
Electrical stimulation, iontophoresis	Pain management, muscle reeducation, decrease swelling	Loss of sensation, open wounds, sensitivity to equipment, implanted pacemakers
Massage		
Effleurage, petrissage, tapotement, friction	Relaxation, muscle spasm, swelling, increase circulation	Open wounds, loss of sensation, discomfort with situation/contact
Therapeutic Exercise		
	Acute/chronic injuries, increase ROM/strength	Overexertion, increased pain, mechanical dysfunction

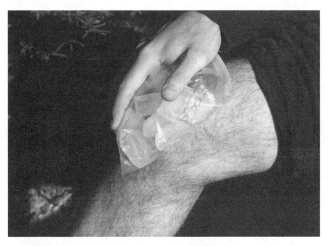

FIGURE 6.1 Ice bag.

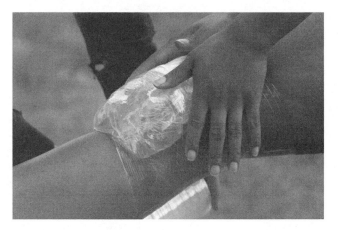

FIGURE 6.2 Ice bag with ace wrap.

compression, and elevation into a comprehensive acute injury management protocol. These four components are utilized together during treatment to decrease tissue damage and swelling. Rest is essential to the healing process of all injuries because it removes unnecessary stress from the injured body part and prevents further damage. Ice decreases secondary tissue damage, reduces swelling, and modulates pain. Compression limits the amount of swelling by squeezing the body part. Elevation uses gravity to assist the lymphatic system in removing the excess fluid and swelling from the injury site. Athletic trainers use several different methods of cryotherapy, each of which has benefits and contraindications associated with use.

Ice Bag

The ice bag (**Figure 6.1**) is the most common form of cryotherapy, most likely because of its ease of use, low cost, and ready availability. Ice bags are very simple to make—requiring only an ice machine and some form of sealable bag—and easy for the athlete to use either in the athletic training room or at home.

The ice bag should be placed on the injury site and compressed with an elastic bandage or plastic wrap (**Figure 6.2**) to both hold it in place and provide a compressive force to minimize swelling and maximize effectiveness. The ice should be left on for 15 to 30 minutes to provide the most therapeutic benefit.[1]

The advantage of using an ice bag over a commercial ice pack is that an ice bag will not be excessively cold and will warm as contact time with the body increases. A commercial ice pack can reach lower temperatures and maintain that temperature for a longer period of time, which could potentially cause frostbite or other cold-related issues.

CONTRAINDICATIONS

Decreased/increased sensitivity to cold, loss of sensation in injured area (could lead to frostbite), and cold allergies.

Ice Massage

Similar to the ice bag, an ice massage provides a therapeutic benefit to the athlete suffering from either acute or chronic injuries. The ice massage, though, has unique characteristics in that it provides the benefit of cryotherapy along with the compressive and circulatory benefits of massage.

Freezing water in either a disposable cup or a specifically designed cryo-cup creates the equipment for an ice massage. The ice, once it is frozen throughout the cup, can be maneuvered over the injury site in an up and down or circular motion to massage the area. The massage should last approximately 7 to 10 minutes for full therapeutic benefit.

CONTRAINDICATIONS

Decreased/increased sensitivity to cold, loss of sensation in injured area, injuries where pressure on the site is inappropriate, and cold allergies.

Cryo-Cuff

A cryo-cuff is a piece of equipment that provides the athlete with the benefits of both cold and compression in one unit. The cryo-cuff surrounds the injured area with a sleeve or cuff that is filled with ice water.

The ice water is kept in a portable cooler that is connected to the cuff by a hose. The cooler then is elevated to add water to the cuff or lowered to remove water from the cuff. Newer models are available with an electric pump to transfer the water in and out of the cuff, which helps to maintain a consistent, lower temperature over the injury site. Treatment should consist of a 20-minute application, with the cooler being lowered and raised halfway through the treatment to refresh the water. This is unnecessary when using a model with an electric pump.

CONTRAINDICATIONS

Decreased/increased sensitivity to cold, loss of sensation in injured area, injuries where pressure on the site is inappropriate, and cold allergies.

■ Cold Immersion

Cold immersion involves dipping the injured body part in a container of water—usually a whirlpool or bucket. The temperature of the cold immersion should be between 50°F and 60°F to provide optimal benefit.[1,3]

Whirlpool

A whirlpool (**Figure 6.3**) uses a turbine to circulate the water at high power, which allows **convection** currents to further decrease tissue temperatures, and water pressure to contact and compress the injured area. Whirlpools can decrease swelling and increase blood flow and **lymphatic return**.[1] Treatment should last from 10 to 15 minutes with the athlete performing range of motion activities throughout the session. Because the cold decreases pain and **hydrostatic pressure** compresses and supports the area, the athlete should be able to complete movements through a larger range of motion in the non-weight-bearing environment (activities known as **cryokinetics**), which can assist in recovery and rehabilitation.

Ice Bucket

Cold immersion may also be conducted with a bucket filled with slushy ice water. The temperature for the ice bucket will tend to be slightly cooler than that found in the whirlpool—typically around 50°F.[1] The treatment time for an ice bucket is 10 minutes of immersion for the injured body part. For some athletes, this treatment can be rather uncomfortable, especially for fingers and toes during treatment for an ankle or wrist injury. To alleviate some of the discomfort, commercial neoprene toe/finger caps are available.

There is a disadvantage with cold immersion in that the injured area is in a gravity-enhanced position rather than elevated as is done with the other cryotherapies. This can lead to increased swelling in the injured site, a concern that should be considered during the inflammatory phase (the first 2 to 4 days post-injury).

CONTRAINDICATIONS

Decreased/increased sensitivity to cold, loss of sensation in injured area, and cold allergies. Cold immersion for

FIGURE 6.3 Whirlpool equipment.

athletes with open wounds could spread infection or disease if others also use the equipment.

Thermotherapy

As with cryotherapy, **thermotherapy** has long been a staple in the treatment of athletic injuries throughout the body. The term *thermotherapy* describes any modality that utilizes heat and is especially effective for chronic injuries or pre-practice treatment (when warming the tissue is beneficial). When heat is applied to the body, it increases blood flow to the area (vasodilation), relieves muscular tension, and reduces pain. Because there is increased blood flow in the

convection The transfer of energy between two objects via a medium, such as air or water, as it moves across the body, creating temperature variations.

lymphatic return A return process similar to that of the venous network, but specializing in the removal of interstitial fluids.

hydrostatic pressure The pressure of blood within the capillary.

cryokinetics Use of cold treatments prior to or in conjunction with an exercise session.

thermotherapy Heat application.

FIGURE 6.4 Hydrocollator pack.

affected area, heating modalities often are contraindicated for acute injuries, particularly during the inflammatory phase because the vasodilation effect increases swelling. Heating tissue also increases cellular metabolism and the need for oxygen, which may increase the degree of secondary hypoxic injury in the surrounding tissue.

Although cryotherapy has traditionally been more popular with athletic trainers, thermotherapy does play an important role in treatments and should be considered as an option after the acute phase of an injury has passed. We discuss several of the thermal modalities, their guidelines, and any affiliated contraindications.

Moist Heat Pack

Moist heat packs (**Figure 6.4**) are one of the more common heat modalities found in athletic training rooms. These heat packs are kept in a temperature-controlled metal water container called a **hydrocollator**. This container maintains a consistent temperature of approximately 160° to 170°F at all times.[1,3] The heat packs absorb the water and, when removed, can maintain that temperature throughout a treatment cycle—usually 10 to 20 minutes. Moist heat packs always should be wrapped in a terry cloth cover and/or within several layers of towels to prevent tissue burning.

Once wrapped in the terry cloth covering, moist heat packs are placed over the injured area for the duration of the treatment. A light weight may be added on top of the pack for stability and improved heating over an uneven surface. In any case, continue to follow up with the athlete to ensure that the treatment is not overheating or burning the underlying tissue. If it becomes too hot, remove the pack, add more toweling between the athlete and the hot pack, and reapply the pack to the treatment area. Moist heat packs only penetrate approximately 1 to 2 centimeters (cm) into the body, and thus are useful in the treatment of superficial injuries, but are not as effective for injuries in deeper tissues.[3]

CONTRAINDICATIONS

Loss of sensation in the injured area, sensitivity to heat, impaired circulation, cancer, active infection, and use dur-

ing the acute injury phase. Do not allow the athlete to lie on the pack because it may cause burning of the tissue.

Warm Whirlpool

Similar to the cold whirlpool/immersion, the warm whirlpool consists of the injured body part being placed in a tank of water that is circulated by a turbine. The whirlpool provides the benefits of thermotherapy along with the advantages associated with the water movement: increased blood flow, hydrostatic pressure, massaging effects of the current, and increased range of motion in the body part. The temperature of a warm whirlpool should be maintained between 90° and 104°F to receive full benefit of the thermotherapy without risking overheating or tissue damage.[3] Treatment time should range between 10 and 15 minutes to maximize the therapeutic benefit.

CONTRAINDICATIONS

Sensitivity to heat, loss of sensation, open wounds, impaired blood flow, cancer, active infection, and acute injuries.

Contrast Bath

Some athletic trainers prefer to utilize both the cold whirlpool and the warm whirlpool in collaboration as a treatment modality called a **contrast bath**. For the contrast bath, an athlete will begin with 3 to 4 minutes in the warm whirlpool and then immediately follow that with 1 minute in the cold whirlpool. The process then is repeated for a treatment time totaling 20 minutes. The ratio of heat to cold may be modified as needed for the treatment.[3] Contrast baths can be especially effective when a slight increase in temperature is needed to increase blood flow to an injured area without causing more swelling to enter the area.[3]

CONTRAINDICATIONS

Same as either of the individual modalities.

Paraffin Bath

The **paraffin bath** (**Figure 6.5**) has become a popular tool for the treatment of injuries in the hands and feet. These

hydrocollator A liquid heating device primarily used to heat/store "hot packs" for therapeutic use.

contrast bath Technique that uses immersion in ice slush, followed by immersion in warm water.

paraffin bath A mixture of paraffin wax and oil that is kept in a liquid state and used to heat hands and feet specifically.

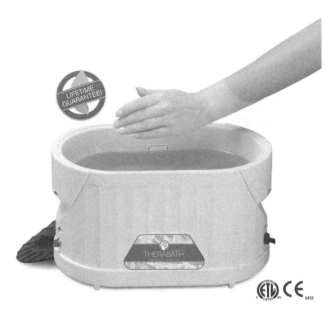

FIGURE 6.5 Paraffin bath.

areas are difficult to treat with moist heat packs because of their shape and uneven surface. The paraffin bath allows heat to effectively reach all areas of the hand or foot.

A paraffin bath contains a combination of paraffin wax and mineral oil that is heated to a constant temperature (130°F), which keeps the wax and oil in a liquid form.[3] To treat the injury, the athlete first should wash the body part thoroughly and remove any jewelry. This will limit the amount of bacteria and dirt that enters the bath and

---

ultrasound A deep-penetrating modality that uses acoustical waves to produce both thermal and nonthermal effects.

frequency The rate of occurrence of a wave measured in hertz (Hz), cycles per second (CPS), or pulses per second (PPS).

intensity The amount or degree of strength of electricity, light, heat, or sound per unit area or volume.

duty cycle The ratio between the pulse duration and the pulse interval: Duty cycle = Pulse duration / (Pulse duration + Pulse interval).

cavitation Gas bubble formation owing to nonthermal effects of ultrasound.

microstreaming Localized flow of fluids resulting from cavitation.

---

could be transferred to other users. The athlete then dips the injured part into the liquid wax 6 to 12 times while avoiding any movement of the body part.

As the injured area is removed from the bath after each dip, the hot wax will cool slightly and solidify to form a solid coating. If the athlete moves his or her fingers or toes between dips, cracks can occur in the coating, which may allow the liquid paraffin to seep underneath on a subsequent dip. This liquid wax will maintain its heat underneath the coating and may cause burning or tissue damage.[1]

Once the dipping is complete, the athlete should place the coated body part into a plastic bag and then wrap a towel around the bag. These layers will maintain a comfortable level of warmth for the athlete throughout the treatment, which should last 15 to 20 minutes. Once the therapy is complete, the wax is removed and placed back into the bath for future use.

CONTRAINDICATIONS

Open wounds, bleeding, loss of sensation, skin infections, and sensitivity to heat.

■ Ultrasound

Ultrasound is a very useful form of thermotherapy that involves a complex piece of equipment. When determining a treatment protocol, the athletic trainer must consider four parameters—**frequency**, **intensity**, **duty cycle**, and duration—prior to beginning the procedure. The type and location of the injury help to determine each of these parameters. Unlike the moist heat packs, ultrasound is a deep-heating modality that is capable of penetrating 1 to 5 centimeters into the tissue and increases the temperature up to 4°C in deep muscles.[1] Because of the depth of penetration, however, ultrasound must be properly indicated and applied to the athlete.

Ultrasound (**Figure 6.6**) derives its effect from acoustic vibrations. The ultrasound units that are found in most athletic training rooms have an applicator (or several of different sizes, depending on the model) that is placed in contact with the skin. This applicator has a piezoelectric crystal inside that, when an electric current is applied to it, expands and contracts causing vibrations that are directed out of the applicator and into the tissues. The vibration travels through the body tissue and causes an increase in temperature, which increases blood flow and relieves muscle tension.

Other, nonthermal effects also occur. **Cavitation** and **microstreaming** occur in the extracellular fluid that helps to deliver pro-inflammatory cellular components, which facilitate tissue healing.[1]

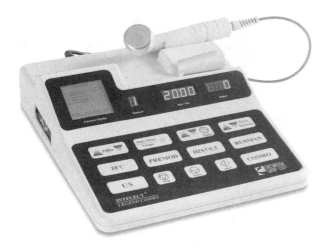

FIGURE 6.6 Ultrasound.

Improper use of this device may cause the crystal to crack or break, which may render them ineffective or increase the risk for injury to the athlete. As mentioned previously, the athletic trainer who is developing an ultrasound treatment protocol must consider several treatment parameters prior to initial use.

Frequency

Frequency is the number of acoustical waves occurring in one second.[1] This parameter determines the depth to which the acoustic vibrations will penetrate. The most common settings are 1 megahertz (MHz) and 3 MHz. When using a 1-MHz frequency, the goal is to reach the deeper tissues. This setting can extend 3 to 5 centimeters into the body tissue.[3] A 1-MHz treatment is most often used for large muscle groups that require this depth (e.g., quadriceps, hamstrings, trapezius muscles). The 3-MHz setting is better suited for more superficial areas (e.g., ankle, elbow, shoulder) because the energy is rapidly absorbed.[1] This setting reaches a depth of 1 to 2 centimeters.[3]

Intensity

The intensity of the treatment determines how much power is given to the vibrations entering the body. The overall range for intensity in athletic settings is 0.1 watts per centimeter squared (w/cm^2) to 3 w/cm^2. Individual institutions may define some standard intensity ranges, but the traditional intensity range utilized for treatments is 0.5 w/cm^2 to 2 w/cm^2. The higher intensities are best for deep tissue or large muscle groups, whereas the more superficial areas are better served with a lower intensity. Treatment times should be adjusted depending on intensity settings.

Duty Cycle

The duty cycle determines the amount of time during the treatment that the ultrasound is active. This can range from 100% down to 20% of the treatment time. A 100% duty cycle often is called continuous ultrasound, where the intensity is maintained throughout the treatment. Continuous ultrasound is useful in producing heating effects within the tissue.[1]

The other duty cycles less than 100% are called pulsed ultrasound. Most machines offer 75%, 50%, and 20% options for pulsed ultrasound, meaning that the intensity that is set is active only during the predetermined percentage of time. Pulsed ultrasound decreases the thermal effect of the treatment while still producing the nonthermal or mechanical benefits to the soft tissue.[1]

The continuous ultrasound is more effective when the goal of the treatment is to gain the heating (thermal) benefits of ultrasound. Pulsed ultrasound provides nonthermal effects, which benefits soft-tissue healing without heating the tissue. This is beneficial in the acute phase of an injury, when heating is contraindicated.

■ Ultrasound Application

To perform an ultrasound treatment properly, the first step—as with any modality—is to determine its appropriateness for the athlete and the specific injury. Once this has been done and the proper frequency, intensity, duty cycle, and duration has been determined, the athletic trainer must prepare the athlete for treatment. The acoustic vibrations in ultrasound do not travel through air and have difficulty penetrating the skin; therefore, to utilize ultrasound effectively, the athletic trainer needs a coupling medium.[1] This medium may be a manufactured ultrasound gel, a thermal or heating lotion, or another form of cream or gel that allows for a smooth surface with an airtight contact to the skin. Other coupling mediums may include placing the body part under water or using some form of bladder or balloon over the affected area.

During treatment, the ultrasound applicator must be constantly moving to avoid burning the athlete. The best pattern of movement is small, slow, overlapping circles. The applicator should be moved in a manner that covers approximately 4 centimeters per second.[1] The typical treatment times for ultrasound range from 3 to 10 minutes depending on the size of the treatment area, frequency, intensity, and goal of the treatment (e.g., vigorous heating, mild heating, nonthermal effects).[1]

CONTRAINDICATIONS

Loss of sensation in affected area. Do not use over the uterus in pregnant women. Do not apply over fractures, open wounds, or acute injuries (when using for thermal effects).

Phonophoresis

Phonophoresis, also known as phono, is a form of ultrasound that utilizes a pharmacologic agent as part of the coupling medium during the ultrasound procedure. The pharmacologic agent, typically hydrocortisone (10%) cream, is spread over the injured area along with the coupling medium.[1] The ultrasound treatment, through its mechanical effects, then transports the medicine through the skin to the affected tissue. Phonophoresis can directly introduce anti-inflammatory medicine that would not otherwise reach the injured area.

CONTRAINDICATIONS

Loss of sensation in affected area. Do not use over the uterus in pregnant women. Do not apply over fractures, open wounds, or acute injuries (when using for thermal effects).

Electrotherapy

Electrotherapy has become a very popular modality in the athletic training setting. Electrotherapy allows a

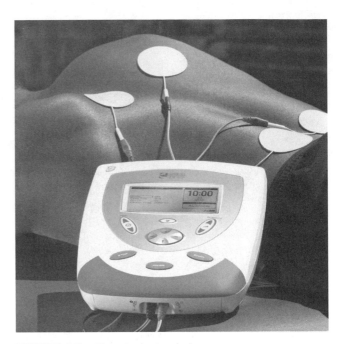

FIGURE 6.7 Electrical stimulation.

variety of treatment options, which are relatively easy to use. Depending on the specific settings utilized, electrotherapy may be used for both acute and chronic injuries, for pain control, to create a muscle contraction, or to deliver medication directly to an injury site. The two most utilized types of electrotherapy are electrical stimulation and iontophoresis.

■ Electrical Stimulation

Electrical stimulation often is abbreviated to stim or e-stim in the athletic training setting. Using different types of currents and **waveforms**, stimulation units (**Figure 6.7**) are able to decrease pain, swelling, and muscle spasm and increase muscle strength—especially post-surgery. Although electrical stimulation is beneficial and has its place in the athletic training room, it is not a substitute for a complete treatment and rehabilitation regimen and should not be overly relied upon.

Determining the treatment goals based on the athlete's stage in the healing process is critical for selecting the proper type of electrostimulating currents. **Biphasic**, **hi-volt**, and **interferential stimulation** are pain modulation currents.[1] These treatments, through several different physiological mechanisms, can decrease an athlete's perception of pain and muscle spasm. **Russian stimulation** and hi-volt stimulation, on the other hand, are very useful in generating a muscle contraction that can reduce swelling in the injured area or increase muscular strength. Russian stimulation,

> **phonophoresis** The introduction of anti-inflammatory drugs through the skin with the use of ultrasound.
>
> **electrotherapy** The therapeutic application of electricity to the body.
>
> **waveforms** The shape of a wave; graphs obtained by plotting the instantaneous values of a periodic quantity against the time.
>
> **biphasic** A pulsed current possessing two phases, each of which occurs on opposite sides of the baseline.
>
> **hi-volt** Electrical stimulation that utilizes a direct current to promote healing and decrease pain in an injured area.
>
> **interferential stimulation** Electrical stimulation that utilizes two channels of alternating current that promotes healing and decreases pain in an injured area.
>
> **Russian stimulation** Electrical stimulation that is used for muscle reeducation and strengthening by creating muscular contractions.

specifically, also is very effective in reeducating muscle in the proper firing patterns following surgery.[1] Because postsurgical swelling can inhibit muscle contraction and brain–muscle neural pathways become less efficient with disuse, this setting can directly stimulate the muscle and decrease recovery time fairly dramatically.[1]

Each type of electrical stimulation utilizes electrodes or pads that are placed on the skin for conduction of the electrical current. The number of pads and placement are dependent on which specific type of stimulation is selected and the location of the injured area receiving the treatment. Most treatments are completed in 15 to 20 minutes and may be accomplished in conjunction with cryotherapy or thermotherapy modalities to increase the therapeutic benefit. Athletes should receive only one to two treatments daily (at least 4 hours apart) to ensure that they gain the full therapeutic benefit.

CONTRAINDICATIONS

Loss of sensation, open wounds, implanted pacemakers, and sensitivity to equipment.

■ Iontophoresis

Iontophoresis is a form of electrotherapy that transports chemical ions through the skin by way of a specific low-voltage direct current. Anti-inflammatory and pain-relieving medicines often are utilized as part of the iontophoresis

---

iontophoresis Introduction of ions into the body through the use of an electrical current.

calibration The act of checking or adjusting (by comparison with a standard) the accuracy of a measuring instrument.

massage The rubbing or kneading of parts of the body especially to aid circulation, decrease muscle spasm, or relax the body.

effleurage Superficial, longitudinal massage strokes used to relax the patient.

petrissage Massage technique consisting of pressing and rolling the muscles under the fingers and hands.

tapotement Massage technique that uses sharp, alternating, brisk hand movements such as hacking, slapping, beating, cupping, and clapping to increase blood flow and stimulate peripheral nerve endings.

friction The force resisting the motion of two surfaces in contact.

---

treatment. The current moves the medicine through the skin directly to the affected area, which can be more effective than taking oral medication.[1] Treatment times typically last 20 to 30 minutes but may vary depending on the injured area and type and dosage of medication. Iontophoresis is especially effective for chronic injuries.

CONTRAINDICATIONS

Loss of sensation, sensitivity to equipment, and open wounds.

▮ Equipment Safety

When utilizing any of the modalities that have been discussed in this chapter, it is essential that each device be updated and maintained in proper working order. An annual assessment and **calibration** of all modality equipment should be completed and the record kept on file for liability purposes. Annual maintenance and upkeep also should be completed to ensure a safe athletic training room for the athletes and to prolong the life of the equipment.

▮ Massage

Massage is one of the oldest modalities in use today. It is a very useful therapy found both in and outside the athletic training room. Massage is defined as the manipulation of the soft tissues of the body in a systematic manner.[3] There are numerous therapeutic benefits to massage including relaxation, decreased muscle spasm, and increased circulation. Four varieties of massage strokes are used in the athletic training setting: **effleurage**, **petrissage**, **tapotement**, and **friction**.

■ Effleurage

Effleurage consists of slow, stroking motions used over the affected areas (**Figure 6.8**). It can be done in both a light and deep manner, allowing for relaxation and increased blood flow (**Figure 6.9**).

■ Petrissage

Petrissage consists of kneading motions similar to a baker kneading bread (**Figure 6.10**). The skin is rolled and twisted in different directions to decrease muscle spasm and remove scar tissue.

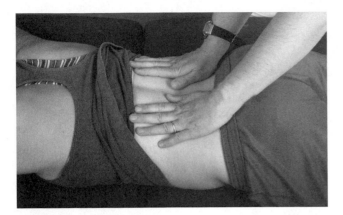

FIGURE 6.8 Effleurage.

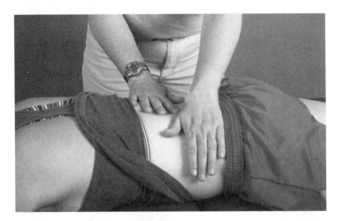

FIGURE 6.9 Cross-body effleurage.

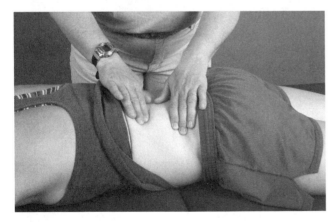

FIGURE 6.10 Petrissage.

■ Tapotement

Tapotement is a percussive massage. This form of stroke uses cupped hands, the side of the hand, or fists to lightly beat on the injured area (**Figure 6.11**). Tapotement can be used to decrease muscle spasm and break up scar tissue.

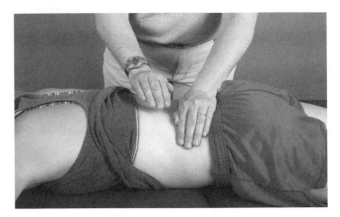

FIGURE 6.11 Tapotement.

■ Friction Massage

Friction massage is utilized to loosen an especially difficult muscle spasm or scar tissue. The hands are moved in a circular pattern pushing deeply into the muscle with the fingers or thumbs (**Figure 6.12**). This form of massage can be painful for the athlete, especially after an acute injury. The athletic trainer should take note of the individual's reaction and adjust the intensity accordingly.

■ Massage Application

In a typical sports massage, all four of these techniques may be used concurrently throughout the treatment. Rarely is one stroke used exclusively; rather each one is performed at different times to highlight each technique's therapeutic benefits. To ensure the athlete's comfort, a massage gel or lotion should be used to decrease friction and skin irritation.

When performing a massage, the athletic trainer always must maintain the highest level of professionalism. When clothing must be removed, a towel should be draped over any private areas to cover them from view. The athlete

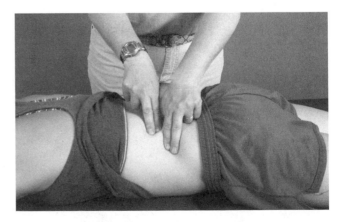

FIGURE 6.12 Friction massage.

should never feel uncomfortable with the situation or the physical contact associated with the massage.

Therapeutic Exercise

In the majority of cases, the most beneficial therapeutic modality following an injury is physical activity.[2] If the appropriate levels of activity are determined (e.g., sprinting is not recommended immediately post-injury), exercise can be extremely valuable in the healing process. Not only does exercise and activity increase the blood flow and therefore the circulation of oxygen to the healing tissue, but it also helps to guide the proper formation and restructuring of the collagen fibers at the injury site.[4]

Any physical activity post-injury should be conducted as part of a systematic rehabilitation protocol that is supervised by a medical professional such as an athletic trainer or a physical therapist. This rehabilitation protocol should take into consideration the ability of the athlete in his or her injured state and not force too much activity too soon. Further injury may occur if the athlete's body is not able to handle the stress placed upon it during rehabilitation.

Four phases or categories of activity should be included in the rehabilitation protocol, depending on the severity of the injury. If the injury is severe, the therapy must focus on the initial phases of rehabilitation until the athlete is capable of completing more difficult activities.

The first phase of rehabilitation is the passive phase, which focuses on regaining range of motion and reducing swelling and other acute symptoms that the athlete may have. In this phase, the athletic trainer is conducting all movements while the athlete is in a relaxed position. The passive nature of the exercises minimizes the amount of stress placed on the healing tissue.

> **therapeutic exercise** Exercise for strengthening, improving awareness of limbs, improving coordination, and improving function.

FIGURE 6.13   Weight lifting.

As the injury improves, the athlete can progress to active-assisted exercises, which include voluntary participation of the patient with the assistance of the athletic trainer. The goal of this phase of rehabilitation is to increase muscle strength while continuing to improve the range of motion of the injured joint.[2]

The active phase is the third category of rehabilitation. During this phase, the athlete is completing the exercises individually with only supervision being provided by the athletic trainer. The athlete strives to increase muscle and tissue strength during these exercises by utilizing gravity as resistance.

The fourth, and final, phase of rehabilitation is the resistive phase, where the athlete utilizes free weights, exercise machines, or the athletic trainer as resistance against joint motion (**Figure 6.13**).[2] Increasing strength is the primary goal of this phase in an attempt to return the athlete to full participation, as well as reduce the risk of reinjury.

Therapeutic exercise is an integral aspect of an athlete's return from injury. It is important for the athlete and the athletic trainer to bear in mind that rehabilitation is an ongoing process that continues past the return to play. The athlete must continue to adhere to the rehabilitation plan to increase strength and range of motion, which will decrease the risk for reinjury.[2]

CHAPTER REVIEW

1. Why is cryotherapy beneficial for the injured athlete?
2. What types of injuries are contraindicated for thermotherapy?
3. What are the four settings that must be determined for an ultrasound treatment?
4. List the types of electrical stimulation used for pain modulation.
5. What are the four stages of therapeutic exercise?
6. How often should electrical modalities be calibrated?

CRITICAL THINKING

How do you avoid falling into a pattern or rut with your modalities prescriptions?

REFERENCES

1. Starkey C. *Therapeutic Modalities for Athletic Trainers*, 3rd ed. Philadelphia: F. A. Davis, 2004.
2. Pfeiffer RP, Mangus BC. *Concepts of Athletic Training*, 5th ed. Sudbury, MA: Jones and Bartlett, 2008.
3. Prentice WE. *Arnheim's Principles of Athletic Training: A Competency-Based Approach*, 12th ed. Boston: McGraw-Hill, 2006.
4. Knight KL. *Cryotherapy in Sports Injury Management*. Champaign, IL: Human Kinetics, 1995.

Evaluation Techniques

In the preceding chapters, we have discussed two of the primary roles and responsibilities of athletic trainers—the prevention and the treatment of athletic injuries. In this chapter, we explore another primary responsibility, the evaluation and assessment of athletic injuries. There are important considerations to understand and procedures to follow when evaluating an injury. The information found in this chapter is what differentiates a medical professional from the average person on the street.

To be considered successful and knowledgeable in assessing injuries, an athletic trainer must be well versed in the basic information—specifically anatomy and nomenclature/medical terminology. Without a thorough understanding of anatomy and terminology, an individual would be incapable of completing the injury history, much less the remainder of the evaluation. Grasping the concept of how the body works and what makes it work is the first step in a student's path to becoming an athletic trainer.

 ## Basic Anatomy

In the coming chapters, we discuss each region of the body and the pertinent anatomy associated with it. Before we reach that stage, though, we examine the basic surface anatomy that correlates to every region of the body. When discussing surface anatomy, the athletic trainer should first visualize the injured person in proper **anatomic position**.

Anatomic position consists of an individual standing in a forward-facing position with his or her arms hanging at the side and the palms of the hands visible from the front. This position dictates the terminology used to describe the injury and the evaluation findings no matter what position the athlete is in at the time of injury. It is not necessary to place an athlete in anatomic position during evaluation as long as you can visualize the proper placement and evaluate based on that position.

> **anatomic position** Used as a universal reference to determine anatomic direction, it is a position whereby the body is erect, facing forward, with the arms at the side of the body, palms facing forward.
> **sagittal plane** A longitudinal (vertical) line that divides the body or any of its parts into right and left portions.
> **frontal (coronal) plane** A longitudinal (vertical) line that divides the body or any of its parts into anterior and posterior portions.

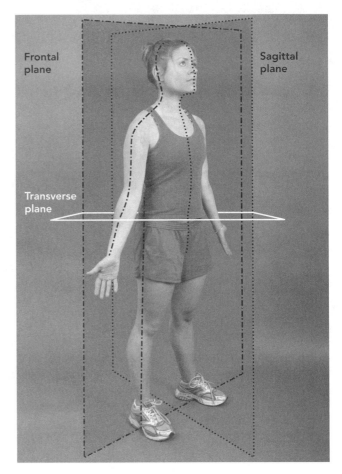

FIGURE 7.1 Planes of body movement.

■ Body Planes

In anatomic position, the body can be divided into three planes. These body planes act as a reference for all movements (**Figure 7.1**). Every movement in the body occurs within one or more of these planes—an important point to bear in mind when evaluating the injury and the motion that caused it. Each of the three planes divides the body equally into halves as though the individual was sliced evenly in two.

The **sagittal plane** is the first plane to be examined. The sagittal plane separates the body down the center into two equal halves. The line of the sagittal plane divides the head through the nose and mouth, down the chest all the way to the belly button, and then to the ground. Each side has one eye, one ear, one arm, and one leg. Any motion that goes forward or backward, such as bending the knee or elbow or nodding your head, occurs in this plane.

The next plane is called the **frontal (coronal) plane**. This plane, as the name suggests, divides the body into front and back at approximately the ears and shoulders. Any motion to the side falls into the frontal plane, such as raising the arms or legs to the side.

Finally, the third plane is the **transverse plane**. The dividing line in this case sits at the waist, separating the top of the body from the bottom. Twisting motions such as rotation at the waist from left to right occur in the transverse plane.[1]

■ Surface Anatomy

With the anatomic position and the body planes in mind, it is now possible to label the directions and descriptions of the body parts that will be recorded during an evaluation. When visualizing the body in proper anatomic position, the front of the body is called the **anterior** portion whereas the back is called the **posterior** aspect. These descriptions are associated with the frontal plane. In the sagittal plane, the imaginary line that divides the body into equal halves is titled the **midline**. The midline of the body becomes important when discussing the next set of descriptors.

Medial and **lateral** directions often are used to describe aspects of a joint such as ligaments or compartments. The medial aspect is the side of the described body part that is closest to the midline. For instance, the inside of the knee is the medial aspect. The lateral aspect is the opposite; it is the part that is farthest from the midline. Medial and lateral can be used to describe the part of the body, or they can be used to compare one part to another. For example, the pinky is medial when compared to the thumb and the shoulder is lateral to the rib cage.

The next set of surface anatomy descriptors is associated with a body part's placement in comparison to the heart or the torso of the body. The **proximal** position is that which is closest to the heart. The **distal** aspect, on the

Fast Fact	
Body Planes	**Description**
Sagittal	Separates the body into equal halves with one arm and leg on each half
Frontal	Separates the body into front and back
Transverse	Separates the body at the trunk into upper and lower halves
Surface Anatomy	**Description**
Anterior	Front of the body
Posterior	Back of the body
Midline	Imaginary line through the middle of the body
Medial	That which is closest to the midline
Lateral	That which is farthest from the midline
Proximal	That which is closest to the heart
Distal	That which is farthest from the heart
Superior	That which is closest to the head
Inferior	That which is farthest from the head

transverse plane A horizontal line that divides the body into superior and inferior portions.

anterior Before or in front of.

posterior Toward the rear or back.

midline An imaginary line drawn down the middle of the body through the nose and umbilicus.

medial Closer to the midline.

lateral Farther away from the midline.

proximal Nearest to the point of reference.

distal Farthest from a center, from the midline, or from the trunk.

superior (cephal) aspect Toward the head.

inferior (caudal) aspect Toward the feet.

other hand, is the aspect that is farther from the torso and closer to the end of an extremity. As before, these can be used as a manner to describe a body part or to compare one part with another. For example, the shoulder is proximal to the elbow whereas the foot is distal to the knee.

The final set of descriptors is used to describe a body part in relation to the head. The **superior (cephal) aspect** is the part closest to the top of the body whereas the **inferior (caudal) aspect** is farther away and closer to the feet. These are fairly similar to proximal and distal but can become especially important when describing the head and neck. For example, the neck is proximal when compared to the head, but it also is inferior.

Nomenclature/Terminology

Understanding the surface anatomy and its descriptors is an essential part of an evaluation. The other basic knowledge that is required is the terminology that an athletic trainer uses to describe movements in the evaluation notes. Specific terms are used to describe the most common movements in the body. To understand these movements fully, it is important to focus once again on the three body planes.

In the sagittal plane, there are two primary motions—**flexion** and **extension**. Flexion is the bending of a joint usually with the distal point of the extremity moving closer to the proximal aspect. Two examples of flexion are bending the elbow so that the hand nears the shoulder and bending the knee to move the foot closer to the butt. Extension is moving the joint in the opposite direction, sending the most distal point back to its farthest position. Extension is often associated with straightening a joint. For instance, extension moves the knee or elbow until the joint locks back into anatomic position.

In the foot and ankle, flexion and extension are distinguished instead as **dorsiflexion** and **plantar flexion**. Dorsiflexion is the movement of the dorsum of the foot (the top) toward the heart. Plantar flexion moves the plantar surface (the sole) away from the heart.

In the frontal plane, the two sets of typical motions are separated by body part. **Abduction** and **adduction**

---

flexion **The act of bending a limb.**

extension **The act of straightening a limb.**

dorsiflexion **Bending toward the dorsum or rear; opposite of plantar flexion.**

plantar flexion **Movement of the foot that flexes the foot or toes downward toward the sole.**

abduction **Movement of the limbs toward the lateral plane or away from the body.**

adduction **Moving of a body part toward the central axis of the body.**

inversion **Turning medially.**

eversion **Turning laterally.**

valgus **An opening on the medial side of a joint caused by the distal segment moving laterally.**

varus **An opening on the lateral side of a joint caused by the distal segment moving medially.**

internal rotation **Movement in which the anterior surface of the distal segment moves toward the midline of the body.**

---

denote mostly shoulder and hip movement whereas **inversion** and **eversion** describe motion in the ankle and foot. Abduction is the movement of the shoulder and hip away from the midline or center of the body. Meanwhile, adduction is moving the extremity back toward the center of the body.

The shoulder presents a unique circumstance in that once it reaches the midway point of movement in abduction—when it is parallel to the ground—it begins to move back toward the midline. Adduction has the opposite effect, actually moving away from the midline for the first half of the motion until it begins to move back toward the center. In either case, the names of the motion do not change. The name is derived from the movement in relation to anatomic position.

In the ankle joint, the motions similar to abduction and adduction are called inversion and eversion. Eversion is moving the ankle outward away from the midline of the body. Inversion is the opposite, moving the ankle and the plantar surface of the foot toward the midline. The inversion motion when done to the farthest degree leaves the athlete standing on the outside (lateral aspect) of the foot.

Also a component of the frontal plane is motion in the knee or elbow that occurs more often as a result of forced movement rather than in a voluntary manner. **Valgus** and **varus** stress placed on the knee or elbow is a frequent cause or mechanism of injury, especially to the protective ligaments in the joint. Valgus movement or stress forces the joint toward the midline of the body and the distal extremity (the hand or foot) away from the midline. Varus stress goes in the opposite direction, forcing the joint away from the midline and the distal extremity toward the midline. Again, this motion is rarely voluntary, unlike the other movements discussed.

The transverse plane has two primary types of motion that are again differentiated by the body part in question. Internal and external rotations are often found at the shoulder and hip whereas pronation and supination are seen in the hands and forearms. **Internal rotation** moves the ball of the shoulder or hip joint toward the midline in a rotatory manner. If the shoulder is against the body and the elbow is flexed, internal rotation moves the fist in toward the stomach. **External rotation** rotates the ball of the joint away from the body and the midline. The fist now moves into space away from the side of the body.

It is important to differentiate the direction of motion for the ball of the joint rather than the distal extremity for hip motion, especially if the knee is flexed during evaluation, which it often is. In internal rotation, the ball of the hip rotates toward the midline while the lower leg and foot rotate in the opposite direction, if the athlete is seated. The reverse is true for external rotation of the hip. It can become confusing during a hip evaluation if you base the motion on the direction of the flexed knee and foot.

Pronation and **supination** are almost exclusively connected to the movement of the hand, although some use the descriptors to discuss the foot as well. Pronating the hand and forearm at the same time rotates the hand from anatomic position to a point where the palm is facing the opposite direction. Supination is the motion that returns the hand to proper anatomic position.

An easier way to visualize the motion is with the shoulder against the side of the body and the elbow flexed. In this position, pronation rotates the hand until it is facing downward. Supination rotates the hand in the opposite direction so that the palm is facing upward. In the supinated position where the elbow is flexed, the hand is upward as if holding a bowl of soup—an easy way to distinguish supination from pronation.

These movements and their descriptors are a very important method for describing injuries and ranges of motion when recording an evaluation. Now that we have discussed surface anatomy and terminology, we can examine issues that are important during an evaluation either on or off the field.

On-Field Survey

When an injury occurs during play, the athletic trainer who responds to the scene will do an immediate assessment of the individual to determine whether there are any life-threatening issues at hand.[2] This preliminary assessment is called a primary or **initial survey** and evaluates an athlete for his or her vital signs and to determine whether there is any severe bleeding or head or neck injuries present.

The vital signs of the athlete consist primarily of the ABCs: airway, breathing, and circulation. If an athlete is breathing and has a pulse, the athletic trainer knows that the athlete is alive at that moment and does not require immediate resuscitation. Other vital signs may include level of consciousness, core temperature, blood pressure, skin color, and the size and reaction of the pupils in the eyes. Each of these vital signs assists in determining whether the athlete is suffering from a life-threatening injury. The athletic trainer must evaluate the individual for these vital signs before continuing to any other injuries.

Once the athletic trainer has ruled out any life-threatening concerns, he or she can focus on what injuries the athlete may have suffered. This assessment is called a **secondary survey** and entails a head-to-toe evaluation to determine any and all injuries that may have occurred.[2] The on-field assessment should be thorough, but also done in a relatively quick manner to ensure the athlete's safety and also to allow the game to return to play.

The primary question that should be answered during the secondary survey is: "Can I safely move the athlete off the field while not exacerbating the injuries or risking the athlete's life?" If the athlete can be safely moved, the athletic trainer should request assistance and transfer the injured player to the sideline for a more in-depth assessment. However, prior to moving the athlete, the athlete should be thoroughly examined to rule out several issues that may pose serious concerns for the athlete and for the athletic trainer's treatment. The first potentially severe concern is whether the athlete has suffered a neck injury that, if moved, could cause paralysis or even death. If there is even a concern that a neck injury is present, the athlete should be stabilized at the neck immediately to prevent additional movement that may cause more damage.

Once in-line stabilization is established (**Figure 7.2**), the athletic training staff can carefully place the athlete on a spine board. The spine board prevents further harm during transport to the hospital for X-rays and treatment. Only trained personnel should assist with the placement

external rotation Movement in which the anterior surface of the distal segment moves away from the midline of the body.

pronation Combination of movements resulting in the rotation of the hand and wrist to the opposite of anatomic position.

supination Movement of the hand and wrist that allows the structure to return to anatomic position.

initial survey Immediate check of airway, breathing, circulation, and other vital signs to rule out life-threatening injuries or conditions.

secondary survey Head-to-toe evaluation of injured athlete to determine the location and extent of injury.

FIGURE 7.2 In-line stabalization.

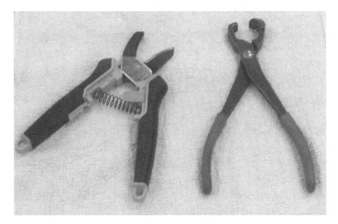

FIGURE 7.4 Facemask removal tools.

of the athlete on a spine board, again to minimize excess motion and prevent further damage. At least four trained people are required to move the athlete onto the spine board properly (**Figure 7.3**).

Several techniques can be utilized for athlete placement. None of the techniques is more effective than the

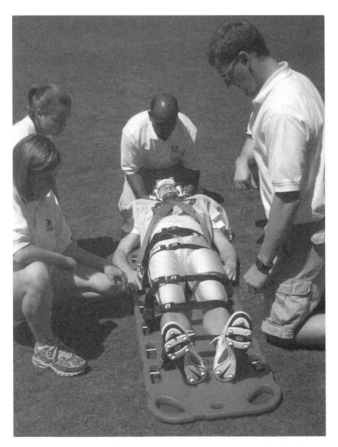

FIGURE 7.3 Spine board.

others. The chosen technique often is preferable because of the position of the athlete or the present situation. It is essential that athletic training staff practice spine-boarding techniques at least once every year and that each technique is practiced so that all staff and students are prepared for any scenario.

An athlete who participates in a sport that requires a helmet (e.g., football, ice hockey, men's lacrosse) presents a unique challenge for spine boarding. In-line stabilization is still the first step that must be taken if a neck injury is suspected, but the stabilization must be conducted with the helmet as the point of contact. A properly fitted helmet can still prevent motion of the head and neck if the athlete is appropriately stabilized.

Once the in-line stabilization is in place, another athletic trainer is tasked with removing the facemask (FM) from the helmet with a facemask removal tool. The facemask must be removed in a timely manner to allow for rescue breathing and/or CPR if the athlete is not breathing.

Numerous versions of facemask removal tools on the market have been shown to be effective (**Figure 7.4**). Research has shown that the FM Extractor tool and cordless screwdrivers are the most effective tools because they complete the task with minimal movement of the head during the facemask removal.[3,4]

The athlete should be spine boarded with the helmet and shoulder pads in place to protect the head and neck from any unnecessary movement that may cause further damage or paralysis. In situations where the helmet and shoulder pads are inhibiting the athletic trainer's ability to provide appropriate care, they may be removed. However, if the helmet is removed, the shoulder pads must also be removed because the two pieces of equipment are developed specifically to provide an even surface for the

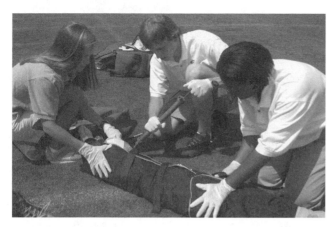

FIGURE 7.5   Vacuum splint.

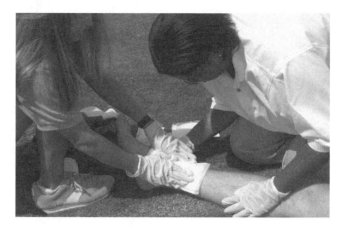

FIGURE 7.6   Applying direct pressure.

athlete to lie on. If only the helmet is removed, the neck will be forced into extension, which may cause further damage or paralysis.

Along with neck injuries, the athlete should also be evaluated to rule out fractures that should be splinted before moving the athlete. The athletic trainer should utilize vacuum splints (**Figure 7.5**) or another form of splinting material to minimize movement of the injured body part and decrease the risk for further damage. Athletic training staffs should practice proper splinting techniques at least once a year so that all staff and students are prepared for any scenario.

Finally, any severe bleeding should be controlled prior to transferring the athlete. Blood loss can quickly turn an injury into a life-threatening situation and should be treated with the proper protocols. In a bleeding scenario, the athletic training staff must use **universal precautions** to avoid disease transmission either to the athletic trainer or to the athlete. After donning gloves, the athletic trainer applies direct pressure to the wound with gauze or other cloth to stop the flow of blood (**Figure 7.6**).

If the blood soaks the first layer of gauze, the athletic trainer should apply a second layer of gauze over the top of the previous layer. Never remove the gauze that is already covering the wound because that will remove the clotting that has already occurred and renew the blood flow to its previous level, if not increase the bleeding. Direct pressure

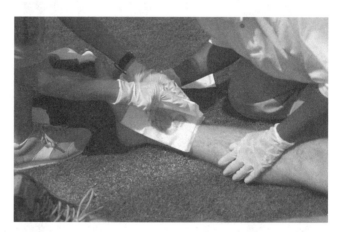

FIGURE 7.7   If blood soaks through the first layer of gauze, a second layer should be placed over the top.

over the wound (**Figure 7.7**) should continue until the bleeding subsides or the athlete arrives at the hospital for further evaluation.

Universal Precautions

When dealing with a bleeding injury—whether severe or not—it is imperative that you follow the standard rules of universal precautions. Universal precautions dictate specific steps for any medical personnel who are treating an injury, especially one involving blood or other body fluids. These steps help protect both the treating individual and the athlete from a transmission of infectious diseases such as hepatitis B or HIV/AIDS. Blood and other body fluids are carriers of these diseases and could threaten the health of the medical staff.

> **universal precautions** Refers to the practice, in medicine, of avoiding contact with patients' bodily fluids by wearing nonporous articles such as medical gloves, goggles, and face shields.

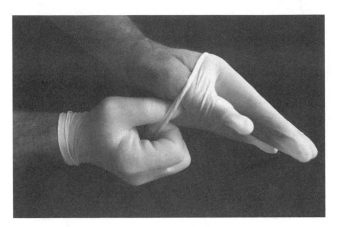

FIGURE 7.8 Protective gloves.

FIGURE 7.9 Wash hands after exposure.

Government regulations have been established requiring that medical personnel follow universal precautions both for their safety and for the safety of the patient. The following guidelines have been approved as universal precautions and should be followed by all athletic trainers.

1. Always wear gloves when handling patients and remove gloves properly (**Figure 7.8**).
2. Always wear protective eyewear or face shield to protect from blood splatter.
3. Wash your hands immediately following contact with a bleeding patient (**Figure 7.9**).
4. Do not recap, reuse, or manipulate used needles or scalpels.
5. Use some form of protective mask when performing rescue breathing or CPR.
6. It is recommended that all medical personnel receive immunizations for tetanus and hepatitis B to assist in the prevention of disease.[5]

Off-the-Field Evaluation

The off-the-field evaluation of the athlete requires most of the athletic trainer's time and energy and is where surface anatomy and terminology become important. When completing an off-the-field evaluation, an athletic trainer uses a systematic process to assess the injured player. This process ensures that the athletic trainer evaluates all of the important components of an injury that then allows for a proper assessment and determination of the nature of the injury and how to properly treat and rehabilitate it.

The systematic process that is used by most athletic trainers is named the **HOPS process**. HOPS is an acronym for history, observation, palpation, and special tests. These steps allow for a thorough examination while proceeding through the categories found in the SOAP (subjective, objective, assessment, and plan) note that was discussed in Chapter 2. The SOAP note is the written format that documents the evaluation and clinical findings throughout the assessment.

■ History

The first aspect of any injury evaluation is the history of the event. This history differs from the previous medical history taken during the preparticipation physical in that it focuses solely on the current injury and any potential causes of the damage. During the evaluation, an athletic trainer asks questions that provide a summary of what happened, when it happened, how, where, and why it happened.

The athletic trainer who is present for the injury and who sees the incident occur will already know some of these answers, but it is still significant to learn the athlete's impression of the incident. Often the athlete's description of what happened and how it felt can lead the athletic trainer to a general notion of what the injury may be even prior to performing any special tests. It is essential for the athletic trainer to ask the right questions and really listen to the answers to develop a proper history.

Asking the athlete what happened to cause the injury is a good introduction for the history. Most of the time, the athlete will describe what he or she was doing during the play and what event occurred to cause the pain—whether it was direct contact with some object, a twist-

HOPS process An acronym used to guide secondary assessment (history, observation/inspection, palpation, special tests).

ing motion, or something else. With this information in hand, the athletic trainer can delve deeper into the event to determine where on the playing surface it occurred, at what point in the game, and what events leading up to it could have caused the injury.

Once the athletic trainer has ascertained the basics of the incident, he or she can evaluate the symptoms that the athlete felt at the time of injury. Did the athlete hear or feel a pop, which would suggest a tear in the injured tissue? Was there immediate pain or swelling or was there a more gradual onset of symptoms? Could the athlete still ambulate if it is a lower-extremity injury? All of these questions provide the examiner with important information on the issue.

Finally, the athletic trainer should investigate the general medical history of the athlete, specifically if the athlete is taking any medications and if there have been any previous injuries at the current site. Medications may play a role in the proper treatment of the injury, and all current medications should be noted to avoid any contraindications or reactions to future treatments.

The previous history at the injury site also is very important to determine whether there is an injury pattern for this specific athlete. For instance, if the athlete has suffered a torn anterior cruciate ligament (ACL) in the same knee before and complains of the same symptoms, he or she might have reinjured the ligament. This information provides a helpful beginning for the examiner's evaluation. The athletic trainer must be certain to ask the athlete about previous injuries to both the involved side and the opposite side of the body to see if the athlete is susceptible to injuries at specific sites on either side. All of the information received during the history portion of the evaluation should be documented in the subjective section of the SOAP note.

■ Observation

The second phase of the evaluation is the observation of the injured area. The examiner is visually checking the injury site for any obvious signs and symptoms. Swelling, redness, discoloration, bleeding, signs of injury (contusions or abrasions), and blatant deformity may all be noticeable during a quick inspection of the involved body part.[6] The examiner also should compare the injured side with the opposite side of the body to determine how the athlete presents normally. What some may consider deformity or swelling could be normal body structure for the injured athlete. A comparison of involved versus uninvolved areas provides a baseline understanding of any anatomic differences caused by the current injury.

However, before this visual inspection is conducted, even before the history is taken, the observation phase

has already begun. True observation begins as soon as the athletic trainer sees the athlete for the first time. How the individual enters the athletic training room or leaves the field often can provide a great deal of information about what has occurred.

Does the athlete have a limp or favor one side more than the other? Does the athlete hold one arm close to the body or is it at an unnatural angle? The way the athlete carries himself or herself and the injured body part can assist the athletic trainer in the evaluation. First of all, the examiner often can immediately determine where the injury is located by the way the athlete is walking. More serious injuries, or lower-extremity injuries, may not allow the athlete to bear weight at all. This observation provides the examiner with an introduction to the injury. The information learned during observation is recorded in the objective portion of the SOAP note.

■ Palpation

After the initial history and visual inspection, the athletic trainer should have a general impression of the injured area and what may be causing the athlete's symptoms. During the palpation phase, the athletic trainer can pinpoint the exact location of injury and determine which special tests should be performed. During this phase, the athletic trainer uses his or her hands as a guide to identify any physical signs and symptoms that are present.

Palpation should begin with a thorough assessment of the uninvolved side (if possible) to determine what is "normal" for the injured athlete. With a general understanding of what is normal for the athlete, the athletic trainer can then move to the involved side and palpate the injured area. When palpating the injury, it is important to begin tenderly to ensure that the athlete does not suffer unnecessary pain.

By palpating the affected area, the examiner can notice pain, muscle spasm, swelling, warmth, or deformity at the injury site.[6] These are signs that might or might not have been apparent during the visual inspection. It is critical from a legal standpoint that the athletic trainer receives consent from the injured athlete prior to palpating any part of the athlete's body. Physical contact without consent can potentially lead to legal action. The information from this assessment should be recorded in the objective section of the SOAP note.

■ Special Tests

The three previous phases of an evaluation provide a general impression of the injury and what may be damaged. They eliminate some injury possibilities and can suggest a potential assessment. The special tests phase is the component of the evaluation that validates that

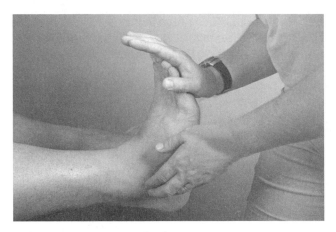

FIGURE 7.10 Tap test for fractures.

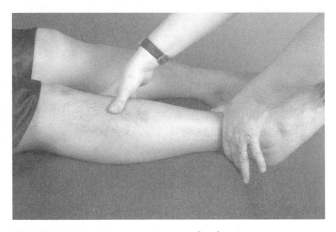

FIGURE 7.11 Compression test for fractures.

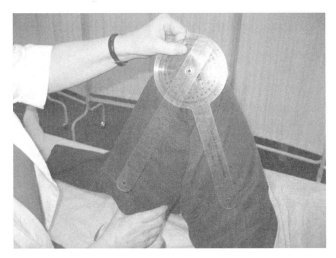

FIGURE 7.12 Goniometer assessment.

information and leads the examiner to an assessment of the injury.

Literally hundreds of special tests that evaluate bone integrity, muscle strength, and soft tissue stability are available. Obviously, all of the tests cannot and should not be performed during a single evaluation. It is the athletic trainer's responsibility to know which tests are appropriate and which are not for a specific injury scenario. The education and practical experience that the athletic trainer has gained will help him or her make this determination.

The integrity of bony structures is tested using one of three techniques. The tap test (**Figure 7.10**) is a very simple, useful procedure to evaluate for fractures. By tapping on different aspects of the bone, the examiner can ascertain painful areas and possible fractures. The compression test (**Figure 7.11**), another technique, is performed when the examiner squeezes the bone from both sides at several different points throughout the structure. Again, this identifies painful areas and potential fractures. The third technique is a **translation** test, or moving one portion of the bone anteriorly while moving another portion posteriorly or moving each portion side to side in opposite directions. The translation test is most often used for the long bones

> **translation** Refers to the anterior gliding of one end of the bone and the posterior gliding of the other end.
>
> **manual muscle tests (MMTs)** A graded strength test performed by applying manual resistance to a segment to evaluate a particular muscle or muscle group.
>
> **range of motion (ROM)** The specific movement provided at a joint by the joint structures (ligaments, joint capsules, cartilage, bones).

of the hands and feet. A positive test finds pain and possible crepitus—a crackling or grinding sound as the edges of the fracture rub against each other.

Manual muscle tests (MMTs) on the major muscle groups surrounding the injured area are conducted once the integrity and stability of the bones have been ascertained. During MMTs, the athletic trainer evaluates the joint's **range of motion (ROM)** and strength in three manners: active, passive, and resistive. Active ROM is the athlete's ability to move on his or her own through a normal pattern such as flexion or extension. The range of this motion is measured in degrees using a goniometer (**Figure 7.12**)—a special tool made specifically for this purpose—and is compared bilaterally.

Passive ROM is the movement through the pattern completed by the examiner with the athlete completely relaxed. This measures the range of the joint without muscle involvement. Resistive ROM is found with the athlete actively moving the body part through its normal ROM against resistance provided by the athletic trainer. For instance, to check hamstring strength, the athletic trainer will resist knee flexion. The resisted ROM determines the athlete's range prior to muscle failure/fatigue or mechanical obstruction possibly resulting from the injury.

Preferably, for a manual muscle test, the athlete should be placed in a position where the movement is conducted against gravity—if that position is not painful for the athlete. This position places an additional force resisting the muscle's action.

MMTs are also used to measure the level of strength that the athlete possesses at different angles during ROM. The examiner tests the athlete's **isometric strength** at several different angles to identify weaknesses or deficits at selected sites within the muscle. Strength levels are based on a scale of 0 to 5 out of 5 with 0 being no strength at all and 5 being full strength without deficit (**Table 7.1**). The athlete's position on the scale is based on a comparison of the injured side to the uninvolved side to determine the athlete's individual strength rather than a random opinion or preconceived guideline of what strength is.

Once the strength of the muscles has been assessed, the examiner can evaluate the other soft-tissue structures to determine whether they have been injured. Each soft-tissue structure has had at least one special test developed to determine its stability and strength. These tests should be utilized to determine whether an injury is present in each structure and the level of damage that was sustained. The special tests for each injury are discussed in more detail in the following chapters.

The information found with the special tests is recorded in the objective portion of the SOAP note. The results of all the special tests, as well as the other phases of

TABLE 7.1
MANUAL MUSCLE TESTS FOR STRENGTH
0/5: No strength, no muscle tone
1/5: No strength, minimal muscle tone
2/5: Minimal strength, full ROM without gravity or resistance
3/5: Moderate strength, full ROM against gravity, no resistance
4/5: Good strength, full ROM against some resistance
5/5: Strength and muscle tone comparable to uninvolved side

evaluation, provide the athletic trainer with the findings on which to base an injury assessment. The assessment is the athletic trainer's professional opinion of the injury. Based on this assessment, the examiner can develop a plan of action that includes treatment, rehabilitation, and possibly referral to a physician.

Now that the proper techniques for evaluations and assessments have been discussed, we can begin exploring each individual region of the body and the specific injuries that may occur. Each of the following chapters is dedicated to one of these regions and reviews the pertinent anatomy, injuries, treatment, and return-to-play guidelines.

isometric strength Strength that does not involve moving the involved body part.

CHAPTER REVIEW

1. What are the three body planes?
2. Which structures does a valgus force damage?
3. What are the steps of universal precautions?
4. What does the acronym HOPS stand for?
5. What are the special tests that evaluate bone integrity?
6. What do manual muscle tests evaluate?

CRITICAL THINKING

How do you evaluate an athlete who you suspect is faking/exaggerating an injury?

REFERENCES

1. Starkey C, Johnson G. *Athletic Training and Sports Medicine*, 4th ed. Sudbury, MA: Jones and Bartlett, 2006.

2. Schottke D. *First Responder: Your First Response in Emergency Care*, 4th ed. Sudbury, MA: Jones and Bartlett, 2007.

3. Decoster LC, Shirley CP, Swartz EE. (2005). Football face-mask removal with a cordless screwdriver on helmets used for at least one season of play. *Journal of Athletic Training*, 40(3):169.

4. Swartz EE, Armstrong CW, Rankin JM, Rogers B. (2002). A 3-dimensional analysis of face-mask removal tools in inducing helmet movement. *Journal of Athletic Training*, 37(2):178.

5. Centers for Disease Control and Prevention. (1987). Recommendations for prevention of HIV transmission in health-care settings. *Morbidity and Mortality Weekly Report*, 36(suppl. 2S).

6. Booher JM, Thibodeau GA. *Athletic Injury Assessment*, 4th ed. Boston: McGraw-Hill, 2000.

Lower Body Evaluation

The Foot

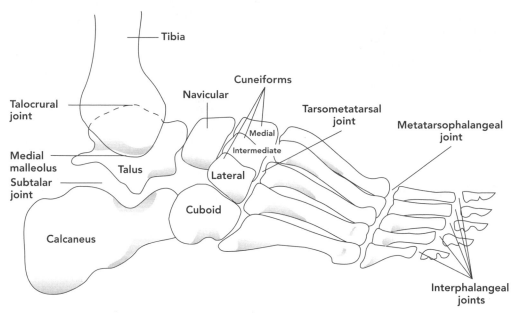

FIGURE 8.1 Anatomy of the foot (lateral view).

The structure and function of the foot make it a mechanical marvel. The two primary roles of the foot, **propulsion** and support, are diametrically opposed to each other. During propulsion, the foot must act as a flexible lever, pushing the individual through the **gait pattern**. In support, the foot is a rigid structure allowing the body to maintain balance.[1]

The foot is an active component in every step an individual takes throughout his or her life. With numerous health organizations suggesting 10,000 steps per day for a healthy lifestyle, the average active person will utilize his or her feet for hundreds of millions of steps during a lifetime. Any injury to the foot structure dramatically restricts both the athlete and nonathlete alike. Estimates reveal that at least 80% of the population has some form of foot issue, many of which can be corrected with proper assessment and treatment.[1]

As discussed in previous chapters, the first step to a successful evaluation and assessment is a proper understanding of anatomy. With the high incidence of injury, it is especially important to understand the makeup of the foot and how the components of the foot work in conjunction. The anatomic structures of the foot are able to distribute and dissipate the many different forces placed on the body through ground contact during the gait cycle. An improperly functioning foot is unable to manage the ground reaction forces effectively and the risk for injury increases considerably.

Anatomy

There are 28 bones found in the foot complex—14 phalanges, 5 metatarsals, 7 tarsal bones, and 2 sesamoids (**Figure 8.1**). The phalanx bones, or phalanges, are the small bones that make up each toe. These bones are important for improved balance and propulsion.[2] The phalanges are assigned a name by their position relative to the torso (e.g., distal, middle, and proximal) and from first to fifth going medial to lateral.

The metatarsals are the long bones between the proximal ends of the toes and the tarsals. These bones play an active role in weight bearing during standing and gait. The metatarsals are numbered medial to lateral from first to fifth. The two sesamoid bones are located beneath the head of the first metatarsal and assist in weight distribution.

The midfoot complex and **subtalar joint** are made up of the seven tarsal bones (**Figure 8.2**). The midfoot complex and subtalar joint are important anatomic points of reference in determining biomechanical issues and overuse injuries. The seven tarsal bones are the cuboid, navicular, calcaneus, talus, and the first, second, and third cuneiforms, as shown in Figures 8.1 and 8.2.

propulsion The movement phase of the gait cycle.

gait pattern Technique of walking.

subtalar joint A joint of the foot located at the meeting point of the talus and the calcaneus

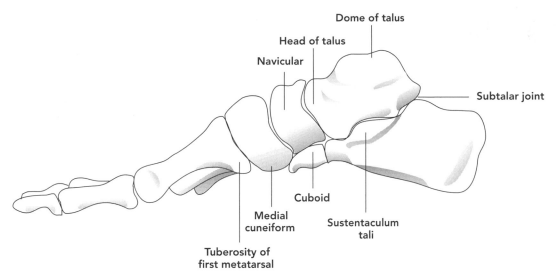

FIGURE 8.2 Anatomy of the foot (medial view).

Ligaments and fascia are interspersed throughout the structure to connect the bones of the foot. This tissue allows for subtle movements of the bones, subsequently improving shock absorption during ground contact.[3] The ligaments and fascia also combine to form the arches of the foot. The longitudinal arch supports the weight of the body and provides room for the nerve and blood supply to travel the length of the foot, while the transverse and metatarsal arches maintain ground contact on uneven surfaces.[2]

The principal movements of the foot complex are inversion (occasionally known as supination) and eversion (or pronation). The movements of the toes are flexion, extension, abduction, and adduction. The tarsal and metatarsal bones are subtly able to flex, extend, and rotate with movement, but measuring these motions is difficult.

Observation of Gait

Observing the gait pattern is a key component of the evaluation of foot **biomechanics**. To begin the initial assessment of the individual, the examiner should evaluate the athlete's shoes to check for abnormal wear patterns, which may suggest inappropriate motion or force during gait. The shoes can offer insight into what to look for prior to the athlete initiating his or her gait pattern.

The athletic trainer can then ask the injured athlete to stand barefoot and place weight, if possible, equally on both feet. Once the athletic trainer has examined the individual in a standing position, he or she should have the athlete walk several steps, turn around, and walk back to the original spot. During this observation, the athletic trainer looks for any signs of foot dysfunction or inappropriate motion. Evaluate the athlete from all sides during walking and standing to ensure that the whole gait pattern is observed.

The gait pattern is divided into two phases: the stance phase and the swing phase. The stance phase is further categorized as the heel strike/initial contact, loading response, mid stance, terminal stance, and toe off. The swing phase is divided into initial swing, mid swing, and terminal swing.[4] It is important to assess the athlete throughout the gait cycle to determine whether issues are present at any point that could be precursors to or signs of an injury.

Abnormal motions or foot dysfunctions include excessive pronation or supination during activity that does not allow the foot to efficiently absorb ground forces. Also, excessive rotation of the foot inward (pigeon-toed) or outward (duck-footed) can lead to foot issues, although these are caused by rotation at the hip or torsion of the lower leg, rather than being the result of a direct foot dysfunction.[2]

The arches of the foot should be inspected bilaterally to determine if the arches are equal for both feet. Arch

biomechanics Branch of study that applies the laws of mechanics to living organisms and biological tissues.

abnormalities may be present in one or both feet. **Pes planus**, or flat feet, occurs when an arch has fallen. **Pes cavus**, or high arch, occurs when the arch is abnormally exaggerated. Pes planus and pes cavus can compromise the weight-bearing role of the foot and may predispose an athlete to injury.

Injuries

Fractures

Most fractures in the foot are caused by direct trauma from contact with the ground or an opponent. In most instances, the athlete is removed from play for evaluation. Fractures in specific areas of the foot that occur frequently are given particular names to designate the location of the injury, for example, **Jones fracture**.

SIGNS AND SYMPTOMS

Fractures of the foot provide the same signs and symptoms as fractures elsewhere in the body.

1. Pain and swelling at the injury site
2. Possible deformity of the bone
3. Discoloration or redness
4. Athlete heard a pop or snap
5. Athlete unable to bear weight effectively
6. Hesitation to ambulate

SPECIAL TESTS

The three special tests for fractures discussed in Chapter 7 should be used for foot fractures. The *compression test*, *tap test*, and *translation test* are positive if pain increases at the site of injury during the test. These fracture tests should not be conducted on an open fracture where part of the bone has penetrated the skin.

TREATMENT

An athlete with a suspected fracture in the foot should be referred to a physician for X-rays. The treatment for a fracture depends on the location of the injury. A fracture of a phalanx may not remove an athlete from competition, whereas a fracture of a metatarsal or tarsal bone requires immobilization with a walking boot and crutches or, in some cases, surgical intervention. A rehabilitation plan can be determined based on the location of the fracture and the severity of the injury.

Stress Fractures

Stress fractures in the foot are becoming increasingly common in athletics. Stress fractures can occur in any bone in the foot but most often are seen in the metatarsals, specifically the second and fifth metatarsals. A stress fracture in the second metatarsal is known as a **March fracture** because of its high occurrence rate in the military during training and marching.[5]

A fifth metatarsal stress fracture occurs at the base of the bone near the articulation with the cuboid. The fifth metatarsal stress fracture is similar to the Jones fracture, although the Jones fracture moniker is utilized only for acute injuries.

SIGNS AND SYMPTOMS

The symptoms of stress fractures are consistent with those of frank fractures, except they are associated with a gradual onset rather than an acute injury. The athlete often complains of having a sensation similar to a rock in his or her shoe with running.

Stress fractures are preceded by stress reactions. The stress reaction occurs when the bone attempts to repair healthy bony tissue to protect itself from abnormal stress. A stress reaction increases to the stress fracture stage as the bone becomes weaker and eventually breaks.

Fast Fact

The Jones fracture is the most common acute injury in the foot.[2] This injury occurs at the proximal base of the fifth metatarsal through acute trauma. This region of the bone does not have a strong blood supply, which can lengthen healing time or cause **disunion** where the two ends of the bone do not reattach. Surgical intervention is becoming increasingly popular as a treatment option because it provides stability and allows the ends of the bone to heal properly.

---

pes planus Flat feet.

pes cavus High arch.

Jones fracture A transverse fracture of the proximal shaft of the fifth metatarsal.

March fracture A stress fracture of the second metatarsal; often seen in new military recruits as a result of the high amount of marching.

disunion A severance of union; separation; disjunction.

SPECIAL TESTS

The three special tests for fractures discussed in Chapter 7 should be used to evaluate stress fractures. X-rays should be taken of the injured area if a stress fracture is suspected, but stress fractures are best examined with a bone scan.

TREATMENT

Several treatment options are available for stress fractures, from immobilization and rest to bone stimulation and surgical intervention. Custom-made **orthotics** inserted into the shoe can be beneficial in the long term to reduce abnormal forces or correct the faulty mechanics that caused the stress fracture. Rehabilitation depends entirely on which treatment option is utilized.

■ Dislocation

Dislocations of the bones in the foot are fairly rare in athletics. The most frequent site of dislocation is in the phalanges; however, even this is less common than fractures are.

SIGNS AND SYMPTOMS

1. Pain and swelling at injury site
2. Obvious deformity
3. Decreased ability or inability to bear weight

TREATMENT

A dislocation of any joint is a very serious condition and should be referred to a physician for X-rays and reduction. Rehabilitation depends on the severity of injury.

■ Arch Strain/Sprain

The *arch of the foot* is an all-encompassing term that designates three separate complexes: the longitudinal arch, metatarsal arch, and transverse arch. The longitudinal arch runs the length of the foot and allows for shock absorption while maintaining the proper structure of the foot.[3] The metatarsal arch sits at the distal heads of the metatarsal bones and provides support to the ball of the foot. The transverse arch is found across the base of the tarsal bones and provides support to the midfoot region.[1] A structural dysfunction in the tendons or ligaments of the arch can decrease the body's ability to adapt to the stresses of normal gait.

The longitudinal arch is the most commonly strained/sprained arch, but all three can be acutely injured. Hyperextension of the midfoot, often resulting from contact with uneven surfaces or twisting motions during running, are

> **orthotics** An orthopedic appliance inserted into the shoe to correct abnormal foot biomechanics.

the most likely cause of an arch strain. Any acute injury to the arch complexes is designated as an arch strain or sprain. In most arch injuries, damage to the muscles, ligaments, and/or fascia that assist in the formation of the arch occurs. Because multiple structures are damaged, both the sprain and strain designations may be utilized.

SIGNS AND SYMPTOMS

1. Pain and tenderness over injury site
2. Swelling (usually seen on medial aspect of arch)
3. Pain with running and cutting

TREATMENT

Rest, ice, compression, and elevation (RICE) treatment should be conducted after an acute injury. Modality use can assist in the alleviation of symptoms. Return to play (RTP) as tolerated. Arch taping may be performed to assist the athlete in return to activity. The athlete should ice after exercise.

■ Spring Ligament Sprain

The spring ligament is an important component of the longitudinal arch and assists in shock absorption and maintaining the integrity of the arch. The spring ligament also is known as the plantar calcaneonavicular ligament.[2] The typical mechanisms of injury for a sprain of this ligament are running on uneven surfaces and stepping into holes or divots.

SIGNS AND SYMPTOMS

1. Pain and tenderness distal to the heel of the foot on the medial aspect of the arch
2. Pain with weight bearing
3. Slight swelling over injury site

TREATMENT

RICE therapy should be completed post-injury. Padding or orthotics can be used to provide support to the injured ligament. RTP is as tolerated for the athlete.

■ Plantar Fasciitis

The plantar fascia (**Figure 8.3**) is a structure of fibrous tissue on the bottom of the foot that runs the length of the foot to help strengthen the arch complex. The fascia can become inflamed as a result of chronic stress. Fasciitis in this area is extremely common, especially in the general population. Plantar fasciitis is a cyclical injury, with the initial stress causing the fascia to tighten, which decreases range of motion in the foot and increases the stress on the fibrous tissue. As the stress increases, the tightness and inflammation increase, causing more damage to the tissue.

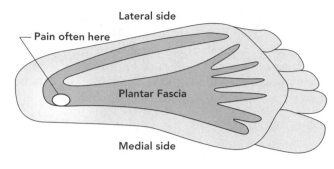

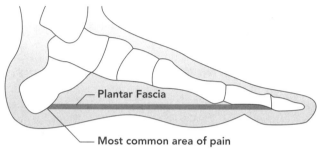

FIGURE 8.3 Plantar fascia.

SIGNS AND SYMPTOMS

1. Pain most often at the distal aspect of the heel on the lateral side
2. Pain that is most severe with the first steps out of bed in the morning
3. Tightness and decreased ROM at the midfoot
4. Slight swelling at injury site

TREATMENT

Early detection and treatment of plantar fasciitis are important because the injury tends to be easily reaggravated. Preactivity ultrasound therapy and postactivity ice massage can help to decrease symptoms. Friction massage with a tennis ball or baseball may be conducted to break up any scar tissue that develops. The athlete can conduct this exercise individually by placing his or her foot on the ball and rolling the injured tissue over the top of the ball.

Stretching the midfoot and toes increases flexibility and ROM in the fascia. A physician may prescribe anti-inflammatory medications and a night splint if pain is persistent. The night splint can decrease morning foot pain by keeping the foot in a dorsiflexed position throughout the night to decrease the tissue tightening that occurs during sleep.

■ Heel Contusion

A heel contusion occurs when an individual injures tissue in the heel of the foot by stepping on a hard object or jumping from a high height. This injury also may develop chronically from repetitive compression, which often results from wearing worn-out shoes without proper cushioning. A pair of cleated shoes also may cause a contusion if the insole does not protect the cleat studs from protruding through the base of the shoe.

SIGNS AND SYMPTOMS

1. Point tender on heel
2. Slight discoloration
3. Pain with ground contact

TREATMENT

Ice helps to decrease the symptoms of a heel contusion. New shoes or adding insoles/orthotics to the current shoes may decrease pain. A heel cup or heel taping technique can be utilized for RTP.

■ Turf Toe

Turf toe is a sprain of the first metatarsophalangeal (MTP) joint, the joint between the first metatarsal and the proximal phalanx. The mechanism of injury is a hyperextension or a hyperflexion motion of the joint. Despite the name, turf toe can occur on any type of surface, not necessarily synthetic turf.

SIGNS AND SYMPTOMS

1. Pain at first MTP joint
2. Pain with flexion or extension of first MTP joint
3. Pain and discomfort with running, especially push-off
4. Slight swelling and discoloration

TREATMENT

RICE is useful post-injury. Referral to a physician may be necessary to rule out a fracture. Rest is the most important treatment for the athlete. A turf toe tape job or steel insole in the shoe to decrease motion may benefit the athlete for RTP.

■ Bunion and Bunionette

A **bunion** (**Figure 8.4**) is a protrusion medially from the first metatarsal head. The bunion is a chronic injury and increases in size over time. A bunion is actually the first metatarsal head moving medially, causing inflammation in the surrounding tissue and forcing the first toe in the

bunion Inflammation of the synovial bursa of the first toe, usually resulting in enlargement of the joint and lateral displacement of the toe.

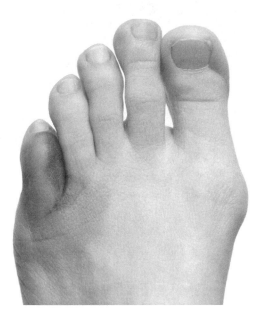

FIGURE 8.4 Bunion.

opposite direction. A **bunionette** is a similar injury except it occurs at the fifth metatarsal.

SIGNS AND SYMPTOMS

1. Pain, especially with shoes on
2. Redness and swelling
3. Obvious protrusion of the first or fifth metatarsal with opposite movement of the associated toes

TREATMENT

Conservative treatment with ice and a shoe change may decrease acute pain and inflammation. Surgical intervention may be necessary if conservative treatment is unsuccessful.

◼ Ingrown Toenail

Ingrown toenails (**Figure 8.5**) are regular occurrences in athletics, especially in athletes who prefer tight shoes (for example, football kickers and soccer players). Ingrown toenails arise when the edge of the nail is pushed into the soft-tissue bed. Pain occurs as the nail lacerates the tissue and an infection enters the area.

SIGNS AND SYMPTOMS

1. Pain at the edge of the nail
2. Swelling and redness in adjacent skin

> **bunionette** A bunion-like enlargement of the joint of the little toe.

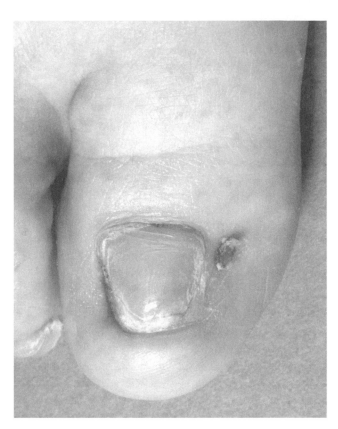

FIGURE 8.5 Ingrown toenail.

3. May have yellow/green discharge from under the nail or the overlying skin

TREATMENT

Initial treatment may consist of a warm water soak with betadine or another antibacterial medium. The soak should last from 10 to 20 minutes. Following the betadine soak, the athlete may be able to maneuver the ingrown portion out of the nail bed. If this is not possible, the athletic trainer or athlete may attempt to wedge a betadine-soaked piece of cotton under the edge of the nail between the nail and the affected tissue. These methods should be continued daily to assist the injured tissue in its healing and the nail to return to its normal growth pattern. If these methods are not successful, the athlete should see a physician to remove the irritating piece of nail or, in the event of chronic problems, the entire nail.

◼ Subungal Hematoma

A subungal hematoma (**Figure 8.6**) is an accumulation of blood under the toenail. A subungal hematoma often results from direct contact, usually from the cleats of an opponent. The pain increases as the pressure of the fluid accumulation pushes on the nail.

SIGNS AND SYMPTOMS

1. Pain at injury site
2. Discoloration under the nail
3. Pain with movement or compression of nail

TREATMENT

The best treatment for a subungal hematoma requires removal of the excess fluid by drilling a hole in the nail until the fluid is released. The procedure should be done in a sterile environment to prevent infection. After the hole is drilled, apply pressure to different areas of the nail until all fluid is removed. Immediate relief for the athlete often results following this procedure. Provide the nail with a protective cover to prevent infection and collect any additional fluid. Have the athlete avoid any further contact to the toe until it has properly healed.

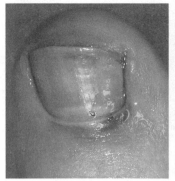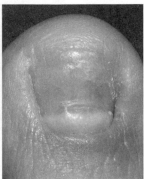

FIGURE 8.6   Subungal hematoma.

CHAPTER REVIEW

1. What are the two roles of the foot?
2. How many bones are found in the foot?
3. What is a Jones fracture?
4. What is the mechanism of injury for turf toe?
5. What is the best treatment for a subungal hematoma?

CRITICAL THINKING

What is your RTP thought process when your star athlete has a fifth metatarsal stress fracture during the season?

REFERENCES

1. Magee DJ. *Orthopedic Physical Assessment*, 4th ed. Philadelphia: W. B. Saunders, 2002.
2. Prentice WE. *Arnheim's Principles of Athletic Training: A Competency-Based Approach*, 12th ed. Boston: McGraw-Hill, 2006.
3. Saltzman CL, Nawoczenski DA. (1995). Complexities of foot architecture as a base of support. *Journal of Orthopaedic & Sports Physical Therapy*, 21(6): 354–360.
4. Perry J. *Gait Analysis: Normal and Pathological Function*. Thorofare, NJ: Slack, 1992.
5. Jones BH, Thacker SB, Gilchrist J, Kimsey JD, Sosin DM. (2002). Prevention of lower extremity stress fractures in athletes and soldiers: a systematic review. *Epidemiologic Reviews*, 24(2):228–247.

The Ankle and
Lower Leg

The ankle and lower leg operate as partners with the foot to allow the propulsion of the body through the gait pattern and supply support and balance for the individual. Because of their constant motion and interaction with the ground, the ankle and lower leg are extremely frequent sites of injury in the athletic population. In fact, ankle sprains are the most common injuries seen in athletics today.[1] Throughout this chapter, we discuss the anatomy of this region, as well as injuries and their treatments.

 ## Anatomy

Compared to the foot, the anatomy of the ankle and lower leg is quite simple. Only three bones are generally considered to be components of this region: the tibia, fibula, and talus. The tibia and fibula are the long bones that form the lower leg between the knee and ankle. The tibia is the larger bone of the two and the second-longest bone in the body (the femur is the longest). The tibia is the primary weight-bearing bone in the lower leg whereas the fibula is a non-weight-bearing accessory bone that serves as an attachment for both major and minor muscle groups.

At the ankle joint, the tibia and fibula link to form a semicircular opening for the talus to articulate. The ends of the two bones encircle the head (dome) of the talus to provide support for the ankle and act as an attachment for the primary ligaments. The distal ends of the bones are each called a malleolus with the tibia distally labeled the medial malleolus and the fibula labeled the lateral malleolus. The opening for the dome of the talus allows for an increased range of motion while also providing support during the gait cycle.

There are three main ligamentous structures in the ankle joint (**Figure 9.1**). Each one connects one of the three bones to another to provide further support for the area. The first ligament group is found on the lateral aspect of the ankle and attaches the fibula to the talus and calcaneus. There are three lateral ligaments in this structure: the anterior talofibular, calcaneofibular, and posterior talofibular ligaments. The anterior talofibular ligament is the most frequently injured ligament in the ankle because it is the first line of defense against forced inversion—the cause of most ankle sprains.

The ligaments on the medial side of the ankle often are referred to collectively as the deltoid ligament (**Figure 9.2**). The deltoid ligament attaches the tibia at the medial malleolus to the talus, as well as the calcaneus and the navicular. This ligament complex stabilizes the ankle joint and works to prevent forced eversion.

The third ligament is an oft-disregarded structure in the ankle joint. The tibiofibular ligament connects the two

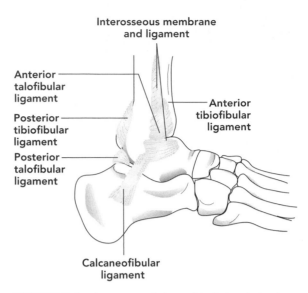

FIGURE 9.1   Anatomy of the ankle (lateral view).

long bones together directly over the talus. This ligament, along with the syndesmosis—a sheath of tissue between the bones—prevents excessive separation of the tibia and fibula during rotation in either direction.

Numerous muscles run throughout the lower leg; however, this chapter focuses only on the major muscles associated with movement and involved in the discussed injuries. Each muscle group can be assigned to a section, or compartment, of the lower leg. The anterior compartment contains the tibialis anterior, the muscle that controls dorsiflexion, and the extensor muscles that initiate the extension of the toes.

The lateral compartment of the lower leg contains the three peroneal muscles, which assist in eversion and dorsiflexion. Finally, the posterior compartment is separated into a shallow and deep category. The shallow muscles—the gastrocnemius and the soleus—combine to form the calf muscle and move the ankle joint into plantar flexion.

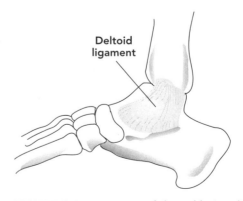

FIGURE 9.2   Anatomy of the ankle (medial view).

The deep muscles include the posterior tibialis and the flexor muscles, which assist in inversion of the ankle and toe flexion. These muscles all work simultaneously to propel the body in movement and provide support to maintain stability.[1]

Injuries

■ Fractures

Each of the three bones in the lower leg and ankle can be fractured and the injuries are seen relatively often in athletics. Fibula fractures are seen the most during sports activities whereas talus fractures occur the least often. The injuries may be caused by either direct force against the bone or indirect abuse, such as a twisting motion.

SIGNS AND SYMPTOMS

1. High levels of pain
2. Swelling and discoloration
3. Obvious deformity, especially with tibial fractures
4. Inability to bear weight, especially with tibial fractures
5. Decreased strength and range of motion in affected extremity

SPECIAL TESTS

The same special tests conducted on foot fractures should be used for lower leg fractures as well. The *tap test*, *compression test*, and *translation test* are positive if pain increases dramatically. If obvious deformity is present, no special tests should be performed.

TREATMENT

A tibial fracture can be a very serious and debilitating injury. Because of its status as the primary weight-bearing bone, the tibia is very painful to injure and makes it nearly impossible for the athlete to walk or run. Splinting with vacuum or rigid splints is required. Any movement or shifting of the bone causes a great deal of pain and could further damage nearby tissue, specifically arteries, veins, and nerves. The distal **neurovascular** structures should be assessed both before and after the splint is applied to ensure that neither the injury nor the splint has compromised the arteries, veins, and nerves.

Many tibial fractures require surgery to repair the bone accompanied by a long period of **immobilization.** The athlete faces a lengthy road to recovery and potentially career-ending or -altering consequences.

Because the force required to fracture the tibia is fairly dramatic, often the injuries that result are a combination fracture of both the tibia and fibula. This injury presents with significant deformity because the primary structures of the lower leg are compromised.

A fibula fracture is less severe than a tibial injury is, but it is still very important to splint and refer to a physician. Because of its mostly non-weight-bearing status, the fibula does not necessarily affect gait dramatically if fractured. Pain and disability are still present and should be treated with traditional electric or cold modalities. Return to play (RTP) is much faster with a fibula fracture than with a tibial injury because the bone is not a weight-bearing bone and the length of immobilization is significantly less. With the decrease in immobilization time, muscle weakening and **atrophy** (decreased size of muscle) are minimized, allowing the athlete to increase activity at a faster rate once he or she is cleared to return.

Talar fractures are much less common than the other two and may be mistaken for ankle sprains. An ankle sprain that does not quite follow traditional criteria or does not heal properly should receive further evaluation for a possible injury to the talus. Talus fractures, if not treated properly, can develop serious complications including **avascular necrosis**.

Avascular necrosis is the death of bony tissue as a result of decreased blood flow to the affected tissue. This condition, if not treated immediately, may necessitate a replacement or removal of the damaged bone. RTP is dependent on the severity of the injury and whether surgery is required.

■ Stress Fractures

Stress fractures in the tibia and fibula are significant in their occurrence rates in athletics. As with metatarsal stress fractures, the exact cause of the injury is unknown; however, training regimen, foot dysfunction, and poor mechanics have all been suggested as possibilities.[2]

SIGNS AND SYMPTOMS

1. Pain that has developed gradually and increased in severity

neurovascular Of or relating to both nerves and blood vessels.

immobilization To prevent, restrict, or reduce normal movement in the body, a limb, or a joint, as by a splint, cast, or prescribed bed rest.

atrophy A wasting away or deterioration of tissue owing to disease, disuse, or malnutrition.

avascular necrosis Death of tissue caused by the lack of blood supply.

2. Pain likely to be worse after activity rather than during motion
3. Pain localized to one specific point

SPECIAL TESTS

The *tap test* and *compression test* can be conducted, but the results could be inconclusive depending on the severity of the injury.

TREATMENT

As with metatarsal stress fractures, it is difficult to identify the lower leg stress fracture with an X-ray. A bone scan may be more appropriate if deemed necessary by the physician. Positive symptoms are often treated in a similar manner as a stress fracture with or without a definitive diagnosis.

The athlete should be removed from weight-bearing activity until pain diminishes—typically 4 to 6 weeks—and given a cross-training regimen including swimming and bicycling. Immobilization may be necessary with severe pain. Gradual RTP may begin once pain has dissipated. Insole orthotics or a shoe change may help the athlete correct any foot dysfunction or biomechanical concerns.

■ Ankle Dislocation

The ankle dislocation (along with a tibia/fibula fracture) may be one of the most grisly injuries to witness in athletics. Often seen after a twisting motion during full weight bearing, an ankle dislocation is readily apparent as the foot is found at an unnatural angle not allowed by a healthy body. With this injury, the talus will tear the supporting ligaments and often fractures either or both of the malleoli because the talar dome is forcibly removed from its normal position.

SIGNS AND SYMPTOMS

1. Extreme pain
2. Obvious deformity
3. Swelling and discoloration at the injury site
4. Loss of range of motion and strength

TREATMENT

This injury requires immediate splinting and referral to a physician for reduction and potential surgery to stabilize the joint. The distal neurovascular structures should be assessed both before and after the splint is applied to

---

> **medial tibial stress syndrome** Another name for shin splints, this often occurs as a result of a sudden increase in duration or intensity of training. Injury presents with pain in the medial aspect of the lower leg.

---

ensure that neither the injury nor the splint has compromised the arteries, veins, and nerves. Crutches and immobilization are required for 4 to 6 weeks with a RTP of 4 to 6 months.

■ Shin Splints

Shin splints, also known as **medial tibial stress syndrome**, are the better-known descriptor for any acute or overuse injury occurring in the anterior compartment of the lower leg. This can include a tibialis anterior strain, microtears in the muscle, microfractures in the tibia, or even a stress fracture.[3] Shin splints generally occur after a change in training regimen, especially after a long layoff. Changing surfaces frequently (for example, from grass to concrete to hard court) and wearing older, worn-out shoes may also result in injury. Any of these injuries—with the exception of the stress fracture—tend to subside within a few days if treated properly and given adequate rest.

SIGNS AND SYMPTOMS

1. Pain increasing with running and dorsiflexion
2. No obvious traumatic mechanism

TREATMENT

Because shin splints are so common in athletes, many overlook the injury and attempt to play through any associated pain. If the injury is ignored, it can develop into a stress fracture; therefore, it should be treated—if only to minimize that risk. Cold modalities—specifically cold whirlpool, ice massage, and ice bags—can help to decrease the pain in the affected area. Ice massage is quite effective because of the dual benefit of a cold modality and the breakdown of scar tissue through the massage.

Stretching the tibialis anterior also benefits the athlete and reduces symptoms. To stretch this muscle, have the athlete remove the shoe on the affected side, curl his or her toes, and stand on the top or dorsal aspect of the toes. Have the athlete rotate the foot medially and laterally until a stretch is felt in the affected area. The stretching assists in the healing process by breaking up any developing scar tissue. RTP may occur within 24 to 48 hours as symptoms resolve.

■ Compartment Syndrome

Compartment syndrome is a very serious injury if not treated appropriately. The muscle compartments that were mentioned before are contained within layers of fascial tissue that help to maintain position and muscle shape. Compartment syndrome may occur either through acute trauma or chronic overuse and is caused by an increase in fluid pressure within the fascial tissue that then compresses the muscles, nerves, and blood vessels. The compression causes a loss of oxygen to the muscle, which can result in tissue death and serious complications.

The chronic version of compartment syndrome is seen far more often than the acute version, which is caused by direct abuse. Chronic compartment syndrome is typically found in runners and causes pain and muscle **ischemia** during activity, and then subsides once the activity is ceased. Many individuals with compartment syndrome complain of foot numbness or tingling during activity caused by the increased tissue pressure.

SIGNS AND SYMPTOMS

1. Pain that increases with activity
2. Numbness/tingling in foot
3. Foot drop resulting from neurovascular damage in the lower leg
4. Pain subsides during rest
5. May occur **bilaterally**

TREATMENT

Symptoms may resolve with a traditional modality regimen; however, if pain and numbness persist, the athlete should be referred to a physician. A physician who suspects compartment syndrome will order an exertion test that measures pressure levels within the legs during running. If the test is positive, the physician may order a surgical release that provides an outlet in the fascia for the excess fluid pressure. The physician could also suggest a cross-training regimen to see whether symptoms resolve without surgery.

In acute cases, any excessive swelling and neurological symptoms, such as numbness and tingling, should be referred to a physician immediately to rule out a medical emergency. If the pressure becomes too great, the athlete may lose all blood flow to and sensation in the affected leg. This can lead to emergency surgery and possibly amputation if not treated in a timely manner.

■ Shin Contusion

A shin contusion (**Figure 9.3**) can be an extremely painful injury because it affects each step that is taken. A shin contusion results from direct trauma to the anterior portion of the lower leg. The injury could develop into a

---

ischemia Local anemia owing to decreased blood supply.

bilateral Having two sides or pertaining to both sides.

osteomyelitis An inflammation of the bone and bone marrow, usually caused by bacterial infection.

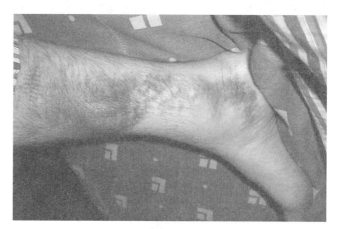

FIGURE 9.3 Shin contusion.

hematoma, which is a collection of blood and other fluids that lasts for a lengthy period of time.

SIGNS AND SYMPTOMS

1. Pain in affected site
2. Swelling and discoloration
3. Decreased range of motion

TREATMENT

Initial treatment should consist of rest, ice, compression, and elevation (RICE) therapy with a pad covering the injured area during competition. The specific pad that should be used is called a *donut pad* because there is a hole in the center that protects the contused area from further injury by avoiding direct pressure over the injury site. Massage and ankle pumps should be used as pain decreases to remove the excess fluid and attempt to prevent a hematoma.

Ankle pumps consist of moving the ankle into dorsiflexion and then plantar flexion in a continuous movement throughout the range of motion. These should be done consistently throughout the day. An athletic trainer may tell the athlete to complete at least 1,000 ankle pumps daily as a potential baseline number.

Timely removal of the excess fluid through proper treatment can prevent chronic conditions that can cause a hematoma or deterioration of the bone (**osteomyelitis**). The athlete may return to play as pain allows with the additional protective padding.

■ Calf Strain

Calf strains occur quite often in athletics, especially during push-off motions or quick steps that stress the calf muscles. The gastrocnemius muscle is the muscle that is most often involved with a strain.

SIGNS AND SYMPTOMS

1. Pain at affected site
2. Decreased range of motion (ROM) in dorsi/plantar flexion
3. Slight swelling
4. Decreased strength

SPECIAL TESTS

A *manual muscle test* of the calf may be conducted to test the strength of the calf muscle versus the unaffected side. Have the athlete lay on his or her stomach in the prone position with both feet off the edge of the table. Resist the feet as the athlete plantar flexes and assign the strength of the injured side on the scale of 0 to 5 (out of 5) as compared to the uninvolved side.

TREATMENT

Electrical and cold modality treatment helps to decrease the initial symptoms. All muscle strains can be treated with electrical modalities. The use of electrical modalities is often dependent upon the individual athletic trainer rather than the injury itself. Stretching and ROM exercises may begin as symptoms allow and RTP as strength increases and pain dissipates. The return time frame is determined by the severity of the strain, a few days to 2 weeks for a grade I, 2 to 4 weeks for a grade II, and 4 to 6 weeks for a grade III injury.

■ Achilles Strain

The Achilles tendon is found at the distal end of the calf muscles as they combine and attach themselves to the calcaneus at the heel. Both acute and chronic injuries can occur at the Achilles tendon. Acute injuries are often the result of a misstep that forces the foot into hyperdorsiflexion (a motion that exceeds the normal range). Chronic injuries result from repeated abuse or a dramatic increase in training regimen.

SIGNS AND SYMPTOMS

Similar to a calf strain, the Achilles strain will have pain at the affected site and possibly slight swelling. The pain will increase with activity, especially during ground contact and push-off.

> **window shade effect** When the tendon detaches from its point of origin and rolls up to the muscle belly.
> **nociceptors** Receptors sensitive to potentially damaging or painful stimuli.

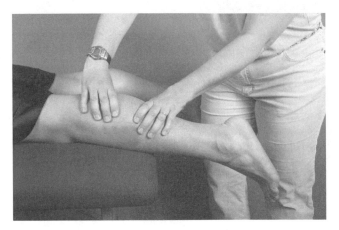

FIGURE 9.4 Thompson test.

TREATMENT

The treatment for an Achilles strain is also similar to that of a calf strain: RICE therapy, stretching, and ROM exercises. There is an Achilles tape job that can be useful during RTP.

■ Achilles Rupture

In some instances, an acute Achilles tendon strain can reach grade III level and cause a tear in the tendon. This injury is seen most often in adults (older than 30 years) who have lost general flexibility, especially weekend warriors or individuals who are starting a new training program after being sedentary for an extended period of time. These injuries may occur in younger athletes, although much less frequently.

SIGNS AND SYMPTOMS

The primary sign of an Achilles tear is a disruption of the structure and rolling of the tendon upward toward the muscle belly. This also is known as the **window shade effect**, owing its name to the look of a rolled-up window shade. Pain is usually intense at the onset of the injury, but often dissipates quickly because of a rupture of the nerves that transmit pain (**nociceptors**).[1] An Achilles tendon rupture frequently occurs in athletes who have had a history of Achilles tendinitis and inflammation. The chronic inflammation degrades the tendon and makes it more susceptible to injury.

SPECIAL TESTS

The *Thompson test* (**Figure 9.4**) is a passive maneuver that determines whether the Achilles tendon is still attached. The patient should be in a prone position with both feet in a relaxed position off of the table. When the legs are relaxed, the examiner squeezes the calf muscle and looks for plantar flexion of the foot. A positive test is found when there is no plantar flexion or a very slight amount attributed to the flexor muscles of the foot.[4]

TREATMENT

The only treatment for an Achilles tear or rupture is surgical intervention to reattach the tendon. Rehab is a lengthy process postsurgery because of the athlete's inability to bear weight and push off for an extended period of time. RTP typically requires at least 1 year of recovery time for full activity.

■ Achilles Tendinitis

The chronic injury to the Achilles tendon is known as Achilles tendinitis. This injury develops gradually with increasing pain directly over the distal insertion on the heel. This injury can affect the athlete for some time if not treated properly and can lead to a tendon rupture if the inflammation remains in the tendon for an extended period.

SIGNS AND SYMPTOMS

1. Pain that increases in the morning and at the start of activity
2. Slight swelling and redness

TREATMENT

If the symptoms have been consistent for a prolonged period of time, a modality regimen—including whirlpool, ultrasound, stretching prepractice, and ice bag or ice massage postpractice—should be conducted. An Achilles tendon taping may be effective and in-sole orthotics may decrease pain. If symptoms are in the initial stages, treating with ice and stretching may prevent chronic inflammation.

■ Peroneal Strain/Tendinitis

The peroneal muscles in the lateral compartment of the lower leg are also prone to both acute and chronic injury. These muscles are responsible for moving the foot into eversion. The peroneal muscles often are injured during inversion ankle sprains, but can incur damage on their own as well. The acute injury to the peroneal muscles is a strain whereas the chronic injury is tendinitis. Both injuries are sometimes referred to by athletes as lateral shin splints.

SIGNS AND SYMPTOMS

1. Pain in lateral compartment that increases with activity
2. Slight swelling or inflammation is possible

TREATMENT

The treatment for a peroneal tendon injury is very similar to a calf or Achilles strain. RICE therapy may be used for initial symptoms along with massage (ice or otherwise) to break up inflammation and scar tissue. Ultrasound may be effective for chronic tendinitis injuries.

Stretching is difficult in the peroneal muscles. It requires an inversion motion that is most effective after warm-up and during activity. Attempting to roll outward onto the edge of the foot may be effective; however, there is concern that an overzealous or unlucky individual may sprain the ankle during stretching. Massage often is more beneficial and safer than attempting the stretching technique.

Ankle Sprains

As was mentioned at the beginning of the chapter, the ankle sprain is one of the most common injuries seen in athletics. Almost every athlete can recall at least one ankle sprain at some point during his or her career. Even with the advances in shoe technology and bracing and taping, the athlete is not protected entirely from an ankle injury.

Because three ligament structures are associated with the ankle joint, there also are three sprains associated with the joint. They are named for the motion that causes them or for their location in the ankle. The most familiar ankle sprain is the inversion or lateral ankle sprain. The other two types are the eversion/medial ankle sprain and the high ankle sprain. We evaluate each one separately to provide a thorough understanding of this widespread problem.

■ Inversion Ankle Sprain

The inversion ankle sprain occurs when the ankle is forcibly moved into inversion and plantar flexion. The lateral ligaments are injured during this motion, typically in order from anterior to posterior. The anterior talofibular ligament (ATF) is the first ligament to be injured because of its placement anteriorly within the joint and the fact that it is the weakest of the three ligaments. The calcaneofibular and posterior talofibular ligaments follow along as the severity of the sprain increases.

SIGNS AND SYMPTOMS

As with all sprains, the inversion ankle sprain is rated on a scale of one to three. A grade I sprain has mild pain and swelling with discoloration increasing after 12 to 24 hours. There is mild disability and relatively little joint

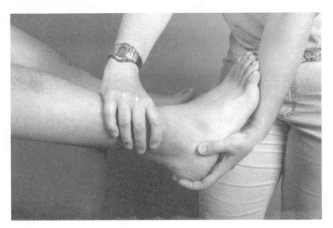

FIGURE 9.5 Talar tilt test.

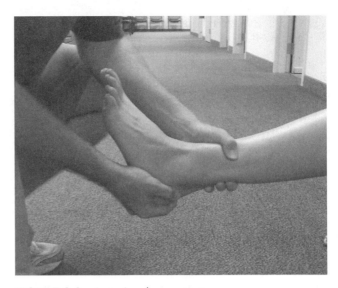

FIGURE 9.6 Anterior drawer test.

laxity because the ligaments are still mostly intact. A grade I sprain typically affects only the ATF ligament and does not cause a complete tear.[4]

A grade II injury causes moderate pain and swelling with discoloration. The athlete may require a walking boot and crutches to immobilize the joint. There is increased joint laxity because the ATF has been injured significantly and the calcaneofibular ligament has sustained damage as well.

A grade III sprain causes severe pain along with dramatic swelling and discoloration. Immobilization is required because weight bearing can no longer be tolerated. All three ligaments have been damaged or torn and subluxation or dislocation may occur.

SPECIAL TESTS

Three tests are specifically used for inversion ankle sprains. The first is the *talar tilt test* (**Figure 9.5**), which examines the calcaneofibular ligament and to a lesser degree the ATF. The patient should be seated or lying on his or her back in a supine position with the foot relaxed. The lower leg is stabilized with one hand while the other hand moves the heel of the foot into inversion. A positive test finds pain with movement and opening of the joint space between the foot and ankle, which suggests joint laxity and ligament damage. As with all tests, this should be compared bilaterally to ensure that a positive test is not caused by an anatomic abnormality found on both sides.[4]

The second test is the *anterior drawer test* (**Figure 9.6**), which examines the ATF ligament exclusively. The athlete should be sitting on the table with the hip and knee bent

and the ankle and foot resting on the table. The test also may be conducted with the athlete in a supine position and the foot hanging off of the table. The lower leg is stabilized just above the malleoli with one hand while the other hand grasps the midfoot region or the heel. The midfoot or heel then is pulled anteriorly while the lower leg is stable. A positive test finds pain and discomfort along with an opening or dimple between the talus and the fibula. The test may be positive with an injured ATF only, but will increase in symptoms and dimple size if the calcaneofibular ligament is also damaged.[4]

The third test is the *posterior drawer test*, which is identical to the anterior drawer except that the midfoot is forced posteriorly. A positive test finds pain and an opening posteriorly and suggests a posterior talofibular injury.

TREATMENT

All inversion sprains are initially treated the same with RICE and immobilization as necessary. Ankle pumps should be initiated as soon as the symptoms allow, followed by range of motion exercises, such as ABCs, which can be completed in a cold whirlpool. ABCs consist of visualizing that the injured foot is holding a pen and writing each letter of the alphabet. The ABCs utilize the entire range of motion and help decrease swelling and discoloration and increase movement. An elastic wrap with a horseshoe pad (as shown in **Figure 9.7**) should be kept on the injury until all swelling subsides. The horseshoe pad provides compression around the bone to prevent swelling in the soft tissue.

As the athlete is able to increase activity without pain, the athletic trainer can advance the ROM exercises

laxity Looseness of the joint whether it is normal or caused by injury/instability.

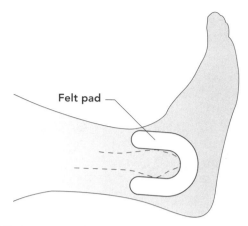

Felt pad

FIGURE 9.7   Horseshoe pad.

and add **proprioceptive neuromuscular facilitation (PNF)** movements and balance activities. The athlete's strength and pain level determine when sports-specific exercises can begin and an RTP schedule implemented (**Figure 9.8**). The athlete should not return to play while symptoms persist. Ankle taping and bracing may benefit the athlete's return to activity. A sample rehab protocol is listed in **Table 9.1**.

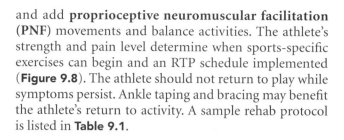

proprioceptive neuromuscular facilitation (PNF) A combination of passive stretching and isometric or isotonic strengthening used to increase flexibility, range of motion, or strength.

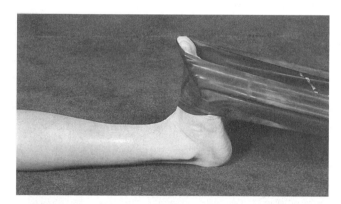

FIGURE 9.8A   Therapeutic exercises.

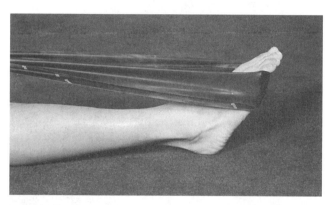

FIGURE 9.8C

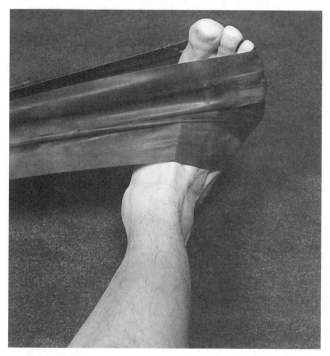

FIGURE 9.8B

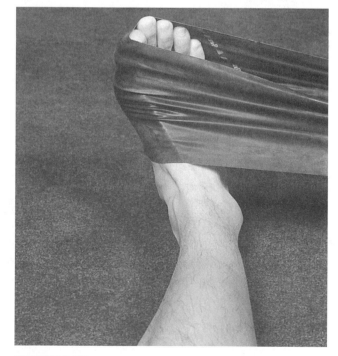

FIGURE 9.8D

TABLE 9.1

ANKLE REHAB PROTOCOL

Phase 1 (0–2 weeks)

RICE

Elastic wrap

Crutches with walking boot if needed

Ankle pumps (repeated ankle dorsiflexion and plantar flexion)

ABCs (moving foot/ankle as if writing the letters of the alphabet)

Biking or swimming for activity

Phase 2 (1–4 weeks)

Cold whirlpool with ROM activity

Therapeutic tubing exercises in dorsiflexion, plantar flexion, inversion, and eversion

PNF exercises

Balance exercises

Heel raises

Toe raises

Achilles stretch (to minimize Achilles pain with return to activity)

Biomechanical Ankle Platform System (BAPS) board with support

Phase 3 (3–6 weeks)

Trampoline exercises

Step-ups

BAPS board without support

Therapeutic tubing exercises

Plyometric exercises

Agility ladder

Slide board

Cuff weights

Sport-specific exercises

In Focus

Proprioceptive Neuromuscular Facilitation

Proprioceptive neuromuscular facilitation, or PNF, is an intricate name for a very effective treatment. PNF is a series of patterned joint movements that form an X. There are several variations of PNF differentiated by the motion of the muscles involved. In each pattern, the examiner resists the desired movement while placing both hands on the muscles that are active.

PNF helps to rebuild sensory and motor nerves that are damaged during injury (**Figure 9.9**). After the injury, an athlete's dysfunction is caused by both the injury itself and the damage to those nerves. The sensory and motor nerves work in unison to create **proprioception**—the body's ability to know where it is in space. As an example of proprioception, stand on one foot and close your eyes. The odds are that your body is able to remain relatively balanced and stabilized because of the proprioception nerves even when you cannot see the ground. Now compare that to an athlete returning from an ankle or knee injury and see how well his or her balance is. (Do not try this with a new injury or further damage may occur.) After the injury, the proprioceptors are damaged and unable to maintain stability sometimes even with the eyes open.

PNF helps to rebuild these nerves and helps the athlete regain balance while also improving strength in the affected muscles and ligaments. PNF can be performed on any joint in the body and should be started as soon after the injury as symptoms allow (**Figure 9.10**). Before attempting PNF patterns, you should gain a more in-depth understanding of the techniques and the patterns than it is possible to give within the scope of this text.

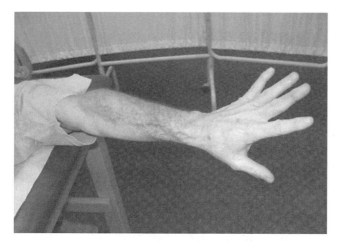

FIGURE 9.9A Upper extremity proprioceptive neuromuscular facilitation (PNF).

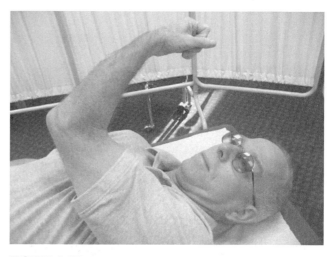

FIGURE 9.9B

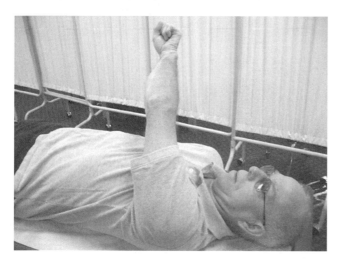

FIGURE 9.9C

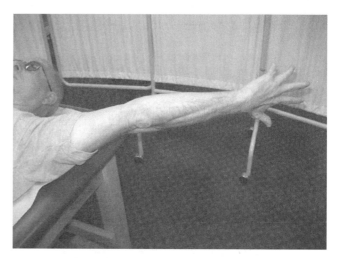

FIGURE 9.9D

A grade II or III ankle sprain should be referred to a physician to rule out a fibular chip or avulsion fracture that may have accompanied the ligament sprain.

■ Eversion Ankle Sprain

Eversion or medial ankle sprains occur in the opposite direction from inversion sprains and affect the deltoid ligament of the ankle. This injury is far less common than the inversion type, occurring in only about 5% of all ankle sprains.[1] An eversion injury, however, may have increased symptoms because of the force required to cause the damage.

SIGNS AND SYMPTOMS

1. Pain and discomfort
2. Decreased ROM
3. Decreased ability to bear weight
4. Swelling and discoloration

SPECIAL TESTS

The *Kleiger test* (**Figure 9.11**) is very similar to the talar tilt test except that it is conducted in the opposite direction. The patient sits on the table with the foot and knee resting off of the edge in a relaxed position. The lower leg is stabilized with one hand while the other hand grasps the foot and moves it into eversion. A positive test is indicated by pain and possible joint opening that suggests deltoid ligament laxity.[4]

TREATMENT

The treatment should be similar to an inversion sprain with a potentially longer immobilization and recovery

> **proprioception** The sense of the position of the body in space and relative to other parts of the body.

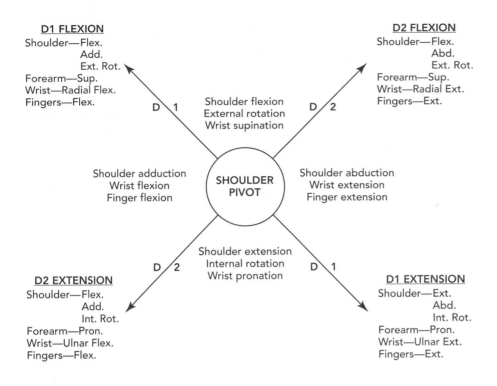

D1 FLEXION
Shoulder—Flex.
Add.
Ext. Rot.
Forearm—Sup.
Wrist—Radial Flex.
Fingers—Flex.

D2 FLEXION
Shoulder—Flex.
Abd.
Ext. Rot.
Forearm—Sup.
Wrist—Radial Ext.
Fingers—Ext.

Shoulder flexion
External rotation
Wrist supination

Shoulder adduction
Wrist flexion
Finger flexion

SHOULDER PIVOT

Shoulder abduction
Wrist extension
Finger extension

Shoulder extension
Internal rotation
Wrist pronation

D2 EXTENSION
Shoulder—Flex.
Add.
Int. Rot.
Forearm—Pron.
Wrist—Ulnar Flex.
Fingers—Flex.

D1 EXTENSION
Shoulder—Ext.
Abd.
Int. Rot.
Forearm—Pron.
Wrist—Ulnar Ext.
Fingers—Ext.

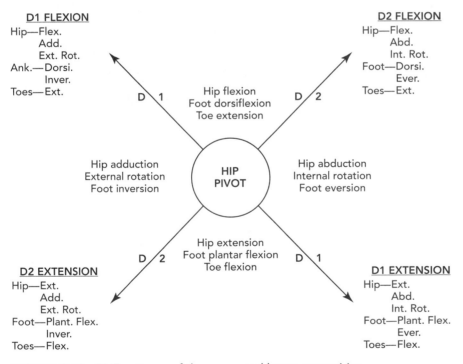

D1 FLEXION
Hip—Flex.
Add.
Ext. Rot.
Ank.—Dorsi.
Inver.
Toes—Ext.

D2 FLEXION
Hip—Flex.
Abd.
Int. Rot.
Foot—Dorsi.
Ever.
Toes—Ext.

Hip flexion
Foot dorsiflexion
Toe extension

Hip adduction
External rotation
Foot inversion

HIP PIVOT

Hip abduction
Internal rotation
Foot eversion

Hip extension
Foot plantar flexion
Toe flexion

D2 EXTENSION
Hip—Ext.
Add.
Ext. Rot.
Foot—Plant. Flex.
Inver.
Toes—Flex.

D1 EXTENSION
Hip—Ext.
Abd.
Int. Rot.
Foot—Plant. Flex.
Ever.
Toes—Flex.

FIGURE 9.10 PNF patterns of the upper and lower extremities.

Source: Prentice WE. *Rehabilitation Techniques in Sports Medicine,* 3rd ed. Boston: McGraw-Hill, 1999. Reprinted with permission.

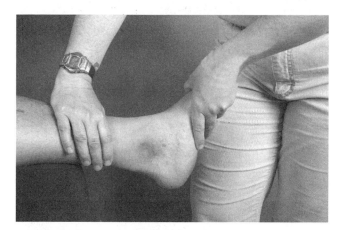

FIGURE 9.11   Kleiger's test.

time. Pain and instability dictate when the athlete is ready to progress.

■ High Ankle Sprain

The high ankle sprain is an injury of either the tibiofibular ligament or the **syndesmosis**—a fibrous sheath of tissue that connects the lateral aspect of the tibia to the medial aspect of the fibula and prevents bony separation. The injury occurs with a forced dorsiflexion and rotation of the ankle at the talar dome that causes a separation of the tibia and fibula. This injury is often associated with more initial pain than other ankle sprains and an even greater disability. The athlete will often have the symptoms of the injury resolve but still be unable to participate because of dysfunction and weakness with activity, especially push off and full-speed drills. The RTP time frame may take several months instead of the few weeks for traditional inversion ankle sprains.

SIGNS AND SYMPTOMS

1. Pain in high ankle/lower leg
2. Pain with weight bearing
3. Slight to no swelling
4. Decreased range of motion
5. Decreased strength

SPECIAL TESTS

In the *squeeze test*, the patient is in a supine position while the examiner grips the lower leg and squeezes the tibia and fibula together just above the ankle. A positive test will indicate pain in the high ankle between the tibia and fibula.

For the *swivel test*, the athlete is in a supine position or sitting with the knee bent at 90° and the foot relaxed. The examiner stabilizes the lower leg with one hand and grasps the heel in the other, pushing it into the joint space.

Then, the examiner rotates the heel and foot medially and laterally without moving it into inversion or eversion (the difference from a talar tilt or Kleiger test). This motion forces the talus into the joint space and separates the tibia and fibula. A positive test will have pain in the high ankle region increasing as the separation increases.

TREATMENT

The treatment for a high ankle sprain is similar to treatment for the other sprains. The concern here is with the psychological impact on the athlete. He or she may feel better after treatment and rehab but still be unable to participate because of dysfunction or lack of strength, especially during push off. The athlete must understand that this injury will take longer to heal than a traditional ankle sprain even if pain resolves. This often is difficult to deal with if the athlete desperately wants to play but cannot return.

■ Preventive Ankle Taping

Preventive ankle taping, as well as post-injury taping is extremely common in the athletic setting. Some athletes will, as a matter of ritual, have both ankles taped before every practice and competition throughout their career, whether they have suffered an ankle injury or not. Numerous studies have been conducted to determine the benefits and disadvantages of taping, yet in the end the individual athletic trainer tends to develop his or her own policy for the prevalence of taping for each team or sport.[5]

Prophylactic ankle braces (**Figure 9.12**) also have been researched thoroughly to determine whether they are more effective than taping techniques are. One study found that ankle braces were as effective, if not more so, than taping is in limiting inversion range of motion over a 30- to 60-minute time frame.[6]

Appropriate and effective ankle taping is both an art and a science.[5] It takes a great deal of practice and trial and error for an athletic trainer to become proficient in all taping techniques. The following figures provide a brief description of one version of ankle taping (see **Figure 9.13** through **Figure 9.26**). Dozens of different steps can be utilized as part of an effective ankle taping. Each athletic trainer will identify the best individual method for taping and then utilize that technique in daily practice.

---

syndesmosis A fibrous structure that connects surfaces that are relatively far apart, as seen between the tibia and fibula.

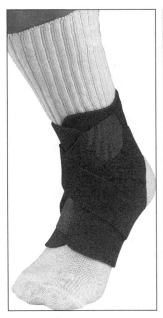
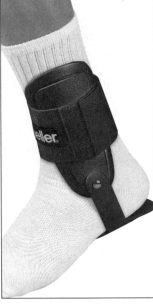

FIGURE 9.12 Types of ankle braces.

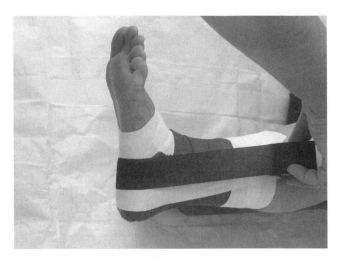

FIGURE 9.14 Stirrups.

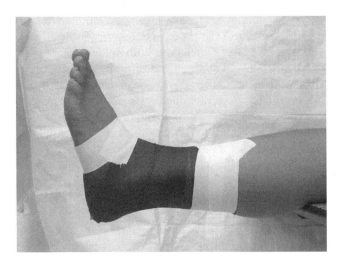

FIGURE 9.13 Anchor strips.

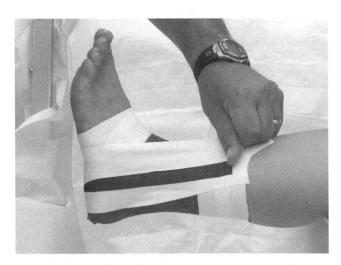

FIGURE 9.15 Overlapping stirrups.

To begin taping, it is important to apply tape adhesive to eliminate loosening or sliding in the taping. The anchors hold the pre-wrap in place and provide the boundaries for the tape job. Stirrups help to keep the ankle in a neutral or slightly everted position, which helps to decrease inversion movements at the joint. The heel locks stabilize the subtalar joint to minimize motion, while the figure-eights stabilize the talocrural and transverse tarsal joints. Finally, the finishing strips ensure that there are no holes or gaps in the taping while also guaranteeing that the tape ends do not roll or wrinkle when the athlete puts on shoes and socks.[5]

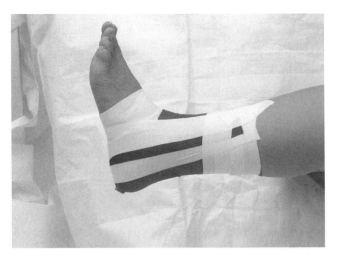

FIGURE 9.16 Anchor strips.

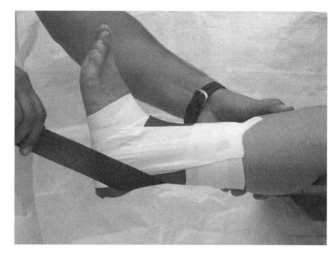

FIGURE 9.17   Heel locks.

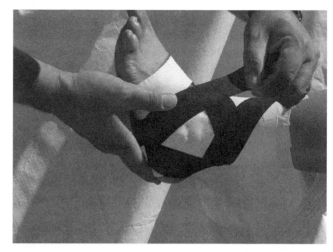

FIGURE 9.20   Second heel lock.

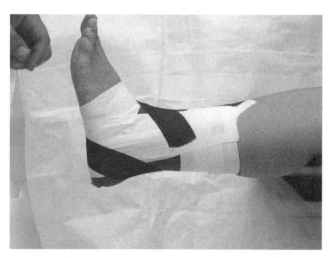

FIGURE 9.18   Completed heel lock.

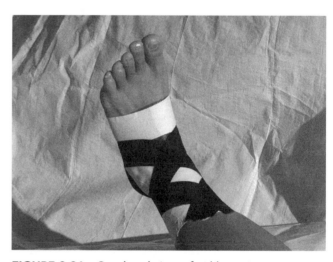

FIGURE 9.21   Overhead view of ankle taping.

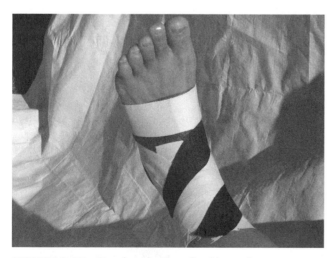

FIGURE 9.19   Overhead view of ankle taping.

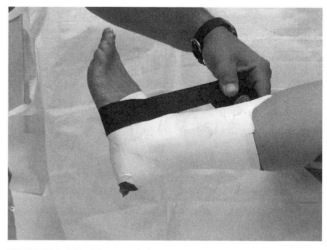

FIGURE 9.22   Figure-eight.

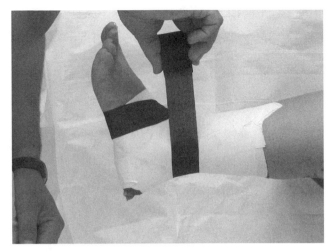

FIGURE 9.23   Completed figure-eight.

FIGURE 9.25   Horeshoe strip.

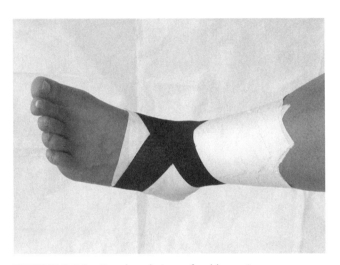

FIGURE 9.24   Overhead view of ankle taping.

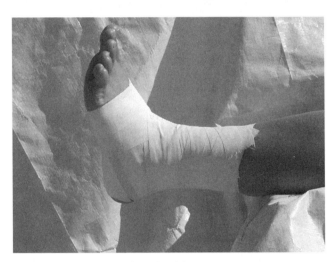

FIGURE 9.26   Completed ankle taping.

CHAPTER REVIEW

1. List the three bones that comprise the lower leg.
2. Which is more severe—a tibia fracture or a fibula fracture?
3. Which injury is treated with a donut pad?
4. List the three special tests for inversion ankle sprains.
5. What does PNF stand for?
6. What percentage of ankle sprains are eversion sprains?

CRITICAL THINKING

How do you determine if an athlete is ready to play after an ankle sprain?

REFERENCES

1. Prentice WE. *Arnheim's Principles of Athletic Training: A Competency-Based Approach*, 12th ed. Boston: McGraw-Hill, 2006.

2. Jones BH, Thacker SB, Gilchrist J, Kimsey CD, Sosin DM. (2002). Prevention of lower extremity stress fractures in athletes and soldiers: a systematic review. *Epidemiologic Reviews*, 24(2):228–247.

3. Couture CJ, Karlson KA. (2002). Tibial stress injuries: decisive diagnosis and treatment of shin splints. *Physician and Sports Medicine*, 30(6):29–36.

4. Magee DJ. *Orthopedic Physical Assessment*, 4th ed. Philadelphia: W. B. Saunders, 2002.

5. Pfeiffer RP, Mangus BC. *Concepts of Athletic Training*, 5th ed. Sudbury, MA: Jones and Bartlett, 2008.

6. Paris DL, Vardaxis V, Kikkaliaris J. (1995). Ankle ranges of motion during extended activity periods while taped and braced. *Journal of Athletic Training*, 30(3):223–228.

The Knee

Because of its configuration and regular use during activity, the knee is one of the most susceptible joints in the body to traumatic injury. It is located at the end of two long levers—the femur and the tibia—and the ends of the bones possess a poor **articulation**, requiring all stability to be provided by the ligaments and muscles.[1] Unlike the other joints in the body, the knee cannot depend on its bony makeup to protect it from injury. The configuration of the knee also makes it a very difficult joint to assess for injuries with numerous possibilities to consider throughout the evaluation.

Anatomy

Four bones work collectively to form the knee joint (**Figure 10.1**). The bones that compose the knee are the tibia and fibula in the lower leg, the femur in the thigh, and the patella—the largest sesamoid bone in the body.[1] Where the three long bones attach to form the joint, they are encapsulated in **synovial tissue**, which helps to protect the structure by creating a joint capsule. The patella (knee cap) sits within the patella tendon, which rests outside of the joint capsule. The patella assists the tibiofemoral joint in its ability to flex and extend throughout its range of motion.

The proximal head of the tibia and the distal end of the femur articulate with each other to form the primary component of the knee joint. The ends of the bones do not correlate well with each other because the femur has a double rounded surface whereas the tibial plateau is relatively flat. The shape difference allows for improved movement and shock absorption but does not offer stability to the joint.[2]

To allow for a better fit between the unequally shaped bones, the tibia is situated with two round cartilaginous structures attached to the plateau on the proximal head. These structures are called the medial and lateral **meniscus** and offer an appropriately shaped point of connection for the femur. The medial meniscus is a C-shaped structure that correlates to the medial condyle—the distal end of the femur—whereas the lateral meniscus is more of an O shape that provides an articulation for the lateral condyle. Each meniscus is thin in the center and thickens as

articulation A loose connection between tissues that allows for movement between the parts.

synovial tissue Soft tissue that lines the noncartilaginous surfaces of a joint.

meniscus A crescent-shaped structure that assists in the formation of a joint and shock absorption.

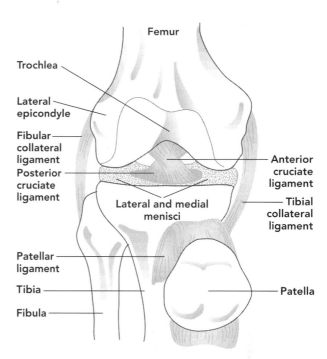

FIGURE 10.1 Anatomy of the knee.

it extends to the outer edges. This thickening allows for a better relationship between the two bones and also assists in the prevention of tibiofemoral joint dislocation.[2]

Along with shock absorption and improved bony correlation, the menisci also lubricate the joint, improve weight distribution, and reduce friction during motion. The concern for any injury to the meniscus is that the cartilage has a fairly poor blood supply, which worsens as you move farther toward the center of the joint. Therefore, an injury to the meniscus has poor healing ability and tends to require surgical repair.[2]

The patella rests between the femoral condyles anterior to the tibiofemoral joint. It has several responsibilities, including guiding the quadriceps muscles and the patella tendon, decreasing friction during movement, and protecting the femoral condyles from injury. It also makes the knee more aesthetically pleasing.[1] During movement, when the patella glides between the condyles of the femur, there is a potential for improper bony tracking to either side. This can create pain with activity and dysfunction in movement. We discuss injuries associated with poor patellar tracking later in this chapter.

■ Muscles of the Knee

Numerous muscles attach to some aspect of the knee joint and work to allow proper movement. Most of them can be lumped into three categories: quadriceps, hamstrings, and calf muscles.

The quadriceps muscles are located on the anterior aspect of the knee and thigh, attaching via the patella tendon to the tibia at the tibial tuberosity. There are four muscles within the quadriceps muscle group. They are the vastus medialis, vastus lateralis, vastus intermedius, and rectus femoris muscles. These muscles work in unison to move the knee into extension.

The hamstring muscles are posterior to the knee and work together to create knee flexion as well as assist with internal and external rotation. The hamstrings include the semimembranosus, semitendinosus, and the biceps femoris muscles (in order from medial to lateral).

The calf muscles are a grouping of the gastrocnemius and soleus muscles and assist the hamstrings in knee flexion. The other smaller muscles that act at the knee include the sartorius, popliteus, plantaris, and gracilis muscles. Each of these muscles assists in movements conducted by the larger muscle groups. The sartorius sits anterior to the quadriceps muscles running lateral to medial from the hip to the tibia. This muscle assists in knee flexion and internal rotation, producing motions that allow the individual to cross his or her leg with the ankle resting on the opposite knee.[1]

The popliteus and plantaris muscles lie directly behind the knee in what is known as the popliteal fossa. These muscles assist in knee flexion, specifically in unlocking the knee from full extension. Finally, the gracilis muscle rests medially to the hamstrings and assists in internal rotation.

Ligaments of the Knee

Four primary ligaments connect the bones of the knee joint. Because their responsibility—along with the joint capsule and meniscus—is to ensure joint stability and integrity, the ligaments are prone to injury in athletics. The four ligaments are divided into two categories differentiated by their placement within the joint. The cruciate ligaments contain an anterior (ACL) and a posterior (PCL) ligament.

---

alignment The orientation of a body part in relation to the surrounding tissue. The maintenance of appropriate positioning of tissue.

genu valgum A lateral angulation of the lower leg in relation to the thigh; knock-kneed.

genu varum A medial angulation of the lower leg in relation to the thigh; bow-legged.

genu recurvatum Hyperextension of the knee.

Q-angle Angle measured from the anterior superior iliac spine to the patella and from the patella to the tibial tuberosity.

The collateral ligaments include a medial (MCL) and a lateral (LCL) ligament.

The ACL and PCL rest within the joint and connect the femur to the tibial plateau. They sit directly in the middle of the joint protected by the patella and femoral condyles, the joint capsule, and a fat pad.[2] It is impossible to palpate either cruciate ligament because of its placement within the joint. These ligaments prevent any excessive anterior or posterior movement (translation) of the tibia. They are termed *cruciate* ligaments because they intersect in the middle forming an X shape or a cross.

The MCL and LCL are found within the joint capsule on the medial and lateral borders of the knee. Each ligament works to prevent excessive movement medially or laterally. The MCL protects from valgus force that pushes the joint medially while the LCL protects from varus force pushing laterally.

Knee Alignment Concerns

One last important consideration that should be discussed prior to reviewing knee injuries is the **alignment** of the knee joint and issues that arise because of malalignment. There are three principal issues to be considered when observing an individual's knee joint alignment. The first is the alignment of the femur in relation to the tibia.

When observing multiple athletes, it is obvious that everyone does not stand the same way whether they are healthy or injured. Each person's stance and bony alignment is slightly different when compared to anyone else. For instance, some athletes' knees bow out while others' angle in toward each other. The alignment of the femur to the tibia is very important because it may be the cause of past, present, or future injuries.

Athletes whose knees are angled toward each other are said to have **genu valgum** (knock knees). This alignment may not cause any direct pain currently, but it places an added stress on the medial aspects of the joint and could predispose the individual to acute injury or chronic knee pain.

Athletes whose knees are angled away from each other are said to have **genu varum** (bow legs). Again, this alignment does not forecast knee problems but does add stress to the lateral aspects of the joint.

Finally, athletes who have knees that extend farther than 0° are called **genu recurvatum**. This places added stress on the posterior aspects of the knee and has the potential to cause further damage to the joint structure.

A similar concern with the alignment of the femur to the tibia is the **Q-angle** (**Figure 10.2**), or angle from the head of the femur through the patella to the tibial tuberosity. An unusually high angle places added stress on the patella, which can lead to knee pain and injury. The

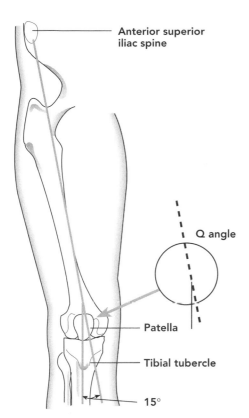

Anterior superior
iliac spine

Q angle

Patella

Tibial tubercle

15°

FIGURE 10.2   Q-angle.

Q-angle is typically higher for females because of wider hips, which are anatomically necessary for childbirth. The average Q-angle for a male is 10° and for a female is 15°. If the Q-angle exceeds 20° in anyone, the individual is more susceptible to patellar tracking issues and chronic knee problems.[3]

To measure the Q-angle of an athlete, the athletic trainer places a goniometer with the center over the patella and one arm tracing the line of both the tibia and femur. The angle that is shown on the goniometer is the Q-angle for that specific athlete. The Q-angle should be measured bilaterally to determine whether there is a discrepancy present. In a healthy individual, the measurement should be similar for both legs.

The third and final consideration in knee alignment is the length of the legs. A leg length discrepancy between the two legs may be caused by any number of issues. It could be caused by a difference in bone length from one leg to the other or pelvis and spine dysfunctions that have forced one side to shorten as compensation. Any leg length discrepancy should be assessed to determine its cause so that the proper treatment may be provided to minimize any knee pain associated with the length discrepancy.

Injuries of the Knee

■ Patellar Fracture

When discussing fractures in the knee, there are several possibilities for injury. It is possible to chip fracture the femur or tibia or fracture the protective cartilage over the femoral condyles (osteochondral fracture), but these injuries are relatively rare in athletics. Fractures can also occur within the joint space, causing loose joint bodies (LJBs) to float within the knee joint and cause pain and swelling. Any athlete that may have sustained one of these fractures should be referred to a physician for an X-ray.

The most frequent fracture, however, is the patellar fracture. Because of its placement within the patellar tendon and its protective position anterior to the rest of the knee, the patella is prone to injury through both indirect and direct force. The patella may suffer a fracture through an extreme contraction of the quad muscles and patellar tendon or through direct contact with the ground or other hard surface.

SIGNS AND SYMPTOMS

1. Pain directly over bone
2. Slight to moderate swelling
3. Pain with flexion and extension, especially in the first 30°

SPECIAL TESTS

A patellar fracture can be assessed using the *fracture tap test*. A positive test is indicated by pain, deformity, and possible crepitus.

TREATMENT

Refer to a physician for X-ray. This injury requires lengthy immobilization because of the stress placed on the bone during normal activities.

■ Patellar Dislocation

The patella, because of its shallow placement between the femoral condyles, is prone to dislocation or subluxation during high-speed motions, especially cutting and pivoting. The patella—when it does dislocate—almost always shifts laterally, coming to a rest on or past the lateral femoral condyle. After this injury has occurred initially, the athlete will be predisposed for repeated dislocations or subluxations along with inappropriate patellar tracking.

SIGNS AND SYMPTOMS

1. Moderate to extreme pain
2. Moderate swelling

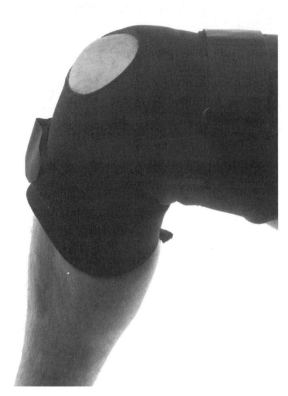

FIGURE 10.3 Patella neoprene sleeve.

3. Complete loss of range of motion (ROM) in knee
4. Obvious deformity laterally

TREATMENT

The athlete should be referred to a physician for reduction if the patella remains out of position and does not return to its normal placement. Using passive extension at a slow pace until the bone realigns will reduce the patella to its proper position. X-rays should be taken postreduction to rule out any associated patellar fracture. Return to play (RTP) is dependent on a resolution of symptoms. A special knee brace with a restrictive pad on the lateral aspect of the patella (see **Figure 10.3**) may be used once the athlete returns to play. Muscle strengthening should be emphasized during rehabilitation to prevent reinjury.

If an athlete has suffered several dislocations/subluxations, it may be wise to consider surgery to repair the injured area and assist in the prevention of other future issues.

■ Patella-Femoral Stress Syndrome

Patella-femoral stress syndrome (PFSS) is an all-encompassing term that includes any chronic pain found in the patellar region that can be blamed on tracking issues. Athletes often complain of pain within the knee, which may be caused by improper lateral tracking of the patella. The change in tracking patterns can be initiated by a number of issues within the musculature of the knee or because of a leg or foot dysfunction.

SIGNS AND SYMPTOMS

1. Pain and tenderness in lateral aspect of patella
2. Slight swelling
3. Crepitus or popping with extension

TREATMENT

The treatment plan depends on the cause of the injury that is found during the evaluation. A strengthening and stretching protocol should be implemented to eliminate any musculature issues.

Numerous exercises are effective for preventing or correcting PFSS involving both the knees and the hips. The athletic trainer should evaluate the injured athlete to determine the location of muscle weaknesses and focus on strengthening those areas using both open and closed kinetic chain activities.

Open kinetic chain activities (**Figure 10.4**) are when the foot and leg are not directly in contact with the ground or another surface. Short arc leg extensions are exercises that will directly benefit athletes suffering from PFSS. For these exercises, the athlete is placed in a seated position with the knee flexed to 90°. The athlete then extends the knee from 90° to 40° against some form of resistance, usually tubing or ankle weights. This motion isolates the quadriceps muscles without causing undue stress and increased symptoms at the patellofemoral joint.[4]

Closed kinetic chain activities involve strengthening while the leg is in contact with the ground or directly against resistance. Two exercises that have been shown to benefit patients with PFSS are wall squats and step-ups. Closed kinetic chain activities should be conducted within

patella-femoral stress syndrome (PFSS) Chronic injury to the knee often seen with patella tracking issues and overuse.

open kinetic chain Exercises that are performed when the hand or foot is free to move. These exercises are typically performed in a non-weight-bearing manner.

closed kinetic chain Exercises that are performed when the hand or foot is fixed and cannot move. The hand or foot is in constant contact with the ground or exercise equipment.

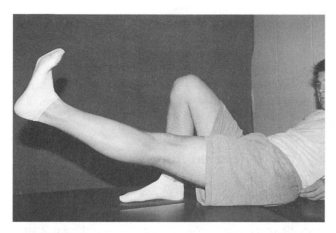

FIGURE 10.4A Open chain kenetic exercises. Flexion.

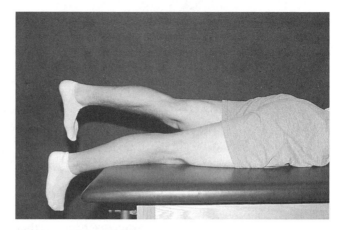

FIGURE 10.4B Extension.

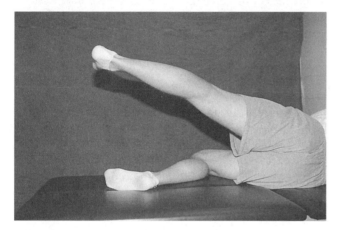

FIGURE 10.4C Abduction.

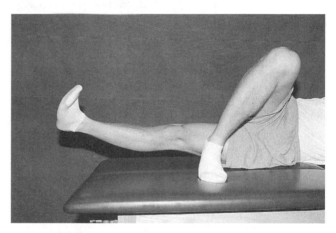

FIGURE 10.4D Adduction.

a knee flexion range of 0° to 40° to minimize stress on the patellofemoral joint.[4]

A taping technique specifically developed for PFSS and patellar tracking issues is called the McConnell technique. This is very effective for some athletes and should be considered during treatment for this issue.

■ Chondromalacia

Chondromalacia is a roughening of the protective cartilage found on the underside of the patella. Abnormal patellar tracking or trauma from an acute injury that has developed into a chronic concern may cause the roughening of the cartilage. Chondromalacia can become quite painful and debilitating for the athlete as it progresses in severity.

SIGNS AND SYMPTOMS

1. Pain underneath the patella
2. Grinding or popping during motion
3. Slight chronic swelling

SPECIAL TESTS

Clarke's sign starts with the athlete lying supine on the examining table. While the athlete is relaxed, grasp the distal aspect of the quad muscles with your thumb and fingers on either side of the patella, forming a semicircle just superior to the patella. Have the athlete actively flex the quadriceps while you attempt to prevent the patella from moving superiorly. A positive test is indicated with pain and grinding underneath the patella during movement.[1]

TREATMENT

Ice therapy will decrease the current symptoms, and strengthening the quadriceps muscles will benefit the athlete in the long term. The athlete should attempt to avoid any activity that causes pain. Anti-inflammatory medication may be useful, as would elastic wrap or a knee sleeve.

If pain persists, surgery may be indicated to smooth the cartilage on the back of the patella. However, the patellar cartilage will not regenerate itself or return to its natural smoothness, which could lead to arthritis in the joint. Repeat surgeries throughout the athlete's lifetime may become necessary.

Osgood-Schlatter's Disease

Osgood-Schlatter's disease is a chronic condition found in adolescents, typically after a dramatic growth spurt. Throughout adolescence and puberty, the tendons are stronger than the bones to which they are attached. This strength discrepancy causes bone damage as the tendon microscopically pulls away from its attachment. At the patella tendon, this damage initiates increased repair that over time develops into an enlarged tuberosity. Pain and tenderness directly over the enlarged tuberosity develop and can lead to disability and difficulty during athletic activities.

SIGNS AND SYMPTOMS

1. Pain at insertion of patella tendon
2. Tenderness to palpation
3. Enlarged tibial tuberosity
4. Pain with jumping or running

TREATMENT

Rest, ice, compression, and elevation (RICE) therapy is a successful modality for this injury. The athlete should decrease activity or cross-train to decrease the stress placed on the tendon. Anti-inflammatory medication may also be useful. A restrictive knee strap placed over the patellar tendon between the patella and the tibial tuberosity may also be beneficial. The patellar strap assists in correcting any abnormal muscle firing patterns. This strap may be useful for the athlete to decrease pain during activity.

Patellar Tendinitis

Patellar tendinitis, which also is called jumper's knee, is extremely common in athletics. A chronic injury, it is often seen in athletes who consistently use repetitive motions in the lower leg such as squatting, jumping, or kicking.

SIGNS AND SYMPTOMS

1. Pain in patella tendon or at inferior pole of patella
2. Pain increases with activity
3. Squeaking noise may occur with knee extension
4. Slight swelling may occur

TREATMENT

An athlete with patellar tendinitis gradually feels increased pain with activity. Modality treatment with ice, ice massage, and ultrasound may be effective to decrease the irritation.

Friction massage may also help to remove inflammation. Anti-inflammatory medicine and a restrictive knee strap placed over the patella tendon between the patella and the tibial tuberosity may also be beneficial. The patellar strap assists in correcting any abnormal muscle firing patterns. Muscle strengthening can also help to improve muscular activity and proper motion.

Patella Tendon Rupture

A patella tendon rupture, much like an Achilles tendon rupture, is relatively rare in younger athletes. It is seen more in athletes—professional or recreational—older than 30 years of age.[5] The injury is caused by a strong contraction of the quad muscles during jumping or running. The tendon can either rupture at the distal insertion on the tibia or just superior to the patella.

SIGNS AND SYMPTOMS

1. Extreme pain immediately followed by a dramatic decrease in pain levels caused by a concurrent rupture of the nociceptors
2. Significant swelling
3. Shifting of the patella out of its normal position into the mid-thigh area (window shade effect)
4. Complete loss of knee extension movement
5. Previous history of chronic tendinitis or inflammation is often present

TREATMENT

Surgical repair is the only reliable treatment for a patella tendon rupture. Because of the movement of the patella into the thigh, the tendon is not in a position to reattach on its own. Rehabilitation time is significant, with a 1-year recovery time often needed for optimal health.

Knee Dislocation

There are two joints in the knee—the patellofemoral and the tibiofemoral (knee) joints. Both of these are capable of subluxation or dislocation injuries. The patellar dislocation has been covered previously. Dislocation of the tibiofemoral joint is a very serious injury that if not treated properly and in a timely manner can risk severe damage and possible amputation of the lower leg.

A knee dislocation is generally the result of tears in one or more of the supporting ligaments caused by a traumatic incident. The displacement of the joint compromises the protective structures surrounding the femoral blood vessels and nerves, causing injury and possibly severing of these essential vessels.[5] If not treated quickly, this injury can lead to tissue death and could require the amputation of the lower leg.

SIGNS AND SYMPTOMS

1. Immediate pain that may decrease dramatically if nerve damage occurs
2. Obvious deformity (usually with the tibia displaced anteriorly)
3. Significant swelling
4. Decreased blood flow and neural sensation in lower leg

TREATMENT

Immediate hospitalization and follow-up with an orthopedic surgeon are essential. The limb should be splinted in the position found and the athlete transported in an ambulance to the nearest medical facility. Surgical intervention is often required for neurovascular and ligament repair. This injury is very traumatic and may be career-ending for the athlete. If the athlete is able to return to play, it will be after a significant recovery time—often 2 or more years.

■ Knee Contusion

Knee contusions are the result of direct contact with the ground or an opponent. The contusion may be to the patella or to the musculature surrounding the knee. These injuries are not severe but can be quite painful for the athlete. Immediately following the injury, the athlete may be unable to bear weight or move through the complete range of motion. However, the symptoms rarely last for more than 1 to 2 days.

SIGNS AND SYMPTOMS

1. Pain at affected site
2. Moderate swelling and discoloration
3. Loss of ROM
4. Decreased weight bearing

TREATMENT

Electrical and cold modality therapy is often enough to alleviate symptoms for the athlete. Ice and compression are the most important treatments to decrease swelling and allow for a faster RTP. Recovery should be possible after 1 to 2 days rest. If pain persists, other injuries may have occurred and the athlete should be reevaluated.

Meniscus Injuries

The menisci are the cartilaginous structures that allow the femur and tibia to articulate despite the bones' awkward connection. Each meniscus is responsible for shock absorption, improving weight distribution, and decreasing friction during knee flexion and extension. Because of these roles, an injury to either meniscus is debilitating to the athlete, often restricting knee motion and decreasing the athlete's ability to compete in sports. As with other structures, the meniscus may be injured in several ways, including contusions or tears, which are the most common.

■ Meniscus Contusion

A meniscus contusion is often associated with a **hyperextension** of the knee caused by a misstep on uneven surfaces. The hyperextension injury can cause bruising of either the meniscus or the femoral condyle as the compression of the two into each other occurs when the knee "locks out" into hyperextension. This injury can cause a great deal of pain for the athlete and may cause him or her to miss several days of activity as symptoms diminish.

It is very important with a hyperextension injury to complete a thorough evaluation of the knee to rule out ligament injury or meniscal tear before assessing it as a contusion. Hyperextension may also cause an ACL injury, which should be ruled out prior to beginning rehabilitation.

SIGNS AND SYMPTOMS

1. Pain, especially as the knee nears full extension
2. Loss of ROM in extension
3. Slight swelling

TREATMENT

RICE therapy helps to decrease symptoms post-injury. RTP can be relatively quick if the athlete is able to regain full range of motion. A hyperextension tape job may be effective for the athlete as he or she returns to activity.

■ Meniscus Tears

The meniscus tear is the more common and more significant injury of the meniscal concerns. Whereas a contusion allows a relatively quick RTP if the athlete has not suffered other injuries, a meniscal tear requires a longer recovery time. Because of the shape of the meniscus, there are several different types of meniscus tears with each one having different RTP implications.

The severity of a meniscal injury depends on which type of tear occurs and in what part of the meniscus. If the injury occurs in the outer one-third of the meniscus, the athlete may be able to avoid surgery and heal with conservative treatment and rest. However, if the injury occurs in the middle or inner one-third, surgery often is

hyperextension Extension that occurs beyond the full range of motion (usually seen as beyond 0°).

recommended because of the limited blood supply of the cartilage and an inability to heal itself.[3]

The medial meniscus is injured more often than its lateral counterpart. Several minor ligaments attach to the medial aspect, which makes it more prone to stresses from different movements. Either meniscus can be torn longitudinally (anterior–posterior), obliquely (at an angle), or transversely (medial–lateral).

The tear can be a tissue laceration or it can produce a flap of injured tissue known as a *bucket-handle tear*. The angle and type of tear also can determine the symptoms that the athlete feels and the ultimate treatment plan.[3]

Several motions can cause injury to the meniscus. The most frequently seen injuries occur when a twisting motion occurs in conjunction with valgus stress. This is found in cutting movements as the athlete attempts to shift and push off of the involved leg. Cartilage damage may also occur with hyperflexion or hyperextension motions and forced rotation of the joint.

SIGNS AND SYMPTOMS

1. Pain, especially when moved similarly to the mechanism of injury
2. Pain with full extension or flexion
3. Diffuse swelling in the joint (**effusion**)
4. Pain along the line of the joint between the femur and tibia
5. Sensation of locking or giving out
6. Clicking or popping sound with movement

SPECIAL TESTS

For the *McMurray's test*, the athlete lies relaxed in a supine position while the examiner passively moves the knee into a 90–90 position (the hip and knee are both flexed to 90°). The athletic trainer then flexes and extends the knee while rotating it medially and laterally (**Figure 10.5**). This motion is done with one hand over the joint space of the knee on either side of the patella and the other hand manipulating the foot through these motions.[1] A positive test may be found with several different results. There may be obvious clicking and popping with movement. There may also be increased pain in one motion or a loss of ROM in one direction.

For the *Apley's compression test*, the athlete lies in a prone position with the knee flexed to 90° (**Figure 10.6**). The examiner stabilizes the thigh with one hand or knee and places the other hand (or hands) at the ankle. The athletic trainer then compresses the lower leg into the knee and rotates the foot/ankle complex medially and laterally. A positive test is indicated by pain or clicking/popping in the joint.[1]

For the *bounce home test*, the athlete is placed in a supine position with the examiner holding the involved leg in the air by the heel. The athlete flexes the knee and then allows slow passive extension. The athletic trainer can either evaluate for full extension or allow the knee to quickly move through the last 10° of extension (bounce home). A positive test is indicated by pain at the joint line or lack of full range of motion.[1]

TREATMENT

As was mentioned earlier, the treatment for this injury often depends on the location and type of damage that the meniscus has incurred. Some athletes are able to compete for long periods of time with meniscal tears because of a lack of extreme pain or disability. Some injuries immediately prevent further play and require surgery before any activity is possible. Referral to a physician will help assess the treatment options available for each specific injury.

If surgery is recommended, there are two principal methods of treatment. The meniscus may either be repaired through reattachment and sutures, or it may be cleaned up by removing the injured tissue. The surgical options often depend on the placement of the injury. The more interior the injury, the less blood flow that the tissue receives and therefore an increased likelihood of removal versus repair. The blood supply for the tissue increases toward the outer edges of the cartilage, which improves the chance for healing, and a repair becomes the better option. Research has shown that the meniscus helps to prevent degeneration of the joint and possible future joint replacement, so it is suggested to attempt repair over removal if that is a possibility.[2]

RTP after surgery is very different in repair versus removal. A meniscal repair requires 3 to 6 weeks of non–weight bearing on crutches followed by progressive rehab. A full recovery may take 3 to 4 months. A removal allows the athlete to begin weight bearing within 3 to 4 days and RTP within as early as 2 to 3 weeks depending on symptoms.

Ligament Injuries

Because there are four primary ligaments in the knee, we will separate them and evaluate each for their specific injuries. All four of them share the traditional ligament sprain categorizations with severity being assigned by grade—I to III. A grade III injury often is categorized as a full tear of the ligament. We begin with the injury that most athletes fear more than any other.

effusion Abnormal swelling found within a joint structure or body cavity.

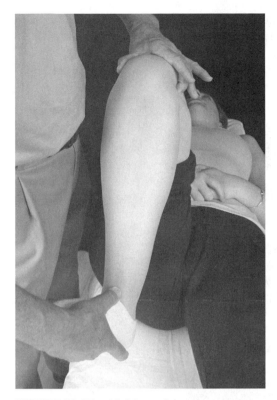

FIGURE 10.5A   McMurray's test.

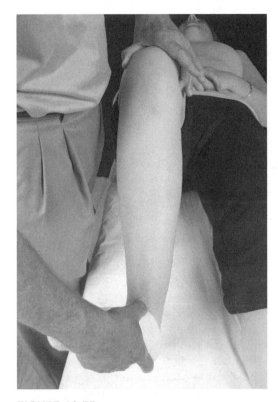

FIGURE 10.5B

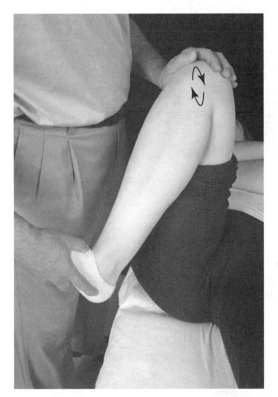

FIGURE 10.5C

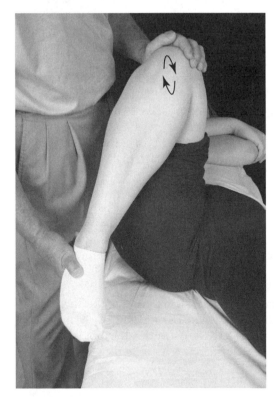

FIGURE 10.5D

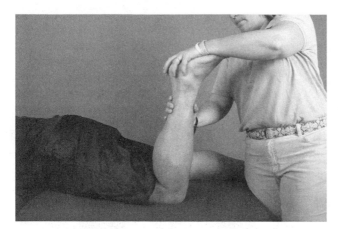

FIGURE 10.6 Apley's compression test.

ACL Sprain

The anterior cruciate ligament (ACL) sprain/tear has become extremely well known as increasingly more high-profile athletes suffer this injury. The ACL's responsibility in the knee joint is to prevent anterior translation or shifting of the tibia in relation to the femur.

The most frequent cause of ACL injuries is noncontact shifting of the knee, often seen with **deceleration**. An ACL injury can be very debilitating to an athlete physically and psychologically, even though surgical repair is fairly straightforward and countless athletes have been able to return to high levels of competition post surgery.

Female athletes are especially susceptible to ACL sprains and tears, specifically the noncontact injuries, for a variety of reasons including several anatomic and physiologic concerns. However, there is no consensus at this point as to the exact underlying reason, and there should be no restrictions to play for any female athlete.[3]

SIGNS AND SYMPTOMS

1. Pain in joint
2. Athlete complains of pop at time of injury
3. Sense of looseness in joint, giving away, or shifting
4. Swelling that increases rapidly post-injury

SPECIAL TESTS

The *anterior drawer test* (**Figure 10.7**) in the knee is quite similar to that of the ankle. The athlete is placed in a supine position with the knee flexed so that the foot is resting on the table. The examiner uses his or her leg to stabilize the

> **deceleration** A decrease in speed or coming to a stop.

foot so that it does not shift during the test. Both hands grip the knee around the joint with the palms and thumbs against the tibial tuberosity, the shaft of the tibia, and the patellar tendon, and the fingers wrapped around the knee gripping the popliteal fossa. The pressure is placed

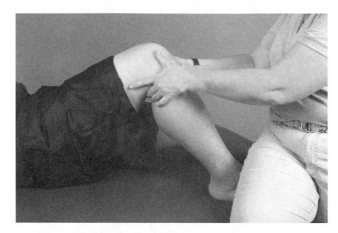

FIGURE 10.7A Anterior drawer test.

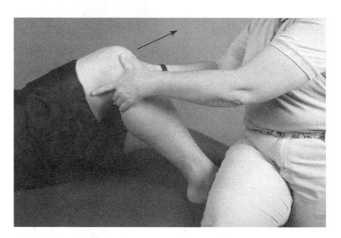

FIGURE 10.7B

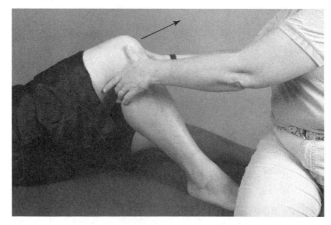

FIGURE 10.7C

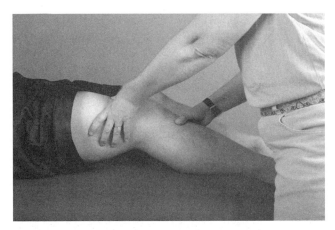

FIGURE 10.8A   Lachman's test.

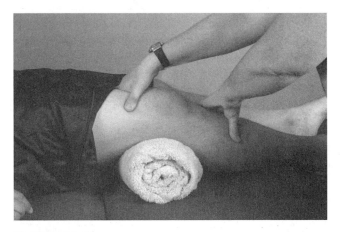

FIGURE 10.8B

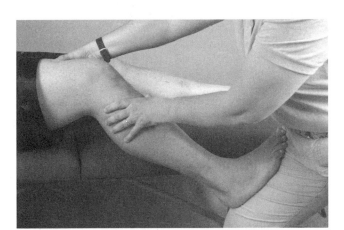

FIGURE 10.8C

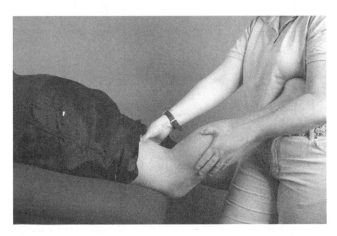

FIGURE 10.8D

on the posterior of the knee by the fingers, forcing the proximal tibia anteriorly. A positive test is indicated by anterior translation of the tibia that exceeds the translation seen in the uninvolved side.[1] A modification for this test places the athlete in a seated position on the table with both legs hanging off the edge. The examiner grasps the foot between his or her legs and grips the knee in the same manner as explained previously. This method may be more effective in assessment during a match or game if a table is unavailable and the athletic trainer is utilizing a bench, chair, or bleacher.

The *Lachman's test* (**Figure 10.8**) is the best indicator of an ACL tear, although it may be difficult to conduct for examiners with small hands or those dealing with larger athletes.[5–7] For this test, the patient is placed in a supine position. The examiner then stabilizes the thigh with one hand and places the other hand around the proximal end of the tibia so that the lower leg is grasped within the hand in the same manner as the anterior drawer test. The examiner

moves the leg into a position between full extension and 30° of flexion, and then pulls the tibia anteriorly several times. The positioning minimizes the effectiveness of the hamstrings to protect the injured ligament and demonstrate a false-negative response.[1] A positive test is indicated by excessive anterior translation of the tibia or a soft or mushy end feel where the ACL should prevent movement. Testing the uninvolved side first and comparing the translation to the injured side may demonstrate a normal end feel for that specific athlete. Several modifications to this test allow assessment for those who cannot grasp the tibia in one hand for one reason or another. Attempting several different techniques will allow each athletic trainer to determine the best method for future tests.

The *pivot shift test* also is an excellent method for assessing ACL injuries. However, it may be difficult to utilize on a patient who is apprehensive or suffering from muscle guarding that can prevent a positive test whether the ACL is injured or not.[1] The patient is placed in a supine position with the hip relaxed and the knee placed in extension and slight medial rotation. The examiner grasps the foot in one hand and the lateral aspect of the tibia in the other. The proximal end of the tibia should be held so that the palm of the hand is over the head of the fibula, the thumb is in the area of the tibial tuberosity, and the fingers are wrapped around the calf to the popliteal fossa. The hand placement with the pressure anteriorly keeps the knee in medial rotation. The examiner then applies a valgus stress to the knee and flexes both the knee and hip to 30° to 40°. A positive test is indicated if the knee shifts anteriorly during the early stages of flexion and then reduces itself to normal position by 40° flexion. The athlete often states that a positive test replicates the feeling of giving away.[3]

TREATMENT

An ACL sprain may be a grade I or II, although the most common injury is a complete tear (grade III). A grade I or II ACL sprain can be treated conservatively with a rehab focus on balance and hamstring strengthening to assist the ACL in stabilizing the knee during the healing process. A complete tear (grade III) requires surgery to repair the ligament. To be able to return to full activity without issue, surgery is necessary. Some athletes have attempted to play with bracing and muscle strengthening alone and may even have had some success. However, long-term capability at a high level requires an ACL and surgery is the sole repair option.

RTP requires 4 to 6 months of rehab with best results seen at approximately 1 year. An ACL derotational brace (**Figure 10.9**) can assist the athlete during his or her return by providing stability and protection. It is especially important during the first year post surgery. **Table 10.1** demonstrates a sample rehab protocol for ACL repair.

■ PCL Sprain

The PCL is a lesser-known component inside the knee. It acts in the opposite direction of the ACL to prevent posterior translation of the tibia in relation to the femur. The PCL is the strongest ligament in the knee and because of its strength and role in the knee's stability and motion, injury is seen less often than in the ACL. The most frequent mechanism of injury is a direct blow to the proximal tibia and knee while flexed at 90°. This takes advantage of the ligament while it is in a vulnerable position.

SIGNS AND SYMPTOMS

1. Pain and tenderness in posterior aspect of knee
2. Slight swelling in popliteal region
3. Joint laxity
4. Loose feeling with walking

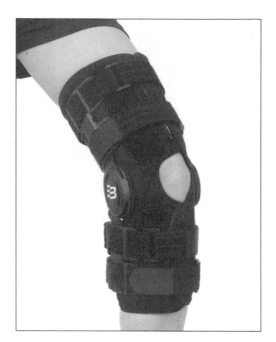

FIGURE 10.9 Knee deroational brace.

SPECIAL TESTS

The posterior drawer test in the knee is similar to the anterior drawer test for the ACL. The athlete is in a supine position with the knee flexed so that he or she can rest the foot on the table or ground. The examiner stabilizes the foot with his or her leg so that the foot does not shift during the test. Both hands grip the knee around the joint line so that the palms and thumbs are against the tibial tuberosity, the shaft of the tibia, and the patellar tendon, and the fingers are wrapped around the knee gripping the popliteal fossa. Pressure is placed on the anterior aspect of the knee, forcing the tibia posteriorly. A positive test is indicated by posterior translation of the tibia greater than that of the uninvolved side.[1] This test may be modified by having the athlete seated on the table with both legs hanging off of the edge. The examiner grasps the foot between his or her legs and grips the knee in the same manner as described previously. This method may be more effective in assessments on the sideline if a table is unavailable and the athletic trainer is utilizing a bench, chair, or bleacher.

The posterior sag test for a PCL tear is a simple passive method of determining ligament rupture. The athlete is placed in a supine position with the hip and knee flexed to 90°. The examiner holds the athlete's foot in place and asks the athlete to relax the muscles of the leg. A positive test is indicated by an obvious sag of the proximal end of the tibia posteriorly.

TABLE 10.1

KNEE REHAB PROTOCOL

Phase 1 (0–4 weeks)

- Immobilizer 0–1 week
- Continuous Passive Motion (CPM) machine for 1–2 weeks until therapy begins
- Post-op brace
- Weight bear as tolerated with or without crutches
- RICE
- E-stim for pain/edema
- Gait training to reach full weight bearing (FWB)
- Exercises: Quad sets
  Straight leg raises
  Squats 0°–40°
  Patellar mobilizations
  Upper body ergometer (UBE)
  Standing Biomechanical Ankle Platform System (BAPS) board (3rd week)

Phase 2 (3–8 weeks)

- Continue phase 1 exercises, increasing weight as tolerated
- Begin isotonic short-arc knee extension 90°–40°
- Proprioceptive activities/PNF
- Exercises: Step-downs
  Wall squats/sits (stopping at 45°–60°)
  Bike
  Hamstring curl

Phase 3 (6–12 weeks)

- Continue phase 2 exercises, increasing weight as tolerated
- Increase isotonic weights
- Rebounder-balancing on one leg
- Initiate lunges
- Isometric wall sits (90°)
- Agility—fast feet, front and side-controlled hopping bilaterally
- Flexibility—hamstrings, Achilles, IT band, quadriceps

Return to Play (12+ weeks)

- The goal is to have full strength
- Once quad strength is 70% begin exercises: Treadmill running
  Plyometrics
  Jump rope
  Figure 8
  Carioca
  Shuttle
  Pogo ball
  Rebounder running

TREATMENT

Grade I and II sprains should be treated conservatively by focusing rehab on balance and quadriceps strengthening. RICE therapy should be conducted until an appointment with a physician. Referral for follow-up testing will assist in determining if the PCL is torn. A grade III PCL tear may only be repaired through surgery with a recovery time similar to an ACL repair. Some physicians believe that an athlete can be successful without a surgical repair of the PCL. The decision ultimately rests with the athlete and his or her doctor.[8]

PCL reconstruction is more difficult than for the ACL because of the proximity of the ligament to major neurovascular vessels. An ineffective repair could preclude the athlete from competition if full strength and flexibility are not recovered. As technology and surgical techniques have improved, this surgery has decreased in risk, a trend that surely will continue in the future, making it easier for athletes to return to competition.[8] A PCL derotational brace may assist the athlete in return to play, especially during the first year of recovery.

■ MCL Sprain

The medial collateral ligament (MCL) is especially susceptible to injury in athletics because of the frequency of contact to the outer side of the knee forcing it medially (**Figure 10.10**). As with all ligaments, there are grades of sprain with a grade I having the least amount of damage and grade III being a complete tear. The severity of

FIGURE 10.10 A valgus stress to the knee.

the injury determines the treatment plans and return to activity.

Unfortunately, because of the MCL's proximity to and relationship with the medial meniscus and the ACL, athletes may injure all three components of the knee, an injury that is relatively common. The tearing of both ligaments and the cartilage is known as either the unhappy or unholy triad, and it causes severe disability to the joint.

SIGNS AND SYMPTOMS

1. Pain increasing with severity
2. Joint stiffness
3. Slight to moderate swelling over ligament
4. Decreased ROM
5. Joint laxity medially

SPECIAL TESTS

The *valgus stress test* (**Figure 10.11**) assesses MCL injury as well as ACL tears if a triad injury has occurred. The athlete is placed in a supine position with his or her leg held in the examiner's hands. The athletic trainer should place one hand around the calf or ankle to stabilize the lower leg and the other hand on the lateral aspect of the knee with the thumb over the tibial tuberosity, the palm over the LCL and lateral joint line, and the fingers wrapped around the popliteal fossa. The examiner then places a valgus stress on the knee, forcing it medially. The test should be performed at both 0° and 30° flexion. At 30° flexion, the knee is open to movement because the femur and tibia are not fully articulated and the ligaments may move freely. At 0° flexion (or full extension) the knee is taut and the ligaments are in a position of strength.[1]

A positive test at either position is seen if the valgus stress opens the knee so that the joint appears to be on a hinge and opening like a door. The more laxity there is,

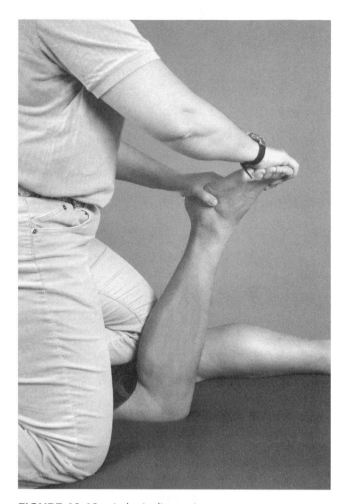

FIGURE 10.12 Apley's distraction test.

the greater degree of damage to the ligament. If a positive test is seen at 0° and there is joint laxity, the test then indicates that there has been damage to the ACL as well as the MCL. Therefore, a positive test at full extension or 0° flexion suggests a possible unholy/unhappy triad—a major knee injury. A positive test at 30° flexion indicates an isolated MCL sprain. The greater the laxity found during the test, the more severe the damage to the ligament.

Another test is the *Apley's distraction test*. Similar to Apley's compression test, for the distraction test the athlete lies in a prone position with the knee flexed to 90° (**Figure 10.12**). The examiner stabilizes the thigh with one hand or knee and places the other hand (or hands) at the ankle. The athletic trainer then distracts the tibia away from the femur and rotates the foot/ankle complex medially and laterally. A positive test is indicated with pain over the MCL or laxity medially.

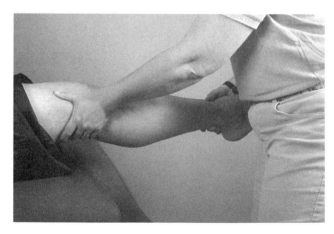

FIGURE 10.11 Valgus stress test.

FIGURE 10.13   Lateral stabilizing brace.

TREATMENT

RICE therapy should be given to any grade injury immediately following the incident. Most isolated MCL injuries (that is, without ACL or cartilage involvement) are treated nonoperatively through conservative therapy and rehab. An unholy/unhappy triad injury requires surgery to repair the ACL and meniscus and possibly the MCL. The athlete should be referred to a physician for follow-up testing to determine the severity of the injury. The physician will place the athlete in a knee immobilizer to provide stability and prevent further injury during gait.

As the athlete returns to activity, he or she will have to demonstrate the ability to sprint and complete sport-specific activities without pain or instability. A lateral stabilizing brace (**Figure 10.13**) or tape job may be utilized during activity to protect from further injury. RTP time frames depend on severity, ranging from 1 to 2 weeks for grade I, 2 to 6 weeks for grade II, and 4 to 16 weeks for grade III sprains, and on whether the athlete has had surgery.

■ LCL Sprain

The lateral collateral ligament (LCL) is injured much less often than the MCL because of its inaccessibility to opponents and outside forces. It is difficult to apply a varus stress to the interior of the knee during competition. Valgus stress to the outside of the knee is a much more frequent mechanism of injury causing MCL injuries than

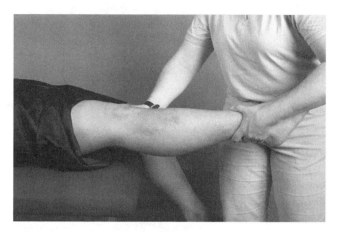

FIGURE 10.14   Varus stress test.

varus stress causing LCL damage. They can occur, but LCL sprains are less prevalent in athletics.

SIGNS AND SYMPTOMS

1. Pain over lateral aspect of knee
2. Slight to moderate swelling over lateral aspect
3. Joint laxity laterally
4. Joint stiffness
5. Decreased ROM

SPECIAL TESTS

The *varus stress test* (**Figure 10.14**) is done in a similar manner to the valgus test for the MCL. The athlete is in a supine position with the injured leg resting in the examiner's hands. One hand stabilizes the lower leg at the calf or ankle while the other is placed on the medial aspect of the knee with the thumb over the tibial tuberosity, the palm over the MCL and medial joint line, and the fingers wrapped around the popliteal fossa. The joint is stressed laterally at 0° and 30° flexion. A positive test is indicated by an opening as though the joint were a hinge opening laterally. A positive test at 0° can indicate ACL involvement as well as a sprain of the LCL. A positive test at 30° suggests an isolated LCL sprain. The greater the laxity found during the test, the more severe the damage to the ligament.

The *Apley's distraction test* also can be used. Similar to Apley's compression test, for the distraction test the athlete lies in a prone position with the knee flexed to 90°. The examiner stabilizes the thigh with one hand or knee and places the other hand (or hands) at the ankle. The athletic trainer then distracts the tibia away from the femur and rotates the foot/ankle complex medially and laterally. A positive test is indicated with pain over the LCL or laxity laterally.

FIGURE 10.15 Double hinged brace.

TREATMENT

The treatment for an LCL sprain is the same as for the MCL. RICE therapy should be conducted initially, followed by a strengthening program and progressive rehab. As the severity increases, so does the length of time for recovery and RTP. An LCL tear by itself is rarely treated surgically, although ACL involvement would indicate surgical repair. RTP is the same as with an MCL sprain, increasing with the severity of injury.

A medial stabilizing brace does not exist because it would create an inability to run effectively with a brace on the inside of the leg. The athlete may benefit with an ACL brace, a double-hinged brace (**Figure 10.15**) that protects both sides of the knee, or an LCL tape job to provide increased stability and protection during activity.

CHAPTER REVIEW

1. What are the four bones that comprise the knee joint?
2. *True* or *False*: You can palpate the anterior cruciate ligament during an injury assessment.
3. What is the difference between genu valgum and genu varum?
4. What is PFSS?
5. Why is a knee dislocation considered a serious injury?
6. What is an unhappy triad?

CRITICAL THINKING

How do you discuss a serious injury, such as a knee dislocation, with an athlete's parents?

REFERENCES

1. Magee DJ. *Orthopedic Physical Assessment*, 4th ed. Philadelphia: W. B. Saunders, 2002.
2. Chhabra A, Elliott CC, Miller MD. (2001). Normal anatomy and biomechanics of the knee. *Sports Medicine and Arthroscopy Review*, 9(3):166–177.
3. Prentice WE. *Arnheim's Principles of Athletic Training: A Competency-Based Approach*, 12th ed. Boston: McGraw-Hill, 2006.
4. Harrison AD. (2006). An evidence-based approach for patients with patellofemoral-pain syndrome. *Athletic Therapy Today*, 11(2):6–10.
5. Booher JM, Thibodeau GA. *Athletic Injury Assessment*, 4th ed. Boston: McGraw-Hill, 2000.
6. Starkey C, Johnson G. *Athletic Training and Sports Medicine*, 4th ed. Sudbury, MA: Jones and Bartlett, 2006.
7. Anderson MK, Hall SJ, Martin M. *Sports Injury Management*, 2nd ed. Baltimore: Lippincott, Williams, & Wilkins, 2000.
8. Orthopedics. *PCL Injury*. Retrieved September 28, 2007, from http://orthopedics.about.com.

The Thigh, Hip, and Pelvis

The hip joint is considered one of the largest and most stable joints in the body. Far fewer injuries occur in the thigh, hip, and pelvis than in the rest of the lower body, although it is important not to overlook this region. The injuries that may occur in the thigh, hip, and pelvis run the gamut from relatively minor to severely debilitating. Because of their role in all movement and posture, the hip and thigh should be thoroughly evaluated to prevent chronic conditions from developing.

 ## Anatomy

The anatomy of the thigh, hip joint, and pelvis should be divided into two categories: (1) the thigh, and (2) the hip/pelvis. They are two distinct regions with separate bones and musculature.

■ Thigh Anatomy

The thigh is defined as the upper portion of the lower extremity from the knee to the pelvis. The femur is the long bone that provides support for this area. It is the longest and strongest bone in the body and has great stability at the hip joint protected by bony structure, **joint capsule**, and numerous ligaments.

The muscles at the thigh are mostly the same as those discussed with the knee. The quadriceps muscles rest anterior to the femur while the hamstrings sit posteriorly. The medial musculature of the femur consists of the adductor muscle group—a collection of three muscles—and the pectineus and gracilis muscles. The adductor muscles, as the name suggests, move the hip and leg into adduction. The lateral musculature consists of the tensor fascia latae (TFL), a thin, wide muscle that narrows into a fascial sheet called the iliotibial (IT) band. The tensor fascia latae and IT band move the hip and leg into abduction.

■ Hip/Pelvis Anatomy

The hip and pelvis are derived from an interaction of several bones and numerous muscles that allow for both small- and large-range movements that improve the body's ability to walk and run while absorbing ground reaction forces during activity.

The pelvic region is composed of three primary bones and three joints (**Figure 11.1**). The sacrum is the bone at the base of the spinal column in the center of the posterior pelvis. It provides the connection between the spine and

> **joint capsule** A collection of fibrous tissue that surrounds and protects a joint from injury.

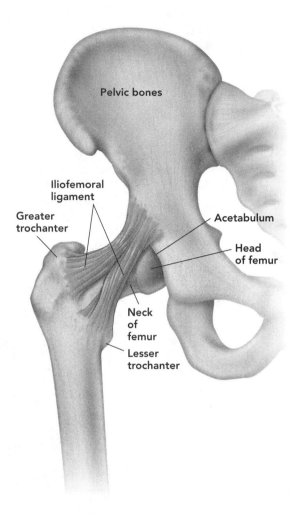

FIGURE 11.1 Anatomy of the hip.

pelvis. On either side of the sacrum are the innominate bones, which connect to the sacrum via the two sacroiliac (SI) joints. These are strong joints that allow for minimal motion between the sacrum and innominates.

The innominate bones are composed of the ilium, ischium, and pubis bones, which are fused together to form the bony pelvis. The innominate bones have a circular structure that protects vital organs and allows proper motion during gait. The symphysis pubis, the attachment of the two pubis bones anteriorly, is the third joint found in the pelvic region. The pelvic bones have a unique interrelationship that allows them to perform all of their essential functions.[1] The complexity of this relationship is far beyond the scope of this text and should be researched in texts that specialize in the pelvic region.

The pelvic musculature is a bit of a misnomer because no muscles directly control the SI joints or the pubic symphysis. Instead, muscles originating from the spine and pelvis serve to move the joint structure.

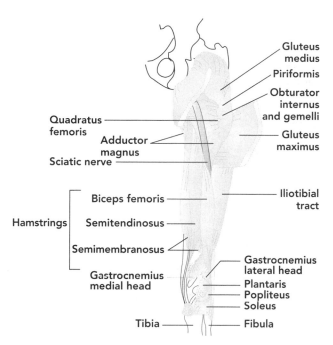

Gluteus
medius

Piriformis

Obturator
internus
and gemelli

Gluteus
maximus

Quadratus
femoris

Adductor
magnus

Sciatic nerve

Iliotibial
tract

Hamstrings

Biceps femoris

Semitendinosus

Semimembranosus

Gastrocnemius
medial head

Gastrocnemius
lateral head

Plantaris

Popliteus

Soleus

Tibia

Fibula

FIGURE 11.2 External rotators of the hip.

The hip is the joint that is composed of the femur and the pelvis (ilium, ischium, and pubis). This joint is very stable, owing to the deep socket formed by the pelvic bones; the large, strong ligaments that surround the joint; and the powerful musculature in the region. A dozen muscles in the hip allow the wide ranges of motion found at that joint. The primary muscles are the iliopsoas (a combination of the iliacus and psoas major muscles), which, along with the rectus femoris, initiates hip flexion; the gluteal muscles (the muscles in the butt), which provide extension, abduction, and rotation; the adductor muscles, which initiate adduction; and the external rotators (the obturators, gemellus muscles, quadratus lumborum, and piriformis), which create external rotation (**Figure 11.2**). All of these muscles help to make the hip stable and allow for better quality of movement during gait.[2]

 Injuries of the Thigh

■ Femoral Fracture

A fracture of the femur is a very serious injury that must be properly stabilized to protect the thigh from further injury and damage. As with a knee dislocation, a femoral fracture threatens the femoral artery, vein, and nerve (the major neurovascular vessels for the entire lower extremity). Fractures of the femur are most often seen in automobile accidents as a result of the knees colliding

with the dashboard. They may occur in athletics, but it is quite rare.

The femur may fracture in one of several places: the shaft, the proximal head, or the neck of the bone. A shaft fracture is the most frequent bony injury found in the femur.[2]

SIGNS AND SYMPTOMS

1. Immediate high levels of pain
2. Crack or pop heard at onset of injury
3. Swelling and discoloration
4. Cannot bear weight
5. Hip may be externally rotated and adducted

TREATMENT

With a femoral fracture, the ends of the bones tend to move and overlap one another making the limb appear shorter than normal. Because of this overlapping, splinting of a femoral fracture should be conducted with a traction splint. The traction splint applies slight pressure in a distal motion to shift the fractured ends of the bone back into proper position. The traction splint helps to prevent further injury to the muscles and neurovascular vessels during transfer to the hospital. The distal neurovascular structures should be assessed both before and after the splint is applied to ensure that neither the injury nor the splint has compromised the arteries, veins, and nerves.

Immediate transport via ambulance should occur with referral to an orthopedic surgeon. Repair of the injury requires surgery to stabilize the bone in its appropriate alignment. The athlete should be monitored throughout his or her rehab to ensure that complications do not arise such as avascular necrosis, osteoarthritis, or neurovascular disorders. Return to play (RTP) will require initial immobilization to allow for recovery followed by 4 to 6 months of progressive rehabilitation.

■ Thigh Contusion

Thigh contusions most often occur as a result of direct contact to the quadriceps muscles. This injury is seen frequently in soccer, lacrosse, and football when an opponent's knee comes in contact with the thigh. The injury may cause a great deal of pain and dysfunction in the injured athlete.

In rare cases, the bleeding in the muscle is so severe that the circulation is compromised and an acute compartment syndrome of the thigh occurs. This is a medical emergency that requires surgery to cut the fascia (a dense connective tissue that surrounds the muscles) and relieve the pressure that is diminishing circulation. If the surgery is not performed, the athlete may lose his or her leg.

Another complication resulting from a thigh contusion is a condition known as myositis ossificans. Myositis ossificans is a calcification of the hematoma that develops from the initial contusion. If not treated properly, this mass will become a bony lump within the muscle belly. Once the myositis ossificans becomes bone, the only treatment option available is surgical removal of the mass.

SIGNS AND SYMPTOMS

1. Pain at affected site
2. Swelling and discoloration
3. Decreased range of motion (ROM), especially knee flexion
4. Difficulty with weight bearing
5. Stiffness developing over time

TREATMENT

Rest, ice, compression, and elevation (RICE) therapy should be offered post-injury. Best results are seen when the ice and compression are combined with knee flexion to stretch the muscle and limit the amount of swelling and loss of motion. As pain dissipates, the athlete should be treated with ice massage, friction massage, and stretching to break up any scar tissue and prevent myositis ossificans. If symptoms persist and a noticeable divot or lump appears, pulsed ultrasound and massage are effective tools to remove the early stages of myositis ossificans.

 Muscular Injuries

■ Quadriceps Strain

A strain of any of the quadriceps muscles (**Figure 11.3**) causes discomfort and disability for the athlete. Because the quadriceps play an integral role in normal gait patterns, it is difficult to participate fully after injuring these muscles. As with all strains, there are three grades of injury ranging from a slight pull (grade I) to a full thickness tear (grade III).

SIGNS AND SYMPTOMS

1. Pain at affected site
2. Swelling
3. Decreased ROM, especially knee/hip flexion
4. Decreased strength, especially knee extension/hip flexion
5. May palpate a divot in muscle with grade II or III strain

SPECIAL TESTS

For the *rectus femoris test*, the athlete is placed in a supine position with the legs hanging off the table at the knee.

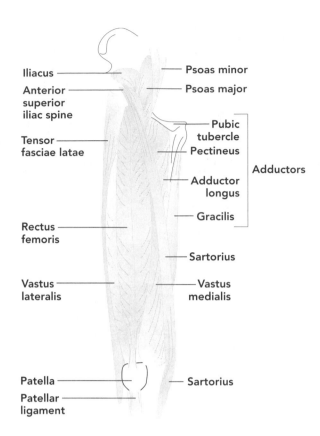

FIGURE 11.3 The quadricep muscles.

The uninvolved leg is brought up to the chest leaving the involved leg on the table with the knee bent and the lower leg hanging off. A positive test is indicated if the lower leg on the involved side extends on its own or the knee lifts off of the table. This test also may show rectus femoris tightness.[3]

The vastus muscles are collectively tested through a manual muscle test with the athlete seated on the table and moving the involved leg into resisted knee extension.

TREATMENT

Again, cold and electrical modality therapy immediately following injury is the best treatment, along with stretching of the quadriceps muscles (**Figure 11.4**). Grade II or III injuries may require immobilization and crutches (initial stretching would not be suggested with the more serious injuries). Strengthening activities may begin as symptoms decrease with an RTP following a successful progressive rehabilitation. A grade I strain may return to activity as quickly as 1 to 2 weeks; a grade II strain as soon as 2 to 4 weeks; and a grade III strain may return

FIGURE 11.4 Stretches for the quadricep muscles.

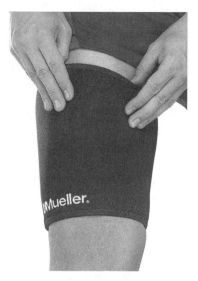

FIGURE 11.5 Thigh compression sleeve.

been properly warmed up or are not utilized very often (i.e., weekend warriors).

SIGNS AND SYMPTOMS

1. Pain in affected area
2. Decreased ROM in knee extension
3. Decreased strength in knee flexion
4. Swelling
5. May palpate a divot in grade II or III strains

SPECIAL TESTS

The *90-90 straight leg raise (SLR) test* is a measure of both flexibility and injury in the hamstrings. The patient is lying supine on a table with the hip and knee flexed to 90°. The athlete then extends the knee fully to a straight leg position. Test bilaterally to determine whether the athlete is unable

anywhere from 4 to 12 weeks depending on the severity and location of the tear. An elastic wrap or thigh sleeve (**Figure 11.5**) may assist in RTP by offering warmth, stability, and compression.

■ Hamstring Strain

Hamstring strains occur more often than quadriceps strains because the hamstrings (**Figure 11.6**) are a principal deceleration muscle group, which helps the body slow down from full speed. Deceleration from a high velocity may cause a muscle strain, especially in muscles that have not

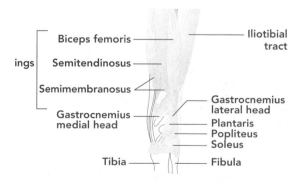

FIGURE 11.6 The hamstring muscles.

to extend as far on the involved side.[3] If there is pain with this maneuver, it is indicative of a muscle strain.

The examiner also may measure strength through a manual muscle test of the distal hamstring musculature. The athlete is seated on a table with his or her legs hanging off. The athlete then performs a knee flexion movement against resistance. The examiner tests bilaterally to determine a strength deficit.

To determine damage within the proximal muscle belly, have the athlete lie in a prone position and extend the hip against resistance provided by the examiner. The test may be conducted with either the knee in full extension or at 90° flexion. Testing bilaterally will assess if a strength deficit is present.

TREATMENT

RICE therapy with stretching is the most effective treatment for hamstring strains (**Figure 11.7**). As symptoms diminish, ice massage and massage may be useful to break up scar tissue. Progressive rehab will allow the athlete to return to play effectively. Recovery time for strains ranges from 1 to 2 weeks for a grade I strain, 2 to 4 weeks for a grade II, and 4 to 12 weeks for a grade III. An elastic wrap or thigh sleeve may assist in RTP by offering warmth, stability, and compression.

■ Tensor Fascia Latae Strain/ IT Band Tendinitis

The tensor fascia latae (TFL) extends distally to the knee, narrowing to become the IT band, and is a major component in hip abduction. The tensor fascia latae can be strained, causing pain at the hip with activity. The IT band also can develop chronic tendinitis that tends to present at the knee. Both injuries are treated similarly despite their different locations and mechanisms of injury.

FIGURE 11.7 Stretch for the hamstring muscles.

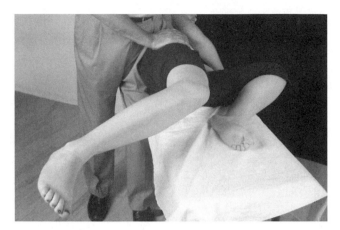

FIGURE 11.8 Ober's test.

SIGNS AND SYMPTOMS

1. Pain at affected site
2. Decreased ROM in abduction/adduction
3. Tightness at affected site

SPECIAL TESTS

The *Ober's test* (**Figure 11.8**) can assess either injury depending on where the symptoms develop. The athlete is placed in a side-lying position with the involved side facing up toward the examiner. The athletic trainer stabilizes the hip with one hand and uses the other hand to pull the thigh into slight extension so that the leg is past the edge of the table. The knee may be extended fully or flexed to 90° as part of this test—either position is effective in assessing the injury. The examiner's hand is positioned at the proximal end of the calf or knee and applies a downward force, moving the leg into adduction. A positive test is indicated if the leg does not adduct past parallel with the table or if the movement causes pain. The location of the pain determines which injury is present.[3]

The *Noble compression test* (**Figure 11.9**) is conducted in conjunction with Ober's test to evaluate IT band irritation at the knee. The athlete is placed in a supine position with the hip and knee flexed to 90°. The athlete slowly extends the hip and knee while the athletic trainer applies pressure over the lateral epicondyle of the femur. A positive test is indicated if the individual complains of moderate to severe pain as the knee moves to 30° flexion.[4]

TREATMENT

RICE therapy at the affected site will decrease any inflammation present. The athlete should stretch the injured area to increase ROM and flexibility using the same technique as that used for the Ober's test. The athlete can modify this stretch by standing while stabilized against the wall

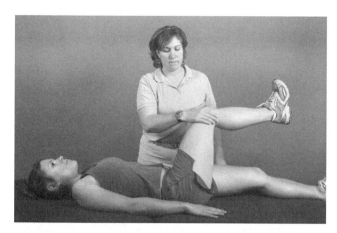

FIGURE 11.9 Noble compression test.

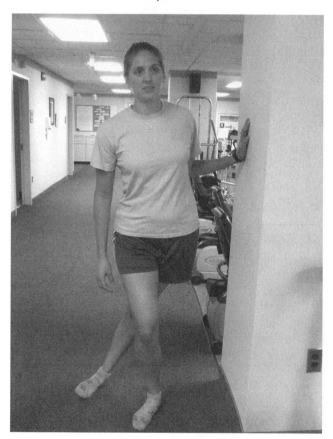

FIGURE 11.10 Stretch for the IT Band.

(**Figure 11.10**). The involved leg is crossed anteriorly or posteriorly to the other leg and then adducted as the athlete shifts laterally. Either stretch will decrease tightness and pain. Electrotherapy and massage may also be useful

> **osteoarthritis** Arthritis characterized by a degradation of the articular cartilage in a joint.

to decrease pain and inflammation. RTP may occur as symptoms dissipate.

 ## Injuries to the Hip/Pelvis

■ Hip Dislocation

A dislocation of the hip is very rare in athletics because of the stable bony structure, strong ligaments, and musculature found at the joint. Although uncommon, it is possible to encounter a hip dislocation in the athletic setting.

SIGNS AND SYMPTOMS

1. Extreme pain
2. Loss of any ROM at the hip
3. Athlete will be lying with the involved leg slightly flexed, adducted, and internally rotated

TREATMENT

Immediate transport via ambulance to the emergency room is required for reduction of the joint. Delayed treatment may complicate matters because the muscles contract and tighten around the joint. The physician and athletic trainer should evaluate the athlete consistently following injury to prevent complications such as sciatic nerve dysfunction, **osteoarthritis**, or avascular necrosis.[2] Recovery requires 2 to 3 months of rehab beginning with bed rest, immobilization, and crutches followed by progressive ROM exercises and strengthening.

Fast Fact

With a hip dislocation, one of the primary concerns is to avoid complications such as avascular necrosis, or death of the bone resulting from a loss of blood supply. Dislocations may require multiple surgeries or even a hip replacement if avascular necrosis occurs. Bo Jackson, a world-class athlete, famously suffered a hip dislocation during a football game. His injury ultimately led to avascular necrosis and required a hip replacement to correct. The injury ended his football career and severely limited his ability to play professional baseball, leading to his eventual retirement.

◼ Hip Pointer

A hip pointer is a general designation for a contusion to the iliac crest and the muscles that attach to the crest. This injury is very painful and causes disability and dysfunction in the athlete. Most often seen in contact sports such as football, basketball, soccer, or lacrosse, hip pointers can make walking difficult and full activity impossible for several days.

SIGNS AND SYMPTOMS

1. Extreme pain at iliac crest
2. Decreased ROM in hip flexion and abduction
3. Decreased strength
4. Discoloration over iliac crest

TREATMENT

Ice and compression are useful to decrease swelling and spasm within the muscle. Stretching, ice massage, and ultrasound may also decrease inflammation and facilitate healing. Relative rest is important for this injury, although the athlete may be able to complete alternative activities such as swimming or biking while they are unable to compete. RTP may occur as the muscular symptoms decrease and the athlete can bear weight and run without pain. A protective donut pad with an **orthoplast** shell placed on the athlete with an elastic wrap will help to prevent reinjury. The athlete should avoid contact, if possible, until symptoms resolve—usually 1 to 3 weeks.

Muscular Injuries

◼ Hip Flexor Strain

There are three primary hip flexor muscles: the iliacus and psoas major (which are collectively referred to as the iliopsoas muscle complex) and the rectus femoris. A strain may occur at any of these muscles, making hip flexion a painful movement.

SIGNS AND SYMPTOMS

1. Pain at affected site
2. Decreased ROM
3. Decreased strength

SPECIAL TESTS

The *Thomas test* (which should not be confused with the Thompson Test of the Achilles tendon) measures flex-

orthoplast A thermomoldable plastic used for casts and splints.

ibility and dysfunction at the hip. The athlete lies supine with both legs resting on the table. The uninvolved leg is brought to the chest and held there by the arms. A positive test is indicated by pain in the involved leg, as well as passive flexion and raising of the involved leg. The knee, and sometimes the lower leg, will no longer be touching the table in a positive test.[3]

The *rectus femoris test* also may be used with this injury, along with a *manual muscle test* of the hip flexors. In the manual muscle test, the athlete is seated on the table with the involved leg hanging off. The athlete attempts to raise the knee off the table (into hip flexion) against resistance. When tested bilaterally, the manual muscle test can assist in determining whether there are any strength deficits.

TREATMENT

RICE therapy and stretching are again useful for this injury. To stretch the hip flexor exclusively, have the athlete kneel on the involved knee while the other leg is positioned forward in a 90-90 position. The athlete should lean forward and then extend his or her back until a stretch is felt. Progressive rehab and strengthening help expedite recovery. RTP is similar to that seen with quadriceps or hamstring strains.

◼ Gluteals Strain

A strain of the gluteal muscles can be a very uncomfortable injury for the athlete both physically and mentally. It is difficult to treat an area that is considered extremely personal. Along with the groin area, an injury to the gluteal muscles requires the athletic trainer to act with added sensitivity and professionalism. A gluteals strain may occur as the result of a forceful movement into hip extension or rotation, causing those motions to be painful for the athlete.

SIGNS AND SYMPTOMS

1. Pain at affected site
2. Decreased ROM in abduction and rotation
3. Decreased strength

SPECIAL TESTS

The *Trendelenberg test* is useful in determining gluteus medius injuries or weaknesses specifically. The athlete stands with hands on hips and raises the uninvolved leg off of the ground. If the involved leg shifts downward at the hip, it is a positive indication of gluteus medius dysfunction.[3] Manual muscle testing of hip extension with the knee flexed to 90° is useful to evaluate the gluteal muscles. If pain and weakness are present, it is indicative of a muscle strain.

TREATMENT

RICE therapy should be conducted. The athlete may opt to sit on the ice to provide compression rather than utilize an elastic wrap. Progressive stretching and strengthening are also useful for recovery. To stretch the gluteal muscles, especially the gluteus medius, have the athlete sit on the floor and bring the involved knee toward the opposite shoulder.

Electrical modalities are difficult to utilize because of the placement of the injury. RTP timelines are similar to that of other strains.

■ Piriformis Strain

The piriformis muscle is the most well known of the external rotators in the hip. Tightness and strains are common in the piriformis because of a lack of routine stretching of the muscle by the majority of athletes.

SIGNS AND SYMPTOMS

1. Pain at affected site
2. Tightness in posterior hip
3. Hip may be externally rotated
4. Decreased strength

SPECIAL TESTS

FABER is an acronym for the motions associated with the piriformis muscle test: flexion, abduction, and external rotation are the movements at the hip that place the athlete in position to conduct the test. The *FABER test* also may be called the figure-4 test or the piriformis syndrome test. To perform the test, have the athlete lie supine on the table. The athlete then moves the involved leg into abduction and external rotation to rest the foot on the uninvolved knee. A positive test is indicated by an inability to rest the leg perpendicular to the uninvolved knee and parallel to the table. The positive test suggests tightness in the piriformis; pain with the motion would suggest a muscle strain. The athlete may also be tested with the hip and knee flexed to 90° and the uninvolved foot resting on the table.

TREATMENT

Treatment is similar to that used for a gluteal strain—RICE and stretching. The FABER test is effective as a stretch if you modify it to include bringing the uninvolved hip into flexion while the involved foot is still resting on the knee (**Figure 11.11**). This movement is an excellent stretch of the piriformis muscle. RTP can be very quick with proper stretching. This injury is rarely debilitating for the athlete.

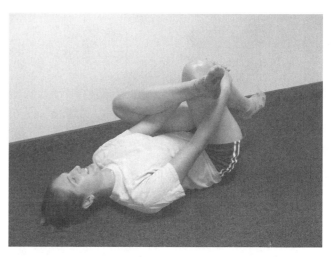

FIGURE 11.11   Stretch for the piriformis muscle.

■ Groin Strain

A groin strain is an injury to the adductor muscle group in the thigh. Groin strains are common injuries in athletics, especially in sports that incorporate regular side-to-side motions such as ice hockey, field hockey, lacrosse, and soccer. Groin strains may occur in conjunction with hip flexor strains or in isolation. Although it is a painful injury, recovery time may be quick if proper treatment is provided.

SIGNS AND SYMPTOMS

1. Pain at affected site
2. Decreased ROM in adduction
3. Decreased strength

SPECIAL TESTS

The best test for a groin strain is a *manual muscle test* of the adductors. Place the athlete in a side-lying position with the involved side closest to the table. The athlete then should attempt to adduct the injured leg against resistance to determine if any strength deficits are present. Pain in the groin area, or weakness compared to the uninvolved side, is indicative of a strain of the adductor muscle group.

An alternative test can be performed with the athlete seated on a table with both legs hanging off the edge at the knees. In this test, the examiner can measure both legs at the same time by resisting the athlete bringing the knees together.

TREATMENT

RICE therapy will decrease the athlete's initial symptoms. Strength, stretching, and balance training will benefit the

FIGURE 11.12 Stretch for the adductor muscles.

athlete in RTP (**Figure 11.12**). A slide board is a very effective therapeutic tool with groin strains because it specifically targets the adductor muscles. RTP time frames for a groin strain are similar to other muscle strains and are based on the degree of muscle damage caused by the injury.

Sacroiliac Joint Dysfunction

As mentioned earlier, numerous low-grade movements occur within the pelvis during normal gait and activity. This area can be very sensitive to excessive or extreme motions and forces, which can cause dysfunction and pain within the pelvis. The most frequent site of pelvic dysfunction is found at the sacroiliac (SI) joints on either side of the sacrum. During movements, the sacrum and the ilia flex, extend, and rotate slightly to allow proper gait. Many times, something as simple as a sneeze or awkward rotation may alter the alignment of the SI joints, which can cause pain and dysfunction with walking or running. Other issues, such as leg length discrepancies or foot malalignment, can cause chronic SI dysfunction in an athlete. SI injuries cause consistent pain for the athlete, which compromises his or her ability to compete at an optimal level.

SIGNS AND SYMPTOMS
1. Pain in low back and butt (specifically one side of the body versus the other)
2. Decreased ROM as a result of pain and dysfunction
3. Pain may increase with activity
4. Possible shooting pain into the thigh

hernia A protrusion of a part or structure through the tissues that typically contain it.

SPECIAL TESTS

For the *Yeoman's test*, the athlete is placed in a prone position. The examiner places one hand on the injured side at the ankle and the other hand under the involved knee. The knee then is flexed to 90° and the hip is extended. The test should be conducted bilaterally. A positive test is indicated by pain that increases with hip extension. SI joint dysfunction causes the pain to localize over the involved SI joint.[3]

The patient in the *flamingo test* stands in a comfortable position and raises one leg off of the ground so that all weight bearing is on the opposite leg. The test is repeated with the other leg raised. A positive test is indicated by pain in the involved extremity localized in the SI joint or pubis symphysis—the site of the injury.[3]

The *stork test* is similar to the flamingo test except that the athlete extends his or her back while standing on one foot. A positive test is indicated by pain localized to the injury site. The stork test incorporates the lumbar spine into the assessment; a positive test that localizes pain in the lumbar region can be indicative of a possible stress fracture in the spine.[3]

TREATMENT

RICE therapy can decrease pain and any inflammation that may be present but will not alleviate the cause of the symptoms. Referral to a physician for X-rays will help to rule out possible fractures. Muscle energy techniques, pelvic stabilization and strengthening, and correcting any underlying issues (such as leg length or foot malalignments) all help to alleviate current and potential SI dysfunction. RTP is dependent on the athlete's pain tolerance and level of dysfunction.

Hidden Injuries

Because of the vast number of interconnected muscles, ligaments, and bones in the hip and pelvis, it often is very difficult to pinpoint exactly what may be causing the athlete's pain and dysfunction. It is essential for the athletic trainer to maintain an open mind when evaluating hip/groin/pelvis injuries because there may be hidden injuries or uncommon issues present. An athlete with hip/groin/pelvis pain could be suffering from any number of injuries including stress fractures, avulsion fractures, muscle tears, **hernias**, internal organ illnesses or damage, cancer/tumors, or many other injuries and illnesses that may cause pain to localize in this region.

If an athlete does not respond to traditional treatment and rehabilitation, an athletic trainer should not hesitate to refer the athlete to a physician to rule out these other possibilities. Specialists only can identify some issues through blood work, diagnostic tests, or thorough evaluations. In the hip/pelvis region, the examiner should not have too narrow a focus.

CHAPTER REVIEW

1. What is the longest bone in the body?
2. *True* or *False*: Several muscles act at the pelvis to move the sacroiliac joints anteriorly and posteriorly.
3. What complications may result from a thigh contusion?
4. Which injury is assessed with the Thomas test?
5. In which sports are groin strains frequently seen?

CRITICAL THINKING

How would you differentiate between pelvic issues and low back injuries such as fractures or disc herniations?

REFERENCES

1. Greenman PE. *Principles of Manual Medicine*, 3rd ed. Baltimore: Lippincott, Williams, & Wilkins, 2003.
2. Prentice WE. *Arnheim's Principles of Athletic Training: A Competency-Based Approach*, 12th ed. Boston: McGraw-Hill, 2006.
3. Magee DJ. *Orthopedic Physical Assessment*, 4th ed. Philadelphia: W. B. Saunders, 2002.
4. Anderson MK, Hall SJ, Martin M. *Sports Injury Management*, 2nd ed. Baltimore: Lippincott, Williams, & Wilkins, 2000.

Upper Body Evaluation

The Spine and Torso

The torso is the largest and most complex anatomic structure discussed in this text. The torso runs from the pelvis to the neck and encompasses the entire chest and **thorax** region. Injuries in this area can range from irritating (muscle strains) to life threatening (spinal cord injuries or cervical spine fractures). This chapter is separated into two sections: (1) the spine and (2) the torso. Anatomy, specific injuries, and treatment options for these regions are described in this chapter.

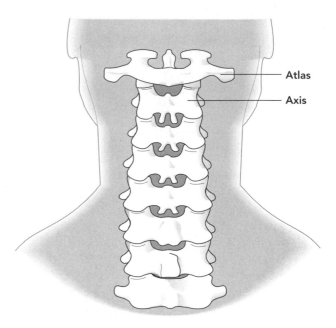

FIGURE 12.1 Anatomy of the cervical spine.

 ## Anatomy of the Spine

The spinal cord is a direct neural link from the brain to all parts of the body. The spinal cord runs through the spinal column and branches into nerve shoots that innervate all of the muscle and tissue in the body. The principal role of the spinal column is protection of the spinal cord from damage. Injury to the spinal cord can be catastrophic, even fatal.

The spine is divided into three regions: cervical, thoracic, and lumbar. Spinal segments are numbered superiorly to inferiorly. The **cervical spine** is the section closest to the skull and provides the neck with a wide range of motion without compromising the spinal cord (**Figure 12.1**). Seven vertebrae comprise the cervical spine. The vertebrae are abbreviated C1 through C7.

Vertebrae C1 and C2 are unique from other vertebrae because they cooperatively support the skull while also

allowing the neck and head to rotate left and right. The C1 vertebra is labeled the atlas because it supports the skull during motion and allows flexion and extension through its articulations with the skull. The atlas contains an opening large enough to allow the medulla (brainstem) to pass through without any compression during motion. The C2 vertebra is named the axis because its primary role is to allow the skull to rotate left and right. The movement of these two vertebrae permits the head and neck to have the range of motion needed during daily activities and athletics.[1,2]

The **thoracic spine** is located directly inferior to the cervical spine and is composed of 12 vertebrae (T1 to T12). These vertebrae protect the spinal cord and also work in conjunction with the ribs (which connect posteriorly to the thoracic spine) to protect the major internal organs in the chest and torso.

The **lumbar spine** is the lowest of the spinal regions and connects the thoracic spine to the pelvis (**Figure 12.2**). Five vertebrae articulate to form the lumbar spine (L1 to L5). The primary role of this region is support and stability of the upper body during standing and activity.

Vertebrae connect to each other through **facet joints** and intervertebral discs. Facets are protrusions from the vertebrae that both allow and restrict motion as needed. The **intervertebral disc (Figure 12.3)** is a sack of fluid and cartilage that lies between the vertebrae. These discs provide a cushion for shock absorption, as well as increase the range of motion of the spine.

---

thorax The chest or torso region of the body consisting of the thoracic vertebrae, the rib cage, and the muscles and organs found within.

cervical spine The most superior aspect of the spinal column. There are seven vertebrae in the cervical spine that support the head and provide for its range of motion.

thoracic spine The middle aspect of the spinal column. There are 12 vertebrae in the thoracic spine that provide shock absorption and support for the torso.

lumbar spine The most inferior aspect of the spinal column. There are five vertebrae in the lumbar spine that provide shock absorption and support during gait.

facet joints Smooth areas of the vertebra that guide and limit motion in the spinal column.

intervertebral disc A fibrocartilage structure found between the vertebrae to improve motion and shock absorption.

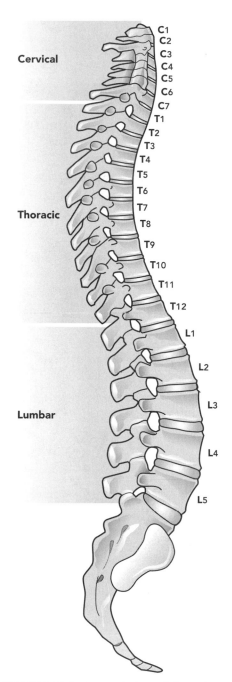

FIGURE 12.2 Lateral view of the spine.

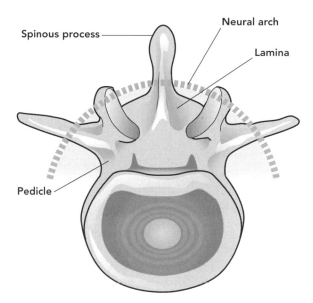

FIGURE 12.3 Anatomy of the vertebra and intervertebral disk.

the erector spinae and paraspinal muscles. The deep spinal muscles are the splenius and multifidus. The spinal muscles work in unison to provide range of motion for the spinal region, especially extension and rotation.[3]

■ Dermatomes and Myotomes

The nerves that branch off of the spinal cord in the cervical and lumbar spine directly innervate the muscles in the upper and lower body, respectively. These neural branches are responsible for both motion and sensation in specific muscles. Neural branches provide sensory innervations (**dermatomes**) and motor innervations (**myotomes**). The cervical and lumbar dermatomes and myotomes are listed in **Table 12.1**.

■ Functional Anatomy

The spine is an engineering marvel. Examination of the spinal column from the side reveals an S shape. The cervical spine has a slight anterior curve, and then the thoracic spine curves back posteriorly before the lumbar spine adjusts anteriorly again. This curvature provides the appropriate shock absorption for gait; provides flexion, extension, side bending, and rotation as required; and

The muscles surrounding the spine (**Figure 12.4**) are responsible for stabilization of the torso, back extension, and rotation. The trapezius and latissimus dorsi are the muscles most often associated with the back but are discussed in the thorax section because of their function during trunk and extremity movement.

The spinal muscles are divided into two groups: superficial and deep. The superficial spinal muscles are

dermatomes The area of skin and its sensation that is supplied by a single spinal nerve.

myotomes The muscles that are innervated by a single spinal nerve.

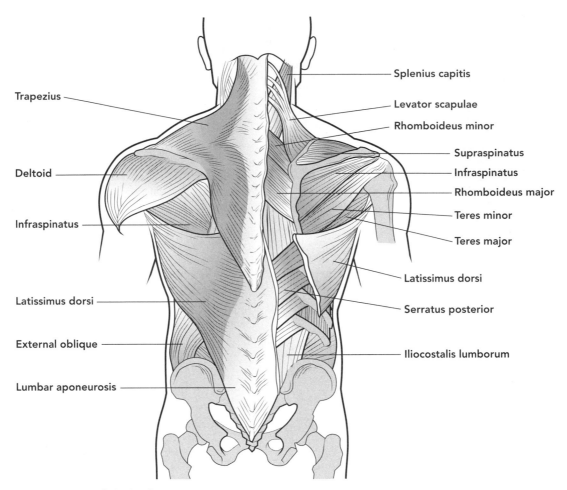

FIGURE 12.4 Musculature of the back.

offers the neck range of motion needed for activities of daily living.[3]

The curve of the spine is unique to each and every person in some small manner. The activities of the individual help to determine what adaptations are needed to provide the optimal spinal curvature for that person. However, malalignments in the curve also may develop as a result of injury or an adaptation to other issues such as leg length discrepancies or weak musculature. For instance, the thoracic spine may curve excessively posterior, creating a **kyphosis**, or hump-backed spine. The lumbar spine may develop alignment dysfunction

> **kyphosis** An excessive posterior alignment of the thoracic spine.
> **lordosis** An excessive anterior alignment of the lumbar spine.
> **scoliosis** An excessive lateral alignment of the spinal column.

by curving too far anteriorly and creating **lordosis**, or the spine may have a decreased curve resulting in a flat back appearance.[1]

The curve of the spine can occasionally shift laterally causing the individual to develop a scoliotic spine. **Scoliosis** is a lateral S shape of the spine, when viewed posteriorly, that may be caused by functional or structural abnormalities.

Lumbar pain is one of the most general complaints in both athletes and nonathletes alike. The forces traveling through this region can cause acute and chronic trauma to the muscles and bones, which results in all manner of lower back pain.

Anatomy of the Torso

The torso, for text purposes, consists of the chest and upper body ranging from the neck to the pelvis. The thorax is

TABLE 12.1

CERVICAL AND LUMBAR DERMATOMES AND MYOTOMES

Upper Extremity

Nerve Root	Dermatome	Myotome	Action
C1	Vertex of skull	None	Neck flexion
C2	Temple, forehead, occiput	Longus colli, sternocleidomastoid, rectus capitis	Neck flexion
C3	Entire neck, posterior cheek, and temporal area	Trapezius, splenius capitis	Neck side flexion
C4	Shoulder, clavicular, and upper scapular areas	Trapezius, levator scapulae	Shoulder elevation
C5	Deltoid area and anterior aspect of entire arm to base of thumb	Supraspinatus, infraspinatus, deltoid, and biceps	Shoulder abduction
C6	Anterior arm, radial side of hand and thumb and index finger	Biceps, supinator, wrist extensors	Elbow flexion and wrist extension
C7	Lateral arm and forearm to index, long, and ring fingers	Triceps, wrist flexors	Elbow extension and wrist flexion
C8	Medial arm and forearm to long, ring, and little fingers	Ulnar deviators, thumb extensors, thumb adductors	Thumb extension and ulnar deviation
T1	Medial side of forearm to base of little finger	None	Finger abduction/adduction
T2	Medial side of upper arm to medial elbow, pectoral and midscapular areas	None	None

Lower Extremity

Nerve Root	Dermatome	Myotome	Action
L1	Back, over trochanter and groin	None	None
L2	Back, front of thigh to knee	Psoas major, hip adductors	Hip flexion
L3	Back, upper buttock, anterior thigh and knee, medial lower leg	Psoas major, quadriceps	Knee extension
L4	Medial buttock, lateral thigh, medial leg, dorsum of foot, big toe	Tibialis anterior, extensor hallucis	Ankle dorsiflexion
L5	Buttock, posterior and lateral thigh, lateral aspect of leg, dorsum of foot, medial half of sole, first, second, and third toes	Extensor hallucis, peroneals, gluteus medius, dorsiflexors	Toe extension
S1	Buttock, thigh, and posterior leg	Gluteals, peroneals, plantar flexors	Ankle plantar flexion and eversion
S2	Same as S1	Same as S1 except peroneals	Same as S1
S3	Groin, medial thigh to knee	None	None
S4	Perineum, genitals, lower sacrum	Bladder, rectum	None

primarily composed of the rib cage and the muscles that flex and extend the spine and upper body. The internal organs found within the rib cage also are considered part of the torso but are discussed in a later chapter.

The rib cage (**Figure 12.5**) is composed of 12 sets of ribs. The superior 10 sets of ribs wrap around the chest and articulate with the sternum anteriorly and the thoracic vertebrae posteriorly. The inferior two sets of

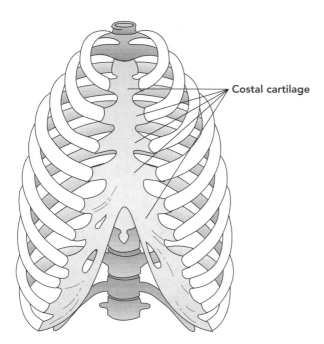

Costal cartilage

FIGURE 12.5   Anatomy of the rib cage.

ribs (number 11 and number 12) are called floating ribs because they attach only to the thoracic vertebrae with no anterior attachments. The rib cage is responsible for the protection of internal organs and assists the lungs in respiration.[3]

The sternum, found at the proximal aspect of the rib cage, is a flat bone that operates as the anterior connection for the ribs. The sternum provides added protection to the heart and allows the ribs to move properly. The sternum tapers into the xiphoid process at its distal end. The xiphoid process is an important anatomic landmark during cardiopulmonary resuscitation (CPR).

The muscles of the torso vary from large major muscle groups to smaller accessory muscles. The trapezius and latissimus dorsi compose the major muscles in the posterior region of the torso. The pectoralis muscles in the chest and the abdominal muscles in the abdomen are the primary anterior torso muscles. Numerous intercostals muscles within the rib cage are accessory muscles that assist in respiration. The diaphragm also is found within the rib cage and is an important muscular component in both breathing and vocalizing.

 ## Injuries of the Spine

■ Cervical and Thoracic Spinal Fractures

A spinal fracture can occur in any vertebra in the spine; however, cervical and thoracic fractures are rarely seen in athletics. Cervical fractures are very dangerous injuries because of the increased risk for potentially life-threatening spinal cord damage and **paralysis**. The extent of paralysis is dependent upon the vertebra fractured, the level of the spinal cord injured/severed, and the damage to the cord. Spinal fractures are almost always very traumatic for the athlete and athletic trainer because of potential life-threatening and sports career-ending consequences.

SIGNS AND SYMPTOMS

1. Pain and tenderness at affected site
2. Restricted range of motion (ROM)
3. Numbness and tingling
4. Weakness in extremities
5. Possible paralysis

TREATMENT

Immediate head, neck, and spine stabilization and immobilization is mandatory for spinal fractures. The slightest movement after injury can potentially increase spinal cord damage and lead to paralysis or death. The athlete must be immobilized with a cervical collar, spine boarded, and transported to a hospital for X-rays to rule out a fracture. Time and care should be taken in the treatment of this injury to avoid any further damage. Rehabilitation will be dictated by the severity and extent of the damage.

■ Lumbar Spinal Fractures

The most common fractures in the spine are in the lumbar region. However, this type of lumbar injury is more often seen in automobile accidents than in athletics.[1] Lumbar vertebrae fractures can cause spinal cord damage and lead to lower extremity paralysis. The two types of lumbar fractures seen in athletics are compression fractures and process fractures.[1]

Compression Fractures

The compression fracture results from severe hyperflexion of the trunk. This motion crushes the anterior portion of the vertebra between the vertebrae above and below the injury site.

SIGNS AND SYMPTOMS

1. Pain at injury site
2. Possible neural symptoms if bone chips damage the spinal cord
3. Slight swelling and discoloration
4. Muscle spasm

paralysis Loss of voluntary movement in a muscle or region of the body as a result of injury or disease.

TREATMENT

The athlete should be referred to a physician for X-rays. If the athlete is suffering from acute neurological (radicular) symptoms, he or she should be spine boarded and transported to a hospital to prevent further spinal cord damage. Return to play (RTP) will depend on the severity of the injury.

Process Fractures

Each vertebra has a spinous process that protrudes posteriorly and two transverse processes that protrude laterally. Any one of these processes can be fractured. These injuries most often occur as a result of direct trauma to the affected area. Process fractures do not place the athlete in immediate danger of neurological complications but must be evaluated appropriately to determine proper treatment.

SIGNS AND SYMPTOMS

1. Pain at injury site
2. Slight swelling and discoloration
3. Muscle spasm

TREATMENT

The athlete should be referred to a physician and X-rays taken to rule out a fracture. The athlete is characteristically cleared for limited activity within his or her pain tolerance following the appointment. The athlete should avoid contact while pain persists. A lumbar brace may assist the athlete in RTP.

■ Spondylolysis/Spondylolisthesis

Spondylolysis and spondylolisthesis often are jointly referred to as a "spondy" injury. Both occur as a result of chronic degeneration of the lumbar vertebrae, specifically a pars defect on the facet of the vertebra.[4] These injuries are frequently seen in offensive linemen in football and in gymnasts because of the repetitive spinal hyperextension motions seen in these specific athletes.

Both injuries display similar symptoms—the primary difference between the two is vertebral shifting. There is no shifting of the vertebral body with a **spondylolysis**, whereas the vertebra shifts anteriorly in comparison to

---

spondylolysis Degeneration or fracture of the pars articularis of a spinal vertebra.

spondylolisthesis Forward movement of a spinal vertebra resulting from a fracture or degeneration of the pars articularis.

core stabilization A series of exercises that focus on the core muscles of the abdomen and lower back.

---

its neighboring vertebrae with a **spondylolisthesis**. The spondylolisthesis is most often a result of a previous spondylolysis injury. Most of these injuries occur between the fifth lumbar vertebra and the sacrum.[4]

SIGNS AND SYMPTOMS

1. Mild to moderate pain, especially during hyperextension and after activity
2. Increased pain with prolonged sitting or standing
3. Weakness or fatigue in lumbar area

TREATMENT

The athlete should be seen by a physician for X-rays to determine whether a spondylolysis or spondylolisthesis is present. The athlete should wear a lumbar brace during activity to decrease symptoms. Activity should be reduced and gradually returned to normal as symptoms allow. **Core stabilization** and lumbar strengthening exercises should be incorporated to prevent reinjury.

Core stabilization and strengthening (**Figure 12.6**) consists of exercises that focus on the musculature of the trunk area: the abdominal muscles, the hip musculature, and the lumbar musculature. Hundreds of exercises can be incorporated in an individual strengthening program. The athletic trainer should evaluate each athlete to determine his or her weaknesses and which muscles should be emphasized in a core-strengthening program.

■ Cervical Sprain

Cervical sprains are generally referred to as whiplash. This injury can be very painful because it often restricts neck motion. A cervical sprain often occurs as a result of the head quickly snapping forward and then backward. This snapping motion is seen during a tackle or contact when the player is not prepared for direct trauma. Cervical sprains often are accompanied by muscle strains and spasms.

FIGURE 12.6 Core strengthening.

Fast Fact

A spondylolysis (**Figure 12.7**) is less obvious during X-ray examination than is the spondylolisthesis (**Figure 12.8**), which has obvious displacement. However, when the X-ray is taken at a posterior oblique angle, it becomes more overt. In this X-ray image, each vertebra takes on the look of a "Scotty dog," or Scottish terrier, with the head facing the vertebral body. A spondylolysis is present if the injured vertebra has a collar on the Scotty dog, which indicates a fracture in the pars.

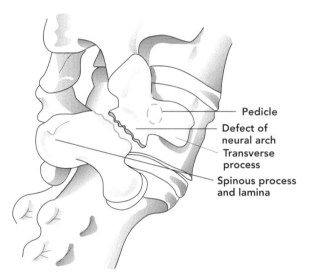

Pedicle
Defect of neural arch
Transverse process
Spinous process and lamina

FIGURE 12.7   Spondylolysis.

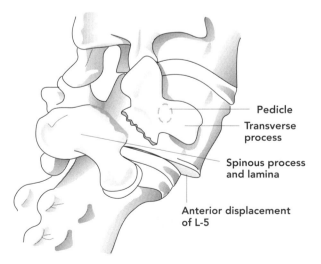

Pedicle
Transverse process
Spinous process and lamina
Anterior displacement of L-5

FIGURE 12.8   Spondylolisthesis.

SIGNS AND SYMPTOMS

1. Pain throughout neck
2. Significant decrease in ROM
3. Muscle spasm

TREATMENT

A physician should evaluate severe injuries to rule out cervical fractures. Symptoms usually decrease in 2 to 3 days. Rest, ice, compression, and elevation (RICE) therapy help decrease pain and muscle spasm. Light stretching and massage increase ROM.

■ Paraspinal Strain

The paraspinal muscles may be strained by forced flexion or rotation of the spine. The injury can be painful and may make standing erect or breathing deeply difficult for the athlete.

SIGNS AND SYMPTOMS

1. Pain just lateral to the spine
2. Pain with back extension and rotation
3. Muscle spasm
4. Slight swelling

SPECIAL TESTS

A *manual muscle test* of the paraspinal muscles assists in the evaluation. Have the athlete lie prone on a table while the examiner places both hands at the shoulders and resists back extension. Pain along the lateral edges of the spine and obvious muscle spasm are positive indicators.

TREATMENT

RICE therapy with electrical stimulation can reduce pain and spasm. Muscle strengthening and core stabilization will allow the athlete to return to play with minimal complications. Recovery time is dependent on the severity of injury.

■ Lumbar Sprain/Strain

Lumbar sprains and strains are extremely common in athletics and are primary causes of lower back pain. Forced flexion, extension, or rotation may cause an injury to the supporting and stabilizing ligaments or muscles.

SIGNS AND SYMPTOMS

1. Pain localized over injury site
2. Muscle spasm
3. Increased pain in certain motions or positions
4. Decreased ROM

TREATMENT

RICE therapy helps decrease pain and muscle spasm in both sprains and strains. Stretching and strengthening exercises are useful to assist in recovery from muscle strains, whereas a strengthening program only is suggested for sprains. A lumbar brace may allow for a faster RTP by providing added protection and stabilization for the injured area. Recovery time is the same as with any other sprain or strain. RTP may occur as symptoms diminish and strength returns.

■ Intervertebral Disc Injury

The intervertebral discs of the spine assist in movement and perform as shock absorbers during gait and activity. There is a potential for damage to the outer shell of the disc (**annulus fibrosis**) or the fluid and material found within (**nucleus pulposus**) because of the forces placed upon them. Injuries to the intervertebral discs occur most frequently in the cervical and lumbar spine.

Several levels of herniation can occur in the intervertebral disc (**Figure 12.9**). If the nucleus of the disc has torn through the annulus—its protective barrier—the injury is known as a **prolapsed disc**. When the nucleus and the intact annulus protrude into the spinal canal and affect a nerve root, the injury is called an **extruded disc**. If the nucleus material separates from the disc and begins to migrate from its traditional position, it is a **sequestrated disc**.[1]

Either repetitive forces or traumatic axial forces loaded onto the neck, most often in contact sports, can cause cervical disc injuries. Lumbar disc injuries can be caused by faulty body mechanics, trauma, or both, and can lead to degeneration of the disc. The discs between the fourth and fifth lumbar vertebrae (L4–L5) and between the fifth

vertebra and the sacrum (L5–S1) are the most frequent sites of injury in the lumbar spine.

SIGNS AND SYMPTOMS

1. Sharp pain over the affected disc
2. Decreased ROM
3. Pain increasing with flexion and decreasing with extension
4. **Radicular pain**
5. Muscle weakness associated with the specific myotome that is compressed

SPECIAL TESTS

For the *valsalva maneuver test*, the athlete is placed in a seated position and asked to hold his or her breath and bear down as if conducting a bowel movement. This force increases pressure in the intervertebral spaces. A positive test

---

annulus fibrosis The outer fibrocartilaginous layer of an intervertebral disc.

nucleus pulposus The interior substance of an intervertebral disc. The jelly-like material provides shock absorption and increased range of motion in the spine.

prolapsed disc Pressure from the nucleus propulsus that pushes the annulus fibrosis outward toward the spinal canal.

extruded disc A tearing of the annulus fibrosis and movement of the nucleus propulsus into the spinal canal.

sequestrated disc When fragments of the annulus fibrosis and nucleus propulsus break off and move into the spinal canal.

radicular pain Pain that radiates along the dermatome of a nerve following injury or damage to that nerve.

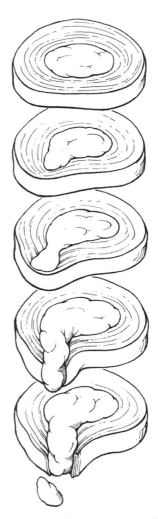

FIGURE 12.9 Injuries to the intevertebral disc.
Source: © 1993 American Academy of Orthopedic Surgeons. Reprinted with permission from the *Journal of the American Academy of Orthopedic Surgeons*, 1(1):33–40.

is indicated if the pain increases at the injury site during the test and decreases once normal breathing has resumed.[3]

TREATMENT

Conservative treatment with joint immobilization may decrease the symptoms and allow the injury to heal. Lumbar disc injuries often benefit from **Mackenzie exercises**, which consist of various extension movements of the lumbar spine. These exercises occasionally force the nuclear material back within the fibrous tissue and help to resolve the symptoms.

If symptoms do not diminish with conservative treatment, a physician may suggest steroid injections, or epidural treatment, to reduce pain and dysfunction. Surgical intervention may be required if symptoms do not resolve. RTP guidelines are based on the pain and dysfunction level of the athlete. Early return to activity may exacerbate the degenerative condition and increase pain and dysfunction.

Injuries to the Torso

■ Rib Fracture/Contusion

The ribs are extremely vulnerable to injury because of their placement in the torso and the large amount of surface area they protect. A direct blow to the ribs can cause a fracture or a contusion of the bone. Rib injuries are seen frequently in collision sports such as ice hockey, football, and lacrosse. This injury can occur at one rib or in several ribs depending on the placement and size of the object that contacts the ribs. A fracture of three or more consecutive ribs on the same side causes a **flail chest**, which can lead to breathing difficulties and other serious injuries.

SIGNS AND SYMPTOMS

1. Moderate to severe pain over injured site (fractures cause the highest level of pain)
2. Pain increases with inhalation
3. Possible swelling and discoloration
4. Possible crepitus at fracture site

Mackenzie exercises A series of exercises that focus on extension of the spine.

flail chest A fracture of three or more ribs in two or more places that causes an aspect of the chest wall to detach and act on its own.

costochondritis An inflammation of the costal cartilage found between the ribs.

SPECIAL TESTS

For the *bucket handle test*, the athlete is placed in a comfortable position either standing or sitting. The examiner places his or her hands on either side of the chest (preferably not directly over the injury site) and squeezes the ribs toward the midline. A positive test is indicated by a dramatic increase in pain. Obvious fractures or deformities should not be tested for the athlete's sake.[3]

TREATMENT

If you are concerned that the athlete may have a rib fracture, the athlete should be referred to a physician for X-rays. Conservative treatment with ice, rest, and a rib brace diminish symptoms. The rib brace (**Figure 12.10**) provides support and stability to the fracture and allows for more comfortable breathing. The athlete may choose to continue wearing the brace after returning to activity, although it can cause breathing difficulties during play.

An alternative for competition is called a flack jacket, which provides protection in the form of a padded vest and does not restrict breathing. RTP is dependent on the athlete's pain tolerance and level of contact seen during activity. One to 3 weeks is a normal recovery time for a RTP with protection; however, some injuries require 6 to 8 weeks.

■ Costochondral Sprain

Costal cartilage is a fibrous structure that surrounds and connects the upper 10 ribs to themselves and to the sternum. The cartilage assists in maintaining the proper position of the ribs and controlling motion. Injury to this tissue occurs more often in athletics than rib fractures do. The cartilage can be damaged by a direct blow or through a forcible twisting motion that involuntarily separates the ribs. A costochondral sprain (**costochondritis**) causes pain at the rib and costal cartilage interface.

SIGNS AND SYMPTOMS

1. Moderate to severe pain over injury site, typically in the space between the ribs
2. Pain increases with inhalation
3. Possible swelling and discoloration
4. Possible crepitus with breathing

TREATMENT

The treatment for a costochondral sprain is the same as for rib fractures. Ice, rest, and a rib brace can help to decrease pain and improve breathing ability. RTP is dependent on the athlete's pain tolerance and level of contact associated with his or her sport. A recovery time of 1 to 3 weeks is possible with rib protection. More severe injuries may require 6 to 8 weeks to heal.

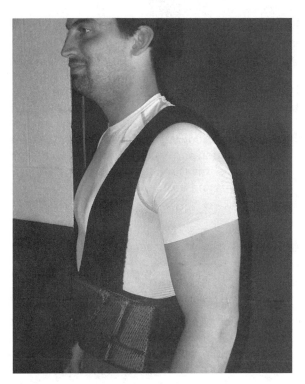

FIGURE 12.10 Protective rib brace.

■ Sternal Contusion/Fracture

A fracture of the sternum is rare, but possible, in athletics. The injury requires a hard impact directly to the center of the chest. Damage to the organs under the sternum, including the heart and lungs, is a major concern because of the great force necessary to fracture the sternum.[1]

SIGNS AND SYMPTOMS

1. Severe pain
2. Pain increases with breathing
3. Possible swelling and discoloration
4. Possible crepitus at fracture site

TREATMENT

Immediate referral to a physician is required to rule out internal injuries. RTP is dependent on any underlying internal damage that occurs. Eight to 12 weeks is not an uncommon recovery time; some athletes require more healing time, depending on severity of injury.

■ Pectoralis Strain

Strains of the pectoralis major and pectoralis minor muscles are very frequent athletic injuries, especially during strength training sessions involving bench press or flies. This injury can cause the athlete some discomfort but is rarely a serious concern.

SIGNS AND SYMPTOMS

1. Pain at injury site
2. Decreased ROM
3. Decreased strength

SPECIAL TESTS

An evaluation should include a *manual muscle test* of the pectoralis muscles. Have the athlete lay in a supine position with arms resting at shoulder level in 90° abduction. The athlete's elbow may or may not be bent depending on comfort. The examiner resists the athlete as the arm horizontally adducts. Compare bilaterally to determine whether strength deficits are present.

TREATMENT

Cold and electrical modality therapy will help to reduce the athlete's symptoms. Decreasing lifting weight or performing alternate lifts during strength training will allow the muscles to heal. RTP can occur immediately depending on the level of dysfunction for the athlete and the severity of the strain.

■ Abdominal Strain

The muscles in the abdominal wall can be irritated or strained with overloading trunk flexion, forced trunk extension, hyperextension, or rotation. The injury can cause the athlete moderate pain and dysfunction. Until they are injured, many athletes are not aware of how often they utilize abdominal muscles in normal gait and activity. These strains are uncomfortable injuries for athletes and can require a longer recovery than other muscle strains do.

SIGNS AND SYMPTOMS

1. Pain at injury site
2. Decreased ROM
3. Decreased strength

SPECIAL TESTS

A *manual muscle test* should be performed to determine the level of strength deficit. For the abdominal muscles, resisting the athlete during a sit-up, crunch, or trunk rotation to the affected side will measure the athlete's strength.

TREATMENT

Ice and rest can benefit the athlete. Progressive rehabilitation involving core stabilization will assist in return to activity. Recovery may take longer than it does for other muscle strains and is dependent on the severity of injury. An RTP of 1 to 4 weeks is a typical range for this injury.

■ Trapezius Strain

The trapezius muscle has the look of a kite with four triangular divisions all connecting at different levels of the spine. The trapezius is responsible for shoulder shrugs, shoulder horizontal abduction, and scapular movements. A strain may occur in any of the four quadrants and can cause dysfunction in several shoulder and upper back movements.

SIGNS AND SYMPTOMS

1. Pain at injury site in upper back
2. Decreased ROM
3. Decreased strength in affected movements

SPECIAL TESTS

Manual muscle tests of the affected motions should be conducted to determine strength deficits. The movements to be tested are determined by the quadrant that is injured. The upper quadrants of the trapezius elevate the shoulders, rotate the scapula upward, and retract the scapula medially. The lower quadrants depress the shoulders, rotate the scapula downward, and retract the scapula medially.[2]

TREATMENT

Trapezius strains should be treated the same as other muscle injuries. A stretching and progressive strengthening program should follow RICE and conservative therapy. RTP is possible as strength is regained and symptoms diminish. The recovery time is dependent on the severity of the injury and follows the same guidelines as other muscle strains, ranging from 1 to 2 weeks for a grade I strain, 2 to 4 weeks for a grade II, and 4 to 12 weeks for a grade III.

■ Latissimus Dorsi Strain

The latissimus dorsi looks similar to a V that is tapered from the bottom resting on the pelvis to a narrow tip attaching to each shoulder. The latissimus is responsible for shoulder adduction and external rotation and lumbar extension. The latissimus is often injured through forced lumbar movements and during strength training.

SIGNS AND SYMPTOMS

1. Pain at injury site in lower back
2. Decreased ROM
3. Decreased strength

SPECIAL TESTS

A *manual muscle test* for the latissimus dorsi consists of placing the athlete in a seated position with 90° shoulder abduction and 90° elbow flexion. The examiner resists the athlete by placing his or her hands at the elbows bilaterally. The athlete then adducts his or her arms toward the body.

TREATMENT

Conservative therapy followed by stretching and strengthening decreases symptoms and allows the athlete to return to play. Recovery time is similar to that seen with other muscle strains.

CHAPTER REVIEW

1. What are alternate names for the first and second cervical vertebrae?
2. Define kyphosis and lordosis.
3. What is the difference between a spondylolysis and a spondylolisthesis?
4. Why are the intervertebral discs important?
5. What tissue is found between the ribs?
6. What are the two primary muscles in the posterior torso?

CRITICAL THINKING

What would you do to remain calm during a spinal cord injury?

REFERENCES

1. Prentice WE. *Arnheim's Principles of Athletic Training: A Competency-Based Approach*, 12th ed. Boston: McGraw-Hill, 2006.
2. Booher JM, Thibodeau GA. *Athletic Injury Assessment*, 4th ed. Boston: McGraw-Hill, 2000.
3. Magee DJ. *Orthopedic Physical Assessment*, 4th ed. Philadelphia: W. B. Saunders, 2002.
4. Moore KL, Dalley AF. *Clinically Oriented Anatomy*, 5th ed. Baltimore: Lippincott, Williams, & Wilkins, 2005.

The Head

The head and its components act as the primary control center for the body in all matters. The brain is responsible for higher order function, such as learning, and all movements and activities—voluntary and involuntary. Injuries to the head range from minor to life threatening and can affect both the external (eyes, ears, nose, or mouth) and internal features (skull or brain).

Anatomy of the Head

The skull is the bony structure that protects the brain from injury and provides each individual with facial definition. The skull is composed of 22 bones with all but one bone joined in immovable joints known as **sutures** (**Figure 13.1**).[1] The mandible, or jawbone, is the sole moveable bone in the skull. Movement of the mandible allows the jaw to open and close and perform important movements such as speaking and chewing food.

The brain is responsible for controlling the entire body. The brain receives and transmits signals throughout the body via the spinal cord. The brain is able to perform multiple acts at any given time because of a predetermined distribution of duties. Without brain activity, an individual is unable to perform any activity, including breathing.

The brain is divided into three parts: cerebrum, cerebellum, and medulla oblongata. The cerebrum is responsible for higher order brain functions such as reasoning, logic, emotions, and learning. The cerebellum is responsible for voluntary muscle activities, voluntary movements, and balance. The medulla oblongata, or brain stem, is responsible for involuntary activities such as breathing, reflexes, and regulating heart rate and blood pressure.[2]

The eyes, ears, nose, and mouth all act as sensory receptors and are responsible for intercepting outside **stimuli** and transmitting it to the brain. Without a sense of smell,

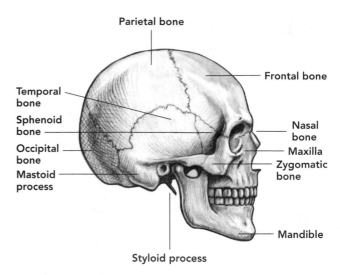

FIGURE 13.1 Anatomy of the skull.

sight, taste, or hearing, an individual is at a disadvantage in receiving stimuli from the outside world. However, a person lacking one principal sense often is capable of adapting with other senses and can often compete in one form of athletics or another quite successfully.

Numerous muscles are found throughout the head and face that allow for facial movements. The facial muscles work cooperatively to create expressions and receive outside stimuli. The nerves that innervate the facial muscles are collectively known as the **cranial nerves**. A head injury may potentially cause damage to these nerves, disrupting their ability to control movements and actions. It is important to complete a cranial nerve assessment any time a head injury is present in an athlete. **Table 13.1** lists the nerves and their roles.

Injuries to the Head

■ Skull Fracture

Skull fractures are generally the result of a direct blow to the head from a blunt object. Skull fractures are dangerous to the athlete because of the damage that occurs in the brain. Intracranial bleeding and swelling can cause serious complications for the injured athlete.

SIGNS AND SYMPTOMS

1. Severe headache
2. Nausea
3. Possible defect or dent in skull
4. **Raccoon eyes**

---

suture An immoveable joint found between the bones of the skull.

stimului Changes in the internal or external environment that cause a response in the tissue.

cranial nerves A collection of nerves that emerge directly from the brain to innervate the motor and sensory systems in the head and neck.

Raccoon eyes Discoloration around the eyes caused by a skull fracture.

TABLE 13.1

CRANIAL NERVES AND THEIR FUNCTIONS

Cranial Nerve	Name	Function
I	Olfactory	Smell
II	Optic	Vision
III	Oculomotor	Eye movement, opening of eyelid, constriction of pupil, focusing
IV	Trochlear	Inferior and lateral movement of eye
V	Trigeminal	Sensation to the face, mastication/chewing
VI	Abducens	Lateral eye movement
VII	Facial	Facial expression, taste, control of tear, nasal, sublingual salivary, and submaxillary glands
VIII	Vestibulocochlear	Hearing and equilibrium
IX	Glossopharyngeal	Swallowing, salivation, gag reflex, sensation from tongue and ear, taste
X	Vagus	Swallowing, speech, regulation of pulmonary, cardiovascular and gastrointestinal functions, taste
XI	Accessory	Swallowing, innervation of sternocleidomastoid muscle
XII	Hypoglossal	Tongue movement, speech, swallowing

5. **Battle's sign**
6. Possible cerebrospinal fluid leaking from ears or nose (yellowish-clear sticky fluid)

TREATMENT

Immediate referral to a physician is necessary to rule out any possible complications that may occur. Recovery time and return to play (RTP) are dependent on the severity of skull and brain trauma.

■ Mandible (Jaw) Fracture

The mandible, because of its placement and relatively small amount of padding for protection, is prone to fracture from blunt trauma to the jaw. The injury may occur in collision sports or from direct contact with high-velocity, low-mass objects such as a baseball, softball, hockey puck, or lacrosse ball.

SIGNS AND SYMPTOMS

1. Pain in injured area, especially with movement or compression
2. Possible deformity
3. Bleeding around teeth or loss of teeth
4. Headache

SPECIAL TESTS

Have the athlete bite down on a tongue depressor, move jaw laterally, or open and close his or her mouth. A positive

test with any of these is increased pain, decreased range of motion, or an inability to complete the task.

TREATMENT

The athlete should be referred to a physician for repair of the jaw, which may include surgery or wiring/banding the jaw shut. A liquid diet may be required for the athlete to minimize jaw movement and allow the mandible to heal. Light activity is allowed for the athlete with progression of exercise as symptoms resolve. RTP may be allowed in 8 to 12 weeks with proper precautions, including custom mouth guards or protective masks. RTP may occur earlier if the fracture is nondisplaced and the risk of reinjury is minimal.

■ Orbital and Zygomatic Fractures

The orbital and zygomatic bones comprise the floor of the eye socket and the upper cheek area. These bones are injured frequently as the result of a direct blow to the eye or cheek. The orbital bone, when fractured, ruptures or explodes, leading to the injury being labeled a **blowout fracture** (**Figure 13.2**).

Battle's sign Discoloration behind the ears caused by a head injury.

blowout fracture Fracture of the orbital floor occurring as a result of a sudden increase in pressure from a direct blow to the eye.

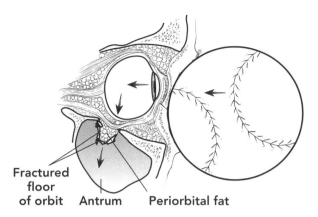

Fractured
floor
of orbit   Antrum   Periorbital fat

FIGURE 13.2   Orbital blowout fracture.

SIGNS AND SYMPTOMS

1. Pain in injured area
2. Double or blurred vision
3. Difficulty in moving eye (orbital fractures can cause an inability to look up)
4. **Photophobia**
5. Bleeding in eye or nose
6. Possible deformity in cheek

TREATMENT

Referral to a physician for X-rays is recommended immediately. Ice—to reduce the swelling—and rest are the best initial treatments. Surgery may be required if there is deformity or dysfunction. RTP will require six to eight weeks if symptoms resolve. Activity should not be allowed until the athlete is cleared to compete to avoid further damage to the bone or the surrounding tissue.

■ Detached Retina

A direct blow to the eye may injure the retina, causing detachment and vision difficulties. A detached retina is typically a painless injury but is a cause for concern because of the potential for permanent damage and diminished vision.

---

photophobia Sensitivity to light.
peripheral vision All that is visible to the eye outside the central area of focus.
sclera A dense, white, fibrous membrane that, with the cornea, forms the external covering of the eyeball.
fluoresceine strips A chemical strip used to assess for a corneal abrasion.
hyphema An accumulation of blood in the anterior chamber of the eye.

SIGNS AND SYMPTOMS

1. Vision difficulties including floating specks, blurred vision, and flashes of light
2. Athlete complains of a curtain falling or coming down at the edge of the eye, reducing **peripheral vision** dramatically

TREATMENT

The athlete should be referred to an ophthalmologist to determine whether surgery is required to repair/reattach the retina. If surgery is not necessary, bed rest with bilateral eye covers can allow the individual time to recover while minimizing further damage. RTP is dependent on the severity of injury and if surgery is required.

■ Corneal Abrasions

The cornea of the eye is the transparent portion of the **sclera**. An abrasion can occur as a result of a foreign object in the eye or a finger or fingernail scraping across the cornea.

SIGNS AND SYMPTOMS

1. Severe pain in the eye
2. Sensation of having something in the eye
3. Watering or tearing from the eye
4. Photophobia

TREATMENT

Referral to a physician is suggested to rule out an abrasion. The physician or athletic trainer can use **fluoresceine strips** and a blue light to determine whether a corneal abrasion is present. An eye patch and antibiotic ointment or drops will heal the injury. The athlete should avoid sunlight until symptoms decrease or resolve. RTP is allowed when the athlete has no vision difficulties and symptoms have resolved, usually in a matter of days.

■ Hyphema

An athlete who suffers a direct blow to the eye by a blunt object may develop a **hyphema**, or collection of blood, in the sclera of the eye (**Figure 13.3**).

SIGNS AND SYMPTOMS

1. Reddish, bloody tinge in the sclera
2. The color may change to brown or green after 24 to 48 hours
3. Vision difficulties

TREATMENT

The athlete should be referred to a physician for evaluation. Bilateral eye patches, sedation, medication, and/or bed rest may be recommended. The bleeding should

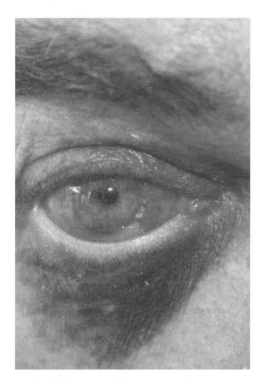

FIGURE 13.3 Hyphema.

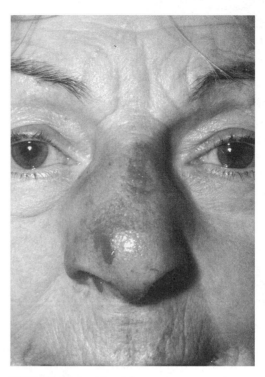

FIGURE 13.4 Nasal fracture.

reabsorb over the course of several days. It is important to remember that this is a serious injury that—if not treated properly—could lead to permanent vision damage.

Nasal Fracture

A fracture of the nasal bone (**Figure 13.4**) is the most common facial fracture seen in athletics. The injury results from direct trauma to the front or side of the nose.

SIGNS AND SYMPTOMS

1. Pain at affected site
2. Profuse bleeding
3. Immediate swelling and discoloration
4. Raccoon eyes
5. Possible deformity in nose or bump on bridge of nose
6. Crepitus
7. Difficulty breathing

TREATMENT

Referral to a physician for X-rays and possible reduction of a **displaced fracture** is required in a timely manner, but not urgently. The athlete with a simple fracture can return to play in a few days with proper splinting or a face shield. Complicated fractures may require surgery to improve the athlete's ability to breathe properly.

Nosebleeds (Epistaxis)

Nosebleeds (**epistaxis**) are extremely common in athletics. Nosebleeds can be caused by a direct blow to the face or nose or by environmental factors such as heat and allergies.

SIGNS AND SYMPTOMS

1. Mild to profuse bleeding
2. Possible pain or swelling depending on cause

TREATMENT

The athletic trainer should first determine the cause of the bleeding to see whether an injury or fracture may be present. The athlete should then apply pressure to the bridge of the nose and bend the head forward. The head should be bent forward not backward to prevent blood from traveling down the throat to the stomach and causing nausea or vomiting. The athletic trainer should provide gauze or a nose plug to collect the blood and can apply ice to the back of the neck to decrease blood flow.

displaced fracture A fracture in which the broken fragments of the bone are separated from each other and not aligned.

epistaxis Nosebleed.

If bleeding does not cease, gauze may be placed within the upper lip to provide pressure to the base of the nose. The athlete can return to play as soon as the bleeding has been controlled, as long as there are no signs of fracture.

■ Cauliflower Ear

Cauliflower ear (**Figure 13.5**) is the general name for a hematoma that develops in the cartilage of the ear. This injury occurs most often in sports that suggest protective headgear but do not require it for all practices and games. Cauliflower ear is most often seen in wrestling, boxing, judo, and rugby. Repeated compression or rubbing directly over the ear causes the injury.

SIGNS AND SYMPTOMS

1. Swelling within the cartilage of the ear
2. Possible bleeding
3. Scarring from a previous injury may be present

TREATMENT

Preventive treatment is preferred with the use of petroleum jelly, skin lube, or protective headgear over the ears during activity. Once the hematoma has formed, the athlete needs to have the fluid drained and a compressive pack placed on the ear, either sutured or taped in place, for at least one week. If the hematoma is not treated, it will calcify and a lumpy shape similar to a cauliflower will remain in the ear permanently. Only cosmetic surgery can remove the tissue after it has calcified.

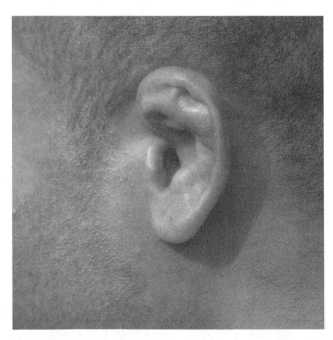

FIGURE 13.5 Cauliflower ear.

Many athletes in the specified sports view this injury as a badge of honor or a symbol of athletic participation. They may resist treatment or remove the compression pack before the damage has healed. The permanence of the injury should be emphasized and appropriate treatment highly recommended. RTP for the athlete is possible as soon as pain is resolved. It is recommended that headgear be worn at all times, especially post-injury until healing is complete.

 ## Special Section: Concussions

Concussions occur frequently in sports and tend to be poorly understood universally. A concussion affects the brain, can range from minor to severe (loss of consciousness), and can have life-threatening consequences. Athletic trainers must clearly understand concussions and take each concussion seriously to minimize present and future consequences.

Concussions are seen most often in contact or collision sports (**Figure 13.6**). Recent research has shown that more than 250,000 concussions occur each year in football alone and 300,000 in all sports.[3–5] Research has also shown that anywhere from 6% to 20% of athletes suffer a concussion annually.[1,3,6,7] Most concussions occur as the result of a direct blow to the head either by equipment, the playing surface, or another player. A concussion can develop after brain contact with the skull when the brain decelerates from the force of the blow. Or, injury may occur to the brain as it rebounds from the initial injury and comes into contact with the opposite side of the skull. This rebounding injury is known as a contrecoup concussion.

The primary concern with concussions is damage to the brain and the permanent issues that may result from this damage. Concussions have a cascading effect; symptoms get progressively worse the more often concussions occur. For instance, an athlete with one concussion may never deal with residual effects, but an athlete with multiple concussions may suffer from memory and cognition deficits long after his or her athletic career has ended.

It is essential to create a head injury history for all incoming athletes so that any future concussions may be considered in the context of the number the athlete has already suffered. Management of the concussion depends on both the severity of the current injury and the athlete's history of head injuries.

concussions Transient alterations in brain function without structural damage caused by injuries that shake the brain.

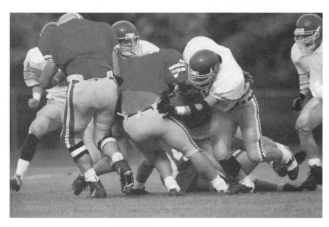

FIGURE 13.6   Football tackle.

SIGNS AND SYMPTOMS

Numerous symptoms are associated with concussions and help in determining the severity of injury. Several concussion-grading scales are used in athletic training.[8,9] Each individual institution can determine which grading system is best for the protection of its athletes.

However, research has shown that perhaps too much emphasis is placed on the specific grading system used. It seems more logical to base the grade of the concussion on the symptoms and their duration only after the symptoms have resolved.[1,9] The following symptoms are derived from the Evidence-Based Cantu grading system.[9] Concussions in this system are graded similarly to sprains and strains on a scale of I to III, with grade I being a mild injury and grade III being severe.

Grade I Concussion:

1. Dizziness/headache
2. Ringing in the ears (tinnitus)
3. Blurred or double vision
4. Nausea
5. Sensitivity to light/noise
6. Possible slight amnesia (**retrograde** or **anterograde**)
7. Disorientation
8. Inappropriate emotional reaction
9. Any change in normal personality
10. Confusion or lack of concentration
11. Possible cranial nerve dysfunction
12. No loss of consciousness

Symptoms will last less than 30 minutes.

Grade II Concussion:

1. This level of concussion demonstrates the same symptoms as a grade I concussion but may be more severe and last longer.

2. Retrograde or anterograde amnesia may last up to 24 hours.
3. There is no loss of consciousness or loss of consciousness lasts less than 1 minute.

Symptoms will last anywhere from 30 minutes to 24 hours.

Grade III Concussion:

1. Preceding symptoms may be more severe and will last longer.
2. Loss of consciousness at onset of injury lasts more than 1 minute.

Symptoms may last more than 7 days.

SPECIAL TESTS

As mentioned before, the treatment plan for concussions is determined by the severity of the present injury and the athlete's history of concussions. When developing a concussion history for each athlete, it is important to have a baseline test of the individual's memory and cognitive ability. Each individual has a different level of memory and ability to comprehend tasks. By administering a *baseline test* (i.e., BESS, ImPACT, SAC), the athletic trainer can measure the athlete's **cognitive ability** prior to injury. The *assessment test* then should be readministered at various intervals post-injury. The scores then can be compared to pre-injury results to determine whether cognitive deficits are present as a result of the current injury.

TREATMENT

Grade I Concussion: The athlete should be monitored to see whether symptoms resolve. If concentration and cognition return to normal and the patient is symptom-free, the athlete may return to competition after 20 minutes.[10] The athlete must pass an on-field assessment prior to RTP. The on-field assessment (**Table 13.2**) determines whether the symptoms have fully resolved. The athlete should be removed from the competition for the rest of the match if symptoms recur or increase with exertion. The day after the game, the athlete should be tested with the cognition

retrograde amnesia Loss of memory and inability to recall events before the traumatic event.

anterograde amnesia Loss of an athlete's immediate memory and ability to recall events that have occurred since the injury.

cognitive ability Brain-based skills and mental functions that assist in the processing of information and applying knowledge.

TABLE 13.2

FIELD MENTAL STATUS EXAMINATION

Response to Items	Yes	No
Orientation:		
Arena		
City		
Opponent		
Month		
Day of the week		
Anterograde Amnesia: (*repeat*)		
truck, blue, golf		
or bike, green, ball		
or boat, red, sport		
Retrograde Amnesia:		
Events of prior period		
Remembers play prior to hit		
Score of game prior to hit		
Memory of hit		
Concentration:		
Days of the week backward		
(*starting with Sunday*)		
Backward digit repetition		
49 (*correct 94*)		
852 (*correct 258*)		
Word List Memory:		
Recall of truck, blue, golf		

Any difficulties should be considered as abnormal. Consult a physician if player has signs/symptoms.

From: Lovell MR, Collins MW, Nogle SE, Monroe J. Field Evaluation of Concussion, 2000.

asymptomatic Having no symptoms of illness or disease.

exertion test A series of exercises that places a progressive physical stress on the injured individual. The test is utilized to determine whether the individual is capable of a return to play.

exam and compared to baseline. The athlete must see a physician if symptoms have recurred, worsened, or the cognition test demonstrates mental deficits.

Grade II Concussion: The athlete should be removed for the remainder of the competition and monitored to ensure that there are no serious complications. The athlete should see a physician the following day for a thorough evaluation. The athlete should be tested periodically using the cognition test with the results compared to the baseline. The athlete must be **asymptomatic** for at least one week both at rest and during an **exertion test** prior to any return to activity. The exertion test consists of different running and cutting drills and sport-specific activities that progressively stress the athlete and increase heart rate. If the athlete is asymptomatic during the exertion test, he or she may begin restricted activities and increase participation as long as symptoms do not recur.

Grade III Concussion: A grade III concussion should be treated as a potential spinal cord injury with the athlete being spine-boarded and removed from the field. He or she should be transported to the hospital for immediate evaluation. The athlete should be tested periodically for cognition and removed from play until he or she returns to baseline levels. Anyone with a grade III injury is removed from play until he or she has been asymptomatic for anywhere from one week to one month, depending on the symptoms, previous history of concussions, and the grading system utilized.[8] At this time, the athlete can return to restricted activity after passing an exertion test. The athlete should continue restricted activity for several days, and then progress to full activity if remaining asymptomatic.[1,8] No athlete should be cleared to participate if any symptoms remain or recur with exertion. Consistent follow-up and communication with the physician should be maintained throughout the recovery process.

During the first 24 hours post-injury, the athlete should be monitored closely to ensure that he or she does not develop serious side effects. The athlete should not be given aspirin or anti-inflammatory medications, including ibuprofen, because of the blood-thinning effects of the medications and the potential for intracranial bleeding.[10] An athlete with a concussion is allowed to sleep post-injury but should be monitored to ensure that symptoms do not worsen.

If at any point post-injury the athlete becomes nauseated or symptoms increase, he or she should be taken to see a physician. If the athlete suffers a second concussion at any time during the remainder of the season, the recovery time should be doubled for whichever grade of concussion the individual suffers.[1]

■ Second-Impact Syndrome

An athlete who has suffered a concussion during a practice or competition may be cleared to return to play that day but should be monitored closely before and after return to play to ensure that second-impact syndrome does not result. Second-impact syndrome is when a subsequent head injury occurs before the symptoms of the previous concussion have resolved. The second impact may be minor and may not even involve the head. Second-impact syndrome results in rapid swelling and herniation of the already-injured brain, causing excessive bleeding and pressure. Athletes under 20 years of age are most susceptible to second-impact syndrome.[1]

An athlete suffering from second-impact syndrome will deteriorate rapidly, leading to unconsciousness and respiratory failure. This is a life-threatening condition with a mortality rate close to 50%.[1] All life-saving measures should be conducted to provide the athlete with the best chance for survival. The best treatment for second-impact syndrome is prevention via a proper and thorough examination following the initial injury. Ensuring that the athlete's symptoms have resolved completely prior to RTP protects the athlete from second-impact syndrome.

CHAPTER REVIEW

1. How many cranial nerves are present in the body?
2. In which sports is cauliflower ear generally seen?
3. How many grades of concussion are listed in the Evidence-Based Cantu System?
4. What is second-impact syndrome?
5. What is a hyphema?
6. List the signs and symptoms of a grade I concussion.

CRITICAL THINKING

What would you do if an athlete with a history of numerous concussions wants to play?

REFERENCES

1. Prentice WE. *Arnheim's Principles of Athletic Training: A Competency-Based Approach*, 12th ed. Boston: McGraw-Hill, 2006.
2. Moore KL, Dalley AF. *Clinically Oriented Anatomy*, 5th ed. Baltimore: Lippincott Williams, & Wilkins, 2005.
3. Mueller FO. (2001). Catastrophic head injuries in high school and collegiate sports. *Journal of Athletic Training*, 36(3):312–315.
4. Oliaro S, Anderson S, Hooker D. (2001). Management of cerebral concussion in sports: the athletic trainer's perspective. *Journal of Athletic Training*, 36(3):257–262.
5. Osborne B. (2001). Principles of liability for athletic trainers: managing sport-related concussion. *Journal of Athletic Training*, 36(3):316–321.
6. Guskiewicz KM, Ross SE, Marshall SW. (2001). Postural stability and neuropsychological deficits after concussion in collegiate athletes. *Journal of Athletic Training*, 36(3):263–273.
7. Powell JW. (2001). Cerebral concussion: causes, effects, and risks in sports. *Journal of Athletic Training*, 36(3):307–311.
8. Bailes JE, Hudson V. (2001). Classification of sport-related head trauma: a spectrum of mild to severe injury. *Journal of Athletic Training*, 36(3):236–243.
9. Cantu RC. (2001). Posttraumatic retrograde and anterograde amnesia: pathophysiology and implications in grading and safe return to play. *Journal of Athletic Training*, 36(3):244–248.
10. Guskiewicz K, et al. (2004). National Athletic Trainers' Association position statement: management of sport-related concussion. *Journal of Athletic Training*, 39(3):280–297.

CHAPTER 1

The Shoulder

The shoulder girdle, which is made up of the upper arm, shoulder, and scapula, is a unique, multifaceted region of the body (**Figure 14.1**). The shoulder has a wide range of motion (ROM) through all three planes of movement. Similar to the hip, the glenohumeral joint in the shoulder is a multiaxial ball and socket joint that allows motion in flexion, extension, abduction, adduction, internal and external rotation, horizontal motion, and **circumduction**.[1] The joint is very shallow and depends on the surrounding joint capsule and musculature for support and stability. Because of its hypermobility and limited support structure, the shoulder is prone to injury, especially in athletic activities.

Anatomy of the Shoulder

The shoulder girdle consists of three bones: the humerus, scapula, and clavicle. The bones articulate and interrelate with each other to allow all of the movements listed earlier. The scapula (shoulder blade) is the linchpin of the shoulder girdle. Both the humerus and the clavicle attach to the scapula to form the two principal joints of the region. The humerus connects to the glenoid fossa, an extension of the scapula, to form the glenohumeral joint—what is generally considered the shoulder joint.[1] The clavicle (or collarbone) attaches to the scapula at the acromion to form the acromioclavicular (AC) joint in the anterior portion of the shoulder girdle (**Figure 14.2**). The clavicle at its medial end attaches to the sternum to

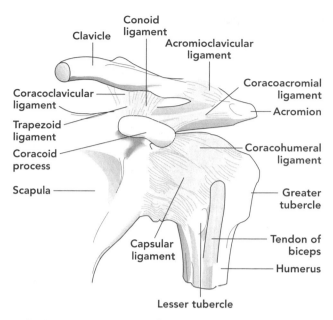

FIGURE 14.2   Anatomy of the AC joint.

form the sternoclavicular (SC) joint, although this joint is rarely injured in athletics.

Numerous muscles throughout the shoulder control its many varied movements. Of those muscles, this chapter focuses on three large muscles and four small muscles. The biceps brachii rests anteriorly on the humerus and is responsible for shoulder and elbow flexion. The triceps brachii sits posterior to the humerus and performs the counteracting movements to the biceps—shoulder and elbow extension. The deltoid is actually a muscle group composed of three smaller muscles found on the proximolateral aspect of the humerus. The three muscles of the deltoid work in unison to move the upper arm into abduction. The deltoid is also responsible for assisting in shoulder flexion and extension.

The four smaller muscles of the shoulder are collectively called the **rotator cuff** (**Figure 14.3**). The supraspinatus, infraspinatus, teres minor, and subscapularis muscles move the upper arm and humerus into abduction and internal and external rotation. These muscles are very important in athletics and are frequently injured, especially in overhead activities found in sports such as baseball, softball, or volleyball.

> **circumduction** Movement of a part (usually the shoulder or hip) in a circular direction.
>
> **rotator cuff** The SITS (supraspinatus, infraspinatus, teres minor, and subscapularis) muscles hold the head of the humerus in the glenoid fossa and produce internal and external rotation.

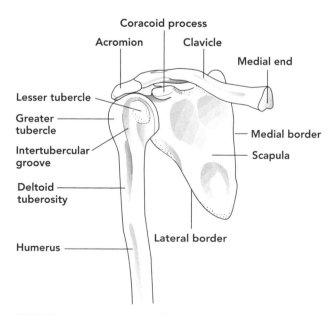

FIGURE 14.1   Anatomy of the shoulder.

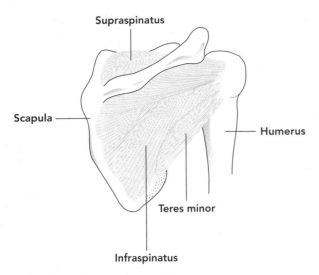

Supraspinatus

Scapula

Humerus

Teres minor

Infraspinatus

FIGURE 14.3 Anatomy of the rotator cuff.

Several accessory, or helper, muscles perform movements at the shoulder girdle. The pectoralis and trapezius muscles assist with the horizontal motions of the humerus and scapula. The latissimus dorsi, teres major, and pectoralis muscles perform adduction of the humerus. The rhomboid muscles, along with the trapezius, allow the scapulas to come together, which is called **scapular retraction**. The opposite motion, **scapular protraction**, is conducted by the serratus anterior and the pectoralis muscles.[2]

The scapula moves in several different patterns and planes, making it able to assist the humerus in its motion. The scapula literally floats over the rib cage with no posterior bony attachment. Its only bony attachments are anteriorly at the humerus and the clavicle. The scapula rests on the posterior musculature in a position that enhances its movement capabilities. Improper motion in the scapula can lead to active dysfunction throughout the shoulder girdle.

The combination of scapular and humeral motion during abduction and adduction is called **scapulohumeral rhythm**. In abduction, the humerus moves from 0° to 30° without any scapular movement. From 30° to 90°, the scapula moves 1° for every 2° of humeral movement. From 90° to full abduction, the scapula and humerus move at

scapular retraction The movement of the scapula toward the midline.

scapular protraction The movement of the scapula away from the midline.

scapulohumeral rhythm The coordinated movement of the scapula, humerus, and clavicle to achieve full shoulder elevation.

the same rate.[3] It is important during an injury evaluation to examine the scapulohumeral rhythm for any irregular motion patterns because they can lead to injury.

Fractures in the Shoulder Joint

■ Clavicle Fracture

The clavicle fracture is the most common fracture seen in the shoulder girdle. A direct blow to the bone or landing on an outstretched arm or on the tip of the shoulder can injure the bone, causing a fracture. The middle third of the bone is the most vulnerable section to fracture.[3]

SIGNS AND SYMPTOMS

1. Pain at the affected site
2. Possible deformity (usually seen in a tent or triangular shape)
3. Decreased ROM
4. Athlete supports injured arm with the opposite arm

TREATMENT

The athlete should be placed in a sling in a comfortable position and referred for X-rays. The X-ray determines whether further action is needed or whether the fracture is in a position to allow for proper healing. The physician may need to reduce the fracture if it is displaced. The athlete is then placed in a figure-8 brace (**Figure 14.4**), which keeps the shoulders back, relieves pressure on the

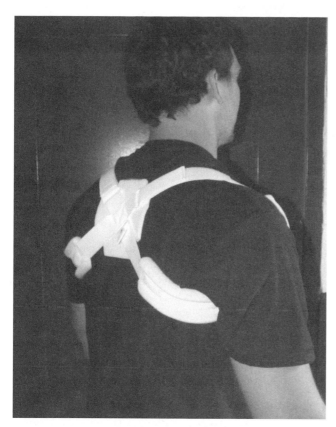

FIGURE 14.4 Clavical figure-8 brace.

clavicle, and allows the ends of the bone to reconnect properly. This brace is worn for 6 to 8 weeks as determined by follow-up X-rays. During immobilization, the athlete may begin progressive strengthening and rehab. Return to play (RTP) is possible in 8 to 12 weeks depending on the athlete's sport and level of recovery.

■ Humeral Fracture

The humerus is generally fractured in one of a few places: the shaft of the bone, the proximal end of the bone, or the head of the humerus. The most frequent site for fracture in athletics is in the proximal end of the bone. Fractures of the head of the humerus, also known as **epiphyseal fractures**, are most common in young athletes (10 years or younger) when the growth plate of the bone has not fused to the shaft.[3]

The primary concern with a humeral fracture is the status of the nearby arteries, veins, and nerves. The

> **epiphyseal fractures** Fractures found at the ends of the bone, usually seen in children/young adults. Also known as growth-plate fractures.

humerus is similar to the femur in that the neurovascular system for the upper arm rests beside the bone, offering an opportunity for potential damage during injury.

SIGNS AND SYMPTOMS

1. Moderate to severe pain
2. Possible deformity
3. Swelling and discoloration
4. Decreased ROM

TREATMENT

The athlete should be splinted and/or placed in a sling (depending on the injury site) and referred for X-rays. The distal neurovascular structures should be assessed both before and after the splint is applied. This ensures that neither the injury nor the splint has compromised the arteries, veins, and nerves.

This injury requires significant recovery time because of the humerus's role in all upper extremity movements. The athlete often is casted and immobilized for 2 to 6 months depending on the site of the damage. Rehab also requires a great deal of time because of the loss of strength and muscle atrophy that occurs with the lengthy immobilization.

■ Scapula Fracture

A fracture of the scapula is a relatively rare injury in athletics because of the strength and density of the surrounding musculature and the protection offered by shoulder pads in many contact sports. The scapula itself, though, is a fairly thin bone that can fracture as a result of direct trauma.

SIGNS AND SYMPTOMS

1. Moderate to severe pain
2. Possible slight swelling and discoloration
3. Decreased ROM
4. Decreased strength

TREATMENT

The athlete should be placed in a sling and referred for X-rays. The athlete may begin a progressive strengthening program as soon as pain allows and can return to play after 6 to 8 weeks if proper healing has occurred. The time frame, though, may be extended if the athlete is vulnerable to reinjury in his or her sport.

 ## Shoulder Sprains

A shoulder sprain is an injury to the ligaments or joint capsule that stabilizes and supports the glenohumeral joint. This injury can occur on its own or in conjunction with a subluxation or dislocation of the humeral head. Shoulder sprains occur quite often in athletics because of the frequent use and vulnerability of the joint.

SIGNS AND SYMPTOMS

1. Pain at the shoulder joint
2. Decreased ROM
3. Decreased strength
4. Slight swelling

TREATMENT

Cold and electrical modality therapy and placing the athlete in a sling help minimize initial symptoms. Progressive range of motion and strengthening allows the athlete to regain motion and promotes recovery. The athlete is cleared to return to play when he or she has full range of motion and strength. A protective brace (i.e., Sully, Max, Duke-Wyre) may be a benefit in the athlete's return to activity to prevent reinjury (**Figure 14.5**).

■ Shoulder Dislocation/Subluxation

Shoulder dislocations and subluxations are extremely common injuries, accounting for up to 50% of all joint dislocations in the body.[3] The glenohumeral joint is relatively unstable—the downside to having such great range of motion—which allows for reasonably easy displacement. Once an athlete has suffered one subluxation or dislocation, that individual is much more likely to suffer reinjury during his or her career. In fact, 85% to 90% of traumatic dislocations recur.[3] Most chronic dislocators require surgery to repair the joint and prevent reinjury. The most frequent type of dislocation is an anterior displacement of the shoulder, which occurs as a result of forced abduction, external rotation, and extension.

SIGNS AND SYMPTOMS

1. Moderate to severe pain
2. Athlete clutches the arm to the side and supports the injured part with the opposite arm
3. Obvious deformity if joint is dislocated with a divot in skin (**sulcus**) where the humeral head normally is
4. Decreased or no ROM
5. Swelling in joint

SPECIAL TESTS

For the *apprehension test*, the athlete is placed in a supine position while the examiner abducts the shoulder and elbow to 90° flexion and externally rotates the shoulder slowly. A positive test is indicated by **apprehension** in the athlete either in facial expressions or movements. The motion replicates the injury force of anterior dislocations and will make the athlete concerned for reinjury.[1]

Administer the *relocation test* after the apprehension test is completed with a positive test. The examiner applies a posterior force over the humeral head and continues external rotation. A positive test is indicated if the athlete's apprehension or pain is relieved or further external rotation is possible.[1]

For the *anterior drawer test*, the athlete is placed in a supine position with his or her arm resting at the side. The examiner stabilizes the scapula by grasping the trapezius and applying downward pressure. The other hand is placed on the proximal humerus and translates it anteriorly and posteriorly. The anterior motion of the shoulder is compared bilaterally to determine whether there is increased movement on the injured side. Increased movement, pain, or apprehension indicates a positive anterior drawer test (**Figure 14.6**).

When completing the *posterior drawer test*, the athlete is placed in the same position as the anterior drawer test with the examiner grasping the injured arm at the forearm. The arm is flexed at the elbow between 90° to 120° and at the shoulder to 20° to 30°. The shoulder is abducted to between 80° and 120°. Once this position is reached,

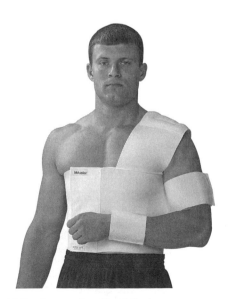

FIGURE 14.5 Protective shoulder brace.

> **sulcus** A deep, narrow furrow or groove, as in an organ or tissue. May be seen as a positive sign of an inferior shoulder dislocation.
>
> **apprehension** When a patient reacts to or limits motion because of a fear or sensation of impending joint dislocation or stress.

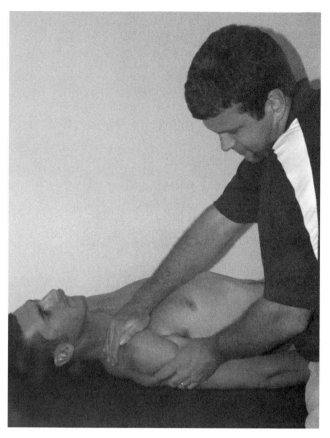

FIGURE 14.6 Anterior drawer test.

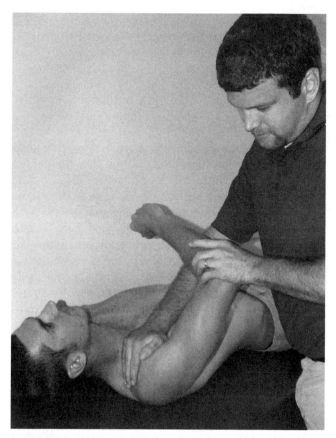

FIGURE 14.7 Posterior drawer test.

the scapula is stabilized and the examiner rotates the arm internally and flexes the shoulder to between 60° and 80° while pushing the humerus posteriorly. This test replicates the motion that causes a posterior dislocation (**Figure 14.7**). A positive test is indicated by increased posterior translation, apprehension, or instability.[1]

Another test is the *sulcus sign*. The athlete is in a seated position with his or her arm resting at the side in a relaxed position (**Figure 14.8**). The examiner grasps the arm below the elbow and pulls distally. A sulcus may appear, which is a dimple or depression at the shoulder between the acromion and the humeral head. This tests for an inferior dislocation or instability. A positive test is indicated if the sulcus is greater than normal on the injured side.[1]

TREATMENT

The injured athlete should be placed in a sling and referred to a physician for reduction if the joint is dislocated. If the athlete suffers a subluxation, he or she should still be placed in a sling and referred to a physician for evaluation, even though the injury has reduced itself.

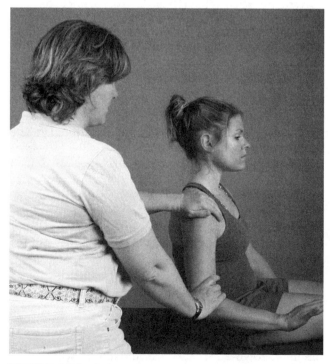

FIGURE 14.8 Sulcus sign.

This injury may be quite painful for the athlete, although pain decreases dramatically with reduction to its normal position. Therefore, a quick referral benefits an athlete who is experiencing high levels of pain. Chronic dislocators may not require as quick of a response because the pain will decrease with repeated injury. X-rays may be taken to rule out a possible fracture of the humerus or glenoid fossa.

Surgery may be necessary for some injuries depending on the severity of the damage to the joint structures or the number of joint injuries that the athlete has suffered. The athlete and the physician should discuss and determine surgical options. If surgery is not required, the athlete is kept in a sling post-injury, but should begin a ROM and strengthening program—as soon as symptoms allow—to decrease any swelling, muscle spasm, and atrophy. Isometric and elastic band exercises may be performed relatively soon after the injury. As the athlete's strength improves and symptoms resolve, he or she may be cleared to return to restricted activity. A shoulder brace will benefit the athlete by providing protection and support while limiting the range of motion.

RTP is dependent on the treatment option selected, the strength of the musculature, and the symptoms of the athlete. If the athlete chooses a surgical repair, the recovery time is 3 to 4 months. Without surgery, the athlete may return in the normal time frame associated with a joint sprain. Recovery time is also dependent on the athlete's sport. Sports that require a lot of upper body movements, such as basketball, lacrosse, or field hockey, may require more recovery time than other sports such as soccer.

■ AC Joint Sprain

The acromion of the scapula is connected by cartilage and ligaments to the clavicle to form the acromioclavicular (AC) joint in the anterior region of the shoulder. The AC joint is also maintained and stabilized by two other ligaments that attach to a spur off of the scapula called the coracoid process. Any or all of these ligaments may be damaged during an injury. When categorizing an AC sprain, there are six classifications or degrees of injury detailed by Rockwood.[4] The sprain is assigned a degree of severity by the number of ligaments injured and the displacement of the clavicle as a result of the ligament damage (**Figure 14.9** and **Figure 14.10**).

Because of its placement in the shoulder, the AC joint is rather vulnerable to injury, specifically in contact sports. The most common mechanism of injury is when the athlete lands on the tip of the shoulder (acromion), forcing it downward, backward, and inward while push-

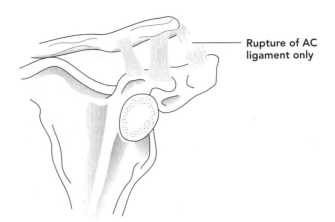

FIGURE 14.9 AC sprain grade I–II.

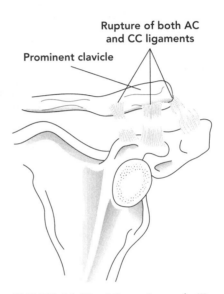

FIGURE 14.10 AC sprain grade III.

ing the clavicle toward the rib cage. AC joint sprains can also occur from a fall on an outstretched arm similarly to clavicle fractures.

SIGNS AND SYMPTOMS

1. Moderate to severe pain especially with shoulder motion above the head or across the body
2. Possible deformity—usually seen when the lateral aspect of the clavicle protrudes upward
3. Swelling and discoloration
4. Decreased ROM in overhead activities and horizontal adduction

SPECIAL TESTS

To complete the *AC shear test*, the patient is placed in a seated position while the examiner cups his or her hands over the superior aspect of the trapezius muscle with one hand on the clavicle and the other on the scapula. The examiner then squeezes the hands together, pushing the clavicle toward the scapula. Pain or abnormal movement at the AC joint indicates a positive test.[1]

For the *AC spring test*, the athlete is in a seated position while the examiner places one hand on the head of the clavicle near the AC joint and presses inferiorly. Pain or abnormal movement of the clavicle indicates a positive test. This test also may temporarily reduce the head of the clavicle to its normal position, which can be seen when observed bilaterally while force is applied.[1]

TREATMENT

The athlete should be placed in an arm sling in a comfortable position and referred to a physician if the sprain is moderate to severe. X-rays help to rule out a fracture of the clavicle as a complication. Rest, ice, compression, and elevation (RICE) therapy helps to reduce acute symptoms. Surgery may be required if the damage is too severe for conservative treatment. Progressive strengthening exercises may begin as soon as tolerated. RTP is dependent on the severity of injury. The athlete should be pain-free with full strength, ROM, and good joint stability prior to return. Commercial AC joint pads are available that provide protection for the returning athlete and help to prevent reinjury.

Labrum Tears

The **labrum** is the cartilaginous structure attached to the glenoid fossa in the shoulder. It acts in a manner similar to the meniscus in the knee. The labrum offers a better fit between the humerus and the glenoid, allows a smooth surface for motion, and provides a cushion for any impacts at the shoulder.

The labrum is often injured or torn at the same time as other shoulder injuries occur, especially shoulder dislocations. Three types of injury may occur in the labrum or humeral head during subluxation/dislocation. The injuries are differentiated by name and location of the damage:

- **Hill-Sachs lesion**: An injury to the posterior lateral aspect of the humeral head
- **Bankart lesion**: A defect in the anterior portion of the labrum
- **SLAP lesion**: An injury to the superior aspect of the labrum that extends posterior to anterior[5,6]

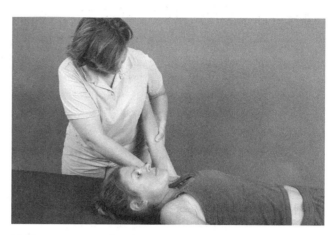

FIGURE 14.11   Clunck test.

SIGNS AND SYMPTOMS

1. Pain in shoulder with motion
2. Clicking or popping with motion
3. Previous history of dislocations
4. Loss of ROM in the specific range affected by injury location

SPECIAL TESTS

In the *clunk test*, the patient is placed in a supine position with the examiner placing one hand on the posterior aspect of the humerus while the other hand is placed over the elbow (**Figure 14.11**). The athlete's arm is fully abducted and externally rotated slightly while the examiner places anterior stress on the humeral head. A clunk, popping, or crepitus at the site of the labral injury indicates a positive test.[1]

---

labrum A ring of cartilage about the edge of a joint surface of the glenoid fossa. Used to provide shock absorption and smooth motion at the shoulder.

Hill-Sachs lesion A small defect usually located on the posterior aspect of the articular cartilage of the humeral head caused by the impact of the humeral head on the glenoid fossa as the humerus dislocates.

Bankart lesion Avulsion or damage to the anterior lip of the glenoid as the humeral head dislocates anteriorly.

SLAP lesion An injury to the superior labrum that typically begins posteriorly and extends anteriorly.

TREATMENT

Labral tears may only be repaired surgically. This can be done in conjunction with a stabilization procedure to correct chronic dislocations or other surgical repairs. RTP is dictated by the rehab protocol designed for the specific repair that the athlete underwent. A sample rehab protocol is listed in **Table 14.1**.

TABLE 14.1

SHOULDER REHAB PROTOCOL

Phase 1 (0–4 weeks)

- Immobilization
- Cryotherapy and/or e-stim to decrease inflammation
- Exercises: Isometrics

    Pendulum (**Codman's exercises**)

    Biceps/triceps strengthening

    Wall crawls

Phase 2 (3–8 weeks)

- Sling to be discontinued
- Continue with e-stim as needed
- ROM: Flexion 0°–90° first 4 weeks

    Flexion to tolerance 4–6 weeks

    Abduction 0°–90°

    Internal rotation (IR) to tolerance

    External rotation (ER) 0°–30° by 6 weeks

- Exercises: Isometrics

    Scapular strengthening

    Elastic band/tubing exercises

Phase 3 (6–12 weeks)

- Continue ROM exercises
- Continue scapular strengthening
- **Progressive resistive exercises** (PREs)
- Rhythmic stabilization/PNF
- Upper-body ergometer (UBE)
- Continue elastic band/tubing exercises
- Joint mobilizations

Return to Play (12+ weeks)

- Isokinetic testing to determine strength
- Sports-specific exercises
- Continue strengthening program

Brachial Plexus Injury

Brachial plexus injuries, or stingers/burners, are a frequent occurrence in athletics, especially contact sports. Football players are particularly prone to these injuries because of the collisions that occur during tackles.

A brachial plexus injury causes the athlete much pain and concern when it occurs. **Stingers** result from an incident where the shoulder and neck are forced away from each other by the playing surface or another athlete. This stretch injures the brachial plexus, which is a large nexus of nerves that travels through the axillary region (armpit) of the shoulder. When the brachial plexus is damaged, it temporarily ceases activity and neural transmission, causing a numbness or "dead-arm" sensation throughout the entire upper extremity. When this injury occurs, it is important for the athletic trainer to first rule out shoulder dislocations or clavicle fractures, which may also cause numbness and tingling post-injury.

SIGNS AND SYMPTOMS

1. Numbness or tingling throughout the arm
2. Loss of ROM or strength lasting anywhere from 5 seconds to several minutes
3. Possible swelling or discoloration from contact

TREATMENT

An athlete with a stinger should attempt to flex and extend his or her fingers and elbow continuously to assist in regaining sensation. After a few minutes, the strength, sensation, and ROM should return to normal levels. The athlete may then return to activity if other injuries have been ruled out. However, an athlete who has suffered one stinger is more likely to suffer recurrent stinger injuries during the course of the game and season and should be monitored closely.

Codman's exercises A form of pendulum movement in the shoulder that helps with regaining or maintaining range of motion after injury.

progressive resistive exercises Exercises that gradually increase in resistance (weight) and repetitions.

brachial plexus The primary neural supply to the upper extremities.

stingers Common name for brachial plexus injuries identified with burning pain or numbness radiating down the arm.

The athlete with a stinger may complain of trapezius muscle spasm and pain the day after the injury. This is treated with ice, electric modalities, and anti-inflammatory medication. If an athlete seems especially prone to these injuries, he or she should be referred to a physician to rule out other serious complications such as an intervertebral disc injury or **spinal stenosis**—a narrowing of the spinal column that impinges on the spinal cord. If the athlete is cleared to participate following the evaluation, he or she can be fitted with protective padding or bracing that prevents excessive neck extension. Several effective commercial devices are on the market including cowboy collars, neck rolls, or Douglas collars.

Muscle Injuries

Deltoid Strain

The deltoid is not injured or strained as often as the other muscles, but the injury can be very painful for the athlete because the muscle is prominent in shoulder abduction, flexion, and extension.

SIGNS AND SYMPTOMS

1. Pain at affected site
2. Decreased ROM
3. Decreased strength
4. Deficit in muscle may be present if injury is severe

SPECIAL TESTS

Because of the multiple movements in which the deltoid is active and the different angles of the three muscles within the deltoid, it is important to complete a *manual muscle test* in flexion, extension, and abduction. For flexion, the athlete may be seated or lying supine with the examiner resisting shoulder flexion. This motion tests the anterior deltoid.

The farther down the arm that the resistance is placed, the more difficult it is for the athlete. The most difficult resistance is when the examiner grasps the wrist.

For extension, the athlete should be placed in a seated or prone position and resisted into extension. Again, the greatest resistance is when the examiner grasps the wrist. This motion tests the posterior deltoid.

For abduction, the athlete should be seated and resisted as he or she moves into shoulder abduction. Movement for

> **spinal stenosis** A development or congenital narrowing of the spinal canal. Increases the risk for spinal cord damage with injury.

this test should be conducted from 0° to 90°. This motion tests the middle deltoid fibers.

A positive test for all three motions is indicated by pain, decreased ROM, or decreased strength when compared bilaterally.

TREATMENT

RICE therapy and a progressive strengthening program provide the athlete with a reduction in symptoms and a proper recovery. RTP time frames are the same as with other muscle strains: 1 to 2 weeks for grade I, 2 to 4 weeks for grade II, and 4 to 6 weeks for grade III.

Rotator Cuff Strain

Rotator cuff injuries are seen quite often in throwing sports or other upper-body activities. Baseball and softball players are especially prone to these injuries, particularly pitchers in either sport. Rotator cuff injuries are prevalent in these athletes because of the velocity of the arm rotations and the deceleration responsibilities associated with the musculature. The rotator cuff may be injured in either an acute or chronic fashion. Grade III strains or tears are unfortunately fairly common in athletics and should be considered when evaluating a rotator cuff injury.

SIGNS AND SYMPTOMS

1. Pain in shoulder, usually deep in the joint
2. Decreased ROM
3. Decreased strength

SPECIAL TESTS

When testing for rotator cuff injuries, the examiner should utilize *manual muscle tests* for each of the four cuff muscles. With the athlete seated, the examiner can measure internal and external rotation at both 0° and 90° shoulder abduction. These two motions test the subscapularis and the infraspinatus/teres minor, respectively.

The subscapularis also may be tested by having the athlete place his or her hand behind the back with the hand resting on the pelvis and the palm facing out. The examiner then resists the athlete as he or she pushes away from the body posteriorly. A positive test in each case is indicated if there is pain, decreased range of motion, or decreased strength.

The examiner also can use the *empty can test*. To test the supraspinatus muscle, place the athlete in a seated position (**Figure 14.12**). The athlete's arms are abducted to 90°, internally rotated, and angled forward 30° where the patient's thumbs point downward as if he or she were emptying a can of food. The examiner then resists the athlete through simultaneous shoulder abduction and

FIGURE 14.12 Empty can test.

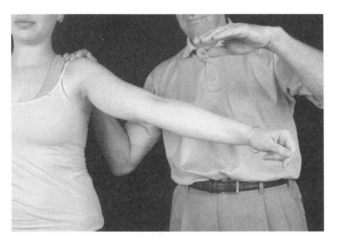

FIGURE 14.13 Drop arm test.

flexion. A positive test is indicated by pain or decreased strength on the injured side.[1]

The *drop arm test* evaluates the likelihood of a tear in any of the rotator cuff muscles (**Figure 14.13**). The athlete should be placed in a seated position with the involved arm abducted to 90°. The examiner then asks the patient to slowly adduct the arm. A positive test is indicated if the athlete is unable to complete the motion slowly or if there is severe pain associated with the movement.

TREATMENT

An athlete with a rotator cuff injury often complains of hearing a pop or feeling a tear when he or she injures the shoulder. Immediate RICE therapy helps to minimize any inflammation entering the muscle and decreases the athlete's initial symptoms. If the athlete has a muscle tear or significant loss of ROM or strength, a physician should see the individual for further diagnostic testing. A complete muscle tear requires surgery prior to any return to activity.

A strained muscle can be rehabilitated through the use of therapeutic tubing in a rotator cuff strengthening program.[7–9] Using tubing for internal and external rotation, in the empty can position, flexion, extension, abduction, and other motions (collectively known as **Jobe exercises**) helps to strengthen the whole shoulder while rehabilitating the injured musculature.

RTP is highly dependent on the athlete's sport and his or her position. A baseball pitcher requires much more time to recover than a football lineman or a field hockey player even though both use their upper bodies for athletic activities as well. The extreme power and velocity found in pitching places a great deal of stress on the rotator cuff and

Fast Fact

Recent literature suggests that glenohumeral internal rotation deficit (GIRD) may be a cause of rotator cuff strains and tears, as well as elbow issues, in athletes.[10–12] Those individuals with an internal rotation deficit of more than 15% to 20% in their throwing shoulder when compared bilaterally are at a higher risk for shoulder and elbow injuries.[12] Specific internal rotation stretches known as sleeper stretches (**Figure 14.14**) can help to minimize the risk for injury in the throwing athlete.

To use the sleeper stretch, have the athlete lie on the side to be stretched (as if the athlete were sleeping on that side) with the shoulder flexed to either 70°, 90°, or 120° (the different angles will alter which muscle fibers are affected). Then, have the athlete flex the elbow to 90° and apply an internal rotation force so that the wrist and forearm are rotating toward the table or the floor. Stretching in this manner decreases the level of GIRD discrepancy and assists in the prevention of shoulder and elbow injuries. The stretching mechanism also may be used to compare the degree of internal rotation bilaterally and determine the level of GIRD in the throwing versus nonthrowing shoulder.

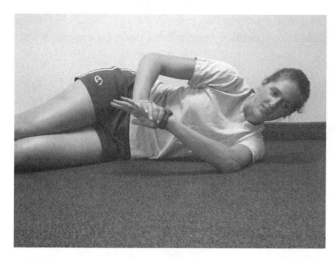

FIGURE 14.14   Sleeper stretch.

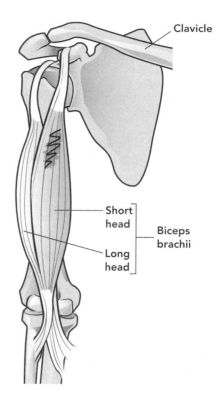

FIGURE 14.15   Biceps muscles rupture.

requires a healthy arm to prevent further injury. Full RTP is allowed when there is pain-free ROM and full strength.

■ Biceps Strain

The biceps brachii may incur injury through a direct blow, forced extension at the shoulder or elbow, or repetitive trauma from activities such as weight lifting. The injury may be quite painful for the athlete, especially in simple daily activities such as brushing teeth or shampooing hair.

SIGNS AND SYMPTOMS

1. Pain at affected site
2. Decreased strength
3. Decreased ROM
4. Possible deficit in muscle (**Popeye deformity**) if injury is severe; a large bulge in the muscle directly beside a noticeable deficit where tear occurred (**Figure 14.15**)

SPECIAL TESTS

The athlete may be tested using a *manual muscle test*. With the individual seated, have the athlete complete a resisted biceps curl. Decreases in strength or range of motion as compared bilaterally are positive signs for a biceps strain.

TREATMENT

Electric and cold modality therapy can help decrease symptoms. All muscle strains can be treated with electric modalities. The use of electric modalities is often dependent upon the individual athletic trainer rather than the injury itself. Progressive strengthening may be conducted as tolerated with an RTP when strength and ROM are returned to normal levels. The recovery time is similar to other muscle strains.

■ Triceps Strain

As with the biceps strain, a direct blow may injure the triceps muscle, or forced movement at the shoulder or elbow (this time flexion), and/or repetitive trauma from activities such as weight lifting. The injury may cause dysfunction in athletes who have to push away or extend against objects or people frequently (for example, football lineman) or athletes in upper-body-dominant sports (such as baseball, softball, volleyball).

> **Jobe exercises** A series of exercises used to strengthen the shoulder musculature. Exercises are completed with either therapeutic tubing or light weights.
>
> **Popeye deformity** A tear of the biceps tendon that is characterized by a deficit in the musculature with a large bulge beside the deficit. Injury is reminiscent of the cartoon character Popeye.

SIGNS AND SYMPTOMS

1. Pain at affected site
2. Decreased ROM
3. Decreased strength
4. Possible deficit in muscle if injury is severe

SPECIAL TESTS

A *manual muscle test* for the triceps assists in the evaluation of this injury. With the athlete seated or lying prone, have the athlete extend the elbow against resistance. A positive test is indicated by pain, loss of range of motion, or a loss of strength when compared bilaterally.

TREATMENT

RICE therapy helps to reduce symptoms, and a progressive strengthening program allows a safe RTP. Recovery time for a triceps strain is similar to that of other muscle strains.

 ## Chronic Injuries

■ Muscle Tendinitis

Chronic injury and inflammation may occur within the tendons of the shoulder, causing tendinitis. This injury is most often found in the biceps and the rotator cuff. Tendinitis is typically caused by overuse or repetitive motion.

SIGNS AND SYMPTOMS

1. Pain with specific motions
2. Decreased ROM
3. Decreased strength

SPECIAL TESTS

The examiner can use the *manual muscle tests* listed in muscle strains for the biceps and rotator cuff as tendinitis tests. The *empty can test* for a strain also is effective for supraspinatus tendinitis.

TREATMENT

RICE therapy, electric modalities, and ultrasound are very effective in treating tendinitis. Anti-inflammatory medicine may also be useful. Tendinitis in the shoulder, as in other muscles, can be extremely painful and restrictive for the

> **impingement** Pressure on the rotator cuff musculature that results when the muscles are rubbed or compressed by the acromion during movement.

athlete. It may also increase the risk for muscle tears if chronic inflammation degrades the tendon. The athlete can participate to tolerance in all activities with treatment and strengthening therapy.

■ Impingement Syndrome

The supraspinatus tendon is situated between the coracoid process and the acromion before it attaches to the humerus. The space between these bony prominences is quite small and any improper mechanics or repetitive overhead motion can lead to compression/**impingement** and inflammation of the tendon. Athletes in sports such as swimming, volleyball, and tennis are especially prone to impingement injuries.

SIGNS AND SYMPTOMS

1. Pain in shoulder around the acromion
2. Pain and decreased ROM with overhead activities

SPECIAL TESTS

The *empty can test* can indicate impingement syndrome if a traumatic injury has not occurred. Another option is the *Hawkins-Kennedy test*. The athlete stands while the examiner flexes the shoulder and elbow to 90°, horizontally adducts the arm in front of the chest, and then forcibly internally rotates the arm while maintaining the position of the elbow (**Figure 14.16**). This motion propels the tendon into the coracoid process causing pain and discomfort.

TREATMENT

RICE therapy, electric modalities, and ultrasound are effective treatments for impingement syndrome. Anti-inflammatory medicines also may be useful. Rehab should attempt to correct the improper mechanics that initially caused the impingement. Therapeutic tubing programs, such as Jobe exercises, should be conducted to strengthen

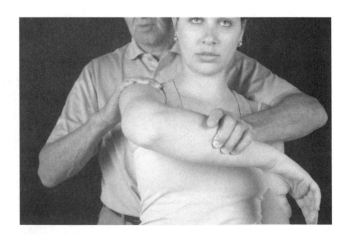

FIGURE 14.16   Hawkins-Kennedy test.

the entire rotator cuff and shoulder complex. The athlete may continue to play as tolerated with modifications to activities that cause pain.

■ Shoulder Bursitis

The bursae in the shoulder assist in cushioning the joint and allowing full range of motion without chronic tendon or bone damage. These bursae often become inflamed and agitated through repetitive motion or improper mechanics.

SIGNS AND SYMPTOMS

1. Pain with specific motion
2. Possible squeaking noise with motion
3. Possible swelling

TREATMENT

RICE therapy with electric modalities or ultrasound can decrease inflammation. The injury may recur if an uncorrected biomechanical issue is to blame. The athlete is cleared to play with this injury as tolerated.

CHAPTER REVIEW

1. What are the two primary joints of the shoulder?
2. Define scapulohumeral rhythm.
3. What percentage of traumatic dislocations recur?
4. What is the most common mechanism of injury for an AC sprain?
5. What are the three types of injuries associated with the labrum or humeral head?
6. What is the more popular name for a brachial plexus injury?

CRITICAL THINKING

What is your suggestion for a baseball pitcher with professional aspirations who is having severe shoulder issues? What do you say to the scouts who ask about him?

REFERENCES

1. Magee DJ. *Orthopedic Physical Assessment*, 4th ed. Philadelphia: W. B. Saunders, 2002.
2. Moore KL, Dalley AF. *Clinically Oriented Anatomy*, 5th ed. Baltimore: Lippincott Williams, & Wilkins, 2005.
3. Prentice WE. *Arnheim's Principles of Athletic Training: A Competency-Based Approach*, 12th ed. Boston: McGraw-Hill, 2006.
4. Pfeiffer RP, Mangus BC. *Concepts of Athletic Training*, 5th ed. Sudbury, MA: Jones and Bartlett, 2008.
5. Starkey C, Johnson G. *Athletic Training and Sports Medicine*, 4th ed. Sudbury, MA: Jones and Bartlett, 2006.
6. Venes D, ed. *Taber's Cyclopedic Medical Dictionary*, 20th ed. Philadelphia: F. A. Davis, 2001.
7. Wilk KE, Meister K, Andrews JA. (2002). Current concepts in the rehabilitation of the overhead throwing athlete. *American Journal of Sports Medicine*, 30(1):136–151.
8. Myers JB, et al. (2005). On-the-field resistance-tubing exercises for throwers: an electromyographic analysis. *Journal of Athletic Training*, 40(1):15–22.
9. Jobe FW, et al. *Shoulder and Arm Exercises for Baseball Players*. Inglewood, CA: Centinela Hospital, 1982.
10. Burkhart SS, Morgan CD, Kibler WB. (2003). The disabled throwing shoulder: spectrum of pathology; Part I: pathoanatomy and biomechanics. *Arthroscopy*, 19(4):404–420.
11. Halbrecht JL, Tirman P, Atkin D. (1999). Internal impingement of the shoulder: comparison of findings between the throwing and nonthrowing shoulders of college baseball players. *Arthroscopy*, 15(3):253–258.
12. Cooper J, Donley P, Verna C, Morgan C. (2002). The relationship between glenohumeral internal rotation deficit and shoulder and elbow pain. *Professional Baseball Athletic Trainers Society Newsletter*, 15(2):4–5.

CHAPTER 15

The Elbow and Forearm

The primary responsibility of the elbow and forearm is placing the hand and fingers in a position so that they can perform their many essential functions. The elbow and forearm fine-tune the hand placement by changing the height, length, and angle of the limb.[1] The forearm is also capable of rotating so that the hand can work effectively in multiple ways.

Anatomy

The elbow and forearm complex is composed of three long bones. The humerus extends from the shoulder distally to the two round knobs (**epicondyles**) on the medial and lateral aspects of the elbow (**Figure 15.1**).

The ulna extends the length of the forearm medially from the elbow to the wrist. The proximal end of the ulna, called the olecranon process, articulates with the humerus to form the hinge joint of the elbow. The olecranon process's articulation with the olecranon fossa of the humerus creates the bony stop that prevents the elbow from hyperextending.

The radius rests laterally beside the ulna to complete the forearm structure. The radius has a rounded head proximally and distally that allows it to rotate, thereby providing the forearm, wrist, and hand with the ability to pronate and supinate.

Numerous muscles assist with motion at the elbow joint. The biceps and triceps muscles both attach distally to the forearm, performing flexion and extension of the elbow, respectively.

The brachioradialis and brachialis muscles also operate at the elbow, assisting the biceps in flexing the joint. The

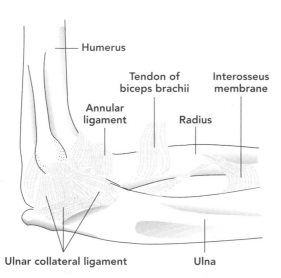

FIGURE 15.1 Anatomy of the elbow.

brachioradialis, also known as the purse muscle, is mainly effective in elbow flexion when the thumb is facing upward. The other principal muscles that act at the elbow are the pronator teres and supinator muscles. These muscles are labeled to describe the actions that they complete. Their motions allow the forearm to properly position itself and the hand to work effectively and efficiently.[1]

Finally, the wrist flexors and extensors also travel through the elbow complex, and although they do not directly act on the joint, the tendons can be injured and cause symptoms to develop at the elbow.

Injuries of the Elbow

■ Elbow Fracture

A fracture at the elbow can occur in any of the three bones in the region, usually as the result of a fall directly on an outstretched arm or direct trauma to the elbow. The fracture causes immediate pain and dysfunction, which do not allow the athlete to continue to play.

SIGNS AND SYMPTOMS

1. Moderate to severe pain
2. Possible deformity
3. Swelling and discoloration
4. Decreased range of motion (ROM)
5. Decreased strength

TREATMENT

The athlete should be splinted and referred to a physician for X-rays. When splinting this injury, it is essential that the athletic trainer check the brachial pulse distally both before and after the splint is applied to ensure that neither the splint nor the injury compromises any vital structures. The neurovascular system for the hand and forearm passes directly beside the olecranon process, so the examiner should be extremely careful to ensure that blood flow and neural input are intact. The examiner should consistently check sensation and capillary refill to rule out neurovascular damage.

Elbow fractures may or may not require surgery depending on the stability and location of the fracture. If surgery is not indicated, the athletic trainer can initiate rest, ice, compression, and elevation (RICE) therapy and ROM exercises. Early ROM exercises are essential for any

---

epicondyles A rounded projection at the end of a bone that serves as an attachment for ligaments or tendons.

elbow injury, especially fractures, because of the risk for permanent loss of range of motion at the joint.

An athlete with an elbow fracture is generally placed in a removable splint that allows for exercises and rehab during the immobilization period.[2] Return to play (RTP) is possible after the fracture has healed and ROM and strength have returned to normal levels. The athlete should be cleared for limited activity within 3 to 4 months with a full return as tolerated.

■ Elbow Dislocation

Elbow dislocations (**Figure 15.2**) are relatively frequent injuries in athletics and result from the same type of trauma as elbow fractures. A fall on the extended elbow will force the ulna, and possibly the radius, to move posteriorly, anteriorly, or laterally and dislocate from the humerus. The conventional method of dislocation is in the posterior direction.[2]

SIGNS AND SYMPTOMS

1. Moderate to severe pain
2. Deformity at elbow
3. Profuse swelling and discoloration
4. Decreased ROM
5. Decreased strength

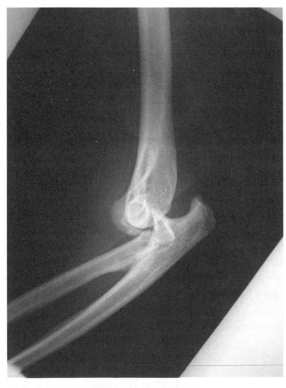

FIGURE 15.2 Elbow dislocation.

TREATMENT

The athlete should be splinted and referred to a physician for reduction of the dislocation. Reduction should only occur after X-rays are taken to rule out an accompanying fracture. The physician also will evaluate the neurovascular status of the arm both before and after reduction to ensure that the arteries, nerves, and veins did not suffer residual damage.

The athlete is then immobilized in a removable splint for approximately 3 to 4 weeks. ROM exercises and strengthening programs are completed during immobilization to minimize the potential for permanent range of motion deficits. RTP is allowed when the athlete has regained full ROM and strength and is symptom-free.

The athlete who has suffered a dislocation may be prone to reinjury and should work to consistently improve strength to avoid repeat injury. It is recommended that the athlete use a brace, sleeve, or tape job for added protection during activity. If recurrent injuries occur, the athlete may require surgery to reconstruct the damaged ligaments.

■ Elbow Hyperextension

The same force that causes an elbow dislocation may also hyperextend the elbow, causing a bone bruise to the olecranon or the humerus as well as soft-tissue damage. An elbow hyperextension is a painful injury because the athlete is unable to fully extend the joint without dramatic pain. The damage that occurs in the joint is relatively minor even though the symptoms may last for several weeks.

SIGNS AND SYMPTOMS

1. Moderate to severe pain
2. Decreased ROM in extension
3. Possible swelling

TREATMENT

Electric and cold modality therapy can help to decrease the initial symptoms. The athlete should be given a ROM program to progressively return to normal movement levels. The athlete is cleared to return to play as soon as tolerated. A hyperextension tape job can be useful in preventing the joint from extending through its full ROM and causing pain during activity.

■ Ligament Sprains

Three principal ligaments support the elbow joint: the ulnar/medial collateral ligament (UCL), the radial/lateral collateral ligament (RCL), and the annular ligament. The RCL is rarely injured during athletics because of the lack of excessive varus stress or force that is applied to the ligament during activity. The annular ligament, which maintains the placement of the radial head in relation to the ulna, is rarely injured by itself. Most annular ligament sprains are associated with elbow dislocations.[2]

On the other hand, the UCL is sprained quite frequently, especially in upper-extremity-dominant sports such as baseball, softball, and tennis. The UCL protects the elbow from the valgus stress that occurs during the late cocking and early acceleration phases of throwing.[2] The UCL can be injured in a variety of manners. Damage can occur as a result of repetitive trauma leading up to one specific incident or movement. UCL sprains or tears may also result from improper mechanics, especially with curveball pitches that place extreme stress on the ligament. Finally, the ligament can suffer damage from an acute traumatic injury similar to that seen with medial collateral ligament (MCL) sprains in the knee.

SIGNS AND SYMPTOMS

1. Mild to moderate pain
2. Slight swelling
3. Athlete will complain of a pop or snap at onset
4. Popping or shifting with further activity

SPECIAL TESTS

The *valgus stress test* for the elbow (**Figure 15.3**) is based on the same concept as that used for the MCL in the knee. The athlete is placed in a seated position while the examiner stabilizes the injured arm with one hand on the wrist and the other at the lateral aspect of the elbow. The elbow is slightly flexed to 20° to 30° and a valgus stress is placed on the outside of the elbow, forcing it medially. A positive test is indicated by pain or joint instability or laxity. The examiner should test bilaterally to ensure that the athlete is not hypermobile.[3]

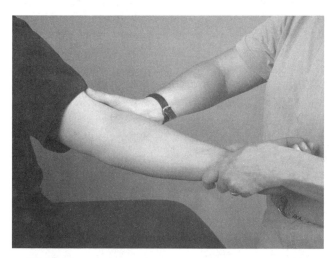

FIGURE 15.3   Valgus stress test.

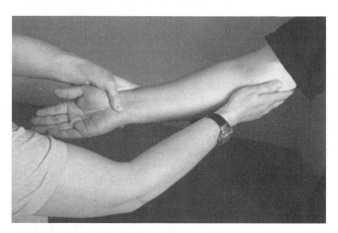

FIGURE 15.4   Varus stress test.

The *varus stress test* (**Figure 15.4**) also is similar to that used in the knee. The varus test determines pain and instability of the RCL ligament. The athlete is placed in a seated position while the examiner stabilizes the injured arm with one hand on the wrist and the other at the lateral aspect of the elbow and stresses the medial aspect of the elbow, forcing it laterally. A positive test is indicated by pain or joint laxity when compared bilaterally.[3]

TREATMENT

The athlete should be referred to a physician for further diagnostic testing. RICE therapy helps to minimize the initial symptoms. Surgery may be required for more serious sprains or tears.

The surgery for UCL injuries, better known as Tommy John surgery, will require 12 to 18 months of recovery prior to RTP. If surgery is not indicated, the athlete may begin a progressive strengthening program and may return when symptoms resolve and the athlete has regained full strength and ROM. The individual would also be wise to evaluate his or her mechanics to determine whether that may have caused the injury.

■ Medial/Lateral Epicondylitis

Inflammation at the medial or lateral epicondyles of the humerus is quite prevalent in athletics. **Medial epicondylitis**, also known as pitcher's or golfer's elbow, occurs when there are repeated forceful flexions of the wrist and valgus torque on the elbow.

> **medial epicondylitis** An overuse injury to the attachments of the flexor and pronator tendons at the medial epicondyle; also known as golfer's elbow.

FIGURE 15.5 Backhand stroke in tennis.

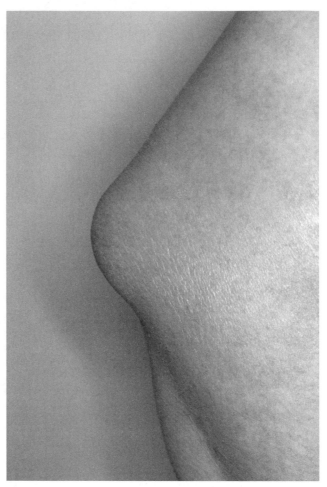

FIGURE 15.6 Elbow bursitis.

Lateral epicondylitis, also known as tennis elbow, is even more common than the medial version and occurs as a result of overuse in the extensor muscles of the wrist and hand. This injury is seen most often with the backhand stroke in tennis (**Figure 15.5**) but can occur in numerous other sports as well.

SIGNS AND SYMPTOMS

1. Pain and tenderness at affected site
2. Pain with activity
3. Decreased ROM

TREATMENT

The athlete is best treated with RICE therapy, anti-inflammatory medication, and ultrasound to reduce the inflammation in the epicondyle and the affected tendons. The pain may persist for several weeks despite treatment. ROM

lateral epicondylitis An overuse injury to the attachments of the extensor and supinator tendons at the lateral epicondyle; also known as tennis elbow.

exercises and wrist and elbow strengthening benefit the athlete in both the short and long term. The athlete may also benefit from a protective sleeve or forearm strap during activity. RTP is allowed when the athlete is able to compete comfortably.

■ Elbow Bursitis

Bursitis in the elbow is a relatively frequent occurrence in athletics (**Figure 15.6**). Also known as olecranon bursitis because of the involved bursa, this injury results from direct acute or chronic trauma to the elbow.

SIGNS AND SYMPTOMS

1. Slight to moderate pain
2. Moderate to severe swelling
3. Decreased ROM

TREATMENT

RICE therapy, specifically the compression aspect, helps to decrease pain and swelling. Chronic swelling may require constant compression with an elbow sleeve or elastic wrap. RTP may occur as soon as tolerated for the athlete with proper compression or padding to prevent reinjury.

Muscle Strains

Biceps Strain

The biceps muscle may be injured through an acute or chronic stress on the distal portion of the muscle/tendon at the elbow that forces the muscle into joint extension or through repetitive flexion motions. Weightlifting pain or strains are more common at the elbow (distal) end of the biceps than at the shoulder (**Figure 15.7**). Football players also tend to strain or irritate the biceps tendon at the elbow during preseason training because of the repetitive stress placed on the muscle with persistent contact. This injury is commonly known as **tackler's elbow**.

SIGNS AND SYMPTOMS

1. Mild to moderate pain
2. Decreased ROM in flexion/extension
3. Pain with motion
4. Possible Popeye deformity if muscle is torn

TREATMENT

RICE therapy with stretching helps to minimize symptoms. The athlete may choose to refrain from full weightlifting sessions until pain subsides because it may cause additional discomfort. Light weights, however, may be beneficial in decreasing the pain and increasing range of motion. Progressive ROM and strengthening exercises help the athlete in his or her recovery. RTP protocols are the same as with other muscle strains. Grade III muscle strains or tears may require surgery and should be referred to a physician.

Triceps Strain

As with biceps strains, the triceps is more often injured at the elbow than at the shoulder. The muscle may be injured through acute or chronic stress that forces the muscle into joint flexion or through repetitive extension motions.

SIGNS AND SYMPTOMS

1. Mild to moderate pain
2. Decreased ROM
3. Pain with motion
4. Decreased strength

TREATMENT

Cold and electric modality therapy with stretching can minimize symptoms and assist in recovery. Progressive

FIGURE 15.7 Weight lifting can cause muscle strains.

ROM and strengthening exercises also benefit the athlete and help in RTP. Protocols for RTP are the same as for other muscle strains. Grade III muscle strains or tears may require surgery and should be referred to a physician.

Injuries to the Forearm

Ulna/Radius Fracture

It is possible to fracture both the ulna and the radius separately, but it is much more common for them to be injured at the same time; therefore, we treat them as one injury. As with other upper extremity fractures, the mechanism of the injury for a forearm fracture is either a direct blow or a fall onto an outstretched arm. It is very

tackler's elbow An overuse injury of the distal biceps tendon that is often seen with football players during preseason as a result of repetitive contact and tackling.

Fast Fact

An acronym often seen during upper extremity evaluations is FOOSH (fall **on** an **o**utstretched **h**and). Many injuries seen in the shoulder, elbow, forearm, and wrist occur as a result of this mechanism. This acronym helps to save time and space in the subjective section of the SOAP note.

common for children and adolescents to fracture these bones during athletics or play.[2]

A specific forearm fracture that occurs at the distal end of the radius and ulna is called a **Colles' fracture** (**Figure 15.8**). This injury occurs as the result of a fall on an outstretched hand, may cause damage to the hand or wrist, and removes the athlete from play for longer than a traditional forearm fracture. A Colles' fracture requires a 1- to 2-month immobilization prior to RTP.[2]

SIGNS AND SYMPTOMS

1. Moderate to severe pain
2. Possible deformity, especially when both bones are fractured
3. Swelling and discoloration
4. Decreased mobility

TREATMENT

RICE therapy, along with splinting, helps stabilize the fracture until a physician sees the athlete. The physician will order X-rays and cast the fractured forearm to prevent further damage. The cast may be left on for 6 to 8 weeks or longer depending on the rate of healing. The athlete may be cleared to return to play, even while still casted, after pain has decreased and symptoms do not recur with activity. An athlete who participates in his or her sport with a cast must cover the cast with foam padding to protect the athlete and other participants from injury.

Any forearm fracture requires an extensive rehab plan after the cast is removed so that the athlete can regain strength in the hand, wrist, and forearm. While immobilized, the athlete should perform hand-strengthening exercises to increase strength and minimize muscle atrophy. Progressive strengthening after immobilization allows the athlete to return to normal functional levels.

Colles' fracture A fracture of the ulna and/or radius in which the distal aspect of the bone displaces dorsally.

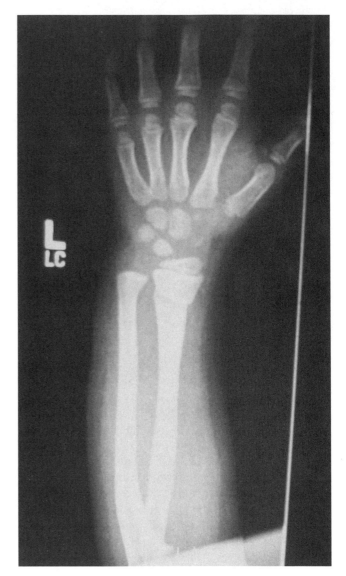

FIGURE 15.8 Colles' fracture.

■ Forearm Contusion

A direct blow to the forearm may also cause a bruise to the underlying muscle and bone. This injury can be painful for the athlete because it may compromise the individual's ability to use his or her hand fully. The contusion may not allow the muscles to have full ROM or strength, which can cause more discomfort than the injury itself.

SIGNS AND SYMPTOMS

1. Pain at the injured site
2. Swelling and discoloration
3. Decreased ROM
4. Decreased strength

TREATMENT

RICE therapy minimizes the symptoms for the athlete. The athlete may return to play as symptoms allow. The use of a protective donut pad can assist in the prevention of further injury for the athlete while also providing peace of mind during activity.

■ Forearm Splints

A strain of the flexor or extensor muscles in the wrist and hand can cause symptoms similar to those seen in shin splints. Therefore, this injury has been labeled forearm splints. It is a repetitive use or repetitive trauma injury often seen in gymnasts, wrestlers, or volleyball players (**Figure 15.9**). Forearm splints typically occur either early or late in the season as a result of the intensity of the preseason or the chronic abuse sustained throughout the year.[2]

SIGNS AND SYMPTOMS

1. Mild pain throughout forearm (pain increases with flexion/extension)
2. Decreased strength
3. Pain with ROM

TREATMENT

Modality treatment for this injury should be based on alleviating the symptoms for the athlete. Ice, cold whirlpool,

FIGURE 15.9   Forearm splints are common among volleyball players.

and anti-inflammatory medicine are especially useful. A compression wrap on the forearm benefits the athlete during activity. Rehab should focus on forearm strengthening and stretching to minimize the risk of recurrence of the injury. RTP is possible for the athlete as symptoms allow. The athlete should practice and compete to tolerance during treatment and rehabilitation.

CHAPTER REVIEW

1. What is the primary responsibility of the elbow and forearm?
2. Why are early ROM exercises essential for elbow injuries?
3. What injury is most often associated with annular ligament damage?

4. *True* or *False*: Biceps and triceps strains are more common at the elbow.
5. What is a Colles' fracture?
6. In which sports do forearm splints frequently occur?

CRITICAL THINKING

How would your rehab change for an athlete with a career-ending (but not life-threatening) injury?

REFERENCES

1. Moore KL, Dalley AF. *Clinically Oriented Anatomy*, 5th ed. Baltimore: Lippincott Williams, & Wilkins, 2005.
2. Prentice WE. *Arnheim's Principles of Athletic Training: A Competency-Based Approach*, 12th ed. Boston: McGraw-Hill, 2006.

3. Magee DJ. *Orthopedic Physical Assessment*, 4th ed. Philadelphia: W. B. Saunders, 2002.

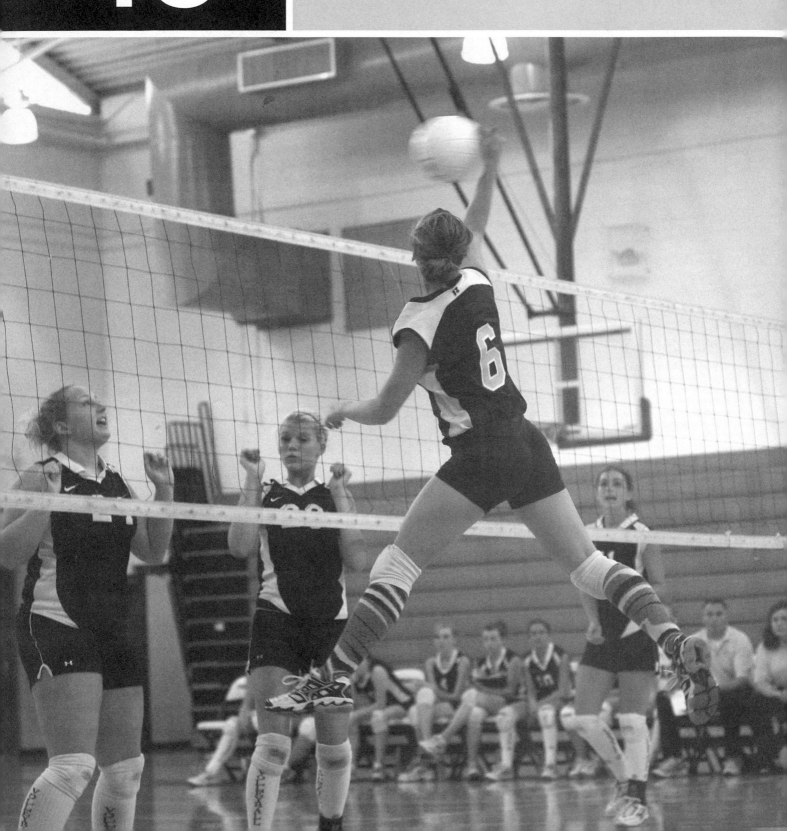

The joints, muscles, and bones that make up the wrist and hand are some of the most active and intricate parts of the upper extremity. The primary functions of the wrist and hand are to gather information for the individual and to allow for dexterous manipulation of objects. The hand acts as a motor and sensory organ that transmits information on temperature, thickness, texture, depth, shape, and the motion of an object.[1] The risk for injury is quite high in this region because the hands are so frequently used and exposed during activity and competition. When the wrist or hand is injured, the athlete's ability to understand, sense, and interact with the outside world is severely compromised.

Anatomy

There are 27 bones found in the wrist and hand. These include the 8 carpal bones, 5 metacarpals, and 14 phalanges (**Figure 16.1**). The carpal bones comprise the main aspect of the wrist and articulate with both the forearm and the hand.

The metacarpals are the bones found in the palm of the hand. These bones are labeled by their position in the hand lateral to medial, beginning with the first metacarpal at the thumb and progressing to the fifth metacarpal at the pinkie.

The phalanx bones, or phalanges, are the bones in the fingers. Each finger has three phalanges with the exception of the thumb, which has two.

Fast Fact

The easy way to remember the carpal bones is to use the mnemonic phrase "Some Lovers Try Positions That They Can't Handle." The first letter of each word relates to the first letter of each carpal bone lateral to medial (in anatomic position) with the proximal row listed first:

Scaphoid
Lunate
Triquetral
Pisiform
Trapezium
Trapezoid
Capitate
Hamate

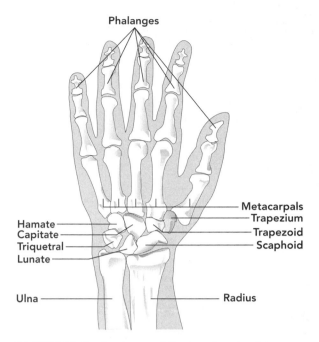

FIGURE 16.1 Anatomy of the hand and wrist.

Numerous joints and ligaments are found throughout the wrist and hand. These joints and ligaments allow for the necessary range of motion while also protecting the region from injury.[2] The only ligament that we discuss specifically is the **triangular fibrocartilage complex** (TFCC), which connects the head of the ulna to the triquetal bone in the wrist.[3] The TFCC ligament is a frequent site of injury in athletics.

The musculature in the wrist, hand, and fingers is quite impressive. There are numerous **intrinsic** (originating in the hand) and **extrinsic** (originating on the forearm) muscles that provide the area with its extreme versatility of movement.

The flexor and extensor muscles of the wrist and hand allow separate flexion and extension of the wrist, hand,

triangular fibrocartilage complex A small cartilaginous structure, similar to the meniscus in the knee, that connects the distal ulna with the triquetrium and lunate bones in the wrist. Also known as the TFCC.

intrinsic muscles Muscles that originate from inside a body segment. In the hand, it is the muscles that originate within the hand.

extrinsic muscles Muscles that originate from outside a body segment. In the hand, they are the muscles that act at the hand but originate in the wrist or forearm.

and fingers, which improves the individual's tactile ability by increasing range of motion.

Each finger contains two flexor tendons and one principal extensor tendon. The separate flexor tendons provide the finger with the ability to flex the proximal interphalangeal (PIP) joint independently of the distal interphalangeal (DIP) joint. The DIP and PIP joints are also capable of flexing independently of the metacarpo-phalangeal (MCP) joint at the knuckles of the hand. Each finger also has intrinsic muscles that allow for individual adduction and abduction.

The thumb and pinkie fingers have their own unique set of muscles and tendons that provide these fingers with an increased range of motion (ROM) over the other three fingers. The muscles and tendons in the thumb are collectively called the thenar muscles, whereas the ones in the pinkie are called the hypothenar muscles.

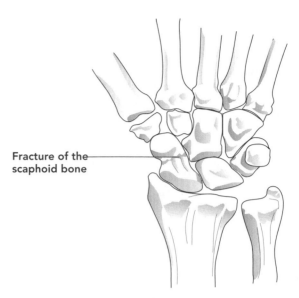

Fracture of the scaphoid bone

FIGURE 16.2 Scaphoid fracture.

 ## Injuries of the Wrist

■ Fractures

The ulna and radius bones end distally at the styloid processes, which when connected form the proximal rim of the wrist. Though the styloid processes may be fractured during a traumatic incident (for example, a Colles' fracture) and labeled as a wrist fracture, it is not a true carpal bone/wrist fracture (**Figure 16.2**). The most common carpal fractures are seen in either the scaphoid or hamate bones.

Scaphoid Fracture

The scaphoid bone is generally injured as the result of a direct fall or impact on an outstretched hand. Often this fracture may be mistaken for a wrist sprain because of their related symptoms. Because the blood supply comes from only one aspect of the scaphoid, if the injury is not treated with proper immobilization, the fractured pieces of the bone may not reunite. When the pieces of the bone do not naturally reattach, a **nonunion fracture** develops. If this occurs, the portion of bone that is separated from the blood supply may potentially become necrotic, which is a precursor to long-term problems.

> **nonunion fracture** Failure of fracture fragments to unite or heal.
> **hypothenar aspect** The fleshy mass of muscle and tissue on the medial (pinkie) side of the palm.

SIGNS AND SYMPTOMS

1. Mild to moderate pain
2. Possible swelling
3. Tenderness in the anatomic snuffbox (where the scaphoid is palpable)
4. Decreased range of motion (ROM) or pain with ROM

TREATMENT

A scaphoid fracture should be treated with immobilization to allow proper healing. The team physician may order X-rays during the first evaluation even though, because of its positioning, a scaphoid fracture is difficult initially to identify on an X-ray. The fracture often does not appear on the X-ray until approximately 10 to 14 days post-injury when the bony healing becomes visible.[4]

Immobilization through casting should be maintained for 6 to 8 weeks to allow for optimal healing. The athlete is cleared to participate with the cast as tolerated as long as the cast is appropriately padded. After the cast is removed, the athlete should continue to tape or brace the wrist to protect from reinjury. If a nonunion fracture occurs, it often requires surgery to reset and pin the bone fragments into their proper position.

Hamate Fracture

The hamate and the spur off of the bone called the hook of the hamate are often injured by a direct blow to the pinkie or **hypothenar aspect** of the hand or a rapid twisting motion associated with bat or racket sports.

SIGNS AND SYMPTOMS

1. Mild to moderate pain
2. Decreased ROM
3. Decreased strength
4. Possible swelling

TREATMENT

As with the scaphoid, the hamate fracture should be X-rayed and immobilized through casting to allow proper healing in the bone. The athlete may return to play as symptoms allow with appropriate padding covering the cast, although this is unlikely in a bat or racket-oriented sport. After the cast is removed (6 to 8 weeks), the hamate is protected with taping and padding over the injured area.

◼ Wrist Dislocation

A dislocation in the wrist is fairly rare in athletics. When the injury does occur, it is often the result of a fall on an outstretched hand (FOOSH) or a forced hyperextension that dislocates one of the carpal bones. The lunate is the most frequently dislocated carpal bone in the wrist.[3] When it is injured; the lunate, located between the radius and the capitate, moves toward the palmar side of the wrist and may place pressure on the tendons and nerves in the carpal tunnel.[5]

SIGNS AND SYMPTOMS

1. Moderate pain
2. Possible deformity
3. Decreased ROM
4. Possible numbness in the hand

TREATMENT

The athlete should be referred to a physician for reduction of the injury. The wrist is then immobilized with a cast to protect from reinjury. After the cast is removed (6 to 8 weeks), the athlete should be taped or braced during subsequent competition for added protection.

◼ TFCC Sprain

The TFCC structure is located between the carpal bones and the ulna. It is a major stabilizer for the wrist, providing rotation and shock absorption.[3] The TFCC can potentially be compared to the meniscus in the knee.

It is injured through an extreme rotation or twist of the wrist usually in bat or racket sports or a forced hyperextension of the wrist. The force may cause a sprain or tear of the structure, causing the athlete great discomfort.

SIGNS AND SYMPTOMS

1. Mild to moderate pain usually on the ulnar side of the wrist

2. Decreased ROM
3. Clicking or popping sound with motion
4. Possible swelling

TREATMENT

The TFCC injury should be treated similarly to a fracture or dislocation. The athlete should be referred to a physician for diagnostic testing and immobilized with a cast. The athlete may play with the cast on if possible—which would not be very likely in a bat- or racket-oriented sport. After the cast is removed, the athlete should be given progressive ROM and strengthening exercises to rehabilitate the injury and protect the wrist from further damage.

◼ Wrist Sprain

A sprain in the wrist is the most common injury seen at this joint. The term *wrist sprain* is a generic, catchall phrase for an injury that occurs to any of the ligaments of the wrist. It is even used erroneously when wrist muscles are strained.[5] It is most often caused by a fall on a hyperextended hand or during a forced twisting motion at the wrist. The sprain is painful and causes dysfunction at the joint.

SIGNS AND SYMPTOMS

1. Mild to moderate pain
2. Possible swelling
3. Decreased ROM

TREATMENT

It is important with this injury to rule out a fracture of any of the bones in the hand and wrist. Once the injury has been correctly assessed as a sprain, it should be treated with cold and electric modality therapy. The athlete should focus on hand and wrist strengthening to prevent reinjury and should be taped or braced when he or she returns to play for added support and protection. The athlete is cleared to return when symptoms subside enough to allow the individual to compete.

◼ Tendinitis/Carpal Tunnel Syndrome

Tendinitis in the wrist is a very common sports injury, especially in racket- or bat-oriented sports. The injury is an overuse condition in the flexor muscles of the wrist. A related injury is often referred to as **carpal tunnel syndrome**. Carpal tunnel syndrome occurs when the flexor

carpal tunnel syndrome A condition of the wrist and hand characterized by compression of that median nerve as it passes through the carpal tunnel.

tendons impinge on the median nerve as a result of repeated wrist flexion activities. This nerve, along with the muscles, arteries, and veins, travels through the tunnel made by the carpal bones and associated ligaments. Either injury can cause discomfort and dysfunction for the athlete when repetitive flexion motions are required.

SIGNS AND SYMPTOMS

1. Mild pain and discomfort
2. Decreased ROM
3. Decreased strength
4. Possible swelling
5. Numbness and tingling in the fingers

TREATMENT

Rest is the best therapy for these injuries. Rest, ice, compression, and elevation (RICE), ultrasound, splinting, and anti-inflammatory medicine also are useful treatments. The athlete should focus on ROM and strengthening exercises and evaluate his or her activity for improper biomechanics. In severe cases of carpal tunnel syndrome, surgery may be warranted. RTP is possible as symptoms subside and to the athlete's tolerance.

Injuries of the Hand and Fingers

■ Metacarpal Fractures

Fractures in the hands and fingers may occur to either the metacarpals or the phalanges. Most metacarpal fractures are the result of a direct blow to the bone from the ground, another player, or a piece of equipment. The force may be directed laterally or longitudinally along the bone.

A common metacarpal fracture is found in the fifth metacarpal and is labeled a **boxer's fracture**. It often results from a punch or direct blow that compresses the long axis of the bone and causes a fracture and possible displacement.

SIGNS AND SYMPTOMS

1. Moderate pain
2. Possible deformity
3. Possible swelling
4. Crepitus

> **boxer's fracture** A fracture specifically involving the fifth metacarpal.

SPECIAL TESTS

The *tap test*, *compression test*, and *rotation test* for fractures are useful with this injury. A positive test is indicated by an increase in pain. The tests should not be conducted if there is obvious deformity.

TREATMENT

The athlete should be referred to a physician for X-rays and casting. Some fractures may require surgery to reset and pin the bone. The need for surgical intervention depends on the location and amount of displacement present at the fracture. In either case, the cast is left on for 4 to 6 weeks followed by ROM and strengthening exercises. The athlete may return to play with the cast as symptoms allow. As before, the cast must be padded for protection of both the individual and other players.

■ Phalangeal Fractures

Fractures in the phalanges happen frequently, especially in the proximal phalanges, and may be caused by a crushing force, direct blow, or twisting motion.[5] The injury is painful for the athlete, but some may choose to continue play if the pain and other symptoms are tolerable.

SIGNS AND SYMPTOMS

1. Mild to moderate pain
2. Possible swelling
3. Possible deformity
4. Decreased ROM
5. Decreased strength

TREATMENT

RICE therapy, along with splinting or taping, is the best treatment for this injury. Phalangeal fractures can be debilitating, but are more often considered a nuisance for the athlete. Depending on the placement of the fracture, the athlete may require casting or splinting for 2 to 4 weeks.

In cases where the fracture is rotated or unstable, surgery may be required to insert an implanted fixation device (i.e., metal screws or plates). If surgery is not required, the athlete is cleared for RTP as symptoms allow. The fingers should be buddy taped (**Figure 16.3**) or braced until all symptoms resolve to protect from further damage. This may take 4 to 6 weeks post-injury. Surgical recovery will take longer, up to 12 weeks for return to play.

■ Finger Dislocation

Dislocation of the finger occurs somewhat frequently in athletics, especially in contact sports such as football. The injury may occur at any of the three finger joints: MCP, PIP, or DIP. With this injury, the joint capsule and/or ligaments stretch or rupture and allow the bones to be

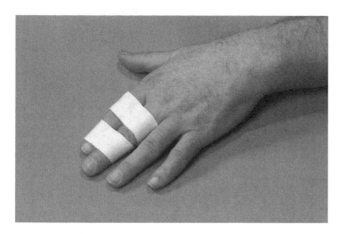

FIGURE 16.3 Finger buddy taping.

displaced. A twisting force, severe hyperextension, or lateral or longitudinal force at the joint causes the dislocation. The injury is quite painful, and there is often significant alarm exhibited by the athlete because of the unnatural-looking deformity that is associated with dislocations.

SIGNS AND SYMPTOMS

1. Moderate pain
2. Obvious deformity
3. Possible swelling and discoloration
4. Decreased ROM
5. Decreased strength

TREATMENT

A trained professional should reduce the finger to its proper position. Further injury to the joint or permanent damage to the neurovascular structures in the finger may occur if the dislocation is reduced by anyone other than a trained professional. It is much more difficult to reduce a first-time dislocation than one that chronically occurs.

Once the injury is reduced, it should be taped or splinted to prevent reinjury and X-rayed to rule out a fracture. The athlete may return to play after symptoms have diminished. The athlete should be taped or braced during activity for at least 2 to 4 weeks to avoid a repeat dislocation.

◼ Gamekeeper's Thumb

Gamekeeper's thumb is an injury to the ulnar collateral ligament (UCL) at the MCP joint of the thumb. The injury is caused by a forced abduction and hyperextension of the joint that sprains or tears the ligament. It is most often seen in either football or skiing athletes.[6]

SIGNS AND SYMPTOMS

1. Moderate pain
2. Joint laxity with valgus stress

3. Decreased ROM
4. Decreased strength

SPECIAL TESTS

The *pinch test* is a manual muscle test of the thumb. The athlete pinches the tips of the thumb and index finger together and attempts to prevent the examiner from separating the two fingers. A positive test is indicated by increased pain or decreased strength in the thumb when compared bilaterally.[1]

The *valgus stress test* for the thumb is completed in the same manner as it is for the knee or elbow. The examiner grasps the thumb at the PIP joint and along the metacarpal. A valgus stress is then placed on the MCP joint to assess the integrity of the ligament. Pain and joint laxity are positive indicators of a sprain or tear.

TREATMENT

The athlete should be referred to a physician for follow-up and possible surgery. Surgical intervention is required if the ligament is completely torn and the joint is unstable. If surgery is not necessary, the athlete will be given a thumb splint or removable cast to protect the joint from further damage. The splint should be used for 2 to 4 weeks or until symptoms resolve. The athlete may play with the splint on as tolerated. After the splint is removed, the athlete should be taped for continued protection.

gamekeeper's thumb Ulnar collateral ligament rupture of the first metacarpophalangeal joint. Also known as skier's thumb.

FIGURE 16.4 Collateral ligament sprain.

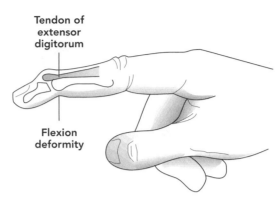

FIGURE 16.5 Mallet finger.

■ Finger Sprain

Finger sprains occur (**Figure 16.4**) similarly to sprains in the elbow or knee. Each interphalangeal joint has collateral ligaments that stabilize it from medial and lateral stress. Injury to these ligaments can range from grade I (minor) to grade III (complete tear). Finger sprains are seen most often in sports such as football and basketball and result from excessive stress on the ligament.

SIGNS AND SYMPTOMS

1. Pain relative to the degree of injury
2. Possible swelling
3. Decreased ROM
4. Decreased strength

TREATMENT

RICE therapy and splinting are useful tools to decrease symptoms and protect the joint structure. The athlete is allowed to return to play with this injury as symptoms allow with appropriate taping or bracing. A collateral or buddy taping helps to prevent reinjury and provide added protection for the joint. The more serious sprains may require an increased healing time and rehabilitation exercises to strengthen the joint.

Tendon Injuries

As was mentioned earlier, there are two flexor tendons and one primary extensor tendon in each finger. Any of these may be injured, resulting in a tear or rupture in the tendons.

■ Mallet Finger

A rupture of the extensor tendon causes what is known as a **mallet finger** (**Figure 16.5**). A mallet injury frequently occurs because of direct contact to the tip of the finger, usually by a ball. The contact causes a quick hyperflexion of the DIP, which tears the extensor tendon from the bone.

SIGNS AND SYMPTOMS

1. Mild to moderate pain in distal phalanx
2. Obvious deformity—distal phalanx is flexed at a 30° angle
3. Loss of ROM/inability to extend DIP joint

TREATMENT

RICE therapy helps to decrease any pain or possible swelling, but full recovery requires consistent splinting. The finger must be braced in full extension for 6 to 8 weeks to allow the tendon to reattach to the bone. If bracing or splinting is not implemented, the athlete will permanently lose extension of the distal phalanx. Surgical intervention is not used for this injury. RTP may occur after symptoms resolve and with proper splinting to prevent further damage and allow healing to occur.

■ Jersey Finger

A **jersey finger** injury is a rupture of the flexor tendon from the distal phalanx (**Figure 16.6**). The injury derives its name from its typical mechanism of injury—the athlete generally ruptures the tendon after attempting to grab an opponent's jersey or getting the finger caught in the uniform and having it forcefully extended at the DIP joint.

mallet finger Avulsion of the extensor digitorum longus from the distal phalanx.

jersey finger Rupture of the flexor digitorum longus tendon from the distal phalanx of the finger.

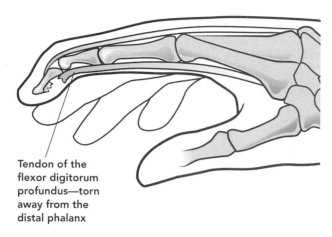

Tendon of the flexor digitorum profundus—torn away from the distal phalanx

FIGURE 16.6   Jersey finger.

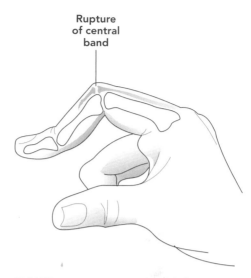

Rupture of central band

FIGURE 16.7   Boutonniere deformity.

SIGNS AND SYMPTOMS

1. Mild to moderate pain
2. Loss of ROM in flexion for distal phalanx
3. Decreased strength

TREATMENT

The athlete will express some level of concern for this injury because he or she is no longer able to flex the finger or properly make a fist. This injury must be repaired surgically for the athlete to regain function. The surgery needs to be scheduled fairly quickly (within 10 days) to ensure optimal recovery. If the surgery is postponed, the athlete risks tendon degradation, thereby making reattachment either impossible or very difficult—often requiring multiple reconstructive surgeries.

Rehab for this injury requires 10 to 12 weeks, using progressive ROM exercises and finger strengthening. ROM is difficult at first because the athlete will have difficulty with even minimal flexion or extension of the finger. RTP is possible following rehabilitation, but the athlete should be braced or taped to protect from reinjury.

■ Boutonniere Deformity

The third tendon injury, the **boutonniere deformity**, occurs when the extensor tendon ruptures at its attachment to the middle phalanx (**Figure 16.7**). The injury causes the PIP joint to flex and the DIP joint to extend forcing the finger into an extremely uncomfortable position that is not easily corrected. The mechanism of injury is typically a direct blow to the tip of the finger.

SIGNS AND SYMPTOMS

1. Moderate pain and discomfort
2. Loss of any ROM
3. Obvious deformity

TREATMENT

As with the mallet finger, the athlete must be splinted with the PIP joint in extension for 6 to 8 weeks. Failure to splint the injury results in permanent deformity of the finger. Rehab exercises should focus on DIP joint flexion. RTP may occur as symptoms resolve and with the appropriate splinting.

■ Swan Neck Deformity

Not technically a tendon injury, the **swan neck deformity** is a finger injury with tendinous involvement.[5] The injury occurs as the result of a severe hyperextension causing the volar plate of the PIP joint to shift or tear. This shifting causes painful hyperextension at the PIP joint, which forces the finger into the shape of a swan neck.

SIGNS AND SYMPTOMS

1. Moderate pain
2. Obvious deformity
3. Loss of ROM

boutonniere deformity Deformity characterized by flexion of the PIP joint and hyperextension of the DIP joint most often resulting from injury to the central slip of the extensor digitorum tendon and its insertion at the base of the middle phalanx.

swan neck deformity A deformity caused by hyperextension at the PIP joint and hyperflexion at the DIP resulting from disruption of the volar plate and tensioning of the flexor tendons.

TREATMENT

The athlete should be treated conservatively with splinting and RICE therapy to minimize symptoms. The PIP joint should be splinted in a flexed position of 20° to 30° for approximately 3 to 6 weeks.[3] The injury may then be buddy taped for continued protection and a progressive rehabilitation regimen started. RTP is possible as soon as symptoms allow with the proper splinting and protection. Surgery may be required if the injury consistently recurs or proper healing does not take place.

Wrist and Thumb Taping

A frequent form of preventive and post-injury taping utilized in athletics is wrist and thumb taping. Taping this area can reduce excessive motion and decrease the risk of injury for the athlete (see **Figures 16.8** through **16.17**). As with the ankle taping, the athletic trainer should practice this taping procedure often to ensure that he or she is proficient in the technique so that the athlete receives the best taping possible.

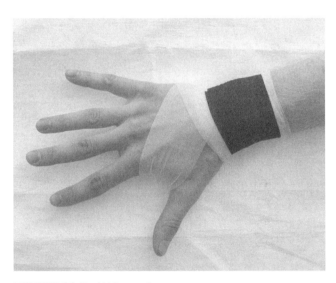

FIGURE 16.8 Wrist taping.

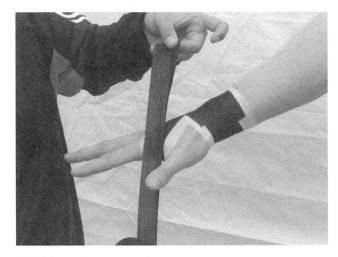

FIGURE 16.9 Figure eight strips.

FIGURE 16.10 Thumb spica strips.

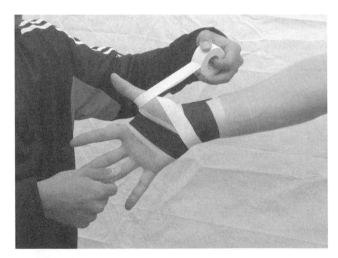

FIGURE 16.11 Thumb spica strips.

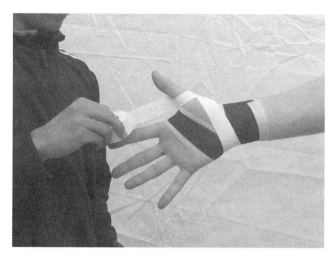

FIGURE 16.12 Apply strips in the opposite direction.

FIGURE 16.15 Alternate strips moving toward the nail.

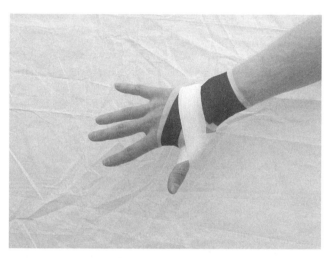

FIGURE 16.13 Stabilize the wrist.

FIGURE 16.16 Figure eight strips.

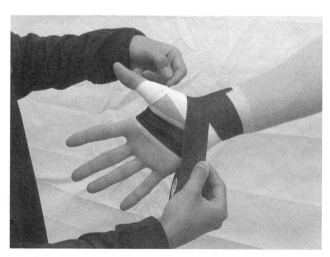

FIGURE 16.14 Stabilize the wrist.

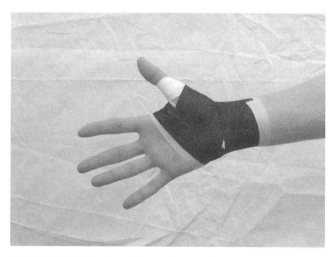

FIGURE 16.17 Complete wrist taping.

CHAPTER REVIEW

1. What is the primary function of the wrist and hand?

2. What are the muscles found in the pinkie collectively called?

3. What two bones are most commonly fractured in the wrist?

4. What ligament is injured in a gamekeeper's thumb?

5. List the four types of finger tendon injuries.

CRITICAL THINKING

How does your athlete's wrist/hand injury affect his or her class work? What can you do to help?

REFERENCES

1. Magee DJ. *Orthopedic Physical Assessment*, 4th ed. Philadelphia: W. B. Saunders, 2002.

2. Moore KL, Dalley AF. *Clinically Oriented Anatomy*, 5th ed. Baltimore: Lippincott Williams, & Wilkins, 2005.

3. Prentice WE. *Arnheim's Principles of Athletic Training: A Competency-Based Approach*, 12th ed. Boston: McGraw-Hill, 2006.

4. Quinn E. *Scaphoid Fracture of the Wrist*. Retrieved October 3, 2007, from http://sportsmedicine.about.com.

5. Pfeiffer RP, Mangus BC. *Concepts of Athletic Training*, 5th ed. Sudbury, MA: Jones and Bartlett, 2008.

6. Hannibal M, Roger D. *Gamekeeper's Thumb*. Retrieved September 18, 2007, from http://www.emedicine.com.

General Medical Conditions

V

CHAPTER 17 General Medical Conditions

General Medical Conditions

General medical conditions in athletics range from minor nuisances (some skin conditions or colds) to major life-threatening issues (**hypertrophic cardiomyopathy** or **pneumothorax**). It is important for athletic trainers to have a broad understanding of the many disorders and illnesses that their athletes may face. The close proximity and contact during both competition and living/housing arrangements offer plentiful opportunities for disease transmission. Proper management of illnesses and disorders provides the healthiest athletic population possible and many fewer concerns for the athlete's safety and well being.

General Illnesses

■ Common Cold

The common cold is the most widespread communicable disease found in both athletics and in everyday life. Colds can be contracted through direct or indirect contact with infectious germs. The germs are spread through the spray expelled by sneezing, coughing, or talking. Cold germs may also spread through contact with an infected object.

SIGNS AND SYMPTOMS

1. Sore throat
2. Coughing
3. Sneezing
4. Stuffy or runny nose
5. Yellow or green mucus

TREATMENT

An athlete suffering from a cold should rest and consume as many fluids as possible, preferably water, juice, or sports drinks. Symptoms associated with the common cold can be treated, but the virus itself is usually present for 7 to 10 days. While suffering from cold symptoms, the athlete should avoid contact with fellow teammates to limit the spread of the virus.

■ Respiratory Infections

Respiratory infections can be categorized into two groups: **upper respiratory infections (URI)** and **lower respiratory infections (LRI)**. Upper respiratory infections produce similar symptoms to the common cold. Athletes with an upper respiratory infection should be isolated from teammates to minimize the risk of disease transmission.

SIGNS AND SYMPTOMS

1. Sore throat
2. Coughing
3. Sneezing
4. Stuffy or runny nose
5. Yellow or green mucus

TREATMENT

Typically, this infection lasts only a few days and should not dramatically affect participation in athletics. The athlete should be monitored and may demonstrate more fatigue than normal, but is cleared to participate as tolerated. If symptoms persist for a longer period of time—more than one week—the athlete should be referred to a physician to ensure that other illnesses are not present.

Lower respiratory infections tend to last longer than upper respiratory infections do—sometimes up to several weeks. Lower respiratory infections may include such serious issues as bronchitis and pneumonia.

SIGNS AND SYMPTOMS

1. Coughing
2. **Malaise**
3. Fatigue
4. Fever
5. Yellow or green sputum

TREATMENT

Athletes with lower respiratory infections should be referred to a physician to ensure that the more serious forms of illness are not present. Return-to-play criteria are determined in consultation with the physician and based on the athlete's capabilities.

■ Influenza

Influenza, or the flu, is essentially an energy-sapping viral attack on the body. Incidents of influenza have become so prevalent that an annual flu shot is recommended for at-risk individuals, including the elderly, children,

hypertrophic cardiomyopathy A disorder in which the heart muscle is enlarged and so strong that it does not relax enough to fill the heart with blood. This leads to reduced pumping ability.

pneumothorax The presence of air or gas in the pleural cavity.

upper respiratory infection Infection of the upper respiratory tract.

lower respiratory infection Infection of the lower respiratory tract.

malaise A vague, general feeling of illness or fatigue.

influenza An acute contagious viral infection characterized by fever, chills, muscular pain, and prostration.

pregnant women, health professionals, and individuals with decreased immune systems.

SIGNS AND SYMPTOMS

1. Fever
2. Cough
3. Sluggishness
4. Headache
5. Runny or stuffy nose
6. General body aches

TREATMENT

As with the common cold, an athlete suffering from the flu should rest and consume fluids to assist in the body's fight against the virus. Treating the symptoms of the illness through over-the-counter (OTC) medicines generally helps the sick individual feel better, although the virus will remain for 7 to 10 days. Contact with teammates should be avoided to prevent the spread of the disease.

■ Mononucleosis

Mononucleosis, often called mono, is an acute viral disease that is quite common in college-aged individuals. It has been called the kissing disease because it is primarily transmitted through saliva. Mononucleosis is a concern in athletics because it can cause extreme fatigue and inflames the spleen, which can increase the risk for a rupture of that organ.[1]

SIGNS AND SYMPTOMS

1. Extreme fatigue
2. Sore throat
3. Swollen lymph nodes
4. Inflamed/enlarged spleen

TREATMENT

An athlete experiencing the symptoms of mononucleosis or one who has been in contact with others who have been diagnosed with the disease should see a physician for a blood test to determine whether the disease is present. Symptoms require approximately 4 to 6 weeks to appear after initial infection.

The athlete should be treated symptomatically and rest as much as possible. The concern with mononucleosis for athletes specifically is the inflamed spleen. The risk for a ruptured spleen increases dramatically if the athlete returns to competition, especially in contact sports, while the organ is still enlarged. A physician must clear the athlete prior to return to play (RTP).

The athlete should avoid interaction with teammates to avoid spreading the disease. As a general protocol, the athletic training staff should sanitize all water bottles, bottle tops, and coolers daily to prevent the spread of this or any other infectious disease.

■ Meningitis

Meningitis is a viral or bacterial infection that inflames the meninges surrounding the spinal cord and brain. Meningitis may be contracted following infections in the ear, throat, or respiratory system. The infection causes swelling in the brain, enlargement of the ventricles, and hemorrhage of the brain stem.[1] Meningitis has recently become more prevalent in the collegiate setting as a result of the close living arrangements and constant interaction present on campus.

SIGNS AND SYMPTOMS

1. High fever
2. Neck stiffness
3. Headache
4. Photophobia
5. Symptoms may progress to convulsions, coma, and possibly death

TREATMENT

Any individual who may be suffering from meningitis should be rushed to a physician immediately to be tested for the disease. A spinal tap procedure is conducted to test the cerebrospinal fluid for infectious materials. If the individual has a positive test, he or she will be quarantined, often in an intensive care unit, and given intravenous (IV) antibiotics and steroids to combat the disease.[1] Anyone who has come in close contact with an individual diagnosed with meningitis should be tested for the disease as a preventive measure.

Many colleges now require or highly recommend a meningitis vaccine for incoming first-year students.

General Medical Trauma

■ Pneumothorax/Hemothorax

A pneumothorax results from an injury to the lungs that causes the **pleural cavity** surrounding the organs to fill

---

mononucleosis A common infectious disease usually affecting young people and characterized by fever, sore throat, swollen lymph nodes, and fatigue. The symptoms may last for several weeks.

meningitis Inflammation of the meninges of the brain and the spinal cord, most often caused by a bacterial or viral infection and characterized by fever, vomiting, intense headache, and stiff neck.

pleural cavity The cavity in the thorax that contains the lungs and heart.

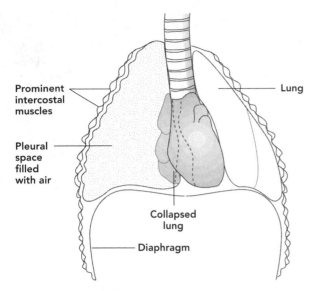

Prominent intercostal muscles

Lung

Pleural space filled with air

Collapsed lung

Diaphragm

FIGURE 17.1 Pneumothorax.

with air (**Figure 17.1**). A **hemothorax** is similar to a pneumothorax, but instead of air, the pleural cavity fills with blood. Blood and air can also enter the cavity at the same time, causing what is known as a **hemopneumothorax**. An injury on one side of the body may also compress the heart and opposite lung, causing what is known as a **tension pneumothorax**.[1]

When the cavity fills as a result of the injury, the lung on the affected side collapses and becomes ineffective. These injuries are caused by direct trauma to the chest, fractured ribs, a puncture of the lungs, or a shearing of blood vessels in the pleural cavity or the lungs.

SIGNS AND SYMPTOMS

1. Moderate to extreme pain
2. Difficulty breathing (**dyspnea**)
3. Bluish skin color (cyanosis)

TREATMENT

This injury requires immediate attention by a physician. The athlete should be transported to a hospital for treatment to avoid major complications. During transport, the athlete's vital signs (i.e., pulse, blood pressure, and respirations) should be constantly monitored. The physician who is monitoring the athlete's progress will determine RTP. This injury requires a lengthy recovery period prior to any return to activity.

■ Liver Contusion

A direct blow to the upper right quadrant of the abdomen may cause a contusion or laceration of the liver. This injury is relatively uncommon in athletics but can cause serious complications, even death, if not treated appropriately.

Fast Fact

Signs of shock include moist, pale skin with a cool, clammy texture; weak and rapid pulse; fast, shallow breathing; decreased blood pressure; and confusion and **disorientation**.[1] Shock by itself is a life-threatening condition and should be treated as such with an immediate referral to a physician.

SIGNS AND SYMPTOMS

1. Bruising over the upper right abdomen
2. Athlete may show signs of shock
3. Pain, which may refer to the right shoulder

TREATMENT

Injury to the liver requires an immediate referral to a physician for evaluation and possible surgery. Any damage to the internal organs can become life-threatening quickly and proper, timely care is essential. The athletic trainer should monitor vital signs throughout transport to the hospital to ensure that the athlete's condition does not degrade and the athlete does not go into **shock**.

■ Commotio Cordis

Commotio cordis results from a direct blow to the chest that causes cardiac arrest. It is a fluke injury where the trauma occurs during a narrow window of 15 to 30 milliseconds in the heart beat cycle.[2] The most common sports in which commotio cordis may occur are baseball,

hemothorax Accumulation of blood in the pleural cavity.

hemopneumothorax The accumulation of air and blood in the pleural cavity.

tension pneumothorax Pneumothorax resulting from a wound in the chest wall that acts as a valve that permits air to enter the pleural cavity but prevents its escape.

dyspnea Difficulty or trouble breathing.

disorientation Mental confusion or impaired awareness, especially regarding place, time, or personal identity.

shock A condition of inadequate peripheral blood flow resulting from a traumatic incident.

commotio cordis A sudden disturbance of heart rhythm. It occurs as the result of a blunt, non-softball, ice hockey, or lacrosse because of the low-mass, high-velocity ball/puck used for these sports.

SIGNS AND SYMPTOMS

1. Onset of **ventricular fibrillation** or **cardiac arrest**
2. Immediate collapse

TREATMENT

An athlete who suffers an incident of commotio cordis should be treated with immediate cardiopulmonary resuscitation (CPR) and use of an **automated external defibrillator (AED)**. Unfortunately, few cases of commotio cordis are successfully resuscitated.[2] If the injury causes cardiac arrest, the AED will be unable to defibrillate the athlete because of the lack of a shockable rhythm. The athlete should receive all possible care in the timeliest manner to provide him or her with the best chance of survival.

■ Sports Hernia

The term **sports hernia** has become widespread in recent years because of an increased public awareness resulting from numerous prominent professional athletes suffering from the injury. A sports hernia is a vague term used to describe a type of weakness in the anterior abdominal wall. The weakness in the wall allows for an abdominal

penetrating impact to the precordial region, often caused by impact of a ball, a bat, or other projectile. This often results in death.

ventricular fibrillation An often fatal form of arrhythmia characterized by rapid, irregular fibrillar twitching of the ventricles of the heart in place of normal contractions, resulting in a loss of pulse.

cardiac arrest Sudden cessation of heartbeat and cardiac function, resulting in the loss of effective circulation.

automated external defibrillator (AED) A portable electronic device that automatically diagnoses the potentially life-threatening cardiac arrhythmias of ventricular fibrillation and ventricular tachycardia in a patient and is able to treat them through defibrillation.

sports hernia A syndrome characterized by chronic groin pain in athletes that results from a weakening of the muscles and tissue in the abdominal wall.

cellulitis An inflammation of body tissue characterized by fever, swelling, redness, and pain.

erythema Redness of the skin.

bulge as the contents of the abdomen push forward. Sports hernias may result from an inherent weakness in the wall that progressively worsens or from one traumatic incident that strains the region and causes abdominal wall damage.[3]

SIGNS AND SYMPTOMS

1. Pinching pain that may gradually become more severe
2. Possible bulge in abdomen
3. Decreased ROM in trunk flexion/extension
4. Dysfunction with athletic or strenuous activities

SPECIAL TESTS

The athlete will be asked to complete the *Valsalva maneuver* by holding his or her breath and bearing down as if conducting a bowel movement, thereby causing the abdominal muscles to contract. A positive test is indicated if the pain increases at the injury site during the test and decreases once normal breathing has resumed.

TREATMENT

A sports hernia is treated according to the symptoms of the athlete and the severity of the injury. The athlete should be referred to a physician for further diagnostic testing. If the injury is minor, the athlete may choose to treat it similarly to a groin strain with RICE therapy, anti-inflammatory medicine, and abdominal strengthening. If the injury is more severe, it may require surgery to strengthen the wall and close any openings in the tissue.

RTP following surgery requires 6 to 12 weeks rest, followed by a gradual return to activity to minimize an increase in symptoms. Conservative treatment allows a faster RTP, but may leave the athlete prone to reinjury.

■ Bacterial Skin Disorders

■ Cellulitis

Cellulitis is an infection of the deep layers of skin, causing inflammation and reddening of the external layers. The infection may be caused by other bodily infections or through contact with unclean surfaces such as game fields, courts, or gymnastics/wrestling mats.

SIGNS AND SYMPTOMS

1. Reddish skin (**erythema**)
2. Warm skin
3. Close-spaced pustules with yellowish discharge
4. Athlete may experience flu-like symptoms

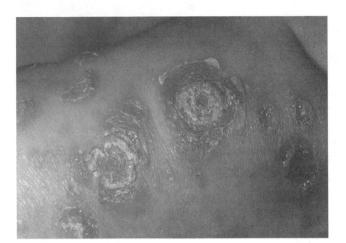

FIGURE 17.2   Impetigo.

TREATMENT

The primary complication associated with cellulitis occurs when the infection becomes systemic and spreads throughout the body. The initial infection is easily treated with antibiotics, but, as it spreads, it becomes more powerful and more difficult to treat. If it becomes **systemic**, the athlete will suffer from flu-like symptoms that progressively worsen. After the cellulitis becomes a systemic concern, the athlete may require IV antibiotics and hospitalization to effectively treat the infection. RTP is allowed for the athlete once the symptoms have resolved and the athlete has returned to full strength.

■ Impetigo

Impetigo (**Figure 17.2**) is a skin disease frequently seen in athletes who are in close contact during practices or competition (for example, wrestlers and boxers). Impetigo is a bacterial infection that causes yellowish-red pustules to form in areas of high friction.

SIGNS AND SYMPTOMS

1. Yellowish-red pustules form in affected area
2. Pustules may itch or burn
3. If pustules rupture, they will create more pustules

---

systemic Pertaining to or affecting the body as a whole.

impetigo A contagious bacterial skin infection, usually of children, that is characterized by the eruption of superficial pustules and the formation of thick yellow crusts.

ringworm Any of a number of contagious fungal skin diseases characterized by ring-shaped, scaly, itching patches on the skin.

TREATMENT

The athlete suffering from impetigo should be given an antibacterial cream as well as prescription antibiotics. The infection tends to resolve quickly with proper treatment. Prior to RTP, the athlete should avoid contact with other athletes or the competition surface to prevent the rupture of the pustules and infection transmission. As the pustules dry and disappear from the skin, the athlete may return to organized practice and competition (48 to 72 hours). During activity, the athlete should cover the affected area with a bandage or tape until the pustules have completely disappeared to ensure that there is no transmission. A reusable elastic wrap or neoprene sleeve should not be used to cover the infection because it may carry the bacteria and transmit it back to the athlete or someone else at a later date.

■ Fungal Skin Disorders

■ Ringworm

Ringworm (**Figure 17.3**) comes in many varieties and can be found throughout the body. From scalp infections to jock itch to athlete's foot, ringworm is the principal fungal infection afflicting athletes (**Figure 17.4**). Ringworm is medically labeled as tinea with the location on the body listed afterward to specify the area affected (**Table 17.1**). This infection is frequently seen in sports with high levels of perspiration and close contact such as wrestling or boxing. The infection also breeds in dark, damp areas such as showers and locker rooms, which leads to cases of jock itch and athlete's foot.[1]

SIGNS AND SYMPTOMS

1. Affected area is circular in shape
2. Reddish outer edges of the circle

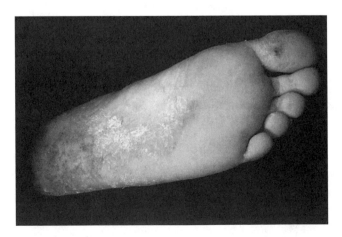

FIGURE 17.3   Ringworm.

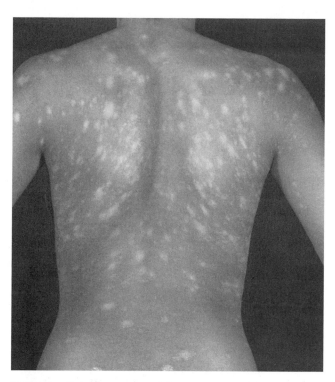

FIGURE 17.4 Tinea versicolor.

3. Scaly, cracking skin throughout infected area
4. Itching or burning

TREATMENT

Topical creams, ointments, or shampoos are especially effective on ringworm. The ointment should be placed on the infection site one to two times a day for several

TABLE 17.1	
TYPES OF RINGWORM	
Types of Ringworm	Affected Areas
Tinea capitis	Head/scalp
Tinea corporis	Trunk/extremities
Tinea unguium	Toe/fingernail
Tinea cruris	Groin
Tinea pedis	Foot
Tinea versicolor	Abdomen/neck/chest

herpes Any of several viral diseases causing the eruption of small blister-like vesicles on the skin or mucous membranes.

weeks to eliminate the condition. If this treatment is ineffective, the athlete may require prescription antifungal medicine. Basic hygiene can help the athlete prevent future outbreaks and decreases transmission to other individuals.

The athlete may practice and compete with ringworm if he or she is treating the infection and it is protectively covered with bandages or tape. A reusable elastic wrap or neoprene sleeve should not be used to cover the infection because it may carry the fungus and transmit it back to the athlete or someone else at a later date.

Viral Skin Disorders

Herpes

Herpes can form in numerous places on the body, including the lips (herpes simplex/cold sores), on the skin (herpes zoster/shingles or herpes gladiatorum), and the genital area (herpes simplex). The most familiar incidence of herpes in athletics is herpes gladiatorum. The herpes gladiatorum form of the virus derives its name from the gladiator sports that include wrestling, judo, and boxing. A herpes infection creates a lesion that has a reddish tinge with a yellow crusty discharge (**Figure 17.5**). Herpes is a highly contagious virus that will return repeatedly throughout the life of the athlete. Once an area is infected, the nerve root for that area becomes a permanent home for the virus where it stays in a resting state until activated by fatigue, stress, illness, or other factors.

SIGNS AND SYMPTOMS

1. Reddish sores with a whitish-yellow center
2. Yellow, crusty discharge
3. Burning or itching sensation

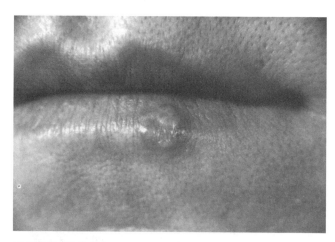

FIGURE 17.5 Herpes.

TREATMENT

An athlete suffering from herpes must be removed from play immediately and remain sidelined until the sores have dried out or dissipated. The discharge from the sores and the open sores themselves are extremely contagious and allow the disease to be transmitted easily to fellow athletes. Several antiviral prescription medicines are available and can minimize the symptoms or shorten the length of outbreak but cannot permanently remove the virus. Because of the risk for infection, all wrestlers must pass a skin check prior to competing in various events.

■ MRSA

Methicillin-resistant *Staphylococcus aureus*, or **MRSA**, (**Figure 17.6**) is a recent addition to the list of concerns for athletic trainers. Within the past several years, increasing incidence of this form of the staph virus in the athletic setting has forced athletic trainers to reconsider cleaning habits and athletic training facility policies to minimize the risk of infection for athletes. Often found in whirlpools, saunas, or hot tubs, MRSA is a highly infectious disease contracted through open wounds. An athlete that develops MRSA requires IV antibiotics and often surgery to remove all infectious cells from the body. Once contracted by one athlete, the disease can transmit rapidly throughout the team/program—if not treated quickly and properly—causing a major epidemic.[4]

SIGNS AND SYMPTOMS

1. Flu-like symptoms
2. Unusual swelling
3. Redness and warmth in affected areas
4. May begin at site of open wound
5. Possibility of developing boils, cellulitis, or open sores

TREATMENT

Isolation from the team, prescription antibiotics, IV antibiotics, and potentially surgery all help to treat the infection and prevent transmission. Proper assessment and rapid referral to a physician may decrease the necessity for surgery for the affected athlete. RTP is possible after all symptoms have resolved and the athlete returns to full strength. Unfortunately, the strength of the infection could require 4 to 6 weeks or longer for the athlete to recover.

■ Management of Skin Disorders

All skin disorders, whether they are bacterial, fungal, or viral, may be prevented through proper cleaning procedures both in the athletic training room and in athletic facilities. All surfaces that athletes come in contact with should be sanitized regularly with a specifically designed

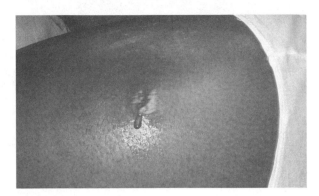

FIGURE 17.6 MRSA.

cleaning agent. Any clothing or equipment worn by athletes should also be washed or cleaned regularly with hot water and a cleaning agent to kill any organisms that may be present.

Finally, if any athletes have been diagnosed with a skin disorder, they should be either kept out of contact with other athletes or have the affected area properly covered to prevent transmission. The participation level of the athlete is determined by the specific skin disorder in question. The National Collegiate Athletic Association (NCAA) has produced a document outlining specific criteria for disqualification because of skin disorders in wrestling—a sport with a long history of dermatologic issues.

General Medical Conditions

■ Diabetes Mellitus

There are two forms of **diabetes mellitus** that can develop in an individual. Type 1 diabetes, also known as insulin-dependent, or juvenile, diabetes, is seen in younger individuals (generally under 35 years of age). Type 1 diabetes is often a congenital disease caused by a genetic abnormality.

MRSA Methicillin-resistant *Staphylococcus aureus*; a bacterium responsible for difficult-to-treat infections in humans.

diabetes mellitus A variable disorder of carbohydrate metabolism caused by a combination of hereditary and environmental factors and usually characterized by inadequate secretion or utilization of insulin.

TABLE 17.2

SIGNS AND SYMPTOMS OF DIABETES

	Type 1 Diabetes	Type 2 Diabetes
Initial Symptoms	1. Frequent urination 2. Constant thirst 3. Weight loss 4. Constant hunger 5. Fatigue	1. Frequent urination 2. Constant thirst 3. Fatigue 4. Peripheral neural dysfunction
Risk Factors	1. Heredity 2. Usually under 35 years of age 3. Active, thin body types	1. Obesity 2. Inactivity 3. Poor nutritional habits 4. High blood pressure 5. Ethnicity

Type 2 diabetes, or non-insulin-dependent diabetes, is directly associated with lifestyle decisions such as obesity, poor nutrition, and inactivity. Type 2 diabetes has previously been associated with older individuals; however, with the obesity epidemic facing American youth, type 2 diabetes diagnoses can no longer be restricted by age.[5]

Either form of diabetes causes a partial or complete inability of the pancreas to release insulin, the primary regulator of glucose levels in the body.[6] Unregulated glucose levels can cause neurovascular disorders, organ damage, and possibly death.

Athletes with diabetes should not be restricted from athletic competition. Research has shown that exercise improves quality of life and may reduce long-term complications of diabetes.[5–7] If there is a diabetic athlete on the team, special care should be taken by the athletic trainer to recognize whether the athlete is suffering from any diabetic episodes and to treat the athlete appropriately (**Table 17.2**).

TREATMENT

An athlete with diabetes must practice proper diet and nutrition and be monitored closely during athletic events, especially during extreme heat, to help prevent diabetic episodes. There are two forms of diabetic episodes: insulin shock and diabetic coma (**Figure 17.7**).

Insulin shock results from having high insulin levels and low blood glucose levels. This may also be referred to as hypoglycemia. **Table 17.3** lists the symptoms for both **insulin shock** and **diabetic coma**. Treatment for insulin shock, or **hypoglycemia**, should include prevention through a proper diet that includes a snack prior to exercise and some form of "pick-me-up" with glucose during lengthy or intense practices. An athletic trainer with a diabetic athlete always should carry sugar packets, fruit juice, glucose tablets/gels, hard candy, or a tube of cake icing to provide a surge of glucose for the athlete in the event of an insulin reaction.[8]

Diabetic coma is the opposite of insulin shock, resulting from too much glucose without insulin regulation. Diabetic coma typically is caused by an inadequate treatment of diabetes by the individual. Poor diet or inactivity may lead to ketoacidosis, which can then lead to diabetic coma.[1] An individual suffering from diabetic coma symptoms rapidly deteriorates from normal activity to unconsciousness. A diabetic coma is a medical emergency that, if not treated immediately, may lead to death. Swift referral to a physician for further treatment is essential.

■ Epilepsy

Epilepsy is a disorder often characterized by recurrent seizures. This disorder may result from genetic abnormalities or numerous neurologic conditions, including a brain tumor or previous head injury. Epileptic seizures range from minor (petit mal) to major (grand mal).

Petit mal seizures last from 5 to 15 seconds and may be as simple as zoning out, random staring, or slight tremors. Grand mal seizures, on the other hand, may last

insulin shock Shock resulting from a severe hypoglycemic reaction caused by an excess of insulin or a lack of glucose.

diabetic coma Unconsciousness caused by a lack of insulin. Also referred to as hyperglycemic shock.

hypoglycemia Low blood glucose.

epilepsy A chronic condition characterized by recurring seizures.

DIABETIC EMERGENCIES

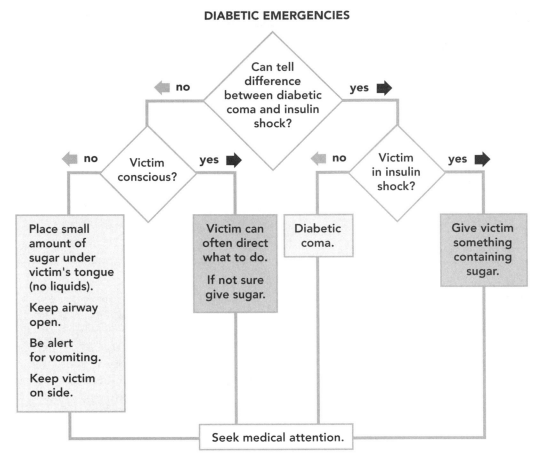

FIGURE 17.7   Procedure for diabetic emergency.

TABLE 17.3		
DIABETIC EPISODE SYMPTOMS	Hypoglycemia/Insulin Shock	Ketoacidosis/Diabetic Coma
Symptoms	1. Sudden onset	1. Gradual or sudden onset
	2. Confusion/disorientation	2. Abdominal pain/cramping
	3. Nausea/vomiting	3. Nausea/vomiting
	4. Increased breathing rate	4. Headache
	5. Pale, clammy skin	5. Blurred/double vision
	6. Inadequate dietary intake	6. Tachycardia
	7. Decreased glucose levels	7. Labored breathing
	8. Lack of coordination	8. Flushed skin
	9. Unconsciousness	9. Fruity smell of breath related to the body's use of acetone
		10. Elevated blood glucose

up to several minutes and include full body convulsions and unconsciousness.[9]

Most epileptics may still participate in some form of athletic play with proper treatment, including anticonvulsant medications.

SIGNS AND SYMPTOMS

1. Each individual has unique symptoms and should be evaluated by the athletic trainer for complete understanding of his or her illness.

TREATMENT

The athletic trainer must be aware of epileptic athletes and monitor them for potential seizures. If an athlete does suffer a seizure, the athletic trainer should remain calm, remove nearby objects that may cause injury, place something soft under the head to cushion it, avoid restraining the athlete, and allow the seizure to run its course. If the athlete suffers injury as a result of the seizure or remains unconscious, the athlete should be referred to a physician by ambulance.

■ Asthma

Asthma is a respiratory disorder that may be caused by a number of factors, such as infection, stress, exercise, allergies, or temperature changes. Asthma is a spasm of the smooth muscles in the bronchi and lungs and a subsequent narrowing of the airway. Asthma attacks may occur suddenly, surprising even the athlete suffering from the attack.

Exercise-induced asthma (EIA) is a specific form of asthma that affects athletes, especially those who participate in continuous activity sports (activity that lasts at least 6 to 8 minutes).[9] The exact cause of exercise-induced asthma is unknown; however, precautions can be taken to minimize the risk of an attack. An athlete who suffers from exercise-induced asthma should avoid activity on

---

asthma A chronic respiratory disease that is characterized by sudden recurring attacks of labored breathing, chest constriction, and coughing.

nebulizer A device that reduces liquid to an extremely fine cloud, especially used for delivering medication to the deep part of the respiratory tract.

ventricular arrhythmia An irregular cardiac rhythm that originates from within the ventricles.

Marfan's syndrome Inherited connective tissue disorder affecting many organs but commonly resulting in the dilation and weakening of the aorta.

---

cold, dry days; avoid extended exercise sessions such as running or biking, if possible; engage in short-burst activities that include periods of rest; and complete an appropriate warm-up prior to all activity.[9] Swimming in indoor pools is an excellent alternative exercise for high-risk athletes because the warm, humid environment decreases the likelihood of an attack.

SIGNS AND SYMPTOMS

1. Shortness of breath/difficulty breathing
2. Chest tightness
3. Coughing/wheezing

TREATMENT

Immediate treatment should come in the form of a fast-acting bronchodilator spray from a prescription inhaler (**Figure 17.8**). An athlete diagnosed with asthma should always have an inhaler on hand and provide the athletic training staff with an extra inhaler for emergencies.

The athlete may need to be removed from play for 20 to 30 minutes and placed in a calm environment to recover fully from an asthma attack. Athletes with asthma may also choose to use their inhaler prior to activity as a preventive measure. Severe cases of asthma may require the use of a **nebulizer** several times a day. A nebulizer transmits the prescription medicine through a steady steam inhaled through the mouth.

■ Hypertrophic Cardiomyopathy

Hypertrophic cardiomyopathy (HCM) is one of the primary causes of sudden death in athletics. HCM is a congenital abnormality that causes a thickened heart muscle—without chamber enlargement—and extensive myocardial scarring.[10] This thickening may cause an increased frequency of **ventricular arrhythmia**.[11] There are numerous other causes of sudden death syndrome in athletes, including Marfan's syndrome, coronary artery dysfunction, and other cardiac abnormalities; however, this text focuses on HCM.

Fast Fact

Marfan's syndrome is a condition that affects the connective tissue found in the body. With this disease, the affected tissue, including tissue in the skeleton, eyes, lungs, heart, and nervous system, is defective and does not act as it should. Over time, the stress on the heart leads to failure and death.[12]

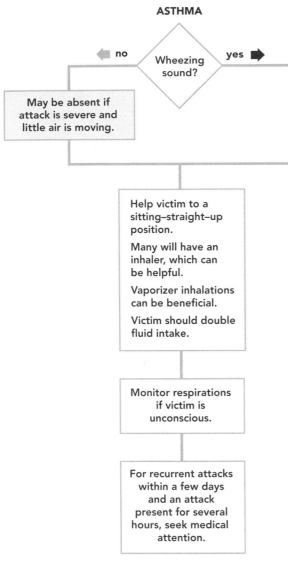

ASTHMA

no ⬅ Wheezing sound? yes ➡

May be absent if attack is severe and little air is moving.

Help victim to a sitting–straight–up position.

Many will have an inhaler, which can be helpful.

Vaporizer inhalations can be beneficial.

Victim should double fluid intake.

Monitor respirations if victim is unconscious.

For recurrent attacks within a few days and an attack present for several hours, seek medical attention.

FIGURE 17.8 First aid procedures for asthma.

SIGNS AND SYMPTOMS

1. Unfortunately, the primary symptom is often collapse and death
2. Previous history of syncope at rest or with exercise
3. Possible chest pain
4. Possible shortness of breath
5. Possible heart murmurs

TREATMENT

The best treatment for HCM and any other cause of sudden death is prevention and proper screening. Screening should include a medical and family history including any sudden deaths in close relatives and a physical exam that includes a heart and lung assessment. If an athlete demonstrates a history or physical exam consistent with HCM or other abnormalities, he or she should be referred to a cardiologist for an **electrocardiogram** (**ECG**) and an echocardiogram to determine whether an abnormality exists.

Preliminary echocardiograms on all new athletes have been suggested as a means to minimize the occurrence and risk of sudden death.[13,14] This policy is rarely implemented at the high school or collegiate level because of the high cost of the testing process and the rarity of the illness.

Treatment for an athlete suffering from a potential sudden death episode or collapse should consist of the use of CPR, an AED, and immediate emergency medical care. All life-saving measures should be attempted to resuscitate the athlete.

electrocardiogram (ECG) Graphic record of the heart's action currents obtained with the electrocardiograph.

CHAPTER REVIEW

1. Why is mononucleosis a concern in athletics?
2. Why is meningitis more prevalent in the collegiate setting?
3. What type of injury may cause damage to the liver?
4. What incidents may cause a sports hernia?
5. What is the principal fungal infection affecting athletes?
6. List the two types of epileptic seizure.

CRITICAL THINKING

How should you screen athletes for potential life-threatening injuries? What precautions do you take if they are cleared to participate with a life-threatening condition?

REFERENCES

1. Venes D, ed. *Taber's Cyclopedic Medical Dictionary*, 20th ed. Philadelphia: F. A. Davis, 2001.

2. McCrory P. (2002). Commotio cordis. *British Journal of Sports Medicine*, 36(4):236–237.

3. WebMD. *A to Z Health Guide: Sports Hernia*. Retrieved July 15, 2006, from http://www.webmd.com.

4. WebMD. *A to Z Health Guide: MRSA*. Retrieved July 17, 2006, from http://www.webmd.com.

5. Case PE, Manore M, Thompson JL. (2006). Stemming the tide: are you prepared for the diabetes epidemic. *ACSM's Health and Fitness Journal*, 10(1):7–13.

6. Tuomilehto J, et al. (2001). Prevention of type 2 diabetes mellitus by changes in lifestyle among subjects with impaired glucose tolerance. *New England Journal of Medicine*, 346:393–403.

7. American College of Sports Medicine. (2000). Position stand: exercise and type 2 diabetes. *Medicine and Science in Sport and Exercise*, 32(7):1345–1360.

8. Jimenez CC, Corcoran MH, Crawley JT, Hornsby WG, Peer KS, Philbin RD, Riddell MC. (2007). National Athletic Trainers' Association position statement: management of the athlete with type 1 diabetes mellitus. *Journal of Athletic Training*, 42(4):536–545.

9. Pfeiffer RP, Mangus BC. *Concepts of Athletic Training*, 5th ed. Sudbury, MA: Jones and Bartlett, 2008.

10. Evans CC, Cassady SL. (2003). Sudden cardiac death in athletes: what sport-rehabilitation specialists need to know. *Journal of Sport Rehabilitation*, 12(3):259–271.

11. McGrew CA. (2003). Sudden cardiac death in competitive athletes. *Journal of Orthopedic and Sports Physical Therapy*, 33(10):589–593.

12. National Marfan Foundation. *What Is Marfan Syndrome?* Retrieved September 20, 2007, from http://www.marfan.org.

13. Save an Athlete. *Prevention Methods*. Retrieved December 26, 2007, from http://www.saveanathlcte.org.

14. Mayo Clinic. *A Heart Condition of the Young*. Retrieved December 26, 2007, from http://www.mayoclinic.org.

Appendix A
Answer Key to Chapter Review Questions

Chapter 1

1. Prevention; clinical evaluation and diagnosis; immediate care; treatment, rehabilitation, and reconditioning of all athletic injuries; organization and administration; and professional responsibility

2. Introduction to athletic training, some level of first aid and CPR certification, and a basic athletic training techniques class; upper- and lower-body evaluation; therapeutic modalities; general medical conditions; rehabilitation and therapeutic exercise; organization and administration, human anatomy, and physiology; exercise physiology; biomechanics; nutrition; sports psychology; and history/philosophy of sports

3. 75 hours of continuing education during a 3-year period

4. College/university, high school, professional sports, clinic, clinic-outreach, industrial, military, academic faculty

5. Licensure, certification, registration, and exemption

6. Commission on Accreditation of Athletic Training Education

Chapter 2

1. Day-to-day operating budget and capital expenses

2. Duty to act, breach of duty, causation, damage

3. A well-developed and deliberate protocol that details the necessary steps required to afford an injured athlete with the optimal level of care

4. Health maintenance organizations (HMOs), preferred provider organizations (PPOs), point-of-service plans (POSs), and exclusive provider organizations (EPOs)

5. Physician exam, height, weight, vision, blood pressure

6. Subjective, objective, assessment, plan

7. Health Insurance Portability and Accountability Act

Chapter 3

1. Intraoral mouth guards

2. Knee pads, shoulder pads, hip pads, butt pad, thigh pads, helmet

3. NOCSAE, ASTM, CSA

4. False

5. Stock, moldable, and custom-made

Chapter 4

1. Dehydration, heat cramps, heat exhaustion, heat stroke

2. Athletes who are obese, out of shape, not accustomed to hot weather, have a previous history of heat illness, or other short- or long-term illnesses

3. A mathematical equation, incorporating both temperature and humidity, that determines how hot it feels to the body

4. Frostbite

5. 5 miles

6. True

Chapter 5

1. Compression forces, tension, and shearing

2. A pooling of blood

3. Abrasion, laceration, incision, avulsion, puncture

4. A sprain is an injury to ligaments. A strain is an injury to a muscle or tendon.

5. A fracture is a break or crack in the bone that causes immediate pain and loss of function directly related to the injury site.

6. Rest, ice, compression, elevation

7. Inflammatory, repair, and remodeling phases

8. Tissues will respond to physical demands, remodeling and adapting to the stress placed on them.

Chapter 6

1. Cryotherapy reduces the swelling in an injured area while still allowing the tissue healing and repair to occur.

2. Acute injuries

3. Frequency, intensity, duty cycle, and duration

4. Biphasic, interferential, hi-volt
5. Passive, active-assisted, active, resistive
6. Annually

Chapter 7

1. Sagittal, frontal, transverse
2. Medial
3. a. Always wear gloves when handling patients and remove gloves properly.
   b. Always wear protective eyewear or face shield to protect from blood spatter.
   c. Wash your hands immediately following contact with a bleeding patient.
   d. Do not recap, reuse, or manipulate used needles or scalpels.
   e. Use some form of protective mask when performing rescue breathing or CPR.
   f. It is recommended that all medical personnel receive immunizations for tetanus and hepatitis B to assist in the prevention of disease.
4. History, observation, palpation, special tests
5. Tap, compression, and translation
6. ROM and strength

Chapter 8

1. Propulsion and support
2. 28
3. A fracture at the base of the fifth metatarsal
4. The mechanism of injury is a hyperextension or a hyperflexion motion of the joint.
5. The best treatment for a subungal hematoma requires removal of the excess fluid by drilling a hole in the nail until the fluid is released.

Chapter 9

1. Tibia, fibula, talus
2. A tibia fracture
3. Shin contusion
4. Talar tilt test, anterior drawer test, posterior drawer test
5. Proprioceptive neuromuscular facilitation
6. 5%

Chapter 10

1. The tibia, fibula, femur, and patella
2. False
3. Genu valgum is when the knees angle toward each other. Genu varum is when the knees angle away from each other (bow-legged).

4. *Patella-femoral stress syndrome* (PFSS) is an all-encompassing term that includes any chronic pain found in the patellar region that may be blamed on tracking issues.
5. The displacement of the joint compromises the protective structures surrounding the femoral blood vessels and nerves, causing injury and possibly severing these essential vessels.
6. An injury to the ACL, MCL, and medial meniscus

Chapter 11

1. The femur
2. False
3. Acute compartment syndrome of the quads and myositis ossificans
4. Hip flexor strain
5. Ice hockey, field hockey, lacrosse, and soccer

Chapter 12

1. The atlas and the axis
2. Kyphosis is an excessive posterior curve of the thoracic spine. Lordosis is an excessive anterior curve of the lumbar spine.
3. There is no shifting of the vertebral body with a spondylolysis, whereas the vertebra shifts anteriorly in comparison to its neighboring vertebrae with a spondylolisthesis.
4. Because they assist in movement and perform as shock absorbers during gait and activity
5. Costochondral tissue
6. Trapezius and latissimus dorsi

Chapter 13

1. 12
2. Wrestling, boxing, rugby
3. Three
4. Second-impact syndrome is seen when a subsequent head injury occurs before the symptoms of the previous concussion have resolved.
5. Collection of blood in the sclera of the eye
6. Dizziness/headache, ringing in the ears, blurred or double vision, nausea, sensitivity to light/noise, possible slight amnesia, disorientation, inappropriate emotional reaction, any change in normal personality, confusion or lack of concentration, possible cranial nerve dysfunction, no loss of consciousness

Chapter 14

1. The acromioclavicular joint and the glenohumeral joint
2. Combination of scapular and humeral motion during abduction and adduction
3. 85–90%

4. The most common mechanism of injury is seen when the athlete lands on the tip of the shoulder (acromion), forcing it downward, backward, and inward while pushing the clavicle toward the rib cage.
5. Hill-Sachs lesion, Bankart lesion, SLAP lesion
6. Stinger/burner

Chapter 15

1. The primary responsibility of the elbow and forearm is placing the hand and fingers in a position that allows them to perform their many essential functions.
2. Minimize the potential for permanent range-of-motion deficits
3. Elbow dislocations
4. True
5. Forearm fracture that occurs at the distal end of the radius and ulna
6. Gymnasts, wrestlers, or volleyball players

Chapter 16

1. To gather information for the individual and to allow for dexterous manipulation of objects
2. Hypothenar muscles
3. Scaphoid and hamate
4. The ulnar collateral ligament
5. Mallet finger, jersey finger, boutonnière's deformity, swan neck deformity

Chapter 17

1. It can cause extreme fatigue and inflames the spleen, which can increase the risk for a rupture of that organ.
2. The close living arrangements and constant interaction
3. A direct blow to the upper right quadrant of the abdomen may cause a contusion or laceration of the liver.
4. An inherent weakness in the wall that progressively worsens or from one traumatic incident that strains the region and causes abdominal wall damage
5. Ringworm
6. Petit mal and grand mal

Glossary

abduction   Movement of the limbs toward the lateral plane or away from the body.

abrasion   An injury resulting from scraping; the result of rubbing or abrading.

acclimatization   Physiologic adaptations of an individual to a different environment, especially climate or altitude.

acute injury   An injury with sudden, traumatic onset.

adduction   Moving of a body part toward the central axis of the body.

air quality   A measurement of the pollutants in the air; a description of the healthiness and safety of the atmosphere.

alignment   The orientation of a body part in relation to the surrounding tissue. The maintenance of appropriate positioning of tissue.

anatomic position   Used as a universal reference to determine anatomic direction, it is a position whereby the body is erect, facing forward, with the arms at the side of the body, palms facing forward.

annulus fibrosis   The outer fibrocartilaginous layer of an intervertebral disc.

anterior   Before or in front of.

anterograde amnesia   Loss of an athlete's immediate memory and ability to recall events that have occurred since the injury.

apprehension   When a patient reacts to or limits motion because of a fear or sensation of impending joint dislocation or stress.

articulation   A loose connection between tissues that allows for movement between the parts.

assumption of risk   An individual, through either express or implied consent, assumes that some risk or danger will be involved in a particular undertaking.

asthma   A chronic respiratory disease that is characterized by sudden recurring attacks of labored breathing, chest constriction, and coughing.

asymptomatic   Having no symptoms of illness or disease.

atrophy   A wasting away or deterioration of tissue owing to disease, disuse, or malnutrition.

automated external defibrillator (AED)   A portable electronic device that automatically diagnoses the potentially life-threatening cardiac arrhythmias of ventricular fibrillation and ventricular tachycardia in a patient and is able to treat them through defibrillation.

avascular necrosis   Death of tissue caused by the lack of blood supply.

avulsion   Forcible tearing away of a part or a structure.

Bankart lesion   Avulsion or damage to the anterior lip of the glenoid as the humeral head dislocates anteriorly.

Battle's sign   Discoloration behind the ears caused by a head injury.

bilateral   Having two sides or pertaining to both sides.

biomechanics   Branch of study that applies the laws of mechanics to living organisms and biological tissues.

biphasic   A pulsed current possessing two phases, each of which occurs on opposite sides of the baseline.

blowout fracture   Fracture of the orbital floor occurring as a result of a sudden increase in pressure from a direct blow to the eye.

bone scan   Diagnostic imaging that detects bone abnormalities through the use of radioactive material that collects at tumors, fractures, and infections.

bony tissue   Any part of the 206 bones that make up the human body.

boutonniere deformity   Deformity characterized by flexion of the PIP joint and hyperextension of the DIP joint most often resulting from injury to the central slip of the extensor digitorum tendon and its insertion at the base of the middle phalanx.

boxer's fracture   A fracture specifically involving the fifth metacarpal.

brachial plexus   The primary neural supply to the upper extremities.

budget   An estimate of expected income and expense for a given period in the future.

bunion   Inflammation of the synovial bursa of the great toe, usually resulting in enlargement of the joint and lateral displacement of the toe.

bunionette   A bunion-like enlargement of the joint of the little toe.

burnout   Fatigue, frustration, or apathy that results from prolonged stress, overwork, or intense activity.

bursa sac A fibrous sac membrane typically found between tendons and bones; acts to decrease friction during motion.

bursitis Inflammation of a bursa.

calibration The act of checking or adjusting (by comparison with a standard) the accuracy of a measuring instrument.

callus Localized thickening of skin epidermis owing to physical trauma. Fibrous tissue containing immature bone tissue that forms at fracture sites during repair and regeneration.

cardiac arrest Sudden cessation of heartbeat and cardiac function, resulting in the loss of effective circulation.

carpal tunnel syndrome A condition of the wrist and hand characterized by compression of that median nerve as it passes through the carpal tunnel.

causation The determination that the actions of a person led to damage and to what extent the person is responsible for the damage caused.

cavitation Gas bubble formation owing to nonthermal effects of ultrasound.

cellulitis An inflammation of body tissue characterized by fever, swelling, redness, and pain.

cervical spine The most superior aspect of the spinal column. There are seven vertebrae in the cervical spine that support the head and provide for its range of motion.

chronic injury Injury with gradual onset and long duration.

circumduction Movement of a part (usually the shoulder or hip) in a circular direction.

closed fracture An uncomplicated fracture in which the broken bones do not pierce the skin.

closed kinetic chain Exercises that are performed when the hand or foot is fixed and cannot move. The hand or foot is in constant contact with the ground or exercise equipment.

closed wound An internal injury that does not disrupt the continuity of the skin.

Codman's exercises A form of pendulum movement in the shoulder that helps with regaining or maintaining range of motion after injury.

cognitive ability Brain-based skills and mental functions that assist in the processing of information and applying knowledge.

collagen The main protein found in connective tissue in the body.

Colles' fracture A fracture of the radius in which the distal aspect of the bone displaces dorsally.

commission When a person commits an act that is not legally his or hers to perform.

commotio cordis A sudden disturbance of heart rhythm. It occurs as the result of a blunt, nonpenetrating impact to the precordial region, often caused by impact of a ball, a bat, or other projectile. This often results in death.

compound fracture A fracture in which the broken bone is exposed through a wound in the skin.

compression A pressure or squeezing force directed through a body or body part in such a way as to increase density.

concussion A transient alteration in brain function without structural damage caused by an injury that shakes the brain.

contrast bath Technique that uses immersion in ice slush, followed by immersion in warm water.

contusion Compression injury involving an accumulation of fluid in a muscle; a bruise.

convection The transfer of energy between two objects via a medium, such as air or water, as it moves across the body, creating temperature variations.

Cooper's ligament A strong ligamentous band that provides support for the breast tissue.

co-pay A relatively small fixed fee required by a health insurer to be paid by the patient at the time of each office visit, outpatient service, or filling of a prescription.

core stabilization A series of exercises that focus on the core muscles of the abdomen and lower back.

costochondritis An inflammation of the costal cartilage found between the ribs.

cramps Painful muscle spasms caused by prolonged contraction.

cranial nerves A collection of nerves that emerge directly from the brain to innervate the motor and sensory systems in the head and neck.

crepitus Crackling or crunching sound or sensation characteristic of a fracture when the bone's ends are moved.

cryokinetics Use of cold treatments prior to or in conjunction with an exercise session.

cryotherapy Cold application.

cyanosis A slightly bluish or purple discoloration of the skin caused by a reduced amount of blood hemoglobin.

deceleration A decrease in speed or coming to a stop.

deductible The amount for which the insured is liable on each injury before an insurance company will make payment.

deformity A deviation from the normal shape or size of a body part.

dehydration Deprivation of water; reduction of water content in the body.

dermatomes The area of skin and its sensation that is supplied by a single spinal nerve.

diabetes mellitus A variable disorder of carbohydrate metabolism caused by a combination of hereditary and environmental factors and usually characterized by inadequate secretion or utilization of insulin.

diabetic coma Unconsciousness caused by a lack of insulin. Also referred to as hyperglycemic shock.

discoloration   A change in color from what is normally seen in an individual.

dislocation   A displacement of a part, especially a bone, from its normal position.

disorientation   Mental confusion or impaired awareness, especially regarding place, time, or personal identity.

displaced fracture   A fracture in which the broken fragments of the bone are separated from each other and not aligned.

disunion   A severance of union; separation; disjunction.

distal   Farthest from a center, from the midline, or from the trunk.

dorsiflexion   Bending toward the dorsum or rear; opposite of plantar flexion.

duty cycle   The ratio between the pulse duration and the pulse interval: Duty cycle = Pulse duration / (Pulse duration + Pulse interval).

dyspnea   Difficulty or trouble breathing.

ecchymosis   Black and blue skin discoloration caused by internal bleeding.

edema   Swelling as a result of the collection of fluid in connective tissue.

effleurage   Superficial, longitudinal massage strokes used to relax the patient.

effusion   Abnormal swelling found within a joint structure or body cavity.

electrocardiogram (ECG)   Graphic record of the heart's action currents obtained with the electrocardiograph.

electrolytes   Salts and minerals found in the body that conduct electricity and that are needed to maintain body fluid function.

electrotherapy   The therapeutic application of electricity to the body.

elevation   The height to which something is elevated above a point of reference such as the heart.

emergency action plan (EAP)   A written document that details the standard of care required in an emergency at a specific institution.

epicondyles   A rounded projection at the end of a bone that serves as an attachment for ligaments or tendons.

epilepsy   A chronic condition characterized by recurring seizures.

epiphyseal fractures   Fractures found at the ends of the bone, usually seen in children/young adults. Also known as growth-plate fractures.

epistaxis   Nosebleed.

erythema   Redness of the skin.

eversion   Turning laterally.

exclusions   A specific situation that is not covered by an insurance policy.

exertional hyponatremia   A condition that occurs when an athlete's blood sodium levels decrease either as a result of overhydration or inadequate sodium intake. If not treated, this condition may become fatal.

extension   The act of straightening a limb.

external rotation   Movement in which the anterior surface of the distal segment moves away from the midline of the body.

exertion test   A series of exercises that places a progressive physical stress on the injured individual. The test is utilized to determine whether the individual is capable of a return to play.

extrinsic muscles   Muscles that originate from outside a body segment. In the hand, they are the muscles that act at the hand but originate in the wrist or forearm.

extruded disc   A tearing of the annulus fibrosis and movement of the nucleus propulsus into the spinal canal.

facet joints   Smooth areas of the vertebra that guide and limit motion in the spinal column.

fascia   Fibrous membrane that covers, supports, and separates muscles.

fasciitis   Inflammation of the fascia surrounding portions of a muscle.

fibroblasts   A cell present in connective tissue capable of forming collagen fibers.

flail chest   A fracture of three or more ribs in two or more places that causes an aspect of the chest wall to detach and act on its own.

flash-to-bang ratio   Number of seconds from lightning flash until the sound of thunder divided by 5. Used as an indicator of the proximity of a thunderstorm.

flexibility   Capable of being bent or moved repeatedly without injury or damage.

flexion   The act of bending a limb.

fluoresceine strips   A chemical strip used to assess for a corneal abrasion.

fracture   A disruption in the continuity of a bone.

frequency   The rate of occurrence of a wave measured in hertz (Hz), cycles per second (CPS), or pulses per second (PPS).

friction   The force resisting the motion of two surfaces in contact.

frontal (coronal) plane   A longitudinal (vertical) line that divides the body or any of its parts into anterior and posterior portions.

frostbite   Local tissue destruction resulting from exposure to extreme cold.

frostnip   Local tissue destruction resulting from exposure to extreme cold. Usually seen as a precursor to frostbite.

gait pattern   Technique of walking.

gamekeeper's thumb   Ulnar collateral ligament rupture of the first metacarpophalangeal joint. Also known as skier's thumb.

genu recurvatum   Hyperextension of the knee.

genu valgum   A lateral angulation of the lower leg in relation to the thigh; knock-kneed.

genu varum   A medial angulation of the lower leg in relation to the thigh; bow-legged.

Good Samaritan law   Provides limited protection against legal liability to any individual who voluntarily chooses to provide first aid.

healing process   A series of predictable reactions to injury that is designed to repair the damaged tissue.

heat exhaustion   A form of reaction to heat resulting from severe dehydration.

heat index   A measurement of the air temperature in relation to the relative humidity.

heat stroke   A severe and often fatal illness produced by exposure to excessively high temperatures, especially when accompanied by marked exertion.

heat syncope   A reaction to heat that causes the individual to faint and momentarily lose consciousness.

hematoma   A collection of blood and other fluids that is found at an injury site.

hemopneumothorax   The accumulation of air and blood in the pleural cavity.

hemothorax   Accumulation of blood in the pleural cavity.

hernia   A protrusion of a part or structure through the tissues that typically contain it.

herpes   Any of several viral diseases causing the eruption of small blister-like vesicles on the skin or mucous membranes.

Hill-Sachs lesion   A small defect usually located on the posterior aspect of the articular cartilage of the humeral head caused by the impact of the humeral head on the glenoid fossa as the humerus dislocates.

histamine   A powerful stimulant of gastric secretion, a constrictor of bronchial smooth muscle, and a vasodilator that causes a fall in blood pressure.

hi-volt   Electrical stimulation that utilizes a direct current to promote healing and decrease pain in an injured area.

HOPS process   An acronym used to guide secondary assessment (history, observation/inspection, palpation, special tests).

humidity   The amount of water vapor in the air, usually expressed as relative humidity.

hydrocollator   A liquid heating device primarily used in physical therapy clinics to heat/store "moist hot packs" for therapeutic use.

hydrostatic pressure   The pressure of blood within the capillary.

hyperextension   Extension that occurs beyond the full range of motion (usually seen as beyond 0°).

hyperthermia   Elevated body temperature.

hypertrophic cardiomyopathy   A disorder in which the heart muscle is enlarged and so strong that it does not relax enough to fill the heart with blood. This leads to reduced pumping ability.

hyphema   An accumulation of blood in the anterior chamber of the eye.

hypoglycemia   Low blood glucose.

hypothenar aspect   The fleshy mass of muscle and tissue on the medial (pinkie) side of the palm.

hypothermia   Decreased body temperature.

immobilization   To prevent, restrict, or reduce normal movement in the body, a limb, or a joint, as by a splint, cast, or prescribed bed rest.

impetigo   A contagious bacterial skin infection, usually of children, that is characterized by the eruption of superficial pustules and the formation of thick yellow crusts.

impingement   Pressure on the rotator cuff musculature that results when the muscles are rubbed or compressed by the acromion during movement.

incision   A cut; a surgical wound.

infection   Invasion of pathogenic microorganisms, which may produce subsequent tissue injury and progress to overt disease through a variety of mechanisms.

inferior (caudal) aspect   Toward the feet.

inflammation   Pain, swelling, redness, heat, and loss of function that accompany musculoskeletal injuries.

inflammatory phase   The first phase of the healing process characterized by swelling, pain, redness, and loss of range of motion. This phase lasts from 24 to 72 hours.

influenza   An acute contagious viral infection characterized by fever, chills, muscular pain, and prostration.

initial survey   Immediate check of airway, breathing, circulation, and other vital signs to rule out life-threatening injuries or conditions.

instability   A joint's inability to function under the stresses encountered during functional activities.

insulin shock   Shock resulting from a severe hypoglycemic reaction caused by an excess of insulin or a lack of glucose.

insurance   The act of insuring property, life, one's person, and so on against loss or harm arising in specified contingencies and in consideration of a payment proportionate to the risk involved.

intensity   The amount or degree of strength of electricity, light, heat, or sound per unit area or volume.

interferential stimulation   Electrical stimulation that utilizes two channels of alternating current that promotes healing and decreases pain in an injured area.

internal rotation   Movement in which the anterior surface of the distal segment moves toward the midline of the body.

intervertebral disc   A fibrocartilage structure found between the vertebrae to improve motion and shock absorption.

intrinsic muscles Muscles that originate from inside a body segment. In the hand, it is the muscles that originate within the hand.

inventory A complete listing of stock on hand that is created annually.

inversion Turning medially.

iontophoresis Introduction of ions into the body through the use of an electrical current.

isometric strength Strength that does not involve moving the involved body part.

ischemia Local anemia owing to decreased blood supply.

jersey finger Rupture of the flexor digitorum longus tendon from the distal phalanx of the finger.

Jobe exercises A series of exercises used to strengthen the shoulder musculature. Exercises are completed with either therapeutic tubing or light weights.

joint capsule A collection of fibrous tissue that surrounds and protects a joint from injury.

Jones fracture A transverse fracture of the proximal shaft of the fifth metatarsal.

kyphosis An excessive posterior alignment of the thoracic spine.

labrum A ring of cartilage about the edge of a joint surface of the glenoid fossa. Used to provide shock absorption and smooth motion at the shoulder.

laceration A torn or jagged wound caused by blunt trauma.

lateral Farther away from the midline.

lateral epicondylitis An overuse injury to the attachments of the extensor and supinator tendons at the lateral epicondyle; also known as tennis elbow.

laxity Looseness of the joint whether it is normal or caused by injury/instability.

lethargy A state of physical and mental fatigue that is characterized by decreased motivation, muscle weakness, and general exhaustion.

liability The state of being legally responsible for the harm one causes another person.

ligament A band of tissue, usually white and fibrous, serving to connect bones and fulfill other bodily functions.

lightning detector Equipment that detects the presence and proximity of lightning strikes produced by thunderstorms.

lordosis An excessive anterior alignment of the lumbar spine.

lower respiratory infection Infection of the lower respiratory tract.

lumbar spine The most inferior aspect of the spinal column. There are five vertebrae in the lumbar spine that provide shock absorption and support during gait.

luxation A complete dislocation of a bone from a joint.

lymphatic return A return process similar to that of the venous network, but specializing in the removal of interstitial fluids.

Mackenzie exercises A series of exercises that focus on extension of the spine.

malaise A vague, general feeling of illness or fatigue.

mallet finger Avulsion of the extensor digitorum longus from the distal phalanx.

manual muscle tests (MMTs) A graded strength test performed by applying manual resistance to a segment to evaluate a particular muscle or muscle group.

March fracture A stress fracture of the second metatarsal; often seen in new military recruits as a result of the high amount of marching.

Marfan's syndrome Inherited connective tissue disorder affecting many organs but commonly resulting in the dilation and weakening of the aorta.

massage The rubbing or kneading of parts of the body especially to aid circulation, decrease muscle spasm, or relax the body.

medial Closer to the midline.

medial epicondylitis An overuse injury to the attachments of the flexor and pronator tendons at the medial epicondyle; also known as golfer's elbow.

medial tibial stress syndrome Another name for shin splints, this often occurs as a result of a sudden increase in duration or intensity of training. Injury presents with pain in the medial aspect of the lower leg.

meningitis Inflammation of the meninges of the brain and the spinal cord, most often caused by a bacterial or viral infection and characterized by fever, vomiting, intense headache, and stiff neck.

meniscus A crescent-shaped structure that assists in the formation of a joint and shock absorption.

metabolism The chemical processes occurring in a living organism that are necessary for the maintenance of life.

microstreaming Localized flow of fluids resulting from cavitation.

midline An imaginary line drawn down the middle of the body through the nose and umbilicus.

mononucleosis A common infectious disease usually affecting young people and characterized by fever, sore throat, swollen lymph nodes, and fatigue. The symptoms may last for several weeks.

MRI Magnetic resonance imaging; a noninvasive diagnostic procedure that provides detailed sectional images of the internal structure of the body.

MRSA Methicillin-resistant *Staphylococcus aureus*; a bacterium responsible for difficult-to-treat infections in humans.

muscle A tissue composed of muscle fibers, the contraction of which produces movement in the body.

myositis ossificans Inflammation in the muscle that is marked by formation of a bony mass within the muscle.

myotomes   The muscles that are innervated by a single spinal nerve.

nebulizer   A device that reduces liquid to an extremely fine cloud, especially used for delivering medication to the deep part of the respiratory tract.

negligence   The failure to use ordinary or responsible care.

neurovascular   Of or relating to both nerves and blood vessels.

nociceptors   Receptors sensitive to potentially damaging or painful stimuli.

nonunion fracture   Failure of fracture fragments to unite or heal.

nucleus pulposus   The interior substance of an intervertebral disc. The jelly-like material provides shock absorption and increased range of motion in the spine.

omission   When a person fails to perform a legal duty.

open fracture   A fracture in which broken bone fragments lacerate soft tissue and protrude through an open wound in the skin.

open kinetic chain   Exercises that are performed when the hand or foot is free to move. These exercises are typically performed in a non-weight-bearing manner.

open wound   An injury that disrupts the continuity of the skin and causes external and/or internal damage to the body.

orthoplast   A thermomoldable plastic used for casts and splints.

orthotics   An orthopedic appliance inserted into the shoe to correct abnormal foot biomechanics.

osteoarthritis   Arthritis characterized by a degradation of the articular cartilage in a joint.

osteoblasts   Bone-producing cells.

osteoclasts   Cells that reasorb bone.

osteomyelitis   An inflammation of the bone and bone marrow, usually caused by bacterial infection.

paraffin bath   A mixture of paraffin wax and oil that is kept in a liquid state and used to heat hands and feet specifically.

paralysis   Loss of voluntary movement in a muscle or region of the body as a result of injury or disease.

patella-femoral stress syndrome (PFSS)   Chronic injury to the knee often seen with patella tracking issues and overuse.

peripheral vision   All that is visible to the eye outside the central area of focus.

pes cavus   High arch.

pes planus   Flat feet.

petrissage   Massage technique consisting of pressing and rolling the muscles under the fingers and hands.

phonophoresis   The introduction of anti-inflammatory drugs through the skin with the use of ultrasound.

photophobia   Sensitivity to light.

plantar flexion   Movement of the foot that flexes the foot or toes downward toward the sole.

pleural cavity   The cavity in the thorax that contains the lungs and heart.

pneumothorax   The presence of air or gas in the pleural cavity.

Popeye deformity   A tear of the biceps tendon that is characterized by a deficit in the musculature with a large bulge beside the deficit. Injury is reminiscent of the cartoon character Popeye.

posterior   Toward the rear or back.

preexisting condition   A condition that is present prior to the current injury that predisposes an individual to damage. Preexisting conditions often are considered exclusions for insurance policies.

primary insurance coverage   All expenses related to an injury that an insurance company provides within a policy.

progressive resistive exercises   Exercises that gradually increase in resistance (weight) and repetitions.

prolapsed disc   Pressure from the nucleus propulsus that pushes the annulus fibrosis outward toward the spinal canal.

pronation   Combination of movements resulting in the rotation of the hand and wrist to the opposite of an atomic position.

prophylactic braces   Braces used to prevent or protect from injury.

proprioception   The sense of the position of the body in space and relative to other parts of the body.

proprioceptive neuromuscular facilitation (PNF)   A combination of passive stretching and isometric or isotonic strengthening used to increase flexibility, range of motion, or strength.

propulsion   The movement phase of the gait cycle.

proximal   Nearest to the point of reference.

psychrometer   An instrument for determining relative humidity by the reading of two thermometers, one with a wet bulb and one with a dry bulb.

puncture   To pierce with a pointed object.

Q-angle   Angle measured from the anterior superior iliac spine to the patella and from the patella to the tibial tuberosity.

Raccoon eyes   Discoloration around the eyes caused by a skull fracture.

radicular pain   Pain that radiates along the dermatome of a nerve following injury or damage to that nerve.

range of motion (ROM)   The specific movement provided at a joint by the joint structures (ligaments, joint capsules, cartilage, bones).

remodeling phase   The third and final phase of the healing process, characterized by scar tissue formation and connective tissue maturation. This phase begins 48 to 72 hours after the injury and may last for up to a year.

repair phase The second phase of the healing process, characterized by initial tissue repair and new tissue generation. This phase begins 48 to 72 hours after the injury and lasts for approximately 2 weeks.

retrograde amnesia Loss of memory and inability to recall events before the traumatic event.

RICE Rest, ice, compression, and elevation.

ringworm Any of a number of contagious fungal skin diseases characterized by ring-shaped, scaly, itching patches on the skin.

rotator cuff The SITS (supraspinatus, infraspinatus, teres minor, and subscapularis) muscles hold the head of the humerus in the glenoid fossa and produce internal and external rotation.

Russian Electrical stimulation that is used for muscle reeducation and strengthening by creating muscular contractions.

sagittal plane A longitudinal (vertical) line that divides the body or any of its parts into right and left portions.

scapular protraction The movement of the scapula away from the midline.

scapular retraction The movement of the scapula toward the midline.

scapulohumeral rhythm The coordinated movement of the scapula, humerus, and clavicle to achieve full shoulder elevation.

sclera A dense, white, fibrous membrane that, with the cornea, forms the external covering of the eyeball.

scoliosis An excessive lateral alignment of the spinal column.

secondary hypoxic injury Additional cellular breakdown and death as a result of a lack of adequate oxygen supply around the primary area of injury.

secondary insurance Insurance coverage that provides for the remaining expenses once a primary coverage plan has completed its payments.

secondary survey Head-to-toe evaluation of an injured athlete to determine the location and extent of injury.

sequestrated disc When fragments of the annulus fibrosis and nucleus propulsus break off and move into the spinal canal.

shearing Force that moves across the parallel organization of the tissue.

shock A condition of inadequate peripheral blood flow resulting from a traumatic incident.

SLAP lesion An injury to the superior labrum that typically begins posteriorly and extends anteriorly.

soft tissue Any part of the body that is not associated with the bones of the body, including muscles, ligaments, tendons, connective tissue, and skin.

spinal stenosis A development or congenital narrowing of the spinal canal. Increases the risk for spinal cord damage with injury.

spondylolisthesis Forward movement of a spinal vertebra resulting from a fracture or degeneration of the pars articularis.

spondylolysis Degeneration or fracture of the pars articularis of a spinal vertebra.

sports drink A drink intended to quench thirst faster than water can and replenish sugar and minerals lost through physical activity.

sports hernia A syndrome characterized by chronic groin pain in athletes that results from a weakening of the muscles and tissue in the abdominal wall.

sprain Injury to the ligaments of the body.

stability The resistance of various musculoskeletal tissue that maintains the integrity of a joint or other skeletal structure.

statute of limitations A statute defining the period within which legal action may be taken.

stimulus A change in the internal or external environment that causes a response in the tissue.

stingers Common name for brachial plexus injuries identified with burning pain or numbness radiating down the arm.

strain Injury to the muscle, tendon, or the junction between the two.

stress fracture A fracture resulting from repeating loading with relatively low magnitude forces.

subluxation Incomplete or partial dislocation of a bone from a joint.

subtalar joint A joint of the foot located at the meeting point of the talus and the calcaneus.

sulcus A deep, narrow furrow or groove, as in an organ or tissue. May be seen as a positive sign of an inferior shoulder dislocation.

superior (cephal) aspect Toward the head.

supination Movement of the foot and ankle that allows the structure to return to anatomic position.

suture An immoveable joint found between the bones of the skull.

swan neck deformity A deformity caused by hyperextension at the PIP joint and hyperflexion at the DIP resulting from disruption of the volar plate and tensioning of the flexor tendons.

swelling An enlargement of an injured area usually resulting from increased fluid.

syndesmosis A fibrous structure that connects surfaces that are relatively far apart as seen between the tibia and fibula.

synovial tissue Soft tissue that lines the noncartilaginous surfaces of a joint.

systemic Pertaining to or affecting the body as a whole.

tackler's elbow An overuse injury of the distal biceps tendon that is often seen with football players during preseason as a result of repetitive contact and tackling.

tapotement Massage technique that uses sharp, alternating, brisk hand movements such as hacking, slapping, beating, cupping, and clapping to increase blood flow and stimulate peripheral nerve endings.

tendinitis Inflammation of a tendon.

tendon A composite of dense, tough, inelastic, white, fibrous tissue, serving to connect a muscle with a bone or part.

tenosynovitis Inflammation of a tendon sheath.

tension Force that pulls or stretches tissue.

tension pneumothorax Pneumothorax resulting from a wound in the chest wall that acts as a valve that permits air to enter the pleural cavity but prevents its escape.

therapeutic exercise Exercises for strengthening, improving awareness of limbs, improving coordination, and improving function.

therapeutic modalities Any treatment conducted on an injured area that is intended to promote healing and minimize or reduce symptoms.

thermotherapy Heat application.

thoracic spine The middle aspect of the spinal column. There are 12 vertebrae in the thoracic spine that provide shock absorption and support for the torso.

thorax The chest or torso region of the body consisting of the thoracic vertebrae, the rib cage, and the muscles and organs found within.

translation Refers to anterior gliding of one end of the bone and the posterior gliding of the other end.

transverse plane A horizontal line that divides the body into superior and inferior portions.

triangular fibrocartilage complex A small cartilaginous structure, similar to the meniscus in the knee, that connects the distal ulna with the triquetrium and lunate bones in the wrist. Also known as the TFCC.

ultrasound A deep-penetrating modality that uses acoustical waves to produce both thermal and nonthermal effects.

universal precautions Refers to the practice, in medicine, of avoiding contact with patients' bodily fluids by wearing nonporous articles such as medical gloves, goggles, and face shields.

upper respiratory infection Infection of the upper respiratory tract.

urine viscosity The thickness or density of the urine, which increases as the water content in the body decreases and dehydration increases.

valgus An opening on the medial side of a joint caused by the distal segment moving laterally.

varus An opening on the lateral side of a joint caused by the distal segment moving medially.

vasoconstriction Constriction of the blood vessels, as by the action of a nerve.

vasodilation Dilation of the blood vessels, as by the action of a nerve.

ventricular arrhythmia An irregular cardiac rhythm that originates from within the ventricles.

ventricular fibrillation An often fatal form of arrhythmia characterized by rapid, irregular fibrillar twitching of the ventricles of the heart in place of normal contractions, resulting in a loss of pulse.

vicarious liability When one person is liable for the negligent actions of another person, even though the first person was not directly responsible.

vital signs The pulse rate, temperature, and respiratory rate of an individual.

waiver An intentional relinquishment of some right or interest.

waveform The shape of a wave; a graph obtained by plotting the instantaneous values of a periodic quantity against the time.

window shade effect When the tendon detaches from its point of origin and rolls up to the muscle belly.

Wolff's law A law that states that bone and soft tissue will respond to the physical demands placed upon them, causing the formation of collagen to remodel or realign along the lines of stress, thus promoting healthy joint biomechanics.

Index

Photo Credits

Chapter 10

Opener Courtesy of J01 Mark D. Faram/U.S. Navy; **10.3** © Matt Baker/Dreamstime.com; **10.4A–D** Reprinted with permission from Starkey C, Johnson G. (Eds). *Athletic Training and Sports Medicine, 4th ed.* Rosemont, IL: American Academy of Orthopaedic Surgeons, 2006; **10.9** Courtesy of Bledsoe Brace System; **10.13** Courtesy of Don Joy; **10.15** Courtesy of Bledsoe Brace System.

Chapter 11

Opener © Photodisc; **11.4A–B** Reprinted with permission from Starkey C, Johnson G. (Eds). *Athletic Training and Sports Medicine, 4th ed.* Rosemont, IL: American Academy of Orthopaedic Surgeons, 2006; **11.5** Courtesy of Mueller Sports Medicine; **11.7** Reprinted with permission from Starkey C, Johnson G. (Eds). *Athletic Training and Sports Medicine, 4th ed.* Rosemont, IL: American Academy of Orthopaedic Surgeons, 2006; **11.10–11.11** Courtesy of Jennifer Eaves and Jessica Hawkins; **11.12** Reprinted with permission from Starkey C, Johnson G. (Eds). *Athletic Training and Sports Medicine, 4th ed.* Rosemont, IL: American Academy of Orthopaedic Surgeons, 2006.

Section Opener IV Courtesy of Lisa Terry McKeown/U.S. Air Force

Chapter 12

Opener © Banannaanna/Dreamstime.com; **12.6** © iofoto/ShutterStock, Inc.; **12.10** Courtesy of Jennifer Eaves and Calvin Bacon.

Chapter 13

Opener © Koji Aoki/age fotostock; **13.3** © Susy56/Dreamstime.com; **13.4** © Dr. P. Marazzi/Science Photo Library; **13.5** © Richard Wareham Fotografie/Alamy Images; **13.6** © PhotoLink/Photodisc/Getty Images.

Chapter 14

Opener © Alan C. Heison/ShutterStock, Inc.; **14.4** Courtesy of Jennifer Eaves and Calvin Bacon; **14.5** Courtesy of Mueller Sports Medicine; **14.6–14.7** Courtesy of Jennifer Eaves and Benji Jones; **14.14** Courtesy of Jennifer Eaves and Jessica Hawkins.

Chapter 15

Opener © Galina Barskay/ShutterStock, Inc.; **15.2** © E.M. Singletary, MD. Used with permission; **15.5** © James M. Phelps, Jr./ShutterStock, Inc.; **15.6** © SPL/Photo Researchers, Inc.; **15.7** © Jacob Yuri Wackerhausen/ShutterStock, Inc.; **15.8** Courtesy of Kevin G. Shea, MD, Intermountain Orthopaedics, Boise, Idaho; **15.9** © Foxjitter/Dreamstime.com.

Chapter 16

Opener © KennStilger47/ShutterStock, Inc.; **16.4** © E.M. Singletary, MD. Used with permission; **16.8–16.17** Reproduced with permission from Pfeiffer RP, Mangus BC. *Concepts of Athletic Training, 5th ed.*

Section Opener V © iofoto/ShutterStock, Inc.

Chapter 17

Opener Courtesy of Tech Sgt. Robert A. Whitehead/U.S. Air Force; **17.2** © Custom Medical Stock Photo/Alamy Images; **17.3** Courtesy of CDC; **17.4** © Medical-on-Line/Alamy Images; **17.5** Courtesy of Dr. Hermann/CDC; **17.6** Courtesy of Bruno Coignard, MD, and Jeff Hageman, MHS/CDC.

Unless otherwise indicated, photographs are under copyright of Jones and Bartlett Publishers, LLC, courtesy of the Maryland Institute for Emergency Medical Services Systems, photographed by Dan Evans Photography, or provided by the author.